THE
IRON ROAD
in the
PRAIRIE STATE

RAILROADS PAST AND PRESENT

GEORGE M. SMERK AND
H. ROGER GRANT,
EDITORS

A list of books in the series appears at the end of this volume.

THE
IRON ROAD
in the
PRAIRIE STATE

THE STORY OF ILLINOIS RAILROADING

SIMON CORDERY

INDIANA UNIVERSITY PRESS • *Bloomington & Indianapolis*

This book is a publication of

Indiana University Press
Office of Scholarly Publishing
Herman B Wells Library 350
1320 East 10th Street
Bloomington, Indiana 47405 USA
iupress.indiana.edu

The paper used in this publication meets the
minimum requirements of the American National
Standard for Information Sciences—Permanence
of Paper for Printed Library Materials, ANSI
Z39.48–1992.

Manufactured in the United States of America

Library of Congress Cataloging-in-Publication Data

Cordery, Simon, 1960- author.
 The iron road in the Prairie State : the story of illinois
railroading / Simon Cordery.
    pages cm. — (Railroads past and present)
 Includes bibliographical references and index.
 ISBN 978-0-253-01906-6 (cloth : alk. paper) — ISBN
978-0-253-01912-7 (ebook) 1. Railroads—Illinois—
History. 2. Railroads—United States—History.
I. Title.
   HE2771.I4C67 2016
   385.09773—dc23

                                        2015022336

1 2 3 4 5   21 20 19 18 17 16

For my fellow enthusiasts,
Stacy and Gareth

CONTENTS

Figure 0.1. The drama of steam: a TP&W double-headed freight between Chatsworth and Piper City (1924). Author's collection.

PREFACE

The history of railroading in Illinois looks from a distance like an orderly sequence of events. The story, seemingly preordained, tells of rise, fall, and tentative renaissance. After a slow, parochial start—so the narrative goes—railroad technology improved and private capital flowed into the industry, which grew into a mighty transportation network, created a national market, and shrank time and space. But storms blew in when the omnipresent and omnipotent railroads alienated employees, customers, and politicians. Reined in by labor unions and government regulators, the railroads suffered a near-mortal blow as people shifted to cars, trucks, and airplanes after 1900. Political and economic pressure squeezed the industry until much of the track became redundant and had to be abandoned. Having redefined how people understood and interacted with the world, railroads almost disappeared. Revived by the elimination of harmful government regulations and saved from the burden of carrying passengers, a smaller but stronger industry entered the twenty-first century by providing vital arteries of commerce and environmentally sound alternatives to trucks and airplanes.

Though this sketch contains a grain of truth, it obscures the lived experience of railroading and the complex development of the industry. For those caught up in the actual events, the narrative arc was far from obvious and mostly imposed after the fact. Disruption, corruption, disaster, scheming, friction, and despair shared the landscape with optimism, dreaming, recovery, expansion, and excitement. Alternative avenues

were frequently present, as was the unknown. Sudden and unanticipated developments caused changes of direction and emphasis across state and nation with local ramifications. The story is clear in retrospect, but the unpredictable, the random, and the tension of the time can only be appreciated by taking ourselves back into the railroad age.

The railroads did not appear out of nothing. True, they brought large numbers of people to the state, but they were not the only force for expansion. The population of Illinois expanded over 200 percent during the decade before the railroad spread across the state as the prairies opened to settlement. In the 1850s Illinois grew by 78.8 percent, and in the 1860s the population more than doubled, but the industry tapped into preexisting trends instead of creating them. The railroads did contribute to the urbanization of the state, with towns and cities growing in double digits every decade from the 1860s on, but even here widespread paving programs in the early twentieth century accelerated the process.

The iron road conditioned Illinois economically and socially, but not in a vacuum. The first tentative steps were taken directly into the abyss of a transatlantic depression, destroying early ambitions and wrecking the state's fiscal health and reputation. Prairie State railroads originated as local interests, and not until after the Civil War did they connect with a growing national system of railroads. Then Illinois became inextricably part of a global economy, sharing in its wealth but subject to its moments of calamity and recession. To speak of Illinois as an independent economic entity became impossible, and the railroads did more than any other business to tie the state into national and international marketplaces during the nineteenth century. Local control became a fiction as Illinois merchants and bankers partnered with and grew dependent upon their counterparts in other states and nations. Any possibility for autarky—the complete economic self-reliance dreamed of by many pioneers—vanished.[1]

The topography of Illinois presents few challenges to railroad building and operation. Mostly flat, with many rivers and streams and almost no truly hilly terrain, the state occupies the territory in which the American railroad network reached its maturity. During the 1850s a dramatic upsurge in railroad building brought trains to every part of the state. Lines radiated out from Chicago; railroads through southern and central Illinois connected Indiana with Iowa and Missouri; and north-south routes linked Wisconsin with Kentucky. By 1880 most settlements of any size were within five miles of an operating railroad, a situation that held until about 1960. Only one of the state's 102 counties—Calhoun, a hilly peninsula trapped between the Illinois and Mississippi Rivers—has never hosted a railroad. Railroads brought in settlers from southern and eastern states and from Europe to carve farms and towns into the frontier. Only the railroad could have carried the lumber, grain, and minerals those settlers and their successors exploited. The young state's remote villages and growing towns would not have existed without the railroads. During the Great Migration of African Americans to the North, railroads provided passage to a new life with new complications in Chicago, Peoria, Decatur, East St. Louis, and elsewhere.

Railroads were ubiquitous across Illinois and the Windy City remains the hub of the North American transportation system, though the separation of operations and financing means Chicago is no longer the home of major railroad headquarters. It is impossible to travel any distance in the state today without encountering railroads or their remnants. From massive yards full of freight cars and lively depots teeming with excited passengers to crumbling bridge abutments or the telltale hump of a disused trackbed, railroads are woven into the cultural and physical fabric of the state. Long-abandoned rights-of-way are still visible from airplane and satellite. The railroad industry shaped the political development, economic growth, and settlement patterns of the state. In return, its topography, politicians, and population have influenced the expansion of railroads across the United States.

Illinois railroading offers a study of railroad development in a microcosm. The costly and futile internal improvements projects imagined by exuberant legislators in Vandalia during the late 1830s found echoes across the young nation. After a decade of despondency, renewed enthusiasm and expansion in the 1850s were duplicated throughout the trans-Appalachian West. The first merger of the railroad age occurred in Illinois, and land grants pioneered by the Illinois Central would spur transcontinental railroad building. Government regulation growing out of lawsuits originating in Illinois in the 1870s and 1880s dramatically altered the relationship between industry and government. Periodic recessions—"panics," as they were called in the nineteenth century—threw Illinois-based railroads into bankruptcy and receivership, allowing many to reorganize but forcing some to disappear.

Illinois railroads encapsulated national trends in the nineteenth century and experienced the growth and decline of the twentieth. When "Little Grangers" built across state lines into Illinois they illustrated one aspect of a new problem: too many railroads and not enough business in an era of competition from interurbans and, more dangerously, the internal combustion engine. The Good Roads movement tilted public policy toward automobiles, buses, and trucks in the 1920s. Good Roads trains spread the gospel of paving while county and state governments subsidized, with federal assistance, the railroads' most powerful competitors by funding road-building programs.

Illinois had one advantage no other state had: Chicago. The Windy City was a barrier and a wealth generator. Because of their origins as unidirectional local projects with territorial limits, railroads ran to but not through the city. This created headaches for passengers

Figure 0.2. Extreme specialization: a 1915 car used by the Illinois Game and Fish Commission to transport fish from hatcheries to rivers. Lake Forest College Library Special Collections.

and freight handlers, but as a center of the grain, meat, and lumber trades Chicago had no parallel. Several attempts to bypass Chicago enjoyed limited success because of the size of its market, its location adjacent to Lake Michigan, and the corporate structures of the railroads themselves.

Politics permeates the story of Prairie State railroading. Two of the state's best-known national figures, Abraham Lincoln and Stephen A. Douglas, cut their teeth on the industry. Municipal and county politicians made their names denouncing corporate power and demanding control over rates and routes. Railroad development in Illinois determined how the federal government could stimulate economic growth and regulate commerce. Trucks, automobiles, and buses subsidized by taxpayers and buoyed by public policy cut deeply into the railroads' customer base. National transportation

priorities in the 1950s and 1960s, particularly an emphasis on building federally subsidized interstate highways and airports, posed a nearly fatal threat to the railroads. Finally, in the late twentieth century, railroad corporations and governments struck an unstable bargain, with huge implications for Illinois.

Most of the railroads named in this book have vanished, their lines absorbed by other corporations or torn up. At their peak in 1920, Illinois railroads had 12,128 route miles; by 2012 that had shrunk to 6,989 miles.[2] How and why that happened is a crucial element in the story told here. Many railroads went bankrupt at least once, with lost investments and shattered dreams, and almost all merged into or were bought by other companies. Rural branch lines laid to serve farming areas and stymie competitors were abandoned in the twentieth century, the track lifted and reused, the land sometimes entering a twilight zone of ambiguous ownership.

Railroads proved expensive to build and maintain. They consumed oceans of capital because they required land, steel, buildings, rolling stock, and lots of people. Railroad corporations needed money to lay track and operate trains, though a fair amount—the exact sums will never be known—went into the pockets of the powerful and occasionally shady people involved. Railroads needed to attract investment from diverse sources, often (in the early days of the industry) foreign banks and financiers. Chasing capital changed the nature of business in the United States and elsewhere. Railroad corporations were the first organizations to systematically utilize funds from investors who were not family members and often did not see the lines in which they invested. Shareholders cared primarily about dividends and bondholders wanted timely interest payments, the local impact of their investments taking a back seat to the search for profits.

This book is also about an industry with some very specific technological and operational jargon. One of the most important terms is "gauge," which denotes the distance or width between the inside heads of the two rails forming a track and is usually 4 feet 8.5 inches. Part of the story of Illinois railroading is how this particular gauge conquered alternatives, though the victory was neither predetermined nor simple. The rails, made of iron and later steel, are attached to wooden or (increasingly) concrete ties sitting on layers of ballast (small rocks) with a graded roadbed beneath. Railroad lines can be classified as either "trunk" (main) or "branch" (minor). Trains are pulled by locomotives, originally steam engines but later diesel and, in a few cases, electric. Runs vary from short hauls of fewer than one hundred miles to interstate trips of two thousand miles or more. People ride in passenger cars while freight travels in ever-increasingly specialized vehicles. The boxcar served many purposes but proved inflexible compared with the intermodal container, its twenty-first-century equivalent. Railroad companies and suppliers developed gondolas, flatcars, tank cars, stock cars, hoppers, auto racks, and others to meet particular needs. At the rear of freight trains were cabooses for crews monitoring rolling stock en route; those cabooses and crews were replaced in the late twentieth century by computers transmitting information from the back of the last car to the locomotive cab.

As the demise of the beloved caboose reminds us, change was and remains a constant feature of railroading, but the history and operation of the industry in Illinois maintains an enduring fascination.

ACKNOWLEDGMENTS

This book has been many years in the making, and the debts incurred are staggering. It is a pleasure to acknowledge them, beginning with two historians who have been incredibly supportive throughout. To Roger Grant I owe massive thanks for his faith in this project, and Don Hofsommer has been unstinting in his support and his conviction that this was a book worth writing. Conversations with Keith Bryant, Al Churella, Jim Ward, Greg Schneider, Brent Glass, Dale Jenkins, Bill Greenwood, and Steve Patterson have helped deepen my understanding of Illinois railroads past and present. John Gruber and Scott Lothes of the Center for Railroad Photography and Art have been very generous with their time and expertise, as have Don Hitchcock and John White.

Traveling around Illinois lecturing about railroads as an Illinois Humanities Council "Road Scholar" has been wonderfully enriching, and it is a pleasure to thank Ryan Lewis and many librarians and archivists for facilitating forty such talks across the years. I learned a lot from listening to audiences on jaunts from Olney to Rockford and many points in between, and I thank them for their thoughtful contributions on this wonderful subject. Many amazing opportunities have come my way thanks to the National Railroad Hall of Fame, and I am grateful to executive director Julie King and board members Bob Bondi and Jay Matson for these experiences.

Numerous dedicated archivists and librarians have contributed to this volume, notably Nick Fry of the John H. Barriger III National Railroad Library, MaryJo McAndrew and Jeff Douglas of Knox College, Anne Thomason of Lake Forest College, Ann Marie Hayes-Hawkinson and Jeff Hancks of Western Illinois University, George Perkins of McLean County Historical Society, and Barb Musk of the Fulton Museum. At Indiana University Press, Sarah Jacobi has been a joy to work with; I am also grateful for the advice of two anonymous readers to whom the press sent the manuscript, which has been greatly improved by their suggestions.

At Western Illinois University I have benefited tremendously from the deep knowledge of railroading of Bart Jennings and from the amazing cartographic skills of Chris Sutton, who designed the maps for this book while introducing me to the magic of GIS. Sarah Ritter helped with the illustrations at a busy time. Students in my Honors Railroading course encouraged me to see the industry in a new light as we traveled through Colorado together, a trip immeasurably improved by Ed Ellis's thoughtful assistance. Many colleagues have assisted with this project. At Western Illinois University these include Bill Thompson, Keith Holz, Bob Welch, Jim Patterson, John Stierman, and William Polley. Former colleagues at Monmouth College have also been generous with their time and expertise, including Pierre "Pete" Loomis, Mark Ogorzalek, Bill Urban, Tom Best, and Fred Witzig. Students in my railroading courses there contributed to my knowledge of the industry, as did the many guest speakers who gave their time so freely to meet with us.

Friends and family have been incredibly helpful. Clive Hanley, photographer extraordinaire, is a wonderful traveling companion with a brilliant grasp of railroading. Lewis L. Gould has offered much good advice and many useful documents. My parents, Ned and Mary Cordery, have long nurtured my interest in the study of railroads and have listened to many a tale with interest and joy. Most of all, Stacy and Gareth have fed my soul and kept me sane on this journey, for which I cannot thank them enough. Without their grounding and encouragement this book would never have seen the light of day.

LIST OF ABBREVIATIONS

A&S	Alton & Sangamon Railroad
AAR	Association of American Railroads
AE&C	Aurora, Elgin & Chicago Railroad
AFL	American Federation of Labor
ARU	American Railway Union
ATSF	Atchison, Topeka & Santa Fe Railway
B&MRR	Burlington & Missouri River Railroad
B&O	Baltimore & Ohio Railroad
B&OCT	Baltimore & Ohio Chicago Terminal Railroad
BCR&N	Burlington, Cedar Rapids & Northern Railroad
BLE	Brotherhood of Locomotive Engineers
BLF	Brotherhood of Locomotive Firemen and Enginemen
BN	Burlington Northern Railroad
BNSF	Burlington Northern Santa Fe Railway
BRC	Belt Railway of Chicago
C&A	Chicago & Alton Railroad
C&EI	Chicago & Eastern Illinois Railroad
C&GE	Chicago & Great Eastern Railroad
C&IM	Chicago & Illinois Midland Railroad
C&NW	Chicago & North Western Railroad
C&OR	Chicago & Ohio River Railroad
C&P	Chicago & Paducah Railroad
C&RI	Chicago & Rock Island Railroad
C&StL	Cairo & St. Louis Railroad
C&V	Cairo & Vincennes Railroad
CB&N	Chicago, Burlington & Northern Railroad
CB&Q	Chicago, Burlington & Quincy Railroad

CCC&StL	Cleveland, Cincinnati, Chicago & St. Louis Railroad (Big Four)
CGW	Chicago Great Western Railroad
CM&G	Chicago, Milwaukee & Gary Railroad
CM&StP	Chicago, Milwaukee & St. Paul Railroad (the St. Paul)
CMStP&P	Chicago, Milwaukee St. Paul & Pacific Railroad (the Milwaukee Road)
CN	Canadian National Railway
COFC	container on flatcar
Conrail	Consolidated Railroad Corporation
CREATE	Chicago Region Environmental and Transportation Efficiency program
CRI&P	Chicago, Rock Island & Pacific Railway
CSX	CSX Transportation
CTH&SE	Chicago, Terre Haute & Southeastern Railroad
DM&FD	Des Moines & Fort Dodge Railroad
EJ&E	Elgin, Joliet & Eastern Railroad
EMC	Electro-Motive Company
EMD	Electro-Motive Division of General Motors
FRA	Federal Railroad Administration
G&CU	Galena & Chicago Union Railroad
GM&O	Gulf, Mobile & Ohio Railroad
GMA	General Managers Association of Chicago
GNR	Great Northern Railroad
IC	Iowa Central Railroad
ICC	Interstate Commerce Commission
ICG	Illinois Central Gulf Railroad
ICRR	Illinois Central Railroad
IGRA	Illinois Good Roads Association
IHIA	Illinois Highway Improvement Association
III	Indiana, Illinois & Iowa Railroad
II&M	Illinois, Iowa & Minnesota Railway
IRA	Illinois Railroad Association
IT	Illinois Traction Railroad
IT	Illinois Terminal Railroad (after 1927)
K&IR	Kankakee & Illinois River Railroad
KCS	Kansas City Southern Railway
L&N	Louisville & Nashville Railroad
LS&BC	LaSalle & Bureau County Railroad
LCL	less-than-carload
M&ORR	Mobile & Ohio Railroad
M&StL	Minneapolis & St. Louis Railroad

MoPac	Missouri Pacific Railroad
MSRR	Michigan Southern Railroad
N&W	Norfolk & Western Railroad
NGRA	National Good Roads Association
NPR	Northern Pacific Railroad
NYC	New York Central Railroad
O&M	Ohio & Mississippi Railroad
ODT	Office of Defense Transportation
OPRI	Office of Public Road Inquiry
ORC	Order of Railroad Conductors
P&BV	Peoria & Bureau Valley Railroad
P&O	Peoria & Oquawka Railroad
P&PU	Peoria & Pekin Union Railway
PD&E	Peoria, Decatur & Eastern Railroad
PD&L	Pekin, Decatur & Lincoln Railroad
Penn	Pennsylvania Railroad
PK&P	Plymouth, Kankakee & Pacific Railroad
RED	Railway Employees Department, AFL
RPO	Railroad Post Office
SP	Southern Pacific Railroad
TC&StL	Toledo, Cincinnati & St. Louis Railroad
TD&B	Toledo, Delphos & Burlington Railroad
TH&A	Terre Haute & Alton Railroad
TOFC	trailer on flatcar
TP&W	Toledo, Peoria & Warsaw Railroad
TP&W	Toledo, Peoria & Western Railroad (after 1879)
UP	Union Pacific Railroad
USRA	United States Railroad Administration (1917–20)
USRA	United States Railway Administration (1973–87)
VRD	Voluntary Relief Department (CB&Q)
WC	Wisconsin Central Railroad
WPB	War Production Board

THE
IRON ROAD
in the
PRAIRIE STATE

PRELIMINARIES

The topography of Illinois is particularly conducive to railroading. Trains move best over flat land, and the state has few hills of any size and nothing that could be mistaken for a mountain. Its 56,400 square miles vary from a low of 279 feet above sea level to the 1,235 feet of Charles Mound on the Wisconsin border near Galena. The glaciated north boasted extensive prairies dotted with stands of timber, while in the heavily wooded south, coal deposits lay concealed beneath the surface. The hilliest section of the state is in the northwest. Here the lead-mining region of Galena escaped the graze of the glaciers, as did Calhoun County in the south. The south offered numerous engineering trials, especially around Cairo, strategically placed at the confluence of the Ohio and Mississippi Rivers but swampy and subject to frequent flooding, while much of far-southern Illinois was viewed as "a hilly extension of the Ozark highland."[1] The state's rivers provided obstacles to emigrants and challenges to bridge builders, while bluffs at Peoria and Alton restricted railroad development at those two important towns. Generally, however, the gentle prairies presented few insurmountable or even challenging hindrances except distance: Illinois is larger than England, birthplace of the railroad industry.

PRAIRIES AND INDIANS

Prior to European settlement successive Indian peoples made the Illinois country their home. When French fur traders and missionaries arrived in the seventeenth century the Illini (or Illiniwek), who had dominated the area for a century, were already being pressured by the Iroquois confederation and left the land bearing their name. Others shared their fate, culminating in 1833 with the federal government's forcible relocation of the remaining Indians. In 1717 the French colony in Louisiana annexed Illinois, where settlers had established outposts on the banks of the Mississippi River, including the town of Kaskaskia. The demography of Illinois changed after Britain defeated France in the French and Indian War (1754–1763). The region became more heterogeneous as British immigrants arrived on the Ohio and Wabash Rivers. Indians clustered around Lake Michigan, and white settlers established trading posts on its banks. Water remained the preeminent means of transportation, and the rivers running around and across Illinois served as highways.

But natural flows were unreliable. Waterways froze, fell, and flooded. Sandbars along the shore of Lake Michigan blocked easy access to the stale stream that would later be named the Chicago River, and the shoreline offered no natural harbors to protect shipping from devastating storms on the giant lake. Just a few miles inland lay a low continental shelf; most of the rivers to its west ran from there down to the Mississippi, while the few to its east flowed into Lake Michigan. The marshy territory on the site of what would—after extensive draining and filling—become Chicago offered an unpromising prospect to hopeful settlers, though small numbers kept arriving nevertheless.

Figure 1.1. Charles Turzak's River and Canal Boats illustrates the brute force needed to move along canals. Collection of Western Illinois University Art Gallery; courtesy of the Fine Arts Program, Public Buildings Service, US General Services Administration.

Dangerous and uncomfortable boats contributed to the risks of river passage. Traveling to Pekin aboard the steamship *Banner* on the Illinois River in the 1830s, Eliza Farnham complained, "The doors were broken, the stairs dilapidated; there was no linen for the berths, the hurricane deck leaked." Tar covering the rough wooden roof melted in the hot sun and dripped onto unsuspecting passengers. Farnham recorded how "the waste of steam was so great that the wheels effected only about four revolutions a minute, and the boat had a strange habit . . . of occasionally running twice or thrice her length with considerable rapidity, and then suddenly

lurching so as to throw everything to the starboard." A decade later Scottish immigrant John Regan spent his first night in Illinois on the banks of the Mississippi after a steamer ran aground.[2] These and a thousand other such tales told of the perils of traveling on the relatively calm rivers forming the state's boundaries. Railroads would seize the competitive advantages their speed and safety offered as an alternative to river travel.

CANALS SHOW THE WAY

Rivers imperfectly met a growing demand for long-distance transportation and were sometimes replaced by canals. These artificial channels enabled humans to harness water for carrying heavy loads over long distances in relative safety. Secure inland haulage on a large scale could boost economic development, as British canal builders demonstrated in the 1760s, but theirs was hardly a recent innovation. While diverting water for irrigation and transportation is as old as civilization, British entrepreneurs pioneered the private, for-profit canal, learning from the public-works engineers who had developed locks for moving barges uphill.[3]

Canal building reached across the Atlantic soon after the American Revolution. Canals in the young republic, often constructed with government funding, carried bulk commodities such as coal and cotton over long distances. As white Americans moved west from the Atlantic seaboard, the states of Virginia and Pennsylvania proposed funding canals to the Ohio River valley. Though not built, these projects whetted an appetite that reached its pinnacle in 1825 with the triumphal opening of the Erie Canal, a state-funded, 340-mile-long ditch linking New York City with Lake Erie via the Hudson River and the Great Lakes, making the country beyond the Appalachians accessible to new immigrants. It was then possible to travel by water from New York City to the young state of Illinois.

STEAM PROVIDES A PUSH

Canals afforded a slow, pastoral means of movement but they could not solve all the problems presented by rivers. Horse-drawn boats did nothing to increase speed and ice could block canals completely, but they did represent a crucial breakthrough. In the realm of technological innovation one improvement frequently leads to others. In this case, proof of the demand for bulk haulage helped convince investors of the need for a faster mode of transportation. Cart horses pulled barges at perhaps five miles per hour while steam locomotives reached twenty-five miles an hour, as rapid as a racehorse. Railroads brought the drama of new technology and the exhilaration of hitherto-unmatched velocity. In one of history's delightful ironies, the world's first public railroad—England's Stockton & Darlington Railway—opened in the same year as the Erie Canal.

The steam locomotive was a strange beast—a "mad dragon" some called it—and it grabbed the American imagination in the 1830s. The pace, noise, and danger of train travel were made culturally safe by applying metaphors such as "the iron horse" to help domesticate the noisy, smelly machines.[4] One Illinois newspaper editor, campaigning in favor of building railroads, wrote in 1851: "A railroad, what an invention! what a blessing! See yon 'iron horse' with his nostrils breathing fire, his long and shaggy mane, in the shape of smoke, streaming far behind, while in his might and strength, with his 'train' in the rear, he comes careering through yon 'neck of timber,' now over that creek, now across the prairie, now again in timber."[5] Excitement and convenience would soon overcome fear of the unknown.

Early locomotives looked like barrels on wheels. Firemen shoveled coal into small fireboxes to boil water, which was released under pressure to power pistons and turn the wheels. The tiny point of contact between wheel and track—less than one-tenth of a square inch—created virtually frictionless motion and demanded ever-improved brakes. The means of slowing and stopping a train was just one innovation railroading inspired. The industry quickly became a leading area for inventions, and Illinois would be the location for many of the workshops, factories, and routes of this technological progress.

Railroads promised a bright future for a young nation. In 1832 one journalist marveled at how "the prosperity and intelligence of the country will be comparatively great" when railroads operated the length and breadth of the land. Modest first steps were being taken at the time of this proclamation. In 1830 the Baltimore & Ohio Railroad (B&O) opened thirteen miles of track from the port of Baltimore to Ellicott's Mills. The company used an American-built steam locomotive constructed by New York businessman, politician, and inventor Peter Cooper. He called his engine *Tom Thumb* because it was "so insignificant," by which he meant it was for demonstration purposes only. Unfortunately, the first run was delayed a week after someone purloined the copper in the pipes and boiler.[6]

Figure 1.2. An "American-type" 4-4-0 locomotive at Disco on the TP&W (April 1894). Author's collection.

Tom Thumb foreshadowed the end of canals, but they did not go quietly. In 1830 several newspapers published "A Canal Stockholder's Outburst," a fictional diatribe complaining that railroads threatened to "set the whole world a-gadding," destroy "local attachments," and "upset all the gravity of the nation." The steam train, the anonymous author declared, was "a pestilential, topsy-turvy, harum-scarum whirligig." But an early traveler on the B&O reported that, far from causing social upheaval, the railroad was reviving Frederick, Maryland, by bringing people and commerce into town and dramatically lowering the cost of sending and receiving commodities.[7] This pattern would be repeated across the nation, but for settlements without railroads the consequences could be dire.

Peter Cooper's diminutive machine boasted one horsepower and was quickly superseded. The first American-built locomotive had been constructed and operated in 1826 by Colonel John Stevens on the grounds of his estate in Hoboken, New Jersey. Stevens became the chief engineer on the Camden & Amboy, refining the designs of British locomotives unable to negotiate the New World's lightweight and poorly laid track. A dozen small workshops sprang up to meet the growing demand for engines, ranging from the short-lived, such as the Taunton Works in Massachusetts, to the durable, including the famous Baldwin Locomotive Works. Established in Philadelphia in 1832, Baldwin turned out some of the iconic locomotives of the steam age and lasted into the diesel era of the mid-twentieth century. After much experimentation, the sturdy and reliable "American-type" locomotive, with its characteristic cow catcher and giant headlight, dominated railroading until after the Civil War.

The Iron Road in the Prarie State

Working with an emerging technology confronting a virtually limitless range of unknown and unfamiliar factors, railroad pioneers woefully underestimated the costs of construction. The first surveys for the B&O, opened in 1830, projected that $5 million would be needed to lay its 290 miles of track, but $16 million, 379 miles, and 22 years later it reached the Ohio River. Investors were cautious: the South Carolina legislature was forced to market and guarantee bonds for the South-Carolina Canal & Rail-Road Company when few individuals or institutions were willing to take the plunge. Building a line from Charleston to Hamburg, it began operations in November 1832 and soon reached its terminus across the Savannah River from Augusta, Georgia. Offering regular passenger services and carrying cotton for shipment to mills in the North and to Europe, it helped make the case for building railroads.[8] Other states took note.

THE PRAIRIE STATE

One of those states was Illinois. Gaining admission to the Union in 1818, the Prairie State covered more territory than New York, Connecticut, Vermont, New Hampshire, Massachusetts, and Rhode Island combined. Settlers attracted by relatively easy passage from Missouri and Kentucky entered from the south, while Native Americans harrying and frightening immigrants in the north delayed colonization there. Chicago did not exist until the owners of a few rough houses clustered around Fort Dearborn boldly declared themselves a city in 1833, the last of the local indigenous peoples having been forced at gunpoint to sell their land to federal Indian agents. An early boost to settlement in the north came with rumors that a proposed canal would be dug to connect Lake Michigan with the Illinois River. This immensely popular project was authorized by the legislature in 1822, but delays in financing and construction meant it did not open until 1848. When finally completed, the Illinois and Michigan Canal linked the Chicago River (which emptied into Lake Michigan) with the Illinois River, joining two watersheds flowing in opposite directions. By then, in another of those wonderful ironies with which history abounds, the first railroad was inching its way out of Chicago. Contemporaries did not know it, but the canal age was drawing to a close.[9]

Horse-drawn stagecoaches also provided long-distance travel before railroads. By 1825, one politically connected stagecoach company, Frink and Walker, controlled almost three thousand route miles in northern Illinois and profited from a firm grip on mail shipments. Beginning with construction of a route toward the village of Naperville, coaches and wagons traversed seven plank roads—essentially wooden beams laid across dirt tracks and constantly needing replacement—leaving Chicago.[10] But these thoroughfares did not offer much improvement on the cart tracks remembered in a poem celebrating the opening of Chicago's first railroad:

> Soon the produce of my fields brought to hand
> So soft were the roads o'er the rich mucky land
> I could not transport in the city a load
> But near half was consumed by the cost on the road.[11]

The writer cursed "the road-dragging toil" and "the mud and the slough" until the seasonal and financial advantages of the railroad had been thoroughly hammered home. Railroads condemned plank roads to an early and unlamented demise. In the late 1840s the entrepreneurial John Frink began investing in railroads, aware that the days of his stagecoaches were numbered. In 1848 he joined the board of the Galena & Chicago Union Railroad (G&CU), the first line out of Chicago, and shortly afterward joined the boards of two Peoria-based railroads.[12] Like canals, the plank roads were rendered redundant by the greater reliability, higher speeds, and lower costs of railroad transportation. To exploit these advantages and open the frontier to settlement, Illinois entered the race to build rail lines with a combination of enthusiasm and naïveté that proved disastrous.

DEVELOPMENT DELAYED

The earliest attempts to build steam-powered railroads in Illinois failed miserably. Several private projects laid a few miles of track before going bankrupt; two short coal lines used animals to haul wagons; and an ambitious state-funded network fell victim to an economic depression—called a "panic" at the time—in 1837. But the seed blown across the Atlantic Ocean from Britain fell on fertile soil. Railroads offered relatively fast, all-weather transportation for people and commodities. Engineering challenges, especially safely and reliably harnessing steam power, proved surmountable, and investment capital became available, but the development of the industry was neither smooth nor simple. The demand was fueled in part by roads so poor that Illinois became a notorious "mud state" when the weather turned foul. In the winter of 1848–49, for example, the people of McLeansboro found themselves isolated. Bereft of "coffee, sugar and other necessaries of life," they survived on what they had stored from previous harvests until the roads dried out the following spring.[1] This was a common occurrence in the harsh Illinois climate, and town and country alike needed a dependable, all-weather mode of transportation to combat snow, ice, and mud.

The 1830s found the young United States wrapping itself ever more closely into a transatlantic economy. Railroad promoters in Illinois hoped to generate growth and boost government revenues by subsidizing railroad construction. Unfortunately, the very forces they sought to employ—transatlantic trade, industrial production,

increasing immigration—proved unhelpful. Even as the young state borrowed money and commenced laying track, credit markets tightened, unemployment rose, and the economy floundered. A debt that would not be fully repaid until 1880 and skepticism among would-be investors resulted.

PRAIRIE DREAMING

Railroad fever gripped Illinois in the 1830s. Canny capitalists extracting grain, meat, lumber, coal, and lead from the resource-rich state required inexpensive and reliable means of transporting their heavy commodities. Western territories were experiencing an unprecedented period of economic and demographic expansion as land sales soared and then peaked in 1836 and 1837. The obvious advantages of railroads, despite the risks and uncertainty of working with a new, untried technology, stimulated a variety of proposals. Politicians gambled that railroads would generate growth and fill government coffers, while reformers saw them as a means to combat frontier licentiousness and laziness with a "great moral improvement."[2] Railroads would create a dynamic economy, their promoters proclaimed, by connecting rivers and encouraging immigration.

The air filled with ideas. Proposals included a railroad from Lake Michigan to the Wabash River through territory "rapidly filling up with a population respectable for enterprise, inteligence [*sic*], and worth." A line from Alton, on the Mississippi, to the future capital at Springfield gained the public support of Abraham

Lincoln as he campaigned for the Illinois General Assembly. Lieutenant Governor A. M. Jenkins drafted an 1832 bill to fund a survey for a railroad from Peru to the future site of Cairo and link the Illinois River with the confluence of the Mississippi and Ohio Rivers. One group of investors proposed building a line from the point at which the Rock River met the Mississippi River through Princeton and Kankakee to the Indiana line, and from there across Ohio to Erie, Pennsylvania, where it would connect with the New-York & Erie Rail Road to New York City. Another prospectus promised that "a Rail-road on this route would open a direct and easy communication with St. Louis and the whole Valley of the Mississippi; it would bring into use some of the best water-power in the Union, surrounded by the most fertile soil in the world and inhabited as it is by a rapidly increasing population."[3] In 1834 Governor Joseph Duncan called for investment in canals and railroads, and the next year the legislature passed its first railroad charters, for the Chicago & Vincennes and for the Jacksonville & Meredosia. In 1836 the legislature issued a further fifteen charters, but virtually none of the required private capital could be raised and the lines were not built. Continuing to look upon railroads as the quickest path to economic development, the Illinois General Assembly unsuccessfully lobbied Congress for land grants.

Everyone in every corner of the state wanted a line, but Illinois was the frontier. People, capital, and equipment remained scarce. The only actual railroads there before 1838 were two coal-mine roads in Little Egypt employing animals to pull rudimentary carts over wooden tracks topped by strips of iron. Both proved short-lived. One of these lines, the Coal Mine Bluff Road—also called the New Pittsburgh & Mississippi Railroad—ran for seven miles from a mine near Belleville down to the Mississippi River and began operations in 1837. The other, which may have begun running beforehand, was located on the Big Muddy near Murphysboro and linked a mine worked for two decades with that river. The donkey on this line walked for about a mile to load barges when the river was too low to permit them to reach the minehead.[4]

Supporters of railroads and other "internal improvements" held meetings across the state in the election season of 1836. In Carlinville, for example, advocates of an iron road from Alton to Springfield announced it would "conduce greatly to the benefit of a line of flourishing counties and develope [sic] with greater rapidity and certainty than any other means the resources of a large portion of the most valuable part of the state of Illinois."[5] Railroad backers called for a statewide convention in Vandalia, then nearing the end of its nineteen-year run as state capital. They outspent, outmuscled, and outraged their opponents, who claimed to have been "threatened and insulted on our way to our boarding houses and denounced in unmeasured terms." Riding a wave of enthusiasm and spouting emotional rhetoric about a bright future for the young state, the prorailroad party swept aside all opposition. The electorate, disconnected from reality and reason, voted the prorailroad faction into office and thereby created "the most irresponsible gathering in the state's history."[6]

One of the leading infrastructure-friendly politicians in 1836 was Morgan County state's attorney Stephen A. Douglas, a Democrat. In Vandalia the energetic Douglas proposed an appropriations bill for improving navigation on the Illinois and Wabash Rivers, completing the Illinois and Michigan Canal, building a south-north railroad from Cairo to LaSalle, and constructing a line from his adopted hometown of Quincy, on the Mississippi, west through his legislative district to the Wabash River. Grandiose and unrealistic by any measure except the spirit of the times, the bill Douglas supported was quickly trumped by other proposals. Another neophyte assemblyman present in Vandalia, Abraham Lincoln, backed internal improvements to gain support for moving the capital to Springfield, whose voters he represented.[7]

After much wrangling over the approximate routes to be followed, a bill passed the assembly in February 1837. The Illinois Internal Improvements Act was a politically astute but financially and technologically implausible attempt to facilitate economic growth. The assembly voted to fund and build eight railroads simultaneously, promising cash to counties not traversed by railroads to gain their support for the project and committing Illinois to building an astounding 1,300 miles of track at an estimated cost of $9.4 million. Such an impressive vision led one contemporary to praise "the high destinies of that young State" for taking what one scholar called "a tremendously bold gamble."[8]

Audacious it certainly was. The Internal Improvements Act authorized construction of four trunk and three branch lines from west to east bisected by a south-north route. The northernmost line traversing the state, appropriately called the Northern Cross, was to connect the Mississippi River at Quincy with the Wabash River at Lafayette, Indiana. This would, it transpired, be the sole line constructed, and even then it reached only Springfield. Another road, from the Mississippi at Warsaw east to Bloomington, was to have a branch from Bloomington to the Illinois River ports of Mackinaw and Pekin. The other two west-east trunk lines would originate in Alton, which Illinois legislators and local boosters promoted as a rival to St. Louis, and terminate on the Wabash. One Alton railroad was to reach the Indiana line at Vincennes, and a second, called the Southern Cross, would do likewise at Mount Carmel with branches to Belleville and Terre Haute, Indiana.

Bisecting the main west-east lines was the south-north Illinois Central. Starting at Cairo, it would terminate in Galena, on the Galena (or Fever) River near the Mississippi River and close to Iowa and Wisconsin. One hundred and twenty miles north of Cairo a secondary line would turn northeast toward LaSalle, where it would link up with the Illinois and Michigan Canal to complete a route into Chicago and Lake Michigan. Darius B. Holbrook, a Cairo businessman with extensive landholdings around the city and a gift for self-promotion, offered to elevate the rails on wooden pilings to conquer the swampy land in his part of the state. Such was the heat of positive feeling when the undertaking was announced that the *American Railroad Journal* proclaimed, "This proposed internal improvement unquestionably is of greater importance to the State, the government, and the whole Union, than any similar work yet projected."[9]

The Illinois internal improvements program mixed giddy ambition with hard-headed politics. It focused on the southern two-thirds of the state because that was where most Illinoisans lived. In 1830 less than 1 percent of the population of the state inhabited the northeast quadrant, and a decade later Cook County still accounted for under 3 percent. In 1840 the five most populous counties were all south of the Illinois River, and the demographic center of the state was a few miles east of Springfield. The internal improvements legislation reflected this reality.[10]

Triumphal bonfires and rapturous editorials greeted passage of the 1837 act. The *State Register* predicted Illinois would "shortly take her place far in advance of her Western sisters," and "this Infant Hercules of the West" earned praise for setting an example other states should emulate. To pay for the proposed lines, the legislature authorized borrowing up to $10 million, eight times the total combined expenses incurred by the state government between its formation in 1818 and passage of the act. To raise money, the legislators appointed three "fund commissioners" and seven public-works officials to sell internal improvement bonds and pay for surveys. Given the state's well-publicized potential, the commissioners anticipated widespread interest among European investors. To sweeten the pot, the assembly guaranteed payment of interest on the bonds.[11]

Work began sporadically across the state. By 1839 construction on five separate segments was under way on the south-north Illinois Central. North of the Illinois River that line was to be raised on wooden posts in order to simplify the building in undulating areas subject to deep frosts. Of the Alton railroads, the line to Mount Carmel was begun in four places, and construction commenced on fifty miles of the road to Shawneetown. Surveys for the Northern Cross were completed, as were twelve miles of line from Meredosia toward Springfield. Bridges and embankments on the projected railroad between Peoria and Warsaw were built, with five miles of track laid from Peoria west. None of these lines would be completed as planned.[12]

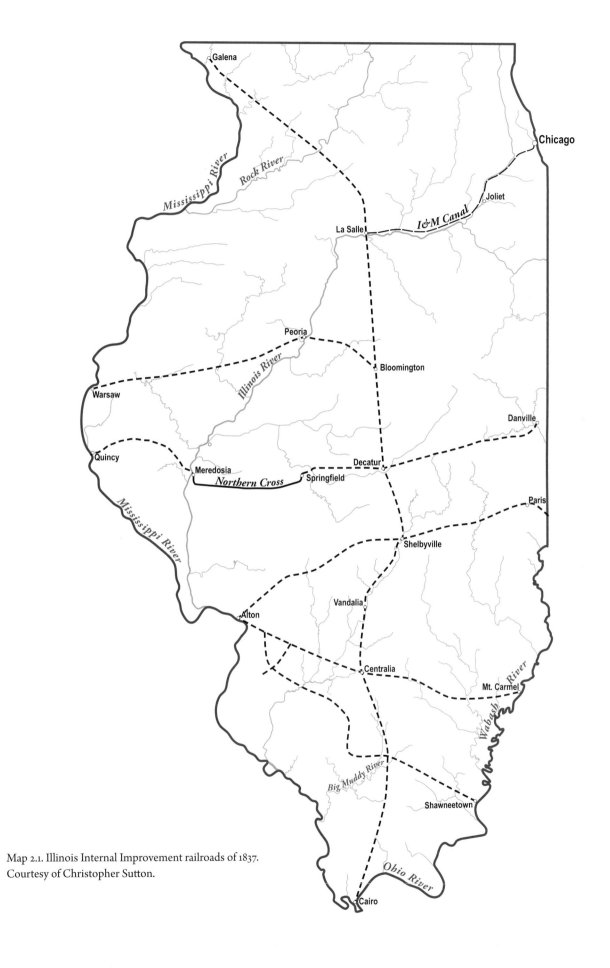

Map 2.1. Illinois Internal Improvement railroads of 1837.
Courtesy of Christopher Sutton.

The 1836–37 state assembly inadvertently demonstrated why early railroads began as local projects. Advertisements calling for "Sealed Proposals" stating "a specific and definite price for the work to be performed" appeared in newspapers statewide, optimistically asserting, "No doubts are entertained of the ability of the State to furnish the money." Despite hopeful notices calling for contractors to bid on "Grading, Bridging and Masonry" through "dry, healthy, and well-settled" territory in which "provisions are easily secured," almost no work was carried out because a transatlantic economic downturn plunged state and nation into a financial crisis.[13]

Periodic economic collapses were one of the growing pains of an industrializing market economy. In 1837 a surfeit of consumer goods—in this case, British textiles—dumped at low prices on the American market undercut domestic production, and American mills closed down. Unemployment, underemployment, dislocation, and uncertainty followed. The downturn made loans impossible to obtain, fatal to a program in which costs had been grossly underestimated. Instead of the "extravagant system of railroads and canals" supporters anticipated, Illinois got "pauper canals and rickety rail roads" standing as "monuments of our folly." Critics charged that the legislature had created "a wild system of speculation . . . which overwhelmed the state in debt and almost [led to] financial ruin." Illinois damaged its creditworthiness by failing to service its railroad loans between 1841 and 1846. Moralists blamed the crash on extravagance, complaining that Americans were spending too much on wine and not enough on iron.[14]

In truth, the taste for luxuries and cheap imports were minor causes of the Panic of 1837.[15] More significant were a Bank of England decision in 1836 to limit the size and number of its loans and British investors' subsequent unwillingness to risk their capital in the United States. The value of American exports plummeted, and the price of cotton tumbled, hurting planters in the South and the northern businessmen who insured, shipped, and sold their harvests. Also in 1836 President Andrew Jackson issued a "specie circular" requiring gold or silver for all purchases of government land, much of which had previously been bought by speculators using paper money drawn on local banks. Land sales fell, eliminating an important source of revenue for the federal treasury and devaluing banknotes. Banks demanded loan repayments, but cash-poor merchants could not oblige and tasted bankruptcy.

By the end of 1837 a substantial number of banks nationally had gone out of business and half a million industrial workers were unemployed. The price of land in Chicago, which had exploded in 1836 on the expectation it would perpetually rise, dropped precipitously. The Chicago branch of the Illinois State Bank closed its doors. Numerous businesses failed and that, combined with an unsuccessful but highly publicized attempt to repudiate the city's debts, made outside investors cautious about lending money there. Moralists revived the Republican critique of credit as ethically dangerous because it produced nothing tangible and advised Americans to avoid speculation and greed. The old virtue of living within one's means—as a family, a community, and a country—became fashionable once more.[16]

The Panic of 1837 was a disaster for the Illinois internal improvements project. Bids were accepted and work was begun, proponents asserting that "the present is a favorable time for putting the works under contract."[17] This could hardly have been further from the truth. Only one segment of one line—fifty-nine miles of the proposed Northern Cross—was actually built, at a cost of $1.5 million in bonds guaranteed by the state. On May 9, 1837, the first track was laid at Meredosia, on the Illinois River. Six months later the first locomotive in the Mississippi Valley, the *Rogers,* arrived from New Jersey. It was supposed to be followed by two other engines, but nature took a dim view of the proceedings and the ship carrying them sank during a storm in the Gulf of Mexico. At Meredosia the inexperienced handlers unloaded the *Rogers* onto the side of the Illinois River and watched helplessly as mud swallowed it. There it stayed for the winter. Rescued and repaired the following spring, the *Rogers* made a short inaugural run exactly one year after track laying had begun. In July 1839 twelve miles of track opened from Meredosia to Morgan City, where passengers connected to a stagecoach for the next dozen miles to Jacksonville. Not until January 1840 did the rails reach Jacksonville, and it took another two years before they finally entered the new state capital of Springfield. Soon afterward the locomotives wore out and sat, abandoned and rusting, as mules pulled trains at walking pace. In 1847 the state decided to get out of the railroad business and auctioned off the line, earning $21,500 on the original $1.5 million investment. The purchasers switched the terminus and renamed it the Sangamon & Morgan Railroad. Extending the line to Danville, they called it the Great Western Railroad and earned a small profit when it merged with the Wabash Railroad in the 1870s.

Illinois did not suffer in solitude. The Internal Improvements Act was one example of "the pervading spirit of the age." Many other states embraced debt, for "the spirit of speculation was rife throughout our entire nation" at the time. By the end of 1837 British investors owned American railroad bonds worth $165 million, many of them losing value rapidly. Nineteen of the twenty-six states in the republic held railroad debt totaling $217.9 million in 1841; Illinois ranked seventh of the nineteen, with $13.6 million, much of it unpaid interest. By 1842 nine states had failed to service railroad loans from British banks, and three of them—Arkansas, Michigan, and Mississippi—defaulted. Obtaining financing from across the Atlantic became virtually impossible. The panic cast a long shadow from which the United States did not emerge for a decade.[18]

Even so, the Panic of 1837 was not solely responsible for the failure of the Illinois internal improvements plan. The project was simply too ambitious for a young, undeveloped state, and it suffered from its political parentage. Everyone wanted "their" line immediately, with the result that none were completed, and only a small fraction of one was built. Instead of concentrating on laying a single line from beginning to end, construction of every railroad began simultaneously. The funds, spent on surveys and grading, were soon exhausted. By the end of 1838 Illinois railroad bonds were worth only twelve cents on the dollar. In his address to the people of Illinois in November 1840, Governor Thomas Carlin lamented how "it is to be deeply deplored that our State is measurably overwhelmed with pecuniary embarrassments." Those "embarrassments" meant that "the bare mention of the word 'railroad' would have the same effect upon our people that flaunting a red rag would have upon a turkey gobbler."[19] Capitalists viewed the Prairie State with caution until a combination of local initiative and federal aid sparked a railroad revolution in the 1850s.

Optimism about the future returned quickly to the prairies. The railroad promise of orderly settlement, rapid cultivation, and improved contact with the rest of the country was too good to be ignored for long. Beginning in 1848, railroad lines pushed out from Chicago, funded by local investors, tax revenues, and land grants. Built by merchants exploiting regional connections, they constituted the infrastructure for improving the lives of ordinary Americans while enriching a new class of capitalists.

OPTIMISM REVIVED

Travelers in Illinois during the 1840s may have paused to puzzle over sporadic strips of artificially flattened ground, mute testimony to the recent infatuation with railroads. In Bureau County, for example, work on the original Illinois Central Railroad (ICRR) got no further than "cutting away strips of timber" and leveling small stretches of territory for rails that never arrived. The Jacksonville & Savannah Railroad used land between Canton and Farmington flattened for the Peoria to Warsaw line. Stone culverts and bridge abutments also remained as a memory of the 1837 Illinois Internal Improvements Act. At the southern tip of the state, ribbons of graded land and a lengthy embankment near Cairo, remnants of "the wild State internal improvement craze," reminded people of how "the State and whole communities were left bankrupt—stranded upon dirt embankments."[1]

Disillusionment lasted barely a decade, however. The passion for railroads reignited in the 1850s, and Chicago emerged as a major commercial center. Trains from the east brought in new inhabitants and departed with grain from the prairies. Developments downstate signaled the temporary prominence of Alton and the permanent rise of St. Louis. On a national scale, the ICRR set an important precedent by using federal land grants to stimulate interest and investment.

Illinois revived dramatically in the 1850s. The population doubled from 851,470 in 1850 to 1,711,871 on the eve of the Civil War, and Illinois had more new track than any other state in the Union. Just 10 miles operated in 1848, 45 miles three years later, 390 miles in 1853, and 1,096 miles at the end of 1854. By 1860 Illinois had 2,679 route miles, and eleven different railroads served Chicago. Only Ohio of the western states could claim more track, and the total decennial growth of Illinois mileage exceeded that of all New England states combined.

The state was becoming incorporated into the national economy by 1860 and slowly recovering from the effects of the Internal Improvements Act. On a local level, the arrival of the railroad initiated a period of growth for many small settlements. Gridley was not unique in claiming that its first train (on the Peoria & Oquawka Railroad [P&O] Eastern Extension) "confirmed the village's birth and guaranteed its existence."[2] The railroad had arrived in time for the Civil War, when it would prove crucial to the movement of soldiers and weapons as military need dictated.

WEST TO THE MISSISSIPPI

After grand ambition came a new reality. The crash of 1837 shook but did not destroy Illinois. During the 1840s, Chicago land prices rose and European financiers looked for new investment opportunities. The first stirrings of renewed progress on the prairies came when railroad advocates met on January 7, 1846, in Rockford to demand recommencing construction of the Galena & Chicago Union Railroad (G&CU). Rockford businessman Thomas D. Robertson, whose vigorous selling of share subscriptions earned him a seat on the board of directors, led a group of energetic and

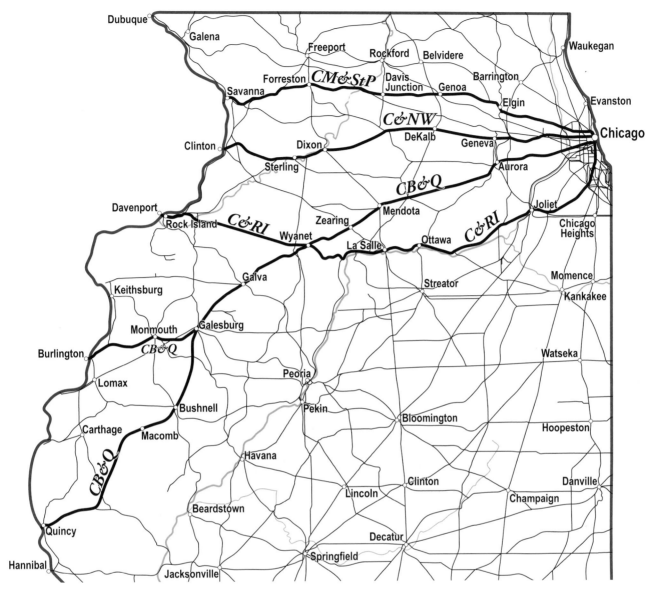

Map 3.1. "Granger roads" main lines. Courtesy of Christopher Sutton.

able investors. Prime among these was New York state senator William Butler Ogden, who supported government aid to railroads and a line from New York to the Mississippi River. In 1835 Ogden "determined to follow the star of empire in the West" and moved to Chicago to represent nonresident landowners there. After two years in the tiny settlement he was elected Chicago's first mayor. Despite losing much of his personal fortune during the panic, he repaid his loans, restored his credit, and saw his landholdings reach over a million acres by 1850.[3]

Inspired by the Rockford gathering, Ogden and other Windy City boosters convinced the Illinois General Assembly to give them the original 1836 G&CU charter. This "Chicago Group" stood to profit from higher land values and set out to raise the capital they needed. Aware that funding would not come from beyond Illinois, they hired agents to sell share subscriptions to farmers along or near the proposed route. Subscribers paid regular installments until reaching a preset amount, making shares affordable while guaranteeing steady income to the railroad. Shopkeepers, artisans, and manual laborers on or near the proposed route took up the stock offering. County politicians created new taxes to invest in the company, hoping farmers would gain access to reliable transportation and reelect them.[4]

Beginning in June 1848, the Galena company laid track to an unincorporated area thirty miles west of Chicago where, in 1849, it met the moribund St. Charles Branch. Here a village called Turner Junction (now West Chicago) sprang up on land owned by company director John B. Turner. To build "a practical and inexpensive road," Ogden and his fellow directors purchased used rolling stock and secondhand strap rail. Consisting of lengths of iron bolted onto wooden beams, strap rail had been outlawed by eastern states after causing several fatal accidents. The G&CU operated mixed freight and passenger services until the first passenger-only train ran on July 4, 1849, from Chicago to Cottage Hill (renamed Elmhurst in 1870). In 1850 the company opened forty-two route miles to Elgin, though the Chicago terminus had to be built outside city limits because Ogden's political enemies blocked him. This stubborn attitude soon changed, and the G&CU constructed a depot near the Chicago River.[5]

Upon reaching Elgin, the directors altered the railroad's destination. The charter gave them tremendous latitude and, aware that another line would reach Galena first, they built to Rockford instead. Asserting that "the present revenue of the Road, and the certain increase from the extension of the Road and growth of the Country tributary to it, renders the bonds now offered of security of a most undoubtable character," the line continued to the Mississippi River at Fulton. An 1854 advertisement promised that "the business of the country through which it passes would furnish a fair dividend to the stockholders." Inflated descriptions and sunny predictions were coins of the railroad realm, but in this case there was cause for optimism: the G&CU paid dividends of 10 percent or more in each of the first five years of its existence. As an early passenger on the line reported, "Never was a railroad more needed, nor one which promised a surer or more continual product for the capital invested in its construction." With its early

profits the company discarded strap rails and replaced them with safer Welsh iron.[6]

In 1855 the G&CU began double-tracking its main line, taking advantage of a far-sighted early decision to build bridges and tunnels wide enough to accommodate two parallel tracks. This gave rise to one of the unique properties of the company: running trains on the left-hand side because its station buildings were north of the original lines. Operating on the right-hand side, as other lines did, would have required Chicago-bound passengers to cross the tracks to get to their trains, a dangerous proposition. G&CU passengers became known as "lantern commuters" because they left their lights at the station in the morning and picked them up at night. In the interim the station attendant would trim the wicks and fill the lanterns with oil.[7]

The only Illinois railroad to cross the Mississippi before the Civil War began life as the Chicago & LaSalle, chartered in 1848. Changing its name to the Chicago & Rock Island (C&RI) in 1851, it reached Joliet in 1853 and the town of Rock Island, at the confluence of the Rock and Mississippi Rivers, a year later. To commemorate the grand occasion two trains carried a thousand people across the state, signifying its connection "with the axis of the commercial system of this country." Stopping en route to allow guests to pick wildflowers and admire the tall prairie grass, the trains made their way slowly west and were greeted at the Rock Island depot by a banner proclaiming, with pardonable exaggeration, "The Mississippi and the Atlantic Shake Hands." Cannons were fired, crowds cheered, and bands played on the decks of steamboats drawn up to the dock. The state had been bridged by the iron road.[8]

The C&RI initiated a race to the Pacific Ocean when it used "a million feet of timber and several hundred thousand pounds of iron" to traverse the Mississippi River. This bridge took three years to build and required its own charter because neither of the lines it joined, the C&RI and the Mississippi & Missouri Railroad, had been authorized to cross the river. Problems dogged construction. The builders had to overcome opposition from President Franklin Pierce's secretary of war, Jefferson Davis, a southerner who feared the Rock Island

Figure 3.1. An "American-type" 4-4-0 locomotive at Aledo on the CB&Q (March 1869). Western Illinois University Libraries, Archives, and Special Collections.

bridge would facilitate a northern route to the West Coast. Davis mobilized the War Department, which owned the island, to deny the company access but attempts to evict railroad laborers and an injunction halting construction both failed. On April 21, 1856, the first train crossed the Mississippi from Illinois to Iowa. The opening ceremony included laying a cornerstone followed by a flag-waving, music-playing, speech-making celebration in Davenport, Iowa. Regular passenger service commenced two days later to the Iowa towns of Muscatine and Iowa City.[9]

The new bridge had a swing section that opened to allow boats to pass, but that did not placate steamboat operators. A "showdown between ships and railroads" erupted on May 6, 1856, when "a newly constructed and very expensive" paddle-wheel steamer called the *Effie Afton* smashed into one of the piers of this swing section. An overturned stove set the boat and then the

bridge alight, prematurely ending the ship's maiden voyage and rendering the bridge unusable. Ships nearby "all started their bells and whistles, rejoicing at the partial destruction of the bridge." John Hurd, captain of the *Effie Afton,* sued the railroad on the grounds that his ship had been pulled into the bridge by currents the piers created. The case dragged on, not least because the St. Louis Chamber of Commerce sued to halt repairs to "so serious an obstacle to navigation in the Upper Mississippi," and the city's businessmen claimed "there can be no doubt but that the bridge company will be beaten." The C&RI hired Abraham Lincoln as its lead defense attorney and the case came before the Chicago Circuit Court in September 1857. Having studied the bridge, the river, and the documentation, Lincoln demonstrated in a lengthy speech to the jury how river currents could not have caused the ship to hit the bridge, pinning blame for the incident on the captain. The jury

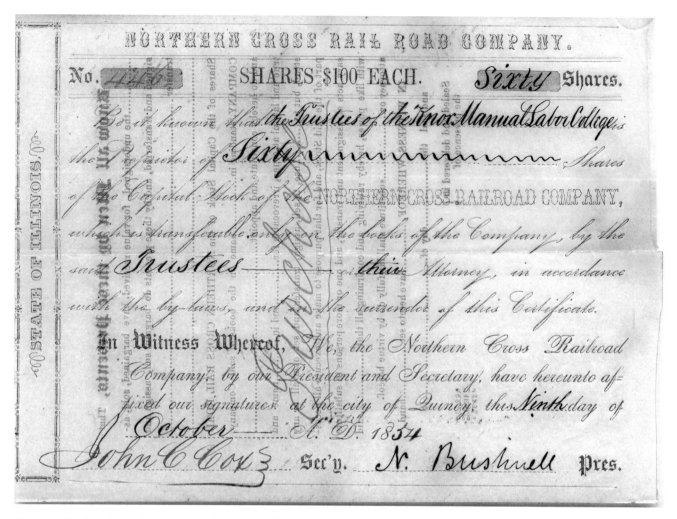

Figure 3.2. Northern Cross share certificate (October 1854). Special Collections and Archives, Knox College Library, Galesburg, Illinois.

failed to return a verdict, the railroad won, and the first stage in establishing a legal precedent for bridging the Mississippi River concluded.[10]

The Rock Island case was one of many that railroad enthusiast Abraham Lincoln argued on behalf of the iron roads.[11] The coming of a railroad, as one newspaper sagaciously put it, "promises to open a rich field for lawyers," and Lincoln took full advantage.[12] He made a name for himself by winning several high-profile, precedent-setting legal cases. In 1851 he defended the Alton & Sangamon Railroad (A&S) from three investors who had defaulted on their stock subscriptions. They argued that they had no legal obligation to continue paying because the company had changed its route after they agreed to purchase shares. Lincoln prevailed before the state supreme court by arguing that subscriptions were nonrefundable because the company had made no promises—real or implied—about its route. Employed on retainer by the ICRR, Lincoln defended that road in court many times, none more spectacularly than in 1854, when he helped it defeat McLean County's attempt to collect property taxes. This turned out to be Lincoln's largest single payday, though he had to sue the company in order to receive his fee.

Following hard on the heels of the G&CU and the C&RI, a third company built west from Chicago. Chartered in 1849, the Aurora Branch was financed by a syndicate led by two Michigan Central Railroad investors, Detroit lawyer James F. Joy and Boston merchant John Murray Forbes. The new railroad began with six miles of track from Batavia to Turner Junction, renting equipment from and running into Chicago over the G&CU.

The Iron Road in the Prarie State

The Aurora Branch built west to Mendota, constructing its own line into the Windy City in 1864.[13]

The Aurora Branch proved to be the first of four separate railroads that all changed their destinations during construction and merged in February 1855 to form the Chicago, Burlington & Quincy Railroad (CB&Q), known for a distinctive "Y" shape. Its main line drove west from Chicago to Galesburg, where it divided and went northwest to Burlington and southwest to Quincy. The second constituent of the CB&Q, the Northern Cross, was built from Quincy to Galesburg using an Internal Improvements Act charter but veering away from the original route. The third was the Central Military Tract Railroad from Galesburg to Mendota. Local business leaders hoped to connect this line with the C&RI at Sheffield, but the Rock Island spurned their advances, and it connected instead with the Aurora Branch at Mendota. The fourth constituent of the CB&Q, the P&O, planned to terminate at the Mississippi port of Oquawka, but apathy there, lobbying by the town of Burlington, and a timely land grant from the Iowa legislature convinced P&O directors to alter its path. They built to a point across the river from Burlington and bypassed Oquawka, which declined into rural obscurity. The P&O received a $90,000 loan from the Central Military Tract Railroad to reach the river, but, unable to repay it, the line became a wholly owned subsidiary of the CB&Q in 1862. It soon relinquished its eastern extension (the route from Peoria east), which would become part of the Toledo, Peoria & Western (TP&W).[14]

The arrival of the railroad was the making of Galesburg. Before it came through, the village did not appear on maps of Illinois but nearby Knoxville did; afterward Galesburg eclipsed Knoxville in size and significance, demonstrating the importance of railroads to economic growth. But all was not plain sailing. Galesburg had been founded by a group of reformers from upstate New York who held strong opinions on the sanctity of the Sabbath. The first train arrived on a fine spring Sunday morning in 1855, whistling loudly. At the depot it encountered a formidable obstacle in the shape of Knox Manual Labor College president Jonathan Blanchard. Though his college invested in the new railroad, Blanchard put faith before profits and strode up to the engineer to demand that he shut off the locomotive. To Blanchard's intense surprise the driver rebuked him and the train chugged away, serving notice of the massive changes America was facing thanks to that irresistible juggernaut, the railroad.[15]

RESUSCITATING THE ILLINOIS CENTRAL

With railroad building gaining traction in the Chicago area, several investors believed it was time to revisit the ICRR project. Only about forty miles had been graded, an embankment built, and no rail laid when the Panic of 1837 had killed it. Two landowners from southern Illinois, politician Sidney Breese and businessman Darius B. Holbrook, retained an interest in the route. In 1836 they had obtained a charter from the state to build a line from Cairo (the site of large tracts of land they owned) to Galena. Breese and Holbrook hired an architect and publicized their new town, for which a railroad was crucial. They surrendered the charter after passage of the Internal Improvements Act of 1837 but remained interested in the project. In the mid-1840s they began building levees to protect Cairo from flooding and to attract railroads.[16] Breese used his influence in the US Senate to claim preemption (the right of settlers to purchase land) along the proposed route of his ICRR. In preparing the way for his legislation, Breese reached out to fellow Illinois politicians, including Stephen A. Douglas.

Douglas smelled a rat. The "Little Giant" believed Breese and Holbrook had no real interest in building a railroad but wanted only to inflate the value of their landholdings near Cairo. Certain that a revived ICRR would strengthen the state and that its terminus should be in Chicago, Douglas threw his weight behind obtaining a land grant. This would, he calculated, earn him support from northern politicians and improve his popularity among voters who suspected he secretly advocated the spread of slavery. More importantly, Douglas believed that solidifying Chicago's status as a railroad hub would bring a transcontinental to the city. His opponents, including former ally Breese, charged Douglas with self-interest. They pointed to how Douglas, upon winning election to the US Senate in 1846, had relocated from Quincy to Chicago and begun purchasing real estate, amassing what his biographer politely calls "a rather substantial investment in Chicago land."[17]

Senator Douglas introduced a bill to grant federal land to the state of Illinois for the proposed railroad in 1847. He played an astute political game to defeat both Breese's preemption strategy and proponents of the southern transcontinental. He brought key southerners on board by including land grants for a railroad from the Gulf of Mexico to Cairo. Douglas and his friends, notably Senator William R. King of Alabama, knew that for fifty years the federal government had been granting land to the states. Illinois had received 46,000 acres of federal land for a seminary, 121,000 acres for salt mines, 996,000 acres for common schools, and half a million acres for other improvements. Abraham Lincoln, then serving his only term in the House of Representatives, sided with Douglas, but the House rejected the bill.[18]

Douglas and King tried again in 1850 by lobbying in Washington, DC, and hosting "a great railroad convention" in Mount Vernon. This time the bill passed. It offered five million acres for settlement, half to be sold by the federal government and half to be granted to the ICRR. The railroad portion, an area of about four thousand square miles, was larger than the state of Delaware. The company got six "sections" of land (each section equaled 640 acres, or one square mile) for every mile of railroad built, alternating with federal sections in a checkerboard pattern. Where land along the proposed right-of-way was already in private hands the company could obtain an equal amount elsewhere in the state. The bill required the federal government to sell its 2.5 million acres before the ICRR could begin marketing its portion. Triumphal voices from the wilderness greeted the land grant. The *Ottawa Free-Trader* proclaimed, "Illinois will be redeemed—her shattered credit recovered, her fame restored," while the New Orleans press praised it for benefiting "the people in all that vast extent of rich and fertile country through which it passes."[19]

Though it had grown since passage of the Internal Improvements Act, Illinois remained the frontier. The state had 851,470 people in 1850, a third of the population

of London, and the three largest towns along the proposed line between Lake Michigan and the Ohio River were Bourbonnais (1,710 people), Jonesboro (584), and Urbana (210). Packs of "prairie wolves"—almost certainly coyotes—ravaged surveyors' camps and squatters attacked company officials delivering eviction notices. Opponents in the southern half of the state, fearful that northern abolitionists might follow northern capital, argued that plank roads or canals would provide better service than the proposed railroad.[20]

The ICRR charter protected the state and the federal government. The largest railroad in the country at the time, the New-York and Erie, was about 300 miles long but the ICRR needed to lay 705 route miles, a daunting task. The charter required the company to build the line within six years or forfeit unsold land to the federal government. Upon completion, the military and the US mail would receive discounts and the company was required to pay 7 percent of gross income to the state in perpetuity, a provision designed to rehabilitate Illinois in the eyes of the capital markets. Some of that money would be used to pay the debt incurred in 1837, and the project did much to encourage new investment in the state.

The Illinois General Assembly set the final route. Many speculators wanted it to follow the 1837 proposal, which would have taken it through Vandalia, Shelbyville, Decatur, Bloomington, and Savanna. Roswell Mason, the chief engineer, wished to build as straight as possible and avoid expensive engineering works. Politicians battled on the floor of the legislature on behalf of their constituents. One of the most successful was state senator Asahel Gridley, "a typical representative of that group so frequently met with in Illinois history, the speculator-politicians," who owned fifteen thousand acres of territory in central Illinois. His supporters owned even more land in an area encompassing five counties around Bloomington. To say Gridley had a vested interest in the route of the proposed railroad would be an understatement. Gridley did not get everything he desired, however, because he encountered an even more powerful politician-speculator, Stephen A. Douglas.[21]

When Douglas left Quincy in 1847 he sold his land-holdings, including a farm in Pike County and town lots in Beardstown, Bloomington, Meredosia, and Virginia. He made a substantial investment in Chicago real estate and then set about promoting railroads. In 1855 he conveyed sixteen acres, thirteen of them submerged beneath Lake Michigan, to the ICRR at a profit of $10,000. Douglas sold only "the right of way to cross my land" and retained most of his holdings in the city. But Chicago was just one leaf in his real-estate portfolio. Land he owned on the western banks of Lake Superior doubled in value when he championed land-grant legislation to construct a railroad from there to Dubuque, Iowa.[22]

Douglas and Gridley won. The ICRR charter passed on February 10, 1851, after intensive lobbying. It authorized a line that would run 120 miles north from Cairo to Centralia, where it split like a wishbone. From Centralia the main line would continue to Dunleith, on the Mississippi across from Dubuque, Iowa, while a "branch line" would veer northeast from Centralia to Chicago. For Douglas, use of the word "branch" was a matter of semantics: he always envisioned Chicago as the principal terminus of his frontier line. Bypassing Peoria and Springfield, the proposed railroad ran through the heart of Gridley's territory, including Bloomington.

The company hosted ground-breaking ceremonies on December 23, 1851, in Cairo and Chicago, 366 miles apart. Cannons, bells, and pontificating signaled the beginning of the gargantuan task ahead. The branch had to be built first in order to bring supplies and people to Chicago through the Great Lakes. Rails had to be bought from Great Britain, at a total cost of just under $4 million, because a railroad boom in the Northeast absorbed domestic iron. When the first new rails arrived in 1852, the company unrealistically announced that it expected to lay ten miles in twenty days. In fact, it would take several months to build the first fourteen miles from Chicago to Calumet.[23]

Construction of that initial section encountered immediate opposition. The proposed route would have to traverse the tracks of the Northern Indiana Railroad, which carried competitor Michigan Southern into Chicago. Denied permission to cross the other's tracks and unwilling to pay for an overpass, ICRR directors authorized an outlaw action. On a cloudy night in April 1852, workers supervised by the ICRR's chief engineer, Roswell Mason, kidnapped the Northern Indiana guard and hastily built a crossing. Instead of negotiating a set of operating rules, the companies simply ignored each other until an 1853 collision killed eighteen people. A bridge solved the problem, but until its completion, trains came to a halt before proceeding, like a four-way stop.[24]

Building ICRR tracks into downtown Chicago proved an arduous undertaking. The directors wanted to enter the heart of Chicago's business district at the south branch of the Chicago River and connect with the G&CU. Unfortunately for the ICRR, the Rock Island and the Northern Indiana owned much of the land it needed, and they refused to sell. The city of Chicago offered an ingenious if expensive solution when, on June 14, 1852, it authorized the ICRR to build along the lakefront. This strip of land lay in the lakebed and had to be reclaimed first. The railroad was also required to build and maintain levees stretching from the city's southern extreme to the Chicago River to protect the city from flooding. Homeowners along the route protested that the value of their property would fall and the city prohibited the ICRR from erecting any building that might block views of the lake. The result was a visually stunning but financially draining entry into downtown terminating at Great Central Station, the city's largest building at the time.[25]

Despite obstacles and controversy, the ICRR did what its promoters hoped it would. The company's agents and brokers sold bonds worth $17 million on the strength of the land grant. By the end of 1855 the company had earned $5.5 million selling five hundred thousand acres to speculators and settlers. Traffic developed rapidly, and within a year of opening it was transporting "grain, lumber, livestock, coal, flour, dressed pork, sugar, molasses, lead, machinery, stone, sand, clay, iron, salt, firewood," and people. The building of the ICRR generated grain-elevator construction, including the largest in the country adjacent to its tracks in Chicago.

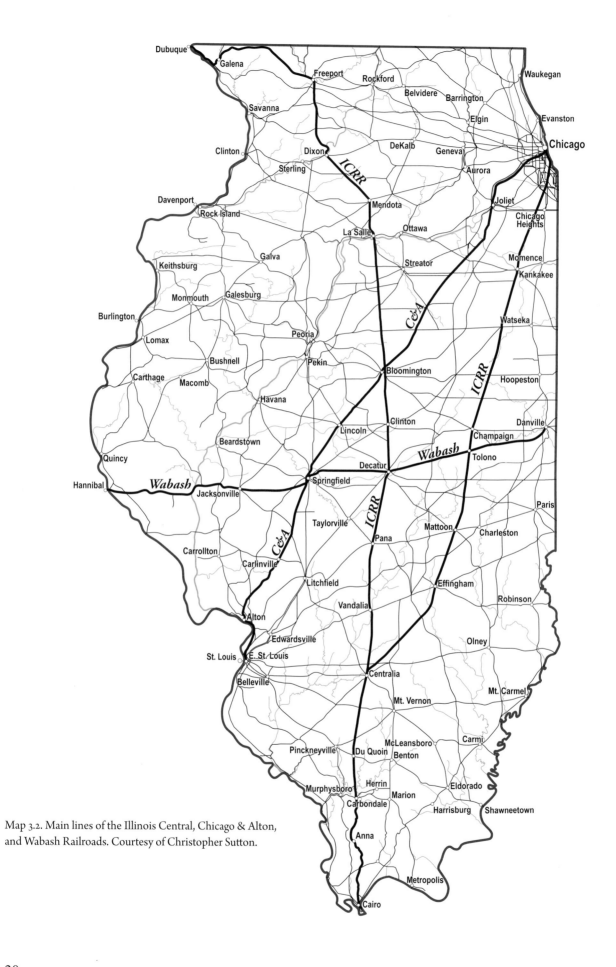

Map 3.2. Main lines of the Illinois Central, Chicago & Alton, and Wabash Railroads. Courtesy of Christopher Sutton.

The first stretch of line, sixteen miles from Chicago to Kensington, opened on May 20, 1852; on September 27, 1856, the last spike was driven at Mason (named for Roswell Mason), bringing construction to a close before the federally mandated deadline.[26]

SERVING THE SOUTH

By the middle of the nineteenth century it was becoming easy to forget that settlers had surged into southern Illinois before they entered the North. The federal government rejected the first applications for land in Chicago because it was too isolated. In 1830, on the cusp of the railroad age, the demographic center of the state was eighty miles northeast of St. Louis. The first institution of higher education in Illinois was Rock Spring Seminary in Alton, established in 1827, followed a year later by Lebanon Seminary (McKendree College today) and then, in 1829, Illinois College in Jacksonville. Alton was a thriving port, and Belleville, Kaskaskia, and Shelbyville were important county seats. The first white settlers to move into Illinois territory after the French came from northern Kentucky and eastern Missouri, bringing slaves with them. Though the 1818 state constitution outlawed the peculiar institution, old habits died hard and Alton made national headlines when defenders of slavery murdered abolitionist publisher Elijah Lovejoy in 1837.

Southern Illinois did not see the kind of economic and social revolution experienced in the North in part because it developed no railroad center comparable to Chicago, but not from want of trying. In 1850 Alton's 3,585 inhabitants believed their excellent natural harbor gave them an advantage over St. Louis. Unfortunately, a limestone bluff looming two hundred feet above the Mississippi River hindered travel inland. Leading citizens wanted Alton to reclaim the central role it held in the 1837 Internal Improvements Act by building the A&S to the state capital. Supported by Abraham Lincoln and other politicians, the railroad was chartered in 1847 but faced numerous obstacles in its early years.[27]

Grading began in January 1851 but by September—facing the high cost of importing iron, competition from other lines for scarce workers, and the wrath of unpaid laborers—the Alton was nearly bankrupt. One of the

original investors, Augustus T. Cowman, withdrew after putting $670,000 of his own money into the project. His business partner, Benjamin Godfrey, a former steamboat captain who was the road's first president, despaired. He traveled to New York City to recruit investors and met Henry Dwight Jr., a financier who claimed without justification to represent one hundred Manhattan banks. Dwight found funding and construction recommenced. A series of financial calamities ensued, but the first train ran from Alton to Springfield on September 9, 1852, cutting travel time from two days to twelve hours. Two daily passenger trains in each direction plied the line, with a regular steamboat service connecting to St. Louis.[28]

Dubious financial arrangements and poor construction dogged its early years, but not all of the problems were of the Alton's making. The Mississippi River proved a treacherous partner: six of the seven boats the railroad owned sank, one of them twice, and in 1864 the company terminated its river service. By then it was running trains over another railroad, the Belleville & Illinoistown, which terminated across the Mississippi from St. Louis. In 1855 the A&S became the Chicago, Alton & St. Louis, and in 1861 a new charter renamed it the Chicago & Alton (C&A), which stuck until the 1930s.[29]

Other railroads extended beyond state lines. Chartered in 1851 in Illinois, the six-foot-gauge Ohio & Mississippi Railroad (O&M) ran its first regularly scheduled passenger trains in May 1857, when it became the western segment of the American Central Line, a loose confederation headed by the B&O. Geographically the shortest route from Illinoistown (renamed East St. Louis in 1861) to the East Coast, travelers had to endure a nine-hour boat ride on the Ohio River between Marietta, Ohio, and Parkersburg, West Virginia. Despite its limitations, the O&M helped confirm Illinoistown as an important railroad junction and gave added impetus to those who argued for making St. Louis the eastern terminus of a transcontinental line. It also resolved a long-running dilemma: the multiplicity of time zones across the country. Every town set its own time, so the American Central Line adopted Baltimore time for trains originating from that city, Columbus time for its Ohio lines, and Vincennes time for operations west of Cincinnati.[30]

Southern Illinois served primarily as a land bridge between east and west, as the Terre Haute & Alton (TH&A) demonstrated. Chartered in 1851, the TH&A connected the Mississippi River with the Wabash River and operated a branch from Belleville to Illinoistown. On the branch lay its future, a connection to St. Louis. This reality was acknowledged when the company rechartered in 1854 as the Terre Haute, Alton & St. Louis Railroad, giving the branch equal status with the main line and driving another dagger into the heart of Alton's boosters.[31]

Westward expansion brought the Pennsylvania Railroad into and through Illinois. In 1858 the Pittsburgh, Fort Wayne & Chicago—heavily financed by the Pennsy—reached the Windy City, followed three years later by a chain of Pennsylvania affiliates linking Chicago with Cincinnati. By 1859 a patchwork of small lines provided freight service from St. Louis to the Pennsylvania at Pittsburgh, traversing southern Illinois over the Terre Haute, Alton & St. Louis Railroad.[32]

Other Illinois railroads avoided Chicago and St. Louis completely. In 1847 the privatized Northern Cross became the Sangamon & Morgan Railroad. This line formed one end of the Great Western Railroad from Toledo, Ohio, to the Mississippi River. The Great Western reached Illinois at Danville in 1856, at which point it entered receivership for the first of its nine times. Building continued until the Great Western met the Sangamon & Morgan in 1857. Another line, the P&O Eastern Extension, was completed to the Indiana state line at Effner in 1859. By then its parent company, the CB&Q, was gazing west and relinquished its claim to the Eastern Extension. Renamed the Logansport, Peoria & Burlington Railroad, it operated a daily passenger train from its terminus in Peoria to Logansport, Indiana, and hosted sleepers between Columbus, Ohio, and Burlington, Iowa. The line also provided a shortcut for the ICRR to connect the Chicago branch with its main line by running trains from Gilman to El Paso. It would soon build to the Mississippi and become the Toledo, Peoria & Warsaw (TP&W).[33]

With the ICRR bisecting the state from north to south and Chicago-based railroads driving west, eastern companies found the new hub attractive. The earliest proposal for extending an eastern road to the settlement at the base of Lake Michigan appeared in an 1836 report to the directors of the B&O, but it had no immediate effect. B&O trains did not reach Chicago until 1874, but in 1852 two lines did enter Chicago from east of Lake Michigan. Connecting Illinois with settled areas of the Union, the Michigan Central and the Michigan Southern were drawn to the Prairie State by the promise of lucrative grain shipments and meat from Chicago's slaughterhouses. They provided precisely the service midwestern farmers needed to ship their products to a world market.

Both Michigan lines began as state-funded infrastructure projects, and both suffered the same fate as their Illinois counterparts. The Michigan Central was purchased by private investors, including James F. Joy and John Murray Forbes of the Aurora Branch, who built west from Michigan's biggest settlement, Detroit. Unable to secure their own route into Chicago, Forbes invested $2 million in the ICRR in return for the right to run trains over its tracks into the city. On May 21, 1852, a Michigan Central train ran into the ICRR's temporary terminus, the first service into Chicago from the East.

The next eastern line to run a train into Chicago, the Michigan Southern Railroad (MSRR), did so one day after the Michigan Central, on May 22, 1852. MSRR trains crossed the Hoosier State over the Northern Indiana Railroad, which joined the Rock Island at Junction Grove (soon to be renamed Englewood and destined to become one of the great transfer points in the United States). Michigan Southern trains then ran over the Rock Island into Chicago, an arrangement facilitated by Henry Farnham, the MSRR director who had convinced eastern investors to buy Rock Island securities when the railroad was in desperate need of financing. The MSRR initiated service from Chicago to Toledo, Ohio, in 1852, and by the end of the year some four hundred passengers arrived in Chicago daily on trains of the two Michigan railroads. In the 1860s these lines offered "the attractions of speed, directness, regularity, comfort and safety—all of which are crowned with the unapproachable beauty and grandeur of its scenery."[34]

"Speed, directness, regularity, comfort and safety" did not exactly describe train travel in the 1850s. Illinois was an inhospitable land with rudimentary railroads. The first trains were so slow that would-be passengers could stand next to the tracks and wave trains to a halt. Ballast and springs were rare. Opening the frontier was a perilous business, and its often harsh realities dampened enthusiasm for the push to territories beyond the Mississippi. One traveler caught in a winter storm declared, "These Illinois snow drifts have put a quietus to the Pacific Railroad by any other than the extreme Southern route." Charles B. George, an engineer running between Chicago and Waukegan, wrote of "a furious storm [that] buried our tracks twenty feet in places" in 1856. It took over a week of shoveling before the line was reopened, only for another blizzard to close it again, leaving engines stuck in snowdrifts and trains abandoned, passengers and crews seeking shelter in nearby houses.[35]

Natural impediments and bad weather could be overcome, as the cultivation of the prairies would demonstrate. Farmers and investors carved fields into the fertile territory, planting wheat and corn, which grew in such abundance that feeding the growing population of Chicago proved relatively straightforward once the railroads began running. Crucial to the rapid settlement of Illinois, the railroads mounted extensive and powerful marketing campaigns to convince potential settlers their futures lay in the state. The arrival of railroads created relatively fast, generally reliable, all-weather means of haulage. Oddly, however, the individual companies all terminated in Chicago. None of them went through the city, and while cars might be transferred from one road to another, the trains stopped there. This accident of history made Chicago the transportation hub for the national railroad network. People, capital, and prosperity flowed into the Prairie State along the narrow ribbons of iron terminating in the Windy City.

CULTIVATING THE PRAIRIE

*I*n the beginning, railroads needed land and the federal government had it. For settlers, it seemed in plentiful supply. The earliest European immigrants entered an apparently empty territory rich in resources and potential. Initial colonization—despite charters from British monarchs—was haphazard and small-scale. Violence against indigenous peoples was commonplace, squatting widespread, and ownership frequently a matter of dispute. Early national land policy was, in the words of historian John Mack Faragher, a matter of "Extinguish Indian title, survey, and sell."[1] Only when the federal government turned to the orderly settlement of the frontier did systematic landownership develop, and only with the arrival of railroads could mass migration occur.

Public land sales in Illinois began in 1814. Land offices in Kaskaskia and Shawneetown did a brisk business and a third office opened in Edwardsville in 1816, all in the southern third of the state. The federal government began planning for settlement north of the Illinois River by setting aside approximately 3.5 million acres—the "military tracts" from which the Central Military Tract Railroad would get its name—between the Illinois and Mississippi Rivers for veterans of wars up to and including the War of 1812. Only after a delegation of territorial leaders, including Governor Ninian Edwards, obtained title in 1816 from the Native Americans living there did land offices make 160-acre plots available to veterans. Purchasers were not required to live on the land, and many veterans sold their allotments to speculators for as

little as ten cents an acre. Soon Illinois land was trading on the open market in New York City for prices ranging from 50 cents to $1.50 an acre. As much as a quarter of the total acreage in the military tract sold that way, violating the principle of establishing small farms to settle the region.[2]

A HUNGER FOR LAND

Landownership could not guarantee success. A case in point was the town of Rockwell, platted along the Illinois River some ninety-five miles south of Chicago. In 1835 John A. Rockwell of Connecticut purchased 640 acres for a temperance community. Rockwell, an agricultural innovator and railroad director, bought the land because it was one of several possible sites for the proposed junction of the Illinois and Michigan Canal and the Illinois River. Unfortunately for his vision and his pocketbook, politicians wishing to sell state-owned land planted a town called LaSalle a few miles upstream from Rockwell. This, it transpired, became the terminus of the canal and spelled the beginning of the end for Rockwell. Construction of a boarding-house, a church, a few stores, and some family homes encouraged settlement, and Rockwell reached nearly two hundred people, most of them from Norwich, Connecticut. Its eponymous founder pondered introducing mining and manufacturing until simultaneous outbreaks of malaria and typhoid decimated the population. Most fled and John A. Rockwell abandoned the project in 1840, though some residents stayed and a visitor in 1848 found it "situated in just the finest position I can recollect."[3]

Unlike Rockwell, railroad officials and politicians were well placed to take advantage of land sales. The state legislature banned the ICRR from establishing new towns, but this did not stop its directors from doing so. Five of them created the Associates Land Company to purchase government land that they knew would soon host stations. They borrowed money from the ICRR to purchase nineteen thousand acres at $2.75 an acre in 1853, and it sold three years later at an average of $12.50 an acre after they had subdivided it into small plots for hotels, grain elevators, general stores, and lumber yards. The associates made what historian John Stover graciously calls "a good return on their original investment." Contemporaries were less polite and labeled such practices "oppressive monopoly," demanding Congress limit the number of acres any single purchaser could buy while restricting land sales "to actual settlers." Full of "speculator-politicians," Congress turned a blind eye.[4]

Land grants dwarfed settlements like Rockwell to the advantage of corporations and large speculators. Between 1850 and 1871 Congress made an area three times greater than New England available to railroad companies, which used the land as security on construction mortgages and bonds. The ICRR received by far the largest land grant in Illinois, though most railroads leaving Chicago for the West benefited from grants beyond the state. The CB&Q, for example, did not receive federal land in Illinois, but its subsidiary, the Burlington & Missouri River Railroad (B&MRR), gained 2.7 million acres of public land in Iowa and Nebraska. Settling that territory took thirty years, and companies processed land applications from large speculators before smallholders because that was faster and more profitable.[5]

ICRR land sales brought settlers who would ship crops and travel by rail. In theory, purchasers would make a down payment of 50 cents and pay $2.50 an acre with up to seven years to repay the balance. When the ICRR began disposing of land in the military tract, it charged veterans who wanted to purchase acreage within six miles of the railroad $4.00 or more an acre,

while speculators paid only $2.56 an acre, pennies over the $2.50 minimum. Bulk purchasers were clearly favored and the policy worked. In 1849 the federal government owned fourteen million acres in Illinois and when it tried to sell land at $1.25 an acre it found few takers. By the end of 1856, however, only one hundred thousand acres remained to be sold.[6]

Attracting settlers was not a simple matter. The ICRR spent some $15,000 annually on newspaper advertising and employed agents to bring people to Illinois. The company was the first American railroad to recruit outside the United States. In 1854 it sent Oscar Malmborg, a Swede employed in its land office, to Scandinavia, where he distributed 1,000 maps and 2,500 circulars in Swedish but enjoyed limited success. In the same year the ICRR launched a campaign in eastern Europe, exploiting the unsettled political and economic situation of the region to attract skilled workers and farmers who wanted to avoid compulsory military service.[7] This effort proved more fruitful.

Company recruiters did not neglect the United States. They distributed over one hundred thousand circulars explaining—and exaggerating—the delights of Illinois. Flyers went to every post office east of Indiana and north of Tennessee, and advertisements appeared in newspapers throughout the Northeast. Like other railroads, the ICRR tried to take advantage of "the tragic decay of rural New England" in order to lure settlers away from the region. Deploying appeals to patriotism and progress, the railroad distributed handbills on the eastern seaboard positioning Illinois as the "Garden State of America." It promised that "children can live in sight of the school, the college, the church, and grow up with the prosperity of the leading state in the Great Western Empire." Farmers could purchase 40- to 160-acre plots and "settle near markets, schools, railroads, churches, and all the Blessings of Civilization." Of course, the posters did not mention breaking the prairie or building those "Blessings" from the ground up.[8]

The railroad published unabashedly glowing depictions of Illinois. It assured would-be settlers that harvests "are not checked by rigorous winters,—nor is the heat of the summers oppressive." The hype did not stop there. Posters promised a land "full of mineral wealth such as Coal, Iron, Lead, Limestone, &c." and claimed that "there is scarcely a county in Illinois in which there is not a supply of timber." Wealth was assured, for "Such is the facility and economy with which these lands can be cultivated, that in two years farmers can readily surround themselves with all the comforts of the old settled farms of the Eastern States." The extraordinary fertility of the land guaranteed, one advert trumpeted, that within six years farmers could repay the loans taken out to purchase their new farmsteads.[9]

Sweetness and light on the printed page disguised a hard-headed approach to publishers. In return for buying space in agricultural journals such as the *Rural New Yorker* and *Prairie Farmer*, ICRR officials demanded editorials directing readers to its advertisements. In at least one case, this meant a complete reversal of editorial policy: the *Prairie Farmer* switched from accusing the company of antifarmer monopolistic practices to praising its approach to land sales.[10] In 1857 the railroad published illustrations in its pamphlets for the first time, mainly woodcuts of bucolic rural homesteads exaggerating the availability of lumber and water. It employed traveling agents to pass out literature at county fairs, special meetings, and rural markets; began purchasing placards on the sides of New York City streetcars; and hired runners to place literature in the hands of immigrants arriving in New York.[11]

The investment paid dividends and the ICRR brought people to the state, initially with a bias to the midsection and the north. Most of the land sold before 1859 was north of Centralia because overblown stories of cholera and malaria in southern Illinois scared off would-be settlers, as did rumors of hostility from old-timers toward "Yankees" and other outsiders. The supposed lack of educational facilities also hurt, and the soil was not conducive to growing wheat, then an important cash crop. The Cairo land company did not sell land but preferred leases, which many prospective settlers did not like, while newspapers elsewhere in the state gleefully reported Little Egypt's floods, insect infestations, and epidemics. But in the rest of Illinois the ICRR generated economic growth, and the population of the thirty-two counties through which it passed more than doubled in a decade. Fueled by railroads, the city of Chicago grew from just under 30,000 people in 1850 to 112,172 in 1860, including "scores of railroad men from the East."[12]

CONQUERING THE PRAIRIES

The first European settlers in Illinois underestimated the fecundity of prairie soil, believing it could only sustain cattle. The grasses actually covered rich loam activated by plowing, but fearsome winter winds, summer swarms of insects, and destructive autumnal fires made life treacherous for pioneers. Immigrants faced massive odds, finding themselves in the wilderness without "the conveniences of civilized life" and prone to dangerous diseases. In some cases, assistance from experienced "backwoodsmen" secured survival, but for many, retreat was the best option.[13]

An important innovation arrived when settlers brought corn cultivation from the uplands of Tennessee and Kentucky. By 1820 it was the state's staple, and in 1839 Sangamon County farmers produced 1.4 million bushels. This equaled the output of the country's premier corn counties, an amazing feat for an area described a decade before as "generally settled with poor, but very kind, people" where barter reigned and "hovels" dominated the housing stock. Corn production on a large scale also developed in the Wabash River valley in the 1840s, while in the 1840s and 1850s livestock farms ranging from 950 acres to 26,000 acres opened in east-central Illinois. Some of these sprang up on land purchased from the ICRR, and many were owned by absentee landlords who hired managers and leased land to tenants. Originally grown to feed hogs and cattle, "cash-corn production began to emerge in eastern Illinois around 1860," the first region to specialize in producing corn for market rather than for feeding a farmer's own animals.[14]

The prairie presented visitors with a vibrant, dynamic landscape. Richard Cobden, a member of the British Parliament and an investor in the ICRR after whom a town in southern Illinois was named, wrote in 1859 that the Grand Prairie was transformed in four years from having "scarcely an inhabitant" to being "dotted with small farm houses built of wood." Another visitor

Figure 4.1. The ICRR grain elevator on the south branch of the Chicago River. Library of Congress Prints and Photographs Division.

from Britain, novelist Anthony Trollope, found a land "rich with the vegetation of thousands of years, [where] the farmer's return is given to him without delay." In truth, taming the prairie took time and effort. Farmers could hope to break one and a half to three acres a day using steel-tipped plows pulled by a team of six oxen, but this was beyond the budgets of all but a few. Only after the widespread introduction of John Deere's steel plow in the 1840s and 1850s could large swaths of prairie be cleared, though swampy land had to wait until the introduction of drainage tiles in the late nineteenth century.[15]

Variety helped promote the appearance of abundance. Illinois farmers grew corn, wheat, rye, barley, and, increasingly, oats to avoid dependence on a single crop. Sheep, pigs, and dairy cows grazed on open fields, while garden vegetables and orchards provided household nourishment. One section of central Illinois saw farms of sixty acres producing a thousand bushels of corn and two hundred bushels of grains, potatoes, and garden crops in the 1830s.[16] Fires periodically swept across the prairies before the arrival of European settlers, keeping trees to a minimum and contributing to the region's fertility, but immigrants tried to stop them.

There were timber stands along rivers and streams, but the relative absence of wood meant railroads had to bring in lumber for buildings, fence posts, and heating.

Development dramatically altered the prairie. The landscape was slowly subdued, and when Trollope visited Dixon to see the "open rolling prairie" he was disappointed at how far he had to ride to escape cornfields. When he eventually reached a field from which no cultivated land was visible it was being used for pasture and the sight of cows ruined the purity of the scene in his eyes.[17] He, like others hoping to find a pristine wilderness, could not help but feel disillusioned.

TO MARKET

In the 1840s market-oriented farmers struggled along dirt tracks to take a steady flow of wagons to Chicago. Hundreds arrived daily at harvesttime bearing wheat, corn, oats, barley, rye, fruits, and occasionally meat. They came for the relatively high prices they received and to shop at Chicago's stores, which offered a greater variety of goods than other towns in the region. Chicago was a true site of exchange where brokers purchased grain for buyers around the world and farmers bought supplies—the necessary and the luxurious—with their earnings.

The grain merchants of Chicago began developing the financial power they would wield over a vast western hinterland in the mid-1840s. Chicago was slowly pulling ahead of its main rival, St. Louis, and other Illinois towns exhibited "a great interest in the prosperity of both, and cannot but wish a spirit of rivalry between them." By 1860 flour and grain receipts in the Windy City outstripped those of St. Louis and the rising cities of Milwaukee, Peoria, and Toledo. During the "prairie boom" the annual production of corn in Illinois rose from 23.6 million bushels in 1840 to 57.6 million a decade later and 129.9 million in 1870. Wheat production had similar spectacular gains, from 3.3 million bushels in 1840 to 30.7 million in 1870.[18]

Railroads played a central role in the development of Illinois agriculture, but so did the choices farmers made. Before railroads arrived farmers floated their harvests to market on rivers and streams. Those near the

Mississippi River and its many tributaries took their produce to St. Louis, where sixty-pound sacks of grain had to be carried one at a time by laborers and piled in the holds of ships or on the floors of warehouses. Adding to the transit time in St. Louis was the need to build storage facilities above the temperamental river to avoid its seasonal rising and falling. In the upstart on Lake Michigan, by contrast, merchants built their grain elevators on the banks of the languid Chicago River.

Slow, seasonal travel initially limited Chicago's market power and restricted the city's growth. Early promoters funded railroads to help farmers "feed the rapidly increasing population in Chicago." Completion of the Illinois and Michigan Canal in 1848 released pent-up demand for reliable mass transportation. Corn shipments to the East, bloated by the product of farmers in the Illinois River valley, increased eightfold. Barges carrying lumber from Wisconsin and Michigan returned with wood for prairie towns and farms. Further evidence of the oncoming commercial storm arrived with the opening of the first ten miles of the G&CU in 1848. Farmers brought what wheat they had—the harvest was poor from then until 1852—to the railhead. By then the company was carrying over half of all wheat destined for the city. As railroads extended, volume, profits, and the value of the land through which they passed increased. After the G&CU opened its line from Rockford to Freeport in 1853, land prices doubled because the Chicago grain market could be reached in half a day. Railroads were more profitable over longer distances because the cost of loading and unloading remained the same regardless of the length of a trip, and the amount charged—the shipping rate—increased with mileage. As a CB&Q official put it, "A Railroad is a cheap means of transportation for long distances and relatively less cheap as the distance diminishes until, when it becomes very small, a wheel-barrow is the cheapest—and for still smaller distances a shovel."[19]

The construction of a massive system of elevators consolidated Chicago's place as the country's premier grain market. An elevator consisted of a building and a process designed to collect, sort, store, and sell grain. Elevators were tall towers of vertical bins with

The Iron Road in the Prairie State

Figure 4.2. Though a late arrival into Chicago, the ATSF built this giant grain elevator to capture a share of the midwestern grain market. Library of Congress Prints and Photographs Division.

steam-powered conveyor belts lifting grain from trains and barges into containers for drying, cleaning, and storage. The complex of elevators, usually tethered to a single railroad, was needed to await the spring thaw on Lake Michigan, across which much of the harvest traveled. Enormous labor savings accrued from the mechanization of storage. In 1855 it took less than an hour to do what had taken a crew of workers a full day just a decade before. By 1857 Chicago's elevators could store as much grain as St. Louis shipped in a year, and in 1860 they held nearly half of all the grain that entered the five largest markets in the United States. In 1858 they

stored four million bushels; by 1888 that number was over thirty million. Viewing Chicago for the first time, Trollope marveled at "rivers of food" being transferred from grain elevators to lake steamers and trains for the trip east.[20]

Ninety percent of the grain sent east traveled on water prior to the Civil War. By rail, grain took nearly six days to reach New York while sailing ships took two to three weeks and steam vessels ten days. Cost outweighed time, however: water-route shippers charged up to a fifth less than rail, and it did not really matter how long grain took to reach the East Coast. For Chicago, the consequence was a fortuitous confluence of low-cost, high-volume eastern trunk lines gathering and forwarding commodities from the lower-volume, higher-cost network of railroads radiating out to the north, south, and west of the city. A transshipment center of unparalleled importance, the Windy City served as a well-remunerated intermediary between farmers and their customers around the globe. Elsewhere in the state similar developments on a smaller scale boosted local economies. Thus the railroads helped make Decatur the largest processing center for agricultural products in the state after 1854.[21]

The centrality of Chicago to the movement of grain throughout the United States could not have developed without the Board of Trade. Created in 1848, this voluntary organization of merchants and bankers set standard weights and established the system of "grades" by which inspectors valued grain. Grading allowed elevator owners to store the harvests of multiple farms in a single vertical bin. Before grading was invented in the 1850s, different farmers' harvests could not be mixed because ownership remained with the original shipper, often the farmer or a local trader, until it reached its final buyer. Accounting for different owners' grain meant operating elevators below capacity, whereas grading allowed elevators to store the products of different farms together. Graded grain was uniform and its origin immaterial, though farmers complained that elevator operators "down-graded" their harvests and consequently lobbied for legislation to regulate the elevators. For buyers, grading provided a secure means of evaluating grain without seeing it, allowing them to lock in prices received by telegraph before the grain traveled from Chicago. The world of futures trading had arrived.[22]

The presence of railroads and a burgeoning demand for wood on the sparsely forested prairies combined to make Chicago a center of the lumber trade. Chicago's lumberyards shipped to settlers in Illinois, Iowa, and southern Wisconsin. By 1868 lumber dealers as far away as Kansas City and St. Joseph, Missouri, relied on Chicago for their supplies, and they in turn shipped the wood to purchasers in Colorado and Wyoming. Lumber moved west from Chicago inexpensively compared with other commodities because it filled cars that would otherwise have run empty. By 1884 Chicago's grip on the lumber markets had become so tight that lumber rates around the country were fixed against those of the Windy City in a series of "differentials" expressing the variance in cents between the Chicago rate and the rates for other towns. But this was the high point, and success bred imitation. After the mid-1880s the railroad network spread farther into lumber regions, making it possible for buyers and shippers to avoid the Windy City.[23]

In three generations of European settlement, an agricultural industry developed on the Illinois prairies. Massive clearing and draining, crops grown for livestock feed and human consumption, the anonymity and efficiencies of the grain elevator, the use of futures contracts, and above all the introduction of the railroad transformed the "wilderness." The process may eventually have unfolded as it did, but the development of a speedy mass transportation system created the infrastructure for settlement, cultivation, and marketing.[24] The prairie became a center of production and selling unparalleled in the world, and Chicago lay at its heart. But much of the capital for that growth came not from the United States at all but from Europe. Innovative financial instruments and the ability to cast aside the shadows of 1837 allowed Illinois to flourish. Inventive means of funding railroad expansion created opportunities for wealth accumulation but also tempted swindlers.

FINANCING RAILROADS

Railroads drew Illinois into a global network of capital and capitalists. Fewer than 50 miles of track existed in the state in 1850; by 1860 the Prairie State's 2,500 route miles connected it with a world marketplace, thanks primarily to foreign money and the growth of Chicago. The iron for all that track was scarce, and much of it had to come from overseas, primarily Great Britain. Rails told only part of the story: railroads needed rolling stock and buildings, workers and coal, managers and paper, bridges and lumber, land and customers. Finding these required capital, raised in the form of stocks and bonds sold in exchanges far from the state and trading outside of local control.

Railroad financing became increasingly complex as capital needs expanded. The experience of the Galena & Chicago Union Railroad—funded in part by progressive artisans and exuberant farmers—was unusual, as was that of the land-grant sustained Illinois Central. There was no such thing as purely private or purely public funding during the first two decades of railroading, if private excludes support of any kind from government entities. Confident assertions like that of Swedish emigrant Gustav Unonius, who wrote "Neither the state nor the city has spent a single dollar" building railroads, bolstered the prevailing laissez-faire ideology but were patently false. The promoters of America's earliest railroad, the Baltimore & Ohio, created a joint-stock company in which the state of Maryland bought five thousand shares worth $500,000, one-sixth of the initial $3 million offered. The South-Carolina Canal and Rail-Road Company built the first line in the South using state guarantees and municipal monies to stimulate interest and investment in the line between Charleston and Hamburg. And the company destined to be the largest corporation in the world during the nineteenth century, the Pennsylvania Railroad, mixed guarantees that government entities would purchase half of its stock with private investment.[1]

Most Illinois railroads mixed government aid, usually stock subscriptions, with private capital. The latter came from foreign banks and financial houses, often in Europe and especially in Britain and Holland. Railroads needed funds for construction costs and initial operations, to say nothing of later expansion. Investment took the form of shares, which ideally earned money for their holders when their worth increased and when the corporations paid a dividend. Investors seeking predictable earnings purchased bonds paying a fixed interest, often between 6 and 10 percent in the first half-century of railroad building. These securities gave their holders part-ownership and a claim on any profit. Specialized brokers and bankers traded stocks and bonds, their prices publicized in newspapers around the world and their travails and successes followed by an eager audience.

STOCKS AND BONDS

Building and operating a railroad was expensive, uncertain, and arduous. Hundreds of investors had to be attracted because, unlike a factory or a ship, no

Figure 5.1. Peoria & Oquawka share certificate (1855). Special Collections and Archives, Knox College Library, Galesburg, Illinois.

individual or family possessed enough money to build a railroad. Local capital, though scarce, could be secured in the 1850s. When Rock Island agents scoured the countryside for funds in 1850 they obtained promises of $25,000 from the Scott County commissioners and a further $10,000 from the city of Davenport, Iowa, while the Rock Island City Council subscribed $13,000 and nearby Henry County another $30,000.[2] But most capital came from New York and beyond. Traded on national exchanges, or bourses, shares theoretically spoke no one language, and their owners could be anywhere in the world. Local control and regional autonomy vanished

while fear of outsiders—of powerful people and groups beyond the reach of the actual customers and employees of a railroad—mounted. Xenophobia and nativism found fertile soil amidst such developments.

Capital could become a metaphorical millstone around the neck of a corporation. Railroads accrued large fixed debts that had to be serviced regardless of whether the economy was thriving or collapsing, whether traffic was extensive or minimal, and whether shipping rates were rising or falling. Factories could close during recessions, but railroads could not decrease their costs by firing or furloughing employees because

The Iron Road in the Prarie State

track and rolling stock needed to be maintained and minimum staffing levels sustained. The physical plant would deteriorate if left unattended. And those obligations—mortgages, bonds, even stocks with shareholders expecting regular dividends—did not vanish just because the economy might hit a rough patch leaving railroad officials helpless in the face of commitments they could not meet. How managers and directors responded to such travails frequently determined the health of the railroad.

The possibility for plunder attracted swindlers. Some of the money disappeared into the pockets of crooks and conmen, but most of it went to pay for construction costs, rolling stock, and wage bills and, all too frequently, to subsidize unexpectedly low traffic volumes. Expenses were routinely underestimated and profits proved transient. Railroad bankruptcies were legion, and Illinois witnessed some of the most spectacular.

The volume of capital involved astounded contemporaries fretting about concentrations of power. Despite setbacks, railroads promoted a new financial system combining extensive landholdings with stocks and bonds, consolidating the preeminence of Wall Street among the nation's financial centers and creating paper instruments sold to millions of investors around the world. Here we meet the first contradiction of the new system of financing. Personal connections were vital for attracting large investors at the very time anonymous ownership became a key characteristic of investing. In September 1851, for example, Robert J. Walker sailed for Great Britain charged with raising $16 million for the Illinois Central. Using relationships forged during his recently concluded stint as secretary of the treasury, he met with Rothschild's, Barings, and other investment banks, but he secured only $1 million in loans, falling far short of his goal. Traveling with Walker was David Neal, an early shareholder in and director of the Illinois Central, who proceeded to Holland to sell shares in the line. Neal had made his fortune trading with Dutch colonies and had numerous contacts in the Netherlands. He used his connections to open doors in Amsterdam, but memories of 1837 stymied his efforts, as they did Walker's. Neither

Walker nor Neal sold a single bond during their 1851 European excursion.[3]

Political clout proved more useful than overseas junkets. A year after Neal and Walker's European jaunt, former United States vice president George M. Dallas, an ally of Walker in the fight for lower tariffs, publicly endorsed the Illinois Central. Dallas wrote that the line "furnishes unusually certain and ample guarantees, that they who purchase will make entirely safe and largely profitable investments of their money. I am of opinion that the income of the road alone (apart from the capital stock of two millions of dollars, and apart from the one-fourth of the lands granted by congress, both of which are reserved to meet deficiencies of interest) would insure to the bondholders the punctual payment of their interest." Investors attracted by the land grant and the expectation that the ICRR would become an important trunk line bought securities through London financial houses, as Dallas predicted they would. British financiers purchased bonds totaling $5 million in 1852, enabling the company to begin construction. The Illinois Central was the first American railroad to float an offer in London, but it would not be the last.[4]

Corruption and scandal undermined early campaigns to sell the Illinois Central to foreign investors. The problem was president Robert Schuyler, a New York City financier. Key investors did not trust him, and their hesitation proved wise when, in 1854, Schuyler was caught selling fraudulent stock in the New York & New Haven Railroad. Schuyler seems to have been a figurehead on the ICRR, but the company was swept into a media firestorm. Newspapers misidentified him as "the originator, and almost sole executive," of the ICRR, publicity the young line did not need. He resigned immediately from and sold his stocks in the Illinois Central, which placed an advertisement in New York City newspapers distancing itself from the disgraced railroader, but the value of ICRR bonds fell to sixty-two cents on the dollar. At that point British investors began purchasing them. This was an astute move, for by August 1855 the bonds had recovered to ninety cents. The affair blew over and by 1857 Dutch investment capital began to arrive. Twenty years later at least 80 percent of the line's common stock was still owned by investors in Holland and Britain.[5]

Foreign investors wanted to protect their capital. With reliable information scarce and the sums of money involved huge, they formed "Protective Committees" and sent investigators across the Atlantic to check on their holdings. One of the first, the London Committee of the Shareholders of the Illinois Central, sent British member of Parliament James Caird to inspect the recently completed line in 1859. Caird met with managers and unraveled the distant mysteries of American railroading, his positive report generating additional investment. Later, in 1874, a group of Dutch investors asked banker Hendrik Jan de Marez Oyens to discover why Illinois Central revenues were falling. After meeting with the board in New York, he traveled on the Chicago branch, testifying favorably on the directors' dedication to improving the road instead of artificially raising dividends. Oyens in turn impressed company officers, who thereafter sent him news of operational and financial problems on competing railroads, just as canal promoters had been telling tales to European investors of the slim chances of success for the Illinois Central. As biased as it may have been, this type of local knowledge was extremely valuable and very difficult for European investors to obtain. Regular newspaper columns in the British trade press—publications such as *Railway News* and *Herapth's Railway Journal*—provided stock quotes, but behind-the-scenes information from personal contacts was rare.[6]

Suspicion was warranted. Foreign investment could result in large gains for financial insiders at the expense of overseas financiers because of the distances and time involved in disseminating information, challenges the first transatlantic cable only partially ameliorated after 1866. Oyens had originally traveled to Illinois on behalf of a committee formed by European capitalists reorganizing the bankrupt Gilman, Clinton & Springfield Railroad. Incorporated in 1867 and completed four years later, the Gilman line issued $2 million in bonds paying 7 percent interest. But by the end of 1873 there were disturbing reports that the company was in trouble, and European investors wanted to know why. In March 1874

no dividends were paid, and the corporation entered receivership.

Speaking with fellow investors, Oyens learned that Gilman officials had engaged in an insider-construction scam. Railroad directors had created a separate company, which they controlled, to pay contractors building the line. The railroad reimbursed the construction company in discounted bonds, which meant the directors were transferring funds to themselves. Then, as directors of the construction company, they sold those bonds at a profit. This was not illegal, but it did give directors serving simultaneously on both boards an incentive to exchange the bonds with the construction company at a discount. Oyens discovered that more than half of the $4.5 million expended on construction had filtered into the pockets of the railroad directors in this way. He tried to track down the lost funds but failed, as did all other investigators. None of the money was recovered, and in 1876 the Illinois Central leased the Gilman road from the international bondholders. The ICRR purchased it the following year, renamed it the Springfield Branch, and ran it as an east-west connection between its two north-south lines. Shareholders lost money because the Illinois Central paid only eighty cents on the dollar. Despite the risks exemplified here, however, capital flowed across the Atlantic in search of opportunity and profit, sometimes to the consternation of European governments fearful of capital shortages in their own countries.[7]

INVESTMENT MORTGAGES

Another form of financing, the mortgage bond, proved popular with investors. Sold in installments and often marketed at a discount to attract buyers, mortgages paid a fixed rate of return and did well when backed by land grants. Mortgage holders frequently had first claim on assets when a company declared bankruptcy. Because the interest had to be paid regardless of the condition of the company, however, mortgages became increasingly unpopular in railroad boardrooms as the nineteenth century wore on.

The checkered history of the Toledo, Peoria & Western (TP&W) in the last quarter of the century demonstrates the advantage of holding mortgage bonds in the event of foreclosure. A Chicago bypass designed to connect the Mississippi River with Indiana, the TP&W rarely experienced profitability and demonstrated one of the enduring verities of Illinois railroad history: trying to work around the Windy City invariably resulted in failure. Built on the ashes of the old Peoria & Oquawka, so ruthlessly jettisoned by the CB&Q, the TP&W experienced this painful truth and entered receivership in 1875, just eight years after it opened as the Toledo, Peoria & Warsaw. The mortgage holders formed a committee to untangle the mess created when company officials failed to consolidate different loans into a single bundle of mortgage bonds, as they had promised they would. It took four years until, in December 1879, the committee incorporated a new company, dropping Warsaw in favor of Western. Mortgage holders salvaged their investments by purchasing the company and leasing it to the Wabash, St. Louis & Pacific Railroad. The Wabash, controlled by Jay Gould and part of a thread of trifling lines loosely strung across the Midwest, guaranteed 4 percent interest on second-mortgage bonds.[8]

The arrangement with Gould lasted only until the Wabash, overextended and failing in a faltering national economy, fell into receivership in 1884. Canceling the Wabash lease hurt those shareholders who had neglected to exchange their TP&W stock for Wabash shares. They lost $464,000, but the first mortgage holders regained ownership of the TP&W during bankruptcy reorganization. Unfortunately, rolling stock, the right-of-way, and even buildings were in terrible shape because cash shortages had forced the Wabash to defer maintenance. Unable to finance rebuilding, the TP&W entered foreclosure again, and mortgage holders bought it once more, in October 1886. The railroad continued to operate, and though the mortgage owners had not received dividends, they did retain ownership in the company, but holders of common stock lost their investments completely.[9]

OUTSIDERS

Robert Schuyler's fall and the damage it caused to the reputation of the Illinois Central demonstrated a growing fear of "brigands who live upon our Railroads to attack it, in hopes that if they can get inside and set fire to it, they can carry off something in the confusion." Here is a second contradiction inherent in the anonymity made possible by the combination of shareholding, the scale of railroad operations, and the personal connections needed to raise money: outsiders controlled much of the vital capital. As early as 1834, Illinois newspapers warned that "Wall Street brokers" were bribing politicians in an attempt to divert federal land grants for canals into railroads. Seventeen years later a chronic shortage of capital led the founders of the Alton & Sangamon Railroad (A&S), predecessor to the Chicago & Alton, to seek assistance from one of those Wall Street brokers, with dramatic and disastrous consequences.[10]

It all began so promisingly. In 1851 Alton president Benjamin Godfrey traveled to New York City in a desperate bid to attract investment capital. There he met Henry Dwight Jr., to whom he confessed that his inability to raise funds brought him close to defaulting on several loans and threatened the future of the Alton. A New York banker, Dwight would prove to be precisely the type of "brigand" locals feared. Sensing blood and profit, he told Godfrey, "I must have the whole of your property and everything I can make from it." Dwight also warned the frantic railroader, "You must put yourself entirely in my hands," and forced Godfrey to authorize him to act on behalf of Alton directors and shareholders in New York City. Using this authority, Dwight gained control of the finances of the Alton by replacing three directors with his own appointees.[11]

The connection appeared to be paying off when construction of the line to Springfield accelerated. What Godfrey did not know was that Dwight himself was overextended and racing against his creditors to obtain cash. The Alton had fallen into his lap at exactly the right time. Unfortunately for Dwight and the railroad, the New York credit market tightened in 1852 and banks began demanding repayment of outstanding loans. Dwight needed cash fast, and he obtained it illegally. He convinced a friendly cashier at a New York bank to give him railroad bonds valued at $230,000 on which he had no legal claim in order to repay a loan in Ohio. He then instructed the directors of the Alton's extension into the Windy City—the Chicago & Mississippi—to issue $2 million in new bonds and awarded himself a $6 million contract to extend the road to Joliet, three times the original estimate.

Dwight grew increasingly frenzied as his access to credit evaporated. In September 1853 he created the fictitious company of Benj. Godfrey & Co. to secure a personal loan. The next month he mortgaged bonds of the Chicago & Mississippi to borrow money from the Litchfield brothers, who controlled the Northern Indiana Railroad. In November, unable to repay his loans, Dwight declared bankruptcy and lost control of the Alton. The Litchfields took over and appointed their own president, superintendent, and directors in place of those allied with Dwight. Undeterred and willfully violating a written agreement not to do so, the New Yorker used proxy votes to oust Litchfield allies from the board. Dwight then ignored shareholder protests to revise the charter and resumed his illegal plundering. He defrauded Godfrey by selling land and property pledged as collateral, secured personal loans using company bonds, pocketed insurance payments owed to others, and submitted duplicate vouchers for bills already paid until, a year later, he was removed from the board.[12]

His absence proved temporary. Dwight convinced four new directors to resign in August 1855 and appointed his own men in their stead. This time he initiated a two-part coup in order to sell the company and repay personal loans totaling $575,000. First he convinced the board to assign a new lease to one of his friends. This lease promised interest payments to the company's many bondholders, but no payments were made. Next, Dwight's allies took control of the company's assets and planned to sell them. On March 1, 1856, the company defaulted on its loans to a New York bank and was foreclosed. Appointed receiver, Dwight sold the line to Edward Litchfield, who made the governor of Illinois, Joel Matteson, its president. This ended Dwight's direct involvement with the Alton while liquidating his personal debt. In 1859 a circuit court ruled that Godfrey was entitled to the property he had lost as a consequence of

Dwight's actions, but the Alton's founder died in 1862 and no reparations were ever made.[13]

The company slowly recovered under Matteson's leadership. In spite of Dwight's malfeasance, construction continued northeast from Springfield and eventually reached Chicago. But the Alton had been built quickly using cheap materials, thus requiring massive renovations. The roadbed sagged, unpainted wooden buildings rotted, bridges disintegrated, and culverts collapsed. In 1860 a new president, James Robb, threw himself into the task of reforming the road. He closed the Bloomington shops for several months to save money, moved the company headquarters to Chicago, hired Roswell Mason to rebuild the Chicago extension, replaced the mostly derelict locomotive fleet, and switched from scarce wood to more readily available coal for fuel. As for Dwight, not only did he "carry off something in the confusion," but he left his mark on the map of Illinois in the form of a town named in his honor some eighty miles southwest of Chicago.[14] The town and the line running through it still exist today.

BUILDING TRAFFIC

New railroads had to create a demand for their services or, where the desire to use trains existed, to expand it. They did so in a variety of ways on the passenger and freight sides. As local businesses they were, in a very real sense, commuter lines from the beginning. When the Galena & Chicago Union built out to Elgin in 1850 it served people who wanted to make the journey east toward the lake. In 1854 the G&CU began operating trains specifically to serve commuters with regular morning and evening runs. In 1856 the Illinois Central cooperated with landowner Paul Cornell to popularize the tract of land that would become Hyde Park. The railroad ran the daily "Hyde Park Special" to Great Central Station in downtown Chicago and out again, though after the Panic of 1857 Cornell was forced to subsidize the service to keep it running. The ICRR also adopted sleeping cars and staterooms for the discerning traveler.[15] Early coaches tended to be rather basic, built of wood with poor ventilation, no springs, bench seating, and link-and-pin couplers,

The Iron Road in the Prarie State

Figure 5.2. Dwight Depot on the C&A, named for Henry Dwight Jr., the banker who almost destroyed the railroad. Library of Congress Prints and Photographs Division.

which encouraged the vehicles to bump each other with some force en route. The ride over unballasted track at even the relatively slow speeds of the 1850s caused many a complaint.

Generating freight traffic was at first quite simple. Farmers welcomed the railroad in most places because of the opportunity to sell their crops in the large markets at the end of the tracks. The railroads in turn assisted farmers by offering expertise and information. Driven by self-interest, railroads promoted agricultural improvements because better stock, stronger plants,

diversified harvests, and bigger yields meant greater volumes of more reliable freight and passenger traffic. In 1858, for example, the Illinois Central provided "almost unbounded liberality" in carrying lumber gratis for organizers of the state fair being held near its line at Centralia. That same year a disastrous harvest convinced ICRR president William H. Osborn to encourage sugar beet cultivation. In 1866 he established a sugar beet processing plant on a farm he owned near Chatsworth. The ICRR also promoted the cultivation of flax and sorghum and fostered agricultural innovation by

Figure 5.3. An example of railroad construction: the East Peoria shops of the TP&W (1928). Author's collection.

transporting reapers and mowers to Salem for State Agricultural Society trials.[16]

When dry summers and falling commodity prices hurt wheat farmers the Chicago & North Western promoted experimentation with relatively drought-resistant alfalfa. In 1861 the price of corn fell from $1.50 to between 23 and 35 cents a bushel; on farms adjacent to the CB&Q and the ICRR the price was below the cost of transporting it, and farmers burned it for fuel. Reacting to farmers' distress, the Illinois Central reduced the cost of transporting corn, but when this proved insufficient the company agreed to pay Chicago prices, minus the cost of transportation, to help farmers service their debts. The consequence was a financial loss to the ICRR but the number of delinquent payments declined. The company then offered a similar deal to wheat farmers, also harmed by low prices. Despite every effort to help settlers, some enforced collections did occur, resulting in public criticism of the Illinois Central.[17]

MERGERS AND ACQUISITIONS

Railroads needed to grow to survive. Expansion generated new customers, kept competing lines at bay, and hinted at higher profitability. To do this, railroads could build branches from their own trunks, purchase existing companies, or fund start-up ventures. Buying publicly traded stock was one way to gain control of another company, but it could be expensive if other investors wanted to purchase the same shares. One railroad could gain control of another by purchasing enough shares to appoint directors to the board or by swapping shares. The first of these strategies enabled the purchasing company to dictate policy while avoiding responsibility for maintenance and debt servicing. Exchanging shares could merge the two companies and block other railroads. The disadvantage, especially for a company in fiscal distress, was the requirement to pay the subordinate's debts.

Figure 5.4. The crowded yards in 1910 at Bushnell, where the CB&Q crossed the TP&W, attest to the close proximity of people and trains in small towns. Western Illinois University Libraries, Archives, and Special Collections.

One relatively low-risk method of merging was the use of lease agreements. In the event investors could not be found, a proposed line would not be built, and the parent company would not lose any of its own money. But if the capital could be raised and the line built, the parent company (whose name often attracted investors) would lease it. Beginning in 1854, the Chicago & Rock Island Railroad (C&RI) leased the Peoria & Bureau Valley (P&BV) for $125,000 annually "in perpetuity" after the P&BV had raised capital, acquired land, and laid rail, all at virtually no cost to the Rock Island, whose trains were destined to run over the new line. This arrangement connected the Rock Island with Peoria while giving P&BV shareholders a guaranteed annual dividend of 8 percent. Collateral trust bonds also limited risk. Under this arrangement the parent company would exchange its own bonds for those of the new railroad, which

would sell those bonds to raise money for construction. This proved an effective way to merge separate corporations and became particularly popular during the early twentieth century. The Atchison, Topeka & Santa Fe used bond exchanges to gain control of the smaller lines it served in Illinois.

Another way to take control of a line was to assume its debt, which could be financially attractive because it was often cheaper than leasing over the long run. Owning a line enabled the larger firm to dictate traffic flows and avoid losing it to a rival. At the end of the nineteenth century the Chicago, Burlington & Quincy (CB&Q) began repaying the debts of the Burlington & Missouri River Railroad (B&MRR), which had been its de facto main line across Iowa. The CB&Q converted "traffic balances" (money the B&MRR owed the Burlington for running its trains over CB&Q rails in Illinois) into B&MRR stock controlled by the CB&Q. In 1872 the larger company, fearing Jay Gould would try to purchase the B&MRR, signed a lease to control it. The CB&Q subsequently reached Denver by extending the Iowa main line of the B&MRR through Nebraska and into Colorado.[18]

Resisting expansion could prove hazardous. Timothy Blackstone, president of the Chicago & Alton from 1864 to 1899, refused to join the race to grow. After the Alton completed a line to Kansas City in 1879 it added virtually no new track. Competing railroads serving its main terminals (Chicago, St. Louis, and Kansas City) and the twenty-four interchange stations along Alton lines siphoned away traffic. The C&A remained profitable through the 1870s and 1880s but, outmaneuvered by more adaptable rivals and handicapped by Blackstone's refusal to carry freight at a loss, it became almost autarkic in its reliance on customers adjacent to its own tracks. Blackstone remained resolutely proud of his stand against expansion, but the Alton stagnated.[19]

Other Illinois railroads pursued policies of careful growth. Marvin Hughitt of the North Western and Charles E. Perkins of the Burlington pursued policies they hoped would strengthen their companies while fending off rivals. Both men shared a commitment to gathering information and acting cautiously. Perkins refused to move his office to Chicago when named president in 1881, preferring to remain in Burlington, Iowa, where he could easily assess the state of the line and its customers. Hughitt and Perkins both considered, and rejected, building to the West Coast, unlike the ill-fated Milwaukee Road. The North Western and the Burlington remained regional railroads that connected with extant transcontinentals, the Union Pacific (at Council Bluffs, Iowa) for both lines and the Northern Pacific (in Montana) in the case of the Burlington.

Extending a main line or developing branches entailed risk, so limiting exposure to the costs of expansion made sense from a financial standpoint. The only major railroad to be completed as a single project in the Prairie State was the Illinois Central, which of course had a substantial land grant to attract investors. Other railroads were built in autonomous segments and

merged later, as with the four original components of the CB&Q. Mergers could be, and would remain, controversial, especially when national figures like Cornelius Vanderbilt and Jay Gould became involved.

BANKRUPTCY AND RECEIVERSHIP

Securities had to be repaid and debts serviced, not always feasible for railroads built through low-density regions or facing economic downturns. When railroads could no longer meet their obligations they declared bankruptcy and entered receivership. Court-appointed receivers were supposed to oversee a corporation while it was being reorganized and had a duty to protect the interests of creditors and customers alike. Receivers could issue certificates to raise money for immediate expenses, such as repairs and wages, but these notes carried high rates of interest and took precedence over all other loans, including first mortgages, in the event a company was foreclosed and its assets sold off.

Receivership could prove beneficial, however, as investors in the Cairo & St. Louis (C&StL) learned. A 151-mile line crossing sparsely populated southwestern Illinois, the C&StL was chartered in 1865, but operations did not commence for a decade. The original promoters failed to raise sufficient capital and lost in court when Cairo taxpayers refused to pay for the interest accruing on its bonds. The lack of funding necessitated a switch from standard gauge to the supposedly cheaper, narrower, three-foot gauge. Just two years after it opened, the longest tunnel on its route collapsed, and its largest shareholder, New York–based car builder Ferdinand E. Canda, forced the road into receivership. A plan to carry it into St. Louis over the Eads Bridge proved impracticable, but the tunnel was rebuilt, and the company enjoyed a moment of profitability. In 1881 it gained a new name, the St. Louis & Cairo Railroad, and its 7 percent bonds were converted into 5 percent first-mortgage income bonds, almost all of which were owned by Dutch investors. In 1885 the Mobile & Ohio Railroad (M&ORR) leased the line to gain entry into St. Louis. This lease had two advantages for bondholders. First, the M&ORR converted the line to standard gauge, allowing it to cross the Mississippi River over Eads Bridge and facilitating interchange with other railroads. Second, the much larger, more prosperous railroad guaranteed the interest payments on bonds that had until then been of uncertain value.[20]

Railroads made, and lost, untold millions of dollars. As the experience of raising, spending, and misplacing money in Illinois suggests, some of that capital vanished into the pockets of speculators and thieves. Most of it did actually find its way into building and operating railroads, many of them profitably. The sheer scale and scope of railroads required raising funds beyond the means of any one individual or family, so railroads ventured into European capital markets. Here, the Illinois Central proved a successful pioneer, demonstrating the importance of personal connections and persistence. The Chicago, Burlington & Quincy could draw on eastern capital markets, while the Galena & Chicago Union convinced farmers and politicians along its route to subscribe to its stock offerings. But local and even regional financing remained relatively less important than capital from Wall Street and from European investors, tying Illinois ever more tightly into the global marketplace. Without those connections, the railroads would not have been built; with them, Illinois became increasingly dependent on external sources of capital and control.

6

CONFLAGRATIONS AND EXPANSION

The railroad-building surge of the 1850s made Chicago into an international marketplace and would help the North win the Civil War. Railroads transformed Illinois by bringing in people and capital, mechanizing and growing the grain trade, and dramatically expanding the labor force. A national financial downturn in 1857 caused an immediate drop in traffic volume, brought expansion to a halt, and tipped many railroads into bankruptcy, but local services temporarily kept them running and allowed the system to adjust to the new mileage.

The 1860s and 1870s witnessed the trauma of Civil War and the excitement of transcontinental railroading. The war caused little direct injury to Illinois railroads, though the closure to civilians of the Mississippi River and additional wartime traffic meant deferred maintenance, damaged track, and worn-out rolling stock. Illinois was the fastest-growing state in the Union during the Civil War because of its network of railroads, migrants entering from the Confederacy, and the increased importance of Chicago as a transshipment center. When the conflict began the industry seemed ready to contribute, though few could have predicted how much the railroads had to offer the war effort.

After the Civil War, railroads were big and getting bigger: physical expansion continued, but even more spectacular was the complexity of the corporations,

the sheer amount of financing needed to keep them running, and the scale of their operations. Local entities had, by war's end, become interlinked corporations regional and even national in scope. The Prairie State was at the heart of this transformation. The completion of the first transcontinental in 1869 connected Illinois with the West Coast and confirmed Chicago as the nation's rail hub. In 1870 the state's 4,823 route miles represented over 9 percent of the nation's total mileage. By 1890 the Prairie State had 9,936 miles, still more than any other state in the Union, and it would continue to grow until reaching 12,128 miles in 1920. Only then did another state, Texas, surpass Illinois's total.[1]

The period between the Civil War and the end of the nineteenth century saw Illinois industrialize, and railroads were a key component in that process. In 1870 the value of manufactured goods equaled that of agricultural products for the first time in the state's short history, and growth continued to favor industry until by 1890 the state stood third in the nation for industrial production. A demographic shift accompanied this change: in 1870, 11.6 percent of the state's people lived in Chicago, but by 1890 that figure had reached almost 29 percent. Between 1890 and 1900 the majority of people lived in urban areas, highlighting the decline of rural Illinois.[2]

Illinoisans split on secession as war loomed. Despite helping to send Abraham Lincoln to the White House, pockets of people—especially in Little Egypt—supported the Confederacy. Fear approached hysteria when Williamson County dissidents met to discuss joining the rebellion while rumors of Southern sympathizers sabotaging railroads gained wide circulation. Some Illinois men fought with Confederate armies, including thirty or so from Marion who joined a company of Tennessee Volunteers. A substantial demonstration of Southern loyalty in Carbondale and pro-Confederacy rallies elsewhere in Little Egypt highlighted the intrastate threat, yet when the call to arms came in 1861 the people of Illinois responded with Northern patriotism. The state raised six Union regiments in five days; within a week of Fort Sumter falling into Confederate hands, Cairo swarmed with Union soldiers preparing to defend the state's southern tip from the expected invasion. Enthusiasm flagged, however, when Illinois failed to send its quota to the Union forces and drafted soldiers for the first time in September 1864. Coercion was not appreciated, and opposition to the war rumbled on, especially in the Far South.[3]

Illinois railroads sent numerous officials to the war effort, though few were as decorated as Ohio & Mississippi Railroad president George B. McClellan. A West Point graduate who had also served as vice president and chief engineer of the Illinois Central, he took command of the Army of the Potomac in August 1861. McClellan had broken into the industry as a surveyor for the Northern Pacific Railroad and understood the importance of railroads for military campaigns. A significant portion of his strategy for winning the war, spelled out in a lengthy report to President Lincoln, drew on his railroading experience.[4]

One of McClellan's first acts was to assign his friend and colleague Captain Lewis B. Parsons of the Army Quartermaster Corps to take charge of transportation in the St. Louis area. A Yale graduate with a law degree from Harvard, Parsons worked alongside McClellan during the 1850s as an attorney for the O&M. In St. Louis

he proved an able administrator, and his duties soon expanded to include the entire Department of the Mississippi. He rapidly reorganized transportation in the West by replacing expensive riverboat charters with short-term contracts. Parsons also reduced government expenditures by restricting free passes and purchasing only as many tickets as the army needed for troop movements rather than bulk buying and leaving seats empty. His logistical abilities were such that in June 1863 he supervised the arrangements for sending ten thousand men from central Kentucky to Vicksburg via Cairo in just four days. By ending the chaotic state of military travel, Parsons earned promotion to Washington, DC, as head of rail and river transportation for the United States Army.[5]

Individual railroads played key roles in the war effort, none more so than the wishbone-shaped Illinois Central. This south-north line lived up to the promise in the original 1836 prospectus to speed armed citizens to the defense of the realm. In 1861 it carried seventy thousand soldiers, and the volume increased the next year. But for the ICRR, military traffic proved a disruptive and unprofitable inconvenience. War trains took priority over others, and as a land-grant railroad the ICRR shipped at a discount, charging only one and one-third cents per troop mile rather than the standard two cents per passenger mile. The road lost money on troop trains, which averaged 1.8 cents per troop mile to operate. Local traffic suffered, and the rising costs of coal and labor also hurt the bottom line, though after 1862 revenue increased, but at a slower rate than the volume of traffic. In 1864 net earnings rose 18 percent, while traffic increased 38 percent, and the final year of the war was the same, with earnings failing to keep pace with record traffic levels.[6]

So many troop trains moved so frequently, and coordinating them became so complicated, that crucial lines and junctions nearly jammed. The 112 miles of the Illinois Central from Centralia to Cairo, nicknamed the "needle's eye" for its strategic importance and narrow confines, proved a particularly troublesome bottleneck. A young official by the name of Marvin Hughitt mastered the eye and gained fame in railroading circles by sending trains down that slim aperture like a skillful embroiderer. Hughitt, an experienced telegrapher working from his office in Centralia, dispatched trains carrying men and matériel along the single track to the South for thirty-six hours without respite. Job done, he walked home and was on the verge of sinking into bed when he was recalled to the apparatus. The original orders had been countermanded by General Ulysses S. Grant, and now those same soldiers and equipment had to return north. For seventy-two hours Hughitt moved military trains around regularly scheduled services without incident. Promotions followed, and he eventually retired as president of the Chicago & North Western.[7]

Soldiers and their equipment were not the only source of passenger traffic during the war. The wounded and the dead returned on hospital and funeral trains with depressing regularity. The Lebanon, Illinois, branch of the Louisville & Nashville Railroad (L&N) operated the first hospital train, designed by the Illinois agent of the Sanitary Commission. Confederate captives also came to the state. After the battle for Fort Donelson, the Illinois Central moved ten thousand prisoners of war from Cairo to points north. The company's standard passenger, the European immigrant settling in the Prairie State, all but vanished when war began. But Illinois Central recruiters found new sources to tap, including Southerners unsettled by the conflict. The US War Department and the ICRR cooperated to introduce cotton farming into Little Egypt to employ refugees from Southern states, particularly Kentucky and Tennessee. In 1862 the company established a land office in Cairo to assist fleeing Southerners and the next year immigration from Europe picked up, and land sales increased as agents found numerous prospective settlers in Germany and Scandinavia.[8]

The federal government made good use of Illinois railroad facilities for the war effort. The ICRR built a three-mile branch to Mound City, on the Ohio River near Cairo, when it became the Union's principal freshwater port in 1862. Already home to the Marine Ways shipyard, Mound City survived having its Indian earthworks dismissed by an English journalist as "a mere heap of earth like a ruined brick kiln" and quickly became a

bustling manufacturing center, living up to its original name of "Emporium City." The Union employed skilled workers in railroad shops to build armored railroad cars, cast capstans, and construct other naval hardware. The government transferred Cairo mechanics to Mound City to convert steamers into gunboats and other floating weapons of war.[9]

No Civil War battles were fought on Illinois soil and the state's railroads suffered no direct physical harm, but this did not mean they were untouched. The draft caused a labor shortage at the very time greater demand for railroad transportation created pressure to expand the workforce, a problem only partly offset when the federal government exempted engineers. The experience of the Chicago & Alton was typical: labor shortages and equipment confiscations for the war effort were inconveniences but did little to damage the long-term health of the corporation. The C&A carried far fewer troops than its counterparts in the state but it benefited from a sharp increase in commodity shipments, including uniforms, ammunition, and food. Projects proposed before the war proceeded as planned: track was replaced, new rolling stock was purchased, and bridges were rebuilt. But shortages of wood and high iron prices delayed rehabilitation as the conflict ground on. In 1865 the C&A temporarily suspended operations because its locomotives were in desperate need of repair and the ranks of skilled mechanics had been depleted by the war effort. To meet shortages elsewhere the company bought stands of timber, set up its own sawmill, began rerolling iron rails at its plant near Chenoa, and recruited three hundred laborers from England to replace workers lost to the military.[10]

Some companies flourished during the war. The Galena & Chicago Union formalized running agreements it had with lines in Wisconsin and Michigan in a "Great Consolidation" from which the Chicago & North Western emerged in 1864, the first major merger of the railroad era. The C&NW enjoyed record earnings during the war but its capacity was constrained by rolling-stock shortages and delays building its extension to Green Bay, Wisconsin. Like many others, the North Western could not acquire new cars and locomotives fast enough to keep up with demand. Nonetheless, its line to Fulton was completed in 1862 and a bridge over the Mississippi River connecting that town with Iowa was opened in 1864. The C&NW then ran the first dedicated postal train across the new structure in August 1864 between Chicago and Clinton, Iowa.[11]

Chicago meatpacking grew almost exponentially as a result of wartime needs. Clustered along a waterway that flowed into the South Branch of the Chicago River, the seven independent meat-rendering facilities helped the Windy City surpass Cincinnati as the nation's leading meat processing center and earned it the title "Hog Butcher for the World." But the packing plants were unpleasant neighbors who spoiled air and water with their smell and waste products. In 1865 the meatpackers moved to a three-hundred-acre area of drained swampland, the Union Stockyards, served by the C&NW from the north and the ICRR from the south. A new neighborhood—Packingtown—and a new industrial area—Back of the Yards—emerged. Cattle from as far away as Texas came to the modern facility, and, after Gustavus Swift produced an effective refrigerator car in 1878, meat products could be shipped from Chicago to anywhere in the United States.[12]

One new line that did open during the war was the Chicago & Great Eastern Railroad, completed in March 1865. The C&GE connected Chicago with Columbus, Ohio, creating another route for grain from Illinois to the Northeast and the Atlantic seaboard. The number of passengers carried by the Chicago, Burlington & Quincy tripled during the war, but the number of cars to carry those passengers rose from forty to only seventy-two. But the railroad was lucky. Many other roads experienced increased traffic volume but had to make do with shrinking car inventories as the War Department requisitioned rolling stock and damaged cars could not be repaired.[13]

The demand for long-distance transportation created by military requirements altered the railroading landscape. From functioning primarily as providers of local services, wartime demands forced separate railroad corporations to cooperate in forming long-distance routes, refocusing them from local horizons to national operations. Longer runs also meant more sleeping cars in service, though these were usually ordinary coaches converted for the purpose. Because of the growing volume of interchange traffic running over two or more roads, groups of lines created informal "communities of interest," which would expand into regional monopolies after the war. One of the first meetings to coordinate operations occurred in March 1862, when six roads serving Chicago met to write rules for passenger and freight routes.[14]

THE HEART OF A TOWN

By the time of the Civil War the railroad depot had become a fundamental element of Illinois towns and villages. Trains carried people from local stations to distant horizons for rest and recreation, business and conventions. They stopped to pick up and set down passengers and freight at specialized buildings, frequently located in town centers. Tickets could be bought and parcels shipped from the station, a gathering place and an economic engine full of possibility and adventure. Bustling cities like Chicago and Peoria, small towns such as Olney and Urbana, and rural outposts from Joy to Harmony had depots. Comings and goings at the depot, which had become simultaneously a gateway and a community center, broke up the monotony of daily life while creating seasonal routines. Townspeople gathered to claim long-awaited packages, many bearing the name Sears Roebuck or Montgomery Ward, from far-off places. Old-timers played pinochle while sizing up newcomers, and children congregated on the platform to gaze in wonder at smoke-belching iron horses. Adults clustered in expectant groups to welcome friends and family. In college and university towns, railroad officials braced for "the annual hegira of students for the homeland," signaled by "a noticeable increase in the amount of out-bound baggage," while every freight station bustled during harvest season.[15]

Train time often shaped the day's contours in small towns and villages around the state. Locals would wander down to the depot to meet incoming arrivals, catch up on the news, and admire the daily train. Growing up in rural Jasper County in southeastern Illinois in

Figure 6.1. Watseka, at the crossing of the TP&W and the C&EI, exemplifies the many junction depots in Illinois. Author's collection.

the 1910s, singer and actor Burl Ives recounted in his autobiography the cultural significance of the railroad. Settling into a new house, the seven-year-old Ives heard someone shout, "Here she comes!" followed by what he described as "a general migration of all the people who were working, trading, and loafing toward the depot. The train was coming." The young lad naturally followed and was rewarded with his first-ever glimpse of a locomotive, which "rolled up majestically and stopped slowly and then gave a great puff, sort of a sigh of relief, and white steam flowed into nothingness. The engine panted like a tired horse. From the cars came squirts of steam and the people gathered around to see who was getting off and what was being taken out of the baggage car." After the train left, "everybody slowly returned to what they had been doing before." The romance of railroading derived from moments like this, and Ives went on to sing about railroads for the rest of his long life.[16]

But railroad corporations were not philanthropies, of course, and depots served hard-headed, practical purposes. Depot employees provided local knowledge to help railroads respond to changing market conditions. Voluminous correspondence between employees and managers covered rates and traffic flows, safety protocols, shipping concerns, and labor issues. The public-spirited Illinois Central, for one, went further and required station agents to collect samples of soil, minerals, grasses, fruits, and crops in their areas to send to the annual state fair. The line also offered reduced tickets to visitors and free transportation for showing cattle and produce.[17]

Mendota provides a characteristic example of an Illinois depot. Mendota earned its name—which translates from Algonquin as "where two trails meet"—when the infant Chicago & Aurora reached the main line of the Illinois Central in the 1850s. This made travel from Chicago to St. Louis possible on a twenty-four-hour "schedule," inviting calamity and delay. The intrepid traveler began on the Galena & Chicago Union, transferring at Turner Junction onto a Chicago & Aurora train to Mendota,

The Iron Road in the Prarie State

where, according to one visitor, "the people look unusually lively, healthy, and well-fed." Passengers paused long enough to enjoy a meal in the station restaurant, orders having been telegraphed ahead to ensure that hot food awaited the train, before boarding the Illinois Central to Bloomington. Here, the by-now-exhausted passenger switched onto the Alton for that line's terminus adjacent to the Mississippi River, from where a riverboat made the final leg of the tortuous trip.[18]

The town expanded rapidly thanks to the railroad. Its population grew by 45 percent between 1860 and 1870 and had surpassed four thousand by 1880. The earliest permanent structures in Mendota were the Illinois Central depot, a roundhouse, and a freight house. The original depot, a small wooden structure, burned down in 1885. It was soon replaced with a modern two-story brick building containing ticket office, hotel, lunch counter, kitchen, baggage room, express office, telegraph office, and waiting room. In 1903 the Milwaukee Road built to and through Mendota on its way to coal fields in Bureau and LaSalle Counties, and within five years passenger traffic reached thirty-nine daily trains in every direction. Fifty years later only ten trains a day, all on the Burlington, stopped to pick up passengers in Mendota. That number had dwindled to six by 1970. Many of the railroad buildings had been shuttered, including locomotive maintenance and repair facilities made redundant by diesels, with an attendant loss of jobs.[19]

During the railroad age the depot was a district. Downtown business and cultural centers developed around the railroad station, which often stood at the end of Main Street. Public buildings such as hotels, restaurants, bars, and law offices could be found there. Warehouses, lumberyards, cattle pens, and grain elevators surrounded the nearby freight station. The announcement of the opening of a depot and the creation of a town site often attracted businesses in the following order: small merchant houses and workshops; hotels; flour mills, sawmills, packing houses, or grain elevators, according to local needs; churches and school buildings; and lastly brick makers and lumberyards. The pattern was repeated across the state and the Midwest, establishing a familiar foundation for town life. When

the St. Charles Railroad established a depot at its terminus in 1871 new industries developed to process and ship local milk supplies, while iron works, piano and glass factories, and a paper mill arrived to take advantage of the town's location on the Fox River. Factory work changed village demographics by bringing in Belgians, Danes, Lithuanians, and Swedes.[20]

The depot was the local symbol of the railroad, the first link between traveler and train. It was the portal to adventure, shopping, vacation, and a day out, and for "drummers" (traveling salesmen) it was the best way to stay in touch with business contacts. Locals eagerly anticipated the arrival of scheduled trains while newspapers recorded the entry of visitors, distinguished and otherwise. Thus, for example, the *Sycamore True Republican* noted in 1892 the appearance in Cortland of "Mrs. A. W. House and grand-daughter" while reporting that "Mrs. M. L. Wilder, of Chicago, has been the guest of her sister, Mrs. M. Mordoff." Such minutiae constituted part of the fabric of daily life in the railway age.

Railroads sometimes literally attracted houses. Most of the towns along the eastern extension of the TP&W, for example, were built after the line came through, often platted by company officials who then recruited the first settlers. Watseka, however, began life as the village of Middleport but moved itself to be adjacent to TP&W tracks. When the Alton & Sangamon Railroad avoided Auburn, south of Springfield, in 1852 the town—an important stop for stagecoaches—virtually disappeared. The villagers moved their houses to the new settlement, called Wineman, and a farmer purchased the abandoned town site and turned it into cornfields. In 1865 the Illinois legislature incorporated Wineman and changed its name to Auburn.[21]

Chicago became home to some of the busiest train stations in America, but no single terminus developed. Early railroads wanted to control their own destinies, and as new lines entered the city after 1880 they rented space in existing stations. Local business and political leaders cultivated separate termini, increasing the amount of traffic forced to use local transfer services and encouraging passengers to stay in the city's hotels. Ubiquitous Parmelee Transfers carried passengers, baggage,

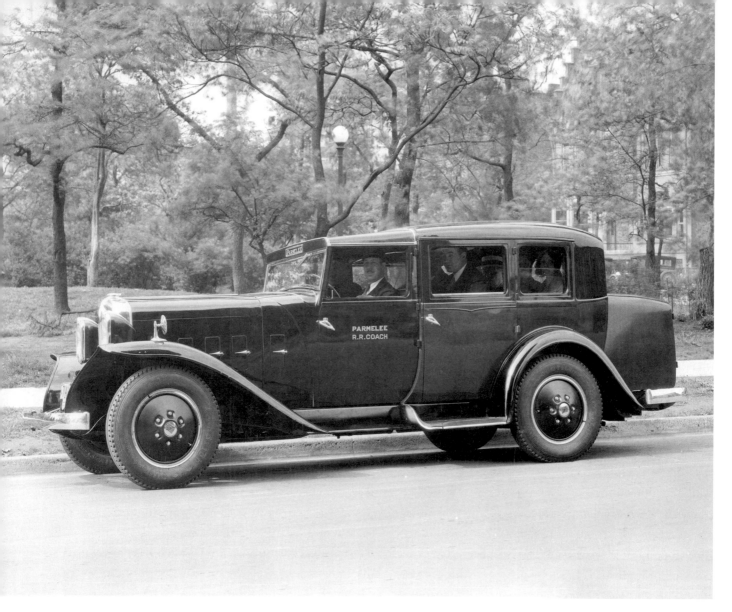

Figure 6.2. Parmelee Rail Taxis moved passengers and their baggage across Chicago to make connections from one terminus to another. Lake Forest College Library Special Collections.

and freight around the city. By 1925 Chicago's passenger network was in full swing, its shape unchanged until the end of private long-distance passenger trains in 1971. After decades of additions, relocations, and renovations, all six principal downtown termini were in their final form, and passengers poured into them at varying rates.[22]

The longest-serving Chicago terminus was the Rock Island's LaSalle Street Station. Opened in 1851 and rebuilt in 1903, it sat adjacent to the Board of Trade building in the heart of the financial district. The North Western brought several stations under one roof at the intersection of Wells and Kinzie Streets in 1881, but

rapid growth demanded a relocation to Clinton and Canal Streets just twenty years later. Unusually, the station continued to serve one railroad, a brief dalliance with the B&O and the Chesapeake & Ohio aside, though it was often the busiest station in the city. In keeping with the monumental architecture of the age, the C&NW built a terminus that, like so many famous stations around the world, reminded passengers of a cathedral or a classical temple. Two blocks south was another key terminus, Union Station, opened in 1882. The original tenants included two Pennsylvania Railroad lines (the Pittsburgh, Fort Wayne & Chicago Railroad and the Pittsburgh, Cincinnati, St. Louis & Chicago Railroad,

The Iron Road in the Prarie State

Figure 6.3. Parmelee passenger agents facilitated movement to and through Chicago's main termini. Library of Congress Prints and Photographs Division.

notable exception, the Atchison, Topeka & Santa Fe Railway (ATSF). From Dearborn Street famous Santa Fe trains like the *Super Chief* carried celebrities to and from California. For dramatic views of the lake it was hard to beat Central Station, the ICRR terminus, built on reclaimed swampland east of the Loop and opened in 1893 in time for the Columbian Exposition. Services from the ambitiously named Grand Central station, owned by the Chicago & Northern Pacific, began running in 1890, but its prominence dimmed after the Panic of 1893. Despite a spectacular tower adding to the skyline it became and remained a minor player, hosting the B&O, the Chicago Great Western, and the Pere Marquette.

Despite progress in the improvement of depots and the development of what could be called a nascent national network, riding the trains in the 1870s remained almost as uncomfortable as it had been in the first years of railroading. This was especially true of long-distance travel. A young carpenter by the name of George Pullman learned that for himself when, in the 1850s, his firm won several contracts to lift buildings out of the mud to allow the city to install a much-needed sewer system. On periodic returns to New York he discovered the agony of overnight train travel. Early experiments using benches for dozing passengers were a start, but in 1856 the first true sleeping cars ran across southern Illinois on the Terre Haute & Alton Railroad, but the ride remained rough. Convinced of the need for a luxurious sleeping car, George Pullman and his friend Benjamin Field, a New York senator who owned a small railroad car–building company, set out to meet the demand. Their first carriage made a test run on the Alton & Sangamon on August 15, 1859. After a brief excursion, during which they demonstrated how the seats could be transformed into commodious bunks, its inaugural revenue run came on September 1, 1859, to St. Louis.

The business thrived, and in 1863 Pullman and Field established a partnership to manufacture sleeping cars. Pullman would, with an unfortunate choice of words, tell an interviewer in 1897 that "good luck" saved his young company when President Abraham Lincoln was assassinated. What he meant was, the Pullman name

often known as the Panhandle), the Milwaukee Road, and the C&A. The CB&Q would become a partner after the ICRR relocated its lakeside depot, making it inaccessible to Burlington trains. Unique among Chicago main stations, it contained platforms facing north and south, separated by the head house but linked by two run-through tracks. Union Station was completely rebuilt in 1925, when dramatic colonnaded concourses and a massive waiting area were constructed. The station owners hired Fred Harvey to provide services ranging from a luxury restaurant and a bookstore to newsstands and a soda fountain.[23] Used today by Amtrak, Union Station is the only remaining long-distance train station in Chicago.

Another terminal with a national reach, Dearborn Station (often called Dearborn Street Station) at Dearborn and Polk Streets, became an instant landmark with its prominent clock tower and majestic redstone head house when it opened in 1885. Owned by the Chicago & Western Indiana, the terminal's tenants (the Chicago & Eastern Illinois [C&EI], the Erie, the Grand Trunk, the Monon, and the Wabash) faced east, but with one

Figure 6.4. The cathedral-like vestibule at C&NW Station in Chicago in 1912. Library of Congress Prints and Photographs Division.

Figure 6.5. Chicago's Dearborn Street Station, known for its iconic clock tower, in 1915. Library of Congress Prints and Photographs Division.

became synonymous with first-class railroad travel after the Pullman sleeper *Pioneer* was used in conjunction with Lincoln's funeral train in 1865. After that train arrived in Chicago from Washington, DC, Lincoln's body lay in state until, on May 2, the *Pioneer,* which was considerably more luxurious on the inside than other opulent railroad cars of the day, was used by dignitaries attending the funeral in Springfield. The Pioneer made an impression, but although it was slightly wider and taller than its contemporaries, there is no evidence to support stories that the C&A had to widen its route to accommodate it.[24]

It was, however, the beginning of a new era for George Pullman. In 1867 he entered into a partnership with six friends who supplied capital for the Pullman Palace Car Company. The firm built sleeping and dining cars, which it rented to railroad companies, and manufactured freight cars. Pullman trained and paid the African-American porters to control the quality of customer care. The company grew so rapidly that Pullman had to build a factory town for his workforce and their families a few miles south of Chicago. The *Chicago Tribune* called the proposed town of Pullman "the most important manufacturing enterprise that has yet been established in Chicago." His model town earned and later lost Pullman a reputation for benevolent paternalism.[25]

Figure 6.6. The grand entrance to the Pullman works near Chicago. Library of Congress Prints and Photographs Division.

THE GREAT FIRE OF 1871

After the Civil War, Illinois continued to grow, and Chicago cemented its place as the nation's crossroads. In 1860 the city's population stood at around 112,000; by 1870 nearly three times that number lived and worked in its wooden and supposedly fireproof brick buildings. In 1870 twenty-one railroads entered Chicago, bringing around 240 trains, evenly divided between freight and passenger, into the city every day. Grain, lumber, cattle, and capital flowed to and through the city. So strongly had it positioned itself at the center of a global commercial network that even one of the nation's deadliest fires could not permanently dampen Chicago's growth.[26]

In October 1871 a massive conflagration temporarily slowed expansion. Chicago had an elaborate network of alarms to alert firefighters to the recurring and dangerous fires plaguing the haphazardly developed city. But on the night of Sunday, October 8, 1871, the system failed. A small fire broke out in a barn probably owned by Catherine O'Leary and perhaps started by her cow, though more likely it was ignited by a careless smoker sheltering from the wind to light up. The blaze spread

The Iron Road in the Prarie State

rapidly from its origins on the Near West Side across the South Branch of the Chicago River and through downtown to the lake. Strong winds pushed the flames ahead of firefighters exhausted from an eight-hour battle the previous day. One Chicago homeowner abandoned his house after "a burning mass, which was as large as an ordinary bed-pillow, passed over my head" while he was pouring buckets of water onto the roof. Little could be done to halt the inferno as it burned through the heart of the city. The "tornado of fire" took three days to extinguish, engulfed 2,100 acres, razed 17,450 buildings, and killed around 250 people. The disaster left more than 100,000 people homeless and destroyed almost one-third of Chicago's taxable real estate.[27]

Railroads experienced extensive damage but rebuilt rapidly. Three of the city's four main termini and a number of smaller depots went up in smoke. LaSalle Street Station, rebuilt in 1868 and featuring a three-story head house at the end of a vast roof supported by limestone walls, was completely destroyed and had to be rebuilt. The Chicago & Alton lost its general offices, a downtown freight house, and rolling stock that could not be moved out of harm's way. The freight and passenger depots shared by the Michigan Central and the Illinois Central were destroyed, along with the latter's "fireproof" land office. Thousands who sought shelter within the brick walls of railroad buildings had to flee when the wooden roofs caught fire. Railroad yards were mostly emptied, but one of the Illinois Central's two elevators was destroyed in a devastating explosion of grain.[28]

The destruction hurt other lines, too. The North Western lost buildings valued at $180,000, of which insurance covered only about a third, along with 133 freight cars. The Chicago, Burlington & Quincy and the Lake Shore both lost buildings and rolling stock, though the former made a significant mark on the memory of one woman who caught the last train to Aurora before services were abruptly halted by the fire. When she returned to the city sometime later she was amazed to discover that her luggage had been saved by railroaders. All told, railroads in Chicago lost buildings worth over $1 million, $2 million in rolling stock and commodities,

and access to grain elevators. Compared with the same month a year earlier, Chicago & Alton earnings fell by $16,051, or 3.3 percent, in October 1871, while the Illinois Central saw them tumble by $141,260, or 15.6 percent.[29]

Railroads in the region contributed to rescue and aid efforts in the immediate aftermath of the fire. Local depots answered telegrammed pleas for assistance by sending blankets, tents, clothing, and food. The Alton ran a special train from Bloomington to Chicago carrying a fire engine and firefighters, covering the 126 miles in a virtually unprecedented 150 minutes. Cities across the Midwest sent equipment, and infantry arrived by rail from Omaha and Fort Leavenworth. Chicagoans seeking refuge outside the city were offered complimentary travel, with over six thousand free passes made available within two weeks of the fire burning itself out. But the city wished to keep the able-bodied around for reconstruction and limited the offer to the sick, the old, and large families with children too young to work. The Illinois Central made a sizeable donation to the relief fund for survivors. Traffic diversions around Chicago continued for months until a semblance of service was resumed in mid-1872. But Chicago recovered.[30]

ACROSS THE CONTINENT

One unanticipated consequence of the Civil War was the first transcontinental railroad. The creation of the Confederate States of America in 1861 inadvertently settled the vexatious question of whether to use a northern or a southern route. That debate had raged since 1845, when New York merchant Asa Whitney lobbied for a line from Milwaukee to the mouth of the Columbia River in the Pacific Northwest. Though several state legislatures supported his plan, Congress did not. For much of the 1840s and 1850s advocates of constructing a railroad to the West Coast deadlocked over whether to follow a northern path or to build across the southern United States. Stephen A. Douglas clashed with Thomas Hart Benton, the railroad-sponsoring senator from Missouri, on this issue. Beginning in Memphis in 1845, conventions designed to arouse popular support for constructing the transcontinental railroad gathered up and down the Mississippi River valley. Thus, for

Figure 6.7. The shops of the Pullman works near Chicago, where luxury passenger and ordinary freight cars were built. Library of Congress Prints and Photographs Division.

example, an 1852 meeting in St. Louis called for a projected Pacific Railroad west from Missouri and declared that "it is the duty of Congress to authorize to provide by means of the public domain, for the construction of such a central national railway, as will unite us by bands of iron, with the State of California and the Territories of New Mexico, Utah, and Oregon."[31]

In 1853 Congress funded surveys along four possible routes. The findings argued forcefully that the best possible path—because it was the shortest, the flattest, and the least expensive—was the southernmost, from Texas to California. Unfortunately, part of the proposed route was in Mexico, but President Franklin Pierce devised an elegant if expensive solution. He authorized James Gadsden, US ambassador to Mexico and a former president of the South-Carolina Rail-Road & Canal Company, to pay $10 million for thirty thousand square miles south of the Gila River in present-day Arizona and New Mexico. This tract of land, known as the Gadsden Purchase, would have made building the southernmost transcontinental feasible had not the Civil War intervened.

The Iron Road in the Prarie State

Other routes had their supporters, and when in 1854 Stephen A. Douglas—apparently forgetting the lessons of 1837—proposed a compromise bill funding three transcontinentals simultaneously (a southern, a central, and a northern route), it seemed likely to pass Congress. But the House failed to act, and attention focused on the implications of the Kansas-Nebraska Act. Drafted by Douglas in an attempt to quicken the pace of westward expansion and make it easier to build a railroad across the continent from Chicago, the act backfired spectacularly. It worsened tensions between North and South by allowing settlers to determine whether the new states would be slave or free.

The war enabled Northerners to build the first transcontinental because there were no Southerners in Congress to oppose them. In 1862 President Lincoln signed the first Pacific Railways Act, authorizing construction of a line from Sacramento, California, to Council Bluffs, Iowa. A company chartered in 1861, the Central Pacific, would build east and connect to the newly created Union Pacific, making its way west from the Missouri River. Following the precedent set by the Illinois Central land grant, the 1862 act gave the two companies right-of-way across government land in alternating sections on each side of the proposed route. They also gained access to thirty-year US bonds. These provisions proved insufficient for the task and the second Pacific Railroad Act, passed in 1864, doubled the land grant and changed the government bonds from first mortgages to second mortgages to attract private investors.[32] Overcoming labor shortages, Indian attacks, and insufficient supplies, the two companies held a formal ceremony on May 10, 1869, at Promontory Summit, Utah Territory, to connect the lines of the two railroads. The simple telegraph message "Done" alerted the nation, and in Washington, DC, a magnetic ball dropped from the dome of Congress to announce the event. Across the newly reunified nation, bonfires and parades demonstrated the importance of connecting the two coasts with an iron ribbon. Chicago, destined to become the terminus of the nation's principal transcontinentals, was now indisputably the hub of a national railroad network.

Running as it did from Council Bluffs to Sacramento, neither of them on a coast, the adjective "transcontinental" seems a little exaggerated, but the label resonated in the age of Manifest Destiny. After 1869 it was possible to board a train on the East Coast and, following a transfer or two, ride "the highway between the oceans" to the Pacific. The symbolic value of reuniting the nation after the bloodletting of the Civil War cannot be underestimated. As one journalist claimed, "The Occident and the Orient, North and South, Saxon, Celt, Mongolian, each clad in his peculiar costume, met and mingled on common ground. All personal and sectional animosities, all prejudices, race, and nationalities were forgotten for the moment in the all absorbing interest of the grand event of history and civilization."[33]

This utopian scene became reality only after the federal government agreed to subsidize the costs of construction. Building across the sparsely inhabited interior was an act of faith aided by land grants. A combination of precedent, foresight, and greed resulted in 164 million acres of federal land being made available to fuel railroad expansion in the twenty years following the chartering of the Illinois Central. Donating the land to state governments bypassed very real concerns about the constitutionality of the federal government subsidizing private corporations. Using this method, railroads obtained 131,350,534 acres. A further 33 million acres were returned to the federal government when proposed lines were not built or the land did not sell.

Land grants are an example of what economists call building ahead of demand. Such investments assume a market will develop in the future for the commodity or service to be produced. Later commentators have been less certain that so much land needed to be granted so quickly, but the consequence was a rapid influx of hopeful capital into the industry and, at a slower pace, people into the seemingly endless open spaces. Most capital-intensive industries build ahead of demand, but the railroads were different because they built into unpopulated areas. Thus, instead of convincing pre-existing customers to purchase their product, railroad companies faced the challenge of creating a market for their services by bringing potential customers into and settling them on the land across which they built. Some economists have argued that "they were an imperfect and inefficient means to accomplish the desired ends," but they certainly accelerated migration and, crucially, gained political traction in the triumphal postwar political climate.[34]

ILLINOIS RAILROAD LABOR

As Confederate forces were winning the Battle of Chancellorsville and Union troops prepared to lay siege to Vicksburg, a group of disgruntled railroad engineers met secretly in Marshall, Michigan. Unhappy about the treatment they were receiving at the hands of their supervisors, they decided to assert their republican rights and defend themselves from arbitrary rule. They formed the Brotherhood of Locomotive Engineers (BLE), a fraternal order fighting for decent working conditions and offering insurance protections. Firemen, conductors, trainmen, and other groups created their own organizations in the 1860s, challenging the conventional belief that capital and labor shared a common interest in the profitable operation of railroad corporations.

A period of often dramatic conflict on the railroads followed formation of the brotherhoods. Wage cuts and layoffs led to strikes but owners and managers fought back. The proud industrial peace of the railroads was shattered by walkouts and murders. Financial panics and technological change led to violence and confrontation in Illinois, most notably in 1877, 1888, and 1894. These were the visible manifestations of a seemingly limitless well of unhappiness and subterranean conflict. But the railroads could bring the nation's economic activity to a virtual standstill, hastening the quest for alternatives. Worse for the industry, federal regulators responded to public complaints about monopoly power by restricting managerial autonomy. The peace of pioneer railroading had been shattered.

RAILROAD WORK

The almost exclusively male railroad labor force fell by 1860 into five different groups: office workers, stationmen, trainmen, shopmen, and trackmen.[1] Managers and clerks kept the books, created timetables, issued orders, purchased supplies, and conducted myriad other tasks in offices located at the main termini and large towns along the route. Station employees—agents selling tickets, telegraphers issuing train orders, and porters carrying luggage—staffed depots along the line. Trainmen—engineers driving locomotives, firemen shoveling coal into fireboxes to heat water for steam, conductors responsible for the safe running of the train, and brakemen operating the brakes to stop a train—kept the services on the move. Shopmen in the construction and repair shops at most junctions and many towns worked as machinists, carpenters, painters, and upholsterers and at other trades. The railroad line was divided into geographical units for maintenance under the supervision of a sectionman and his section gang, who walked their stretch of track fixing defects and clearing brush or other obstacles.

Railroad labor hierarchies developed haphazardly and usually in response to operational problems. Eastern railroads provided early models, often following military examples, and Illinois contributed to this process. The Chicago, Burlington & Quincy established formal job qualifications by setting age minimums, administering literacy tests, and experimenting with blacklists of workers. During the 1850s Illinois lines began hiring

Figure 7.1. ICRR commuters arriving in downtown Chicago (1907). Library of Congress Prints and Photographs Division.

Figure 7.2. Record keeping was a crucial part of the work of station agents. Library of Congress Prints and Photographs Division.

experienced officials from older eastern roads. When he was appointed general superintendent of the Illinois Central at the beginning of 1856, for example, John H. Done brought a cadre of managers with him from the Baltimore & Ohio to reproduce that line's administrative systems. Done created the first suburban services outside of New York and Philadelphia but died when he fell in front of a Chicago commuter train during its first week of operation.[2]

Railroad work was physical, dangerous, and mostly outdoors. It demanded intense concentration for long periods of time, and even the indoor labor of station

Figure 7.3. Working on the caboose entailed numerous jobs, including applying the brakes. Library of Congress Prints and Photographs Division.

agents required diligence and attention to detail along with literacy. Trainmen on cabooses set brakes while yard work included setting switches, signaling engineers, and moving quickly but carefully around heavy equipment in motion. Locomotives required regular maintainence in repair shops located at most junctions and yards of any size. Here again the dizzying array of tasks and tools along with the sheer noise of machinery and hammers created a distinctive workplace with its own rhythms and risks.

The Iron Road in the Prarie State

Figure 7.4. Throwing switches to move trains from one track to another was one of many tasks in the yard.
Library of Congress Prints and Photographs Division.

The rewards of railroad labor came in the form of relatively steady work, high community status, and fringe benefits. As railroads crisscrossed the state, the power they wielded grew commensurately, much of it directly influencing the lives and labor of the men and, very occasionally, women who kept the machines in action. By 1881 forty-nine railroads employed a combined 48,673 workers in Illinois, 5 percent of the total workforce in the state. Visible at depots and on trains, unseen in office buildings and repair shops, they kept

Figure 7.5. The C&EI Oaklawn shops illustrate some of the heavy equipment of railroad repair facilities. John W. Barriger III National Railroad Library, St. Louis Mercantile Library, University of Missouri at St. Louis.

the railroads running. Railroaders often experienced an intrinsic satisfaction from the work they performed, a trait evident in the loyalty many felt toward the industry.[3]

BUILDING THE ILLINOIS CENTRAL

Construction of the original Illinois Central Charter Lines in the 1850s illustrates the challenges facing the earliest railroad builders. Railroads ran best on level ground, which meant filling depressions and digging through hills. The only tools available for moving thousands of tons of earth were spades, shovels, buckets, mule-drawn carts, and animal-powered scrapers. The

work demanded a strong back and a diligent disposition. No particular skill was required of those who performed the bulk of the labor, but hard work it most definitely was.

Railroad construction offered steady employment and relatively high pay, up to $1.25 a day when the average daily wage for common laborers in Illinois ranged from 25 cents to $1.00. The problem was finding enough people to do the work. In 1852 the Illinois Central advertised for laborers in newspapers across the northern United States, and the chief engineer of the line, Roswell Mason, paid New York City labor agents $1.00 for each worker who stayed with the railroad at least one

The Iron Road in the Prairie State

month. The company brought recent immigrants from Germany and Ireland to Chicago to work on the line. By the fall of 1853 the Illinois Central had recruited a workforce of approximately ten thousand, and though the number fluctuated, the demand for new workers abated.[4]

Other railroad corporations faced the same pressure because a concurrent railroad-building boom created labor shortages. Competition for workers caused Mason to complain about the absence of "honor and fair dealing among contractors" who, he noted, "send agents to each others [sic] work and entice men away." Contractors building adjacent stretches of line sometimes bid against each other for laborers. Harvest seasons were particularly vexing because farmers would offer men two dollars a day plus food to help bring the crop in. Some railroad laborers quit to buy land along the line they had just built, cultivating the land for themselves. It is impossible to know exactly, but historians estimate that building the Charter Lines brought about one hundred thousand people into the state, many of whom remained once construction ended.[5]

Recruiting and retaining workers was only the beginning of the labor-management challenges companies and contractors faced. The men overheated in summer and froze in winter. Crowded, isolated, and unhealthy work camps nurtured epidemics. Laborers shared beds and mugs, increasing the likelihood of transmitting disease. Malaria and dysentery were feared throughout the works, and cholera outbreaks at LaSalle in 1854 claimed the lives of thirty or more workmen. In the summer of 1855 another cholera epidemic spread south from Galena, killing laborers all the way to Decatur. Men threw down their tools and fled in fear.[6]

Violent clashes could be ignited by a volatile mix of ethnic rivalry and gossip. In Decatur, Irish workers heard a rumor that German laborers were killing their fellow countrymen on a nearby line. Equipping themselves with axes and shovels, they marched through the town to do battle, but local people armed with old muskets turned them back. In LaSalle, thirty-two men were arrested for killing a contractor after he announced a reduction in wages. Alcohol played a role in this December 1853 incident, as it had in many others, leading the ICRR to ban the sale of liquor at construction sites.[7]

DISCIPLINING LABOR

Enforcing discipline on the railroads was a constant challenge. Company rule books explained lines of authority, proscribed personal behavior (drunkenness was a commonly highlighted sin, but so were gambling and tardiness), advocated self-control and promptness, and enunciated specific duties for each job. Rule violations could mean unemployment. Managers told supervisors to keep a close watch on the men under their authority and fine or fire those who disobeyed the rules. Using two sets of unusually detailed documents, historian Walter Licht found that "between 4 and 7 percent of the men employed were discharged annually for disciplinary reasons" on the CB&Q and discovered a similar proportion on the Erie Railroad. He speculates that this was only the tip of an arithmetic iceberg of punishment. The data revealed an unequal distribution of discharges: on the CB&Q they fell disproportionately on trainmen, while white-collar employees were more likely to lose their jobs on the Erie.[8]

Local supervisors enforced the sometimes ambiguous regulations. Strict adherence to a company's rules against alcohol consumption would have meant losing many of the skilled workers in its shops. James C. Clarke of the ICRR asked division superintendents to tell "discontented men" to leave the company and in 1857 fired a station agent who publicly criticized the board of directors. Forceful, even abusive, treatment was particularly pronounced against laborers, who could be easily let go by their superiors. An Illinois Central track supervisor paid laborers below the listed rate and pocketed the difference, a form of corruption exacerbated during economic downturns, when labor gangs were assembled and dispersed with dizzying rapidity. CB&Q managers discovered during the 1870s that the absence of formal grievance procedures led to arbitrary local decisions and multiple complaints against supervisors. In the same decade the problem of supervisors demanding gifts from job seekers and selling their staff "voluntary" insurance policies to remain employed plagued the CB&Q.[9]

Illinois railroads pioneered the use of "spotters" to guard passengers, protect freight, and inform on employees. Spotters documented CB&Q supervisors using company labor and materials to build houses, shopmen taking home company tools and materials, and conductors stealing cash. In 1855 Chicago railroads signed an agreement with the National Detective Agency to have its "Pinkertons" spy on railroaders. Testimony by one of its agents led to the conviction of a CB&Q conductor of "respectability and high standing" who was sentenced to one year in the Alton penitentiary for "embezzling" thirty dollars. Similarly, several C&A conductors lost their jobs after being caught stealing fare money. As there were no laws against entrapment, Pinkertons tested employee honesty by shipping and monitoring packages. This led to the capture of two light-fingered station agents at Wappella.[10]

Railroad cars carried valuable goods that were tempting to criminals and those down on their luck. In 1879 three boys were arrested in Chicago for taking wheat from B&O freight cars, a practice they had engaged in for some time. A pail of candy and several dozen eggs that vanished from Illinois Central boxcars in the Mattoon yards in 1904 are just two examples among thousands across the years. Quick-thinking employees could stymie would-be thieves. When four men tried to rob a Rock Island passenger train near Peoria they were thwarted by the conductor, Robert Murray, who disarmed one of the men as he tried to board the train after forcing it to a halt by placing ties across the track.[11]

On Christmas Eve 1912 an attempt to dynamite safes on the *Hummer*, a C&A express between Chicago and Kansas City, captured the nation's attention.[12] Here again railroaders foiled the robbers after the *Hummer* came to a stop at busy Iles Junction, south of Springfield. Two men fired shots into the air, warning passengers to stay inside. They then uncoupled the passenger cars and forced the engineer to move the locomotive and a baggage car several hundred yards up the track. The masked bandits then attempted to dynamite safes but failed. After exchanging gunfire with "a sheriff's posse which

had been summoned by telephone and arrived on a switch engine they fled into the night." But the men, whose actions "had all the Wild West trimmings," left their overcoats in a field beside the track. Containing rope, a candle, and "high grade candy" stolen from the train, these simplified the job of identifying them after they had been "caught in a dragnet spread by the police over Springfield and the surrounding country." John "Swede Kid" Hartnett, a former Chicago saloon-keeper, and Elmer Vigus of Springfield were imprisoned, but the getaway driver, who supposedly "brought the men to Springfield in a buggy," escaped. Dramatic and memorable episodes like this were few and far between, but small-scale pilfering was commonplace.

ACCIDENT COMPENSATION

Railroad work could be brutally dangerous even without outlaws. Railroaders feared the accidents that regularly took limbs and lives because of the hardships they and their families might subsequently endure. The earliest attempts to pay compensation to workers injured or killed were haphazard and unreliable. The Galena & Chicago Union gave the survivor of an employee a sewing machine to enable her to make a living, while the Illinois Central presented another widow with three hundred dollars. It assigned disabled trainmen to work as flagmen and watchmen. Railroads in the 1850s and 1860s kept sick employees on the payroll and even, in one case, paid a worker while he nursed sick relatives.[13] But there was no guarantee of compensation, and companies favored "deserving" cases, which usually required meeting a moral standard acceptable to managers and board members.

Railroad officials and employees slowly developed welfare programs, constrained by uncertainty about a railroad's legal responsibility for compensating accident victims. Railroad managers were divided on the issue of liability. The Illinois Central's James C. Clarke and Charles E. Perkins of the CB&Q both rejected the idea that a private corporation owed its employees anything beyond the payment of wages. By way of contrast, William Ackerman of the ICRR and CB&Q general superintendent Robert Harris wanted employees to feel the company was concerned for their welfare. Harris provided free passes to all employees and their family members and opposed every attempt to create blacklists.[14]

During the 1860s and 1870s Illinois railroads experimented with insurance funds for injured and sick employees. The Illinois Central briefly operated a relief club and the Railway Employees Mutual Benefit Association of the West attracted members, but neither survived for long. In 1868 Chicago railroad executives created the Provident Life Insurance and Investment Company to entice employees away from the newly created insurance funds of railroad brotherhoods. In 1870 Harris sanctioned half-pay plus medical costs for men injured at work and authorized the CB&Q to renovate the house of a machinist who had lost an arm. Such initiatives proved short-lived, and in 1872 Harris contracted with the Travelers Life and Accident Insurance Company to sell policies directly to Burlington employees and deduct premiums from payroll.[15]

Some managers hoped pension schemes would generate loyalty. The Chicago & North Western provided a "yearly gift" of pension contributions to cultivate "the harmonious relations that should exist between capital and labor, whether skilled or unskilled." Employees on the Wabash, a line known for good relations between officers and men, formed an insurance society, funded railroad employees' hospitals in Danville and Springfield, and became widely known as a pioneer in the railroad YMCA movement. Housing in remote towns and villages, passes for free travel and discounted shipping, and even guaranteed promotions were designed, as Harris of the CB&Q wrote, "to cultivate among all the employees of the Co. a feeling of sympathy with the Road." For engineers, "railroading became not only a job . . . but, indeed, a way of life" that held "emotional appeal." Working for the railroad could bring community prestige and, despite the image of the "boomer" wandering at leisure from job to job, railroaders showed no more geographic mobility than other groups of workers. The advantage to railroad companies of loyalty and stability was a relative absence of conflict between management and labor. American railroad workers developed a reputation for being "disciplined . . . and

conservative," characteristics the brotherhoods did little to diminish.[16]

THE BROTHERHOODS

Railroad employees unhappy with the power their supervisors wielded organized fraternal labor unions in the 1860s and 1870s. The BLE blazed the trail from Marshall, Michigan, in 1863. Train conductors organized next. They established the Conductors Union, predecessor of the Order of Railroad Conductors (ORC), in Amboy, Illinois, in 1868, followed in 1873 by the Brotherhood of Locomotive Firemen and Enginemen (BLF) in Port Jervis, New York. These early organizations were craft unions limited to employees in one occupation and pursuing mutualist strategies based on the assumption that members were as interested as managers and owners in the safe and profitable operation of the railroads. They offered disability and life insurance, though their main impact seems to have been generating "loyalty and pride" toward the brotherhoods.[17]

The first railroad workers' organizations claimed to promote mutual labor relations. Charles Wilson, an early leader of the BLE, "believed that workers and employers shared a common interest" and his successor, Peter M. Arthur, "lectured at brotherhood conventions on the mutual interest of labor and capital." Arthur and other railroad labor leaders believed that "the workingman today may be the capitalist five or ten years from now" and strove "to acquire the respect of employers and the community at large." The BLE planned to "win the good graces of the employers through elevating the character of its members and thus raising their efficiency as workmen" and another brotherhood promised "to establish mutual confidence, and create and maintain harmonious relations, between employer and employe."[18]

Brotherhood mutualism did not stretch to African American or women workers, of whom there were virtually none until the First World War. Reflecting the racism of the time, brotherhood rules contained whites-only clauses, excluding African Americans from membership. Black railroaders worked as porters, maids, cooks, waiters, and red caps. Despite the color barrier, African American workers could be found in other ranks, notably as firemen, but the brotherhoods tried to keep them out of the higher-paying occupations through intimidation and strikes. White railroaders waged a continuous "undeclared war against black trainmen," resulting in the murder of several African American railroad employees.[19]

THE TURNING POINT

Mutual relations fell victim to a changing economy. Railroads had experienced strikes (when engineers struck the Galena & Chicago Union in 1864 other Chicago-based roads had supplied strike breakers), but the events of 1877 indicated conflict of an unprecedented magnitude.[20] The Panic of 1873, triggered by the collapse of a bank owned by railroad financier Jay Cooke, reverberated around the country. Anger at wage cuts, longer hours, and other changes harming railroad workers' quality of life fueled the strikes, which broke out with virtually no prompting from and often against the wishes of brotherhood leaders. Construction all but stopped as traffic plummeted. Railroads desperate for customers reduced their rates, forcing others to follow suit. Wages continued to fall. In July 1877 trainmen on the Baltimore & Ohio Railroad responded to a 10 percent wage cut by stopping all freight trains at Martinsburg, West Virginia. The local militia refused to reopen the line, so the governor requested federal troops, whose arrival ended the strike.

The Martinsburg example emboldened disaffected railroaders elsewhere to take action. The strike spread to the Pennsylvania Railroad because it announced plans to run "double-headed" freights using two engines. This cut costs by reducing the number of trains and allowed the company to lay off trainmen. On the first day of double-headed running, July 19, 1877, trainmen closed Pittsburgh to all rail traffic by blocking key switches, at which point the governor sent in a National Guard detachment. Guardsmen shot into a group of protesters and killed twenty-six people, causing fury in the city. Suddenly confronted by a massive crowd of locals—only some of whom were railroaders—the troops took shelter in a Pennsylvania Railroad roundhouse but fled when the crowd set it on fire.

The strike soon reached Illinois. Beginning with Michigan Central switchmen in Chicago, the stoppages spread to the B&O and the Illinois Central. Police killed thirty striking workers, and demonstrators forcibly closed the Chicago yards of the ICRR by firing shots into the caboose of a train attempting to leave the Windy City on the night of July 25. Striking railroaders and sympathizers blocked the Illinois Central at Mattoon, Carbondale, Decatur, and Effingham, stranding passengers. Strikers in Carbondale allowed fruit and passenger trains to proceed, electing an executive committee and reporting to a coordinating committee in East St. Louis. Galesburg railroaders who occupied the CB&Q yard also permitted selected trains to run but stopped and even derailed others.[21]

American railroads ground to a halt, causing fears that "the whole lawless and criminal population... have taken command of the strike, and have assumed control of the entire railroad commerce of the United States." The *Chicago Tribune* shuddered that "the suddenness of the strike, and its extent, was a surprise," while the *Sycamore True Republican* called for military intervention and blamed "lazy, vicious, tramping bummers who would not work if they could and who swarmed to the scene of violence as vultures to the battlefield."[22] The situation deteriorated and the federal government mobilized troops fighting Indian Wars on the Great Plains to patrol the streets of Chicago, St. Louis, and other cities.

The events of 1877 marked a turning point in relations among working people, business owners, and politicians. Sympathy and understanding across class lines appeared to be waning. The dramatic and unexpected use of federal troops to protect private property stunned many Americans, and a strike wave rolled through the 1880s like an aftershock. In 1881 there were 471 labor conflicts involving 101,000 workers in all industries; five years later 407,000 workers participated in 1,432 strikes nationwide. In 1886 Wabash Railroad employees in Illinois walked out to protest a 10 percent wage reduction, one episode in a series of strikes against railroads controlled by Jay Gould. Six people were killed in violent confrontations with guards and police in the East St. Louis yards.[23] The 1880s would be remembered

The Iron Road in the Prairie State

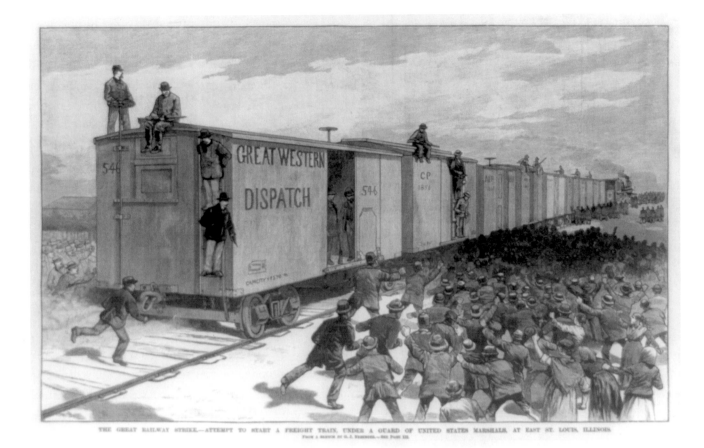

THE GREAT RAILWAY STRIKE.—ATTEMPT TO START A FREIGHT TRAIN, UNDER A GUARD OF UNITED STATES MARSHALS, AT EAST ST. LOUIS, ILLINOIS.
FROM A SKETCH BY G. J. DERGREDE.—SEE PAGE 138.

Figure 7.6. US marshals protect a freight train from striking railroaders in East St. Louis during the 1886 turnout.
Library of Congress Prints and Photographs Division.

as one of the most tumultuous periods in American history, signaling a new stage in the development of industrial capitalism.

THE GREAT BURLINGTON STRIKE OF 1888

Turbulence returned to Illinois in 1888 on the Chicago, Burlington & Quincy. In February CB&Q engineers and firemen struck against low wages and unacceptable work rules. BLE and BLF members complained that other roads paid considerably more for the same work, a fact widely circulated in union newspapers. The Chicago & North Western paid engineers $175.00 per month for the run from Rockford to Chicago, but the CB&Q paid only $104.00 for the comparable Rockford-to-Aurora route. The C&NW paid engineers $120.00 for twenty-six days' work on its fast mails, whereas the CB&Q paid $87.50 for equivalent runs. Other assignments showed similar—if less glaring—disparities.[24]

Bigger than wages was the issue of "classification." This policy allowed managers to hire firemen temporarily as engineers at a lower rate of pay. Firemen feared this as a way to reduce their income and the BLE perceived it as a threat to the brotherhood's ability to control the number of qualified engineers. By creating more than it needed, the company increased the supply and reduced the cost. To brotherhood members classification represented "the power which a great company has to coerce, or to punish," its employees.[25]

The strike began on February 26, 1888, when engineers and firemen refused to work. This happened after Burlington general manager Henry Stone rejected a pay scale drawn up by the BLE that omitted classification completely.[26] Believing the strike would end quickly, Stone telegrammed Perkins not to bother traveling to Chicago from his home in Boston. This was a mistake. Within a day of the strike call being issued,

2,137 enginemen and firemen in the company's employ stayed home, leaving only forty-five engineers to operate hundreds of trains and firmly planting egg on Stone's face.[27]

For Stone, Perkins, and other Burlington officials, the strike brought into the open the question of who should manage the railroad. Officials believed the brotherhoods were trespassing on their territory, because demanding that switch-engine drivers "shall have regular engines," stating that hostlers (who moved engines in the yards) "shall not be required to knock fires," and telling the railroad where to assign personnel took decision making out of the hands of management. The brotherhoods also demanded that seniority govern all regular runs. Crews in need of rest—a condition they should be allowed to determine for themselves—would not be required to work, and there should be "no more examinations or tests." The brotherhoods also demanded respectful treatment, requesting that "all officers, engineers and firemen will observe strict courtesy of manners in their intercourse with each other."[28]

Refusing to negotiate, let alone accede to, a lengthy list of demands, Burlington managers hired replacement workers and kept passenger services running. A month after the strike began, on March 23, 1888, the Switchmen's Mutual Aid Association joined in sympathy after engineers promised to form one large rail workers' union. On at least two occasions the brotherhoods attempted to convince engineers and firemen on other roads to demonstrate their support for CB&Q strikers by boycotting its freight cars. Managers on connecting lines were willing to honor the boycott as a way to punish a wealthy and powerful competitor. On the Wabash Railroad one yardmaster eager to rid his territory of Burlington cars moved them as quickly as possible with little concern for their contents, giving rise to the term "Wabashing."[29]

The CB&Q obtained injunctions against the Wabash and the Union Pacific on the grounds that, as common carriers, they were legally obliged to handle Burlington traffic. The courts agreed and banned boycotts. The strike continued and Perkins, replacing Stone as chief negotiator on the company's side, promised to match the wages paid by other roads and to negotiate with the brotherhoods. But his willingness to compromise had limits: he refused to abolish classification and blacklisted strikers convicted of violence.[30] The brotherhoods rejected his offer. Attacks on replacement workers ("scabs") and Pinkertons increased.

But the brotherhoods could not afford to support striking workers forever and officially ended the strike in the fall. By then the union movement was split, as the engineers reneged on their promise to combine with other brotherhoods into a single organization. Switchmen returned to work on December 11, 1888, and, after securing a promise that employees who had not participated in violent actions would be rehired or recommended to other companies, engineers and firemen followed suit on January 4, 1889. By then the two sides had spent over $4.5 million, and Burlington stock dividends would not reach prestrike levels until long after Perkins had retired. The 1888 strike demonstrated the isolation of the Burlington and a strategic weakness of the brotherhoods. The refusal of general managers on other roads to accept Burlington cars until forced to do so by the courts revealed cracks in the ranks of management, while unemployed enginemen and firemen fired elsewhere flocked to replace Burlington employees. The solidarity of labor was broken by need and opportunity, as were the shared interests of railroad managers.[31]

The Burlington experienced the most dramatic turmoil in 1888, but it was not alone. On the Illinois Central in the same year, several localized disputes broke out unconnected to the Burlington strike. At Scales Mound, for example, sectionmen demanded the same pay as temporary laborers sent in by the company in February. Their boss told them that "if they wish to quit they may and we will fill their places." In July 1890 laborers at nearby Council Hill demanded a pay raise after learning their counterparts in East Dubuque earned an hourly wage of 15 cents compared to their own 12.5 cents. Their supervisor supported the demand, but his backing proved worthless as management rejected their claim. They left, and the company hired "a floating gang to do this work."[32] As the railroads knew all too well, strikes large and small punctuated the Gilded Age and

The Iron Road in the Prairie State

the large pool of unemployed workers made it easy to replace strikers.

CONTROL THROUGH FRINGE BENEFITS

The 1888 strike convinced Burlington directors of the need to pay closer attention to labor relations. In April, as the strike turned violent, Forbes sent Perkins the rule book of an insurance society for employees of the Calumet and Hecla Copper Company with the comment that such a society was "rather a popular idea among stockholders." Perkins unequivocally opposed company-subsidized insurance plans, which, he felt, gave the men "something for nothing." Instead, he argued, the company should encourage esprit de corps by limiting promotions and restricting pay raises. The board overrode Perkins and established the Voluntary Relief Department (VRD) in 1889. Undeterred, Perkins continued to argue that the company's responsibility for its workforce stopped with the payment of wages.[33]

Forced to accept his bosses' fait accompli, Perkins used the VRD to control costs and discipline workers. VRD members' dues paid for physicians, drugs, and hospitalization while the Burlington met administrative costs, paid 4 percent interest on monthly balances, and covered deficiencies. A committee of thirteen, six elected by the members and six by the board, administered the VRD. The general manager cast the deciding vote in the event of a tie, soothing Perkins's fears of worker control. In 1891 he wrote an internal memorandum stating that "in employing men in any department, preference shall be given, other things being equal, to applicants who will become members of the Relief Fund; also, in reduction of force, members of the Relief Fund are to be retained, other things being equal." Hardly a convert to mutualism, Perkins made the best of what was, from his perspective, a bad situation by reshaping the carrot into a stick.[34]

THE 1894 PULLMAN STRIKE

The Burlington strike left the brotherhoods weak and divided, revealing an inherent flaw in craft organizing. But the railroad industry was not much stronger and by 1893 renewed depression and rampaging

unemployment once again created the preconditions for conflict. During an economic downturn between 1893 and 1898, nearly two hundred railroads declared bankruptcy, causing layoffs and wage cuts that stoked the embers of antagonism.[35]

In 1893 Eugene Debs, secretary of the BLF and future Socialist Party candidate for US president, helped create the American Railway Union (ARU). Unlike the brotherhoods, which organized along craft lines, the ARU invited all railroaders regardless of position to join. It found an especially receptive audience on the principal western lines—the Santa Fe, Southern Pacific, and Union Pacific—whose workers feared the effects of bankruptcy, but the first test of the ARU came in the North. In 1893 three railroads in receivership—the Great Northern, the Northern Pacific, and the Union Pacific—began cutting salaries and wages. In February 1894 the Union Pacific secured a federal injunction forbidding its employees from striking, but the ARU appealed and the injunction was overturned on the grounds that it violated the constitutional guarantee of free assembly. The prestige and attractiveness of the new union shot up among railroad workers and its sudden popularity prepared the way for further conflict.

It soon arrived. The Great Northern Railway cut wages in an attempt to provoke a strike and destroy the ARU. Debs traveled to St. Paul to meet with the local Chamber of Commerce. He and James J. Hill, president of the Great Northern, spoke with leading industrialists, many of whom relied on the railroad for shipping raw materials and finished products. Swayed by Debs and mindful of how a strike would hurt their own businesses, they demanded an immediate settlement on terms favorable to the union. Debs had unexpectedly defeated the mighty "Empire Builder" and by the end of the year the ARU claimed 150,000 members, a third more than the combined membership of the brotherhoods.

The ARU's first major victory proved to be its last. In the spring of 1894 the Pullman Company cut wages in its factories in the town bearing its name. Most Pullman employees rented houses and shopped in stores owned by the company, making them dependent on it for food and housing. Living and working together

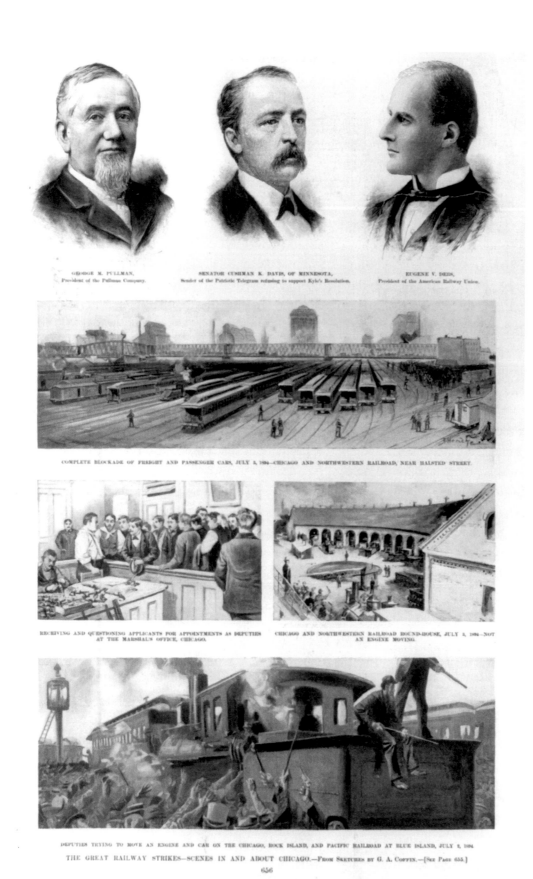

GEORGE M. PULLMAN,
President of the Pullman Company.

SENATOR CUSHMAN K. DAVIS, OF MINNESOTA,
Sender of the Patriotic Telegram refusing to support Kyle's Resolution.

EUGENE V. DEBS,
President of the American Railway Union.

COMPLETE BLOCKADE OF FREIGHT AND PASSENGER CARS, JULY 5, 1894—CHICAGO AND NORTHWESTERN RAILROAD, NEAR HALSTED STREET.

RECEIVING AND QUESTIONING APPLICANTS FOR APPOINTMENTS AS DEPUTIES AT THE MARSHAL'S OFFICE, CHICAGO.

CHICAGO AND NORTHWESTERN RAILROAD ROUND-HOUSE, JULY 5, 1894—NOT AN ENGINE MOVING.

DEPUTIES TRYING TO MOVE AN ENGINE AND CAR ON THE CHICAGO, ROCK ISLAND, AND PACIFIC RAILROAD AT BLUE ISLAND, JULY 2, 1894.

THE GREAT RAILWAY STRIKES—SCENES IN AND ABOUT CHICAGO.—FROM SKETCHES BY G. A. COFFIN.—[SEE PAGE 635.]

656

Figure 7.7. Contemporary illustration of activity in the Chicago area during the 1894 Pullman strike. George Pullman is at the top left, Eugene Debs the top right. Library of Congress Prints and Photographs Division.

created solidarity, which in turn developed into a unified stand against the company when Pullman reduced wages during the economic downturn of 1893. Pullman claimed his factories were filling orders at a loss, and rents and prices did not change. Spurning Pullman's offer to open the books and angered by selective wage cuts (managers were exempted) and the continued payment of dividends to shareholders, a deputation of workers petitioned for restoration of their pay on May 10, 1894—the twenty-fifth anniversary of the first transcontinental. Despite promises that there would be no retribution, the company fired the leaders of the delegation. The intimidation backfired when Pullman employees went on strike and appealed to the ARU for support. Despite Debs's characteristic hesitancy, on June 12, 1894, the union called for a nationwide boycott of Pullman cars.[36] The sympathy strike by ARU members turned a local affair into a national event, pitting the combined power of the federal government and corporate leaders against the young union.

The General Managers Association (GMA) immediately grasped the gravity of the situation and hired Edwin Walker, former manager of the Great Western Railroad, to coordinate the association's response. The Chicago-based GMA enjoyed the not-insignificant assistance of US attorney general Richard Olney. Olney had worked as a railroad lawyer before being elevated to the head of the US Department of Justice in 1893 at the urging of CB&Q president Charles E. Perkins. As general counsel he had earned a well-deserved reputation for helping the Burlington evade government regulations. Despite federal appointment he stayed on the payroll of the Burlington and, rumor had it, of the Santa Fe, earning himself the nickname "the Champion of the Trusts."[37]

The ARU instructed its members not to interfere with trains carrying US mail, but railroad officials claimed the mails were not getting through. From Chicago, US Army general Nelson Miles sent alarmist dispatches to Olney warning of anarchy and street violence while newspapers reported the "absolute and complete paralyzation of railway traffic throughout the west." Olney suddenly found virtue in the legislation he had helped

his railroad clients dodge. He deployed the Sherman Antitrust Act to justify injunctions banning interference with any railroad property, which extended to uncoupling cars. The injunctions, one of which blanketed the entire Chicago area, even forbade strikers from discussing their activities publicly.[38]

On July 2, 1894, strikers at Blue Island, a railroad center a few miles south of Chicago, ignored an injunction ordering them to leave railroad property. Walker, whom Olney had appointed his special counsel in Chicago, dithered but finally called for federal troops. No injuries were reported and no property was damaged, but the Blue Island action and persistent urging by Olney gave Walker the pretext he needed, and soldiers arrived from Fort Sheridan on July 4. The mobilization of federal troops and Illinois National Guard detachments led to escalating attacks on railroad property, including the torching of freight cars, until a July 6 pitched battle resulted in the deaths of four rioters and serious injuries to five militiamen. Beyond the yards, the buildings of the White City erected for the 1893 World's Columbian Exposition on Chicago's south side were burned down during a gun battle between army troops and striking railroaders. National Guard troops were dispatched to Cairo to clear the tracks, and in Decatur state militia kept the peace after some six hundred men struck the Wabash shops. As the conflict spun out of control, Debs attempted to negotiate a truce, but the press smeared him, calling him "Dictator Debs" and the strike "the Debsian Rebellion." Debs and other union leaders were arrested, and the "undisciplined, and impecunious" ARU imploded. Members of the ARU around the country were fired and the strike collapsed.[39]

The brotherhoods flourished after the strike. In July 1894 brotherhood leaders publicly supported the ARU but refused to help it. Tactically this was brilliant: they were tacitly condemning a pesky rival to death while seeming to show solidarity with the railroad workforce. The findings of an investigation by the US Strike Commission labeled the brotherhoods beacons of "conciliation, arbitration, conservatism, and responsibility" in contrast to George Pullman's stubborn refusal to negotiate and ARU members' alleged use of violence.[40]

The strikes of the last quarter of the nineteenth century threw into stark relief the changing relations between railroad workers and managers. They also demonstrated how interconnected with other states Illinois had become. A railroad strike originating in West Virginia and Pennsylvania traveled by rail into the Prairie State and caused a shutdown there. But bigger challenges awaited on the horizon as government regulation and competition threatened to bring down the railroad empire. City governments across Illinois would enact laws to reduce smoke pollution and improve crossing safety. State and federal legislation reduced the railroad corporations' ability to respond to changing market conditions. The longer-term impact of rate regulations would be felt when unregulated cars and trucks began to compete with the railroads for traffic.

A KALEIDOSCOPE OF REGULATIONS

trikes alienated customers, angered politicians, and fomented a climate of mistrust. Passengers and shippers began to feel that railroad corporations wielded too much influence. Politicians at every level—from municipal to federal—created regulations to address their concerns. Legal precedents based on US Supreme Court cases originating in Illinois gave the federal government the authority to establish minimum and maximum prices for transporting people and products. These regulations restricted railroad managers' power to set the prices ("rates") or negotiate with customers from the 1870s to the 1980s. Lowering or raising rates was painfully slow, hurting railroads' ability to respond to market conditions and contributing to the ossification of the industry in the twentieth century.

THE IOWA POOL AND THE
ORIGINS OF REGULATION

By 1870 three railroads—the Chicago & North Western, the Rock Island, and the Burlington—were crossing Illinois and Iowa and preparing to converge on Omaha, the eastern end of the original transcontinental. They earned increased traffic from the new connection, augmenting the grain, pork, and beef they hauled into Chicago from the rich agricultural region they served. But cutthroat competition among the three lines lowered rates and profits, putting pressure on other parts

of the systems to compensate. To dampen the competition, the three railroads agreed to share the traffic across Iowa. This informal "pool" collapsed in the face of economic depression, but after 1874 formal, regional associations emerged to share revenues and eliminate competition.[1] From the perspective of the railroads, pools were a rational response, but shippers thought they deliberately stifled competition in the name of higher profits. Regulation ensued.

Nicknamed the "Granger roads" by their enemies, the members of the Iowa pool along with the Chicago, Milwaukee & St. Paul served nine states in the Midwest (Illinois, Missouri, Kansas, Nebraska, Iowa, Wisconsin, Minnesota, North Dakota, and South Dakota); all entered Chicago. "Grangers" were members of a fraternal order called the Patrons of Husbandry. Founded in 1867 by one-time US Department of Agriculture official Oliver Hudson Kelley, the Patrons of Husbandry (commonly referred to as the Grange) combined insurance provisions with social gatherings in rural areas. From the Granger perspective, railroads "make themselves superior to [the law], and when occasion suits them, they do not hesitate to violate and defy it." Farmers believed the railroad corporations operated "for their own benefit only, and are utterly regardless of the rights of others. The sole object of the directors is to wring money from those who are forced to use the line, and the public, for whose convenience the road is supposed to have been built, are denied the simplest privileges."[2] Such sentiments resonated with farmers as they gathered in Grange meetings across Illinois.

The label "Granger roads" was not meant as a compliment. Farmers grew to mistrust and even hate the railroads that conveyed their harvests to the Windy City. Farmers were particularly unhappy about seemingly irrational rates that discriminated (a key word in this context) against customers in small, isolated towns. In the 1870s, for example, a farmer in Elgin paid thirty cents to ship butter to New York City because he could choose from among several competing railroads. Another farmer in a town served by a single railroad would pay seventy cents or more to send the same quantity of butter just 170 miles.[3] To shippers it appeared the railroads were playing favorites; to the railroads this was simply good business.

Alienating their early boosters, the railroads found themselves under attack, and Rockford led the charge. This was ironic, given the town's crucial role in reviving the Galena & Chicago Union Railroad in 1846. Public demands for railroad regulation in Illinois seem to have originated there in May 1858, when businessmen gathered to protest the rates charged by the very railroad they had helped create. Speakers at a mass meeting condemned the Galena Road for setting unnecessarily high rates. Irritation was contagious. Farmers in Annawan threatened to boycott the Chicago & Rock Island Railroad unless it restricted the power of its local employees. Fury at "the monopoly," which was "extorting an unjust charge from the producer," contributed to calls for regulating railroads and warehouses. Complaints about the Springfield legislature acting like "the hired attorney of the railroads" followed failed attempts to regulate the industry.[4]

STATE REGULATION

Railroad regulation originated in New England, but there it was voluntary. The Illinois legislative and judicial systems pioneered compulsory guidelines in response to farmers' complaints about "collusion between railroad companies and the owners of elevators." A new state constitution, ratified in 1870, gave Illinois the power to regulate railroads and elevators, including the authority to establish "reasonable maximum rates." Watched closely and emulated by Nebraska, Texas, and other states, the legislature prohibited differential charges ("discrimination") for transporting commodities over equal distances. The state commission established in 1871 to set rates drafted maximum freight charges, much to the disgust of the railroad companies, which ignored them. The state could in theory have revoked the charter of railroad companies that repeatedly refused to follow the state regulations, but it did not.[5]

Beginning in 1871, the state of Illinois regulated grain elevators by publishing maximum rates for storage. The intent was to curb price fixing and require owners to obtain a state license. This was a victory for farmers who felt the elevator operators were overcharging for storage and underestimating the quality of their grain, but it angered railroad executives. The commissioners justified regulations on the grounds that railroad corporations were not meaningfully competitive and hurt the businesses that relied on them. Resulting state laws could be financially burdensome because they were often forged in the heat of a political moment to punish railroads for perceived overcharging. Formulated without reference to their economic effects, they created a patchwork of often punitive legislation, much to the distress and dismay of railroad officials.[6]

RESISTING REGULATION

Railroad corporations objected to regulation. In his 1871 report to the Illinois Railroad and Warehouse Commission, a Toledo, Peoria & Warsaw Railroad Company vice president aired the frustration of many industry executives when he wrote, "But I protest, on behalf of said company, that it is not legally bound to make any report whatsoever, and deny the right of the Legislature in any way to interfere with its property and franchises, and that this report has been made simply through courtesy." The directors of the Rockford, Rock Island & St. Louis Railroad took their complaint one step further, arguing that the law was "unconstitutional and a violation of vested rights, and not applicable to this corporation."[7] Regulations were a bitter pill for the laissez-faire individualists who made up the ranks of railroad officials to swallow.

The railroads mounted a counterattack to blunt the new directives. Grain elevator operators, many of them connected with and even paid by railroad corporations, ignored the 1871 requirement to obtain state licenses. In September of that year the Railroad and Warehouse Commission emerged victorious in a suit against the Chicago grain elevator company of Ira Munn and George Scott. Munn appealed and, though he fled the state after his company collapsed in a failed bid to corner the wheat market, his appeal reached the US Supreme Court. In 1877 the court ruled in favor of the state. *Munn v. Illinois* established the constitutionality of state regulations enacted in the "public interest."[8]

Grain elevators were not alone in feeling the effects of the new regulatory regime. In 1872, a year after passage of the Illinois Railroad and Warehouse Act, the state charged the Chicago & Alton with discriminatory pricing practices based on evidence of different rates charged to ship lumber from Chicago to the downstate towns of Lexington and Bloomington. Shipping to Bloomington was cheaper even though it was sixteen miles farther from Chicago than Lexington. The C&A answered the charges in court by pointing to differing competitive positions in the two markets: it enjoyed a monopoly on rail service to Lexington but competed against the Illinois Central for traffic out of Bloomington. The court ruled in favor of the plaintiffs, and the C&A appealed to the Illinois Supreme Court, which overturned the lower court decision. The Illinois legislature responded by strengthening the powers of the Railroad and Warehouse Commission. One long-term consequence was a tiered passenger rate in which the largest companies (the Alton, the Burlington, the Illinois Central, the Rock Island, and the North Western) could charge no more than 3 cents a mile, while roads with less mileage in Illinois could charge between 3.5 and 4 cents a mile. New freight rates soon followed.[9]

Regulation flowed from the railroads too. An 1881 convention of railroad officials gathered in Chicago to discuss the problem of time. Stations had originally set their clocks according to astronomical observations,

as had been customary from the origin of timepieces. The result in the railway age was something akin to chaos. To cite only one case, when the sun stood at noon in Chicago it was 11:48 a.m. in St. Louis. Though the nation did have about one hundred haphazard "railroad-time" sectors, standardization was desperately needed. The General Time Convention of 1881 asked William F. Allen, managing editor of the *Official Guide of the Railways,* to devise a solution. This he did, drawing lines down the 75th, 90th, 105th, and 120th meridians to create four separate time zones. After railroad officials met in Chicago to adopt the new system, depots around the country reset their clocks and railroaders synchronized their watches on November 18, 1883.[10] With minor modifications these are the time zones in effect today, a product of railroaders' need for uniformity.

THE *WABASH* CASE

Even as the railroads began telling time for the rest of the country, critics renewed their calls for regulation. The railroads, they contended, had been established in the public interest and should operate that way. Railroads, so the argument ran, "owe their existence to the State; their charters specify certain conditions under which they shall exist and conduct their business." It followed that the railroads "are created not only that their stock holders may make money, but with special reference to the service they are expected to render the public, and their utility to the public was the controlling cause of their creation by the state."[11] The concept of public interest lay at the heart of the *Munn* ruling and would guide future regulation.

Many farmers depended on a single railroad to carry their harvests to market, leaving them particularly exposed to seasonal rate adjustments. Company officials called this supply and demand, but farmers saw it as an injustice that shipping rates rose at harvesttime. Farmers believed they were not being fully rewarded for producing the wealth of the nation. They understood the laws of supply and demand but did not like them, believing legislators had a duty to oversee economic relations based on justice and fairness. And justice for

Figure 8.1. Time became a crucial commodity as the railroads expanded, and in 1883 the railroad industry introduced four standardized time zones. Here, the Chicago Union Station watch inspector is kept busy adjusting timepieces. Library of Congress Prints and Photographs Division.

the farmers meant charging the same price for hauling their grain in October as in March, regardless of demand.

That philosophy informed the second phase of the legal attack on railroads. In this stage, regulators grappled with companies claiming exemption from state laws because they operated across state lines. The breakthrough came in 1886, once more in a case originating in Illinois. The Supreme Court, in October of that year, overturned an earlier ruling by the state high court in *Wabash, St. Louis, and Pacific Railway v. Illinois.* This suit arose because the Wabash charged different rates to ship similar products to New York for two customers, one in Peoria and one in Gilman, in violation of state law. The Gilman business had paid nearly twice as much as the Peoria company for each one-hundred pounds carried to the Empire State. The *New York Times* labeled it "Unjust Discrimination" and demanded an end. The Illinois Supreme Court found against the Wabash, which appealed on the grounds that the shipment from Peoria was less expensive to transport because it was larger, and therefore cheaper on a per-unit basis, than the Gilman load. The US Supreme Court agreed with the Wabash and ruled that no state could legally regulate a company operating across state lines because state powers ended at the border, and to go beyond risked restraining interstate commerce. But there was a sting in the tail: the Court declared that when companies operated across state lines, the commerce clause of the US Constitution (Article I, Section 8, Clause 3) gave the federal government the right to do so. Railroad regulation, it ruled, "must be, if established at all, of a general or national character."[12]

The *Wabash* ruling strengthened regulatory legislation (praised by the *Chicago Tribune* as the "anti-monopoly and anti-extortion policy of Illinois") and heightened calls for passage of a pending interstate commerce bill by Congress. All in all, *Tribune* editors believed, the *Wabash* case had reinforced "the foundations of Grangerism." The *Wabash* ruling upheld the principle that railroads acted in the public interest and therefore the public, through their elected representatives, had a right to regulate them. The immediate consequence was formation of the first regulatory agency within the federal government, the Interstate Commerce Commission (ICC), in February 1887. The bill signed into law by President Grover Cleveland adopted vague language about "reasonable and just" rates, and the ICC proved unable to ban the types of pricing policies at stake in the *Wabash* case, but federal regulation of economic activity would only increase.[13]

One area in desperate need of regulation was the safety of travelers and employees. Railroads were becoming more and more dangerous as rolling stock grew larger and speeds increased. People experimented incessantly in a quest to stop the trains more effectively, to couple and uncouple them safely, and to keep them at a secure distance from each other. But railroads were loath to adopt new technology on the grounds of expense, especially when labor remained relatively cheap and therefore disposable. Link-and-pin devices required brakemen to risk life and limb by standing between cars to couple and uncouple them, but Eli Janney, a clerk in Alexandria, Virginia, patented an automatic coupler in 1868. New Yorker George Westinghouse solved the problem of slowing and stopping trains when, by 1872, he created a system using compressed air to apply the brakes. Both men continued to improve their inventions.

Invention is one thing, adoption quite another. Air brakes, automatic couplers, and other safety devices did not become standard equipment in the railroad industry until the federal government intervened. Pushed by Lorenzo S. Coffin, an Iowa railroad commissioner who convinced the CB&Q to test air brakes, the Benjamin Harrison administration acceded to demands for improved railroad safety measures. In 1893 President Harrison signed into law the Railroad Safety Appliance Act, requiring railroads to equip all rolling stock with automatic couplers and air brakes. Accident rates fell, the number of railroaders injured and killed tumbled, and compensation payments dropped. Around the same time the first "interlocking" mechanisms to keep trains apart were introduced, though their use would not become general until being required by the ICC in the 1920s.

Figure 8.2. Elevating tracks was a common means of avoiding street congestion. Here, an "L" service glides above Wabash Avenue in 1900. Library of Congress Prints and Photographs Division.

MUNICIPAL REGULATION

Railroads made Chicago what it was. As one wag wrote in the 1890s, that meant "the town lay under a pall of smoke and the rushing trains bore down on their victims at every crossing." A hundred people died annually at the end of the nineteenth century from collisions between road traffic and trains in the city, stimulating demands for separating railroad tracks from ever-more-congested city streets. One response was the elevated railroad in downtown Chicago, which would become known as the Loop, built in conjunction with the World's Columbian Exposition. Another response

came in the form of an 1899 Chicago City Council regulation requiring the Chicago & Alton to elevate its tracks within the city limits. The C&A spent $11 million over fourteen years, and the Pennsylvania Railroad undertook a similar project at the beginning of the twentieth century. Aurora, at the junction of two main CB&Q lines, required that corporation to elevate its tracks for the safety of road vehicles and pedestrians in 1917. The project took five years and cost $3 million in land acquisition and track relocation.[14]

These and many similar regulations of great importance to local politicians and a nuisance to railroad officials consumed time and money but saved lives. In 1891,

The Iron Road in the Prarie State

Figure 8.3. Chicago's Loop at Wabash and Van Buren in 1907. Library of Congress Prints and Photographs Division.

for example, the town council of Pana, on the Illinois Central near Decatur, passed an ordinance requiring flagmen to guard two crossings within the municipality, reduced to a single person after the ICRR appealed the rule. Making the most of the situation, the general manager instructed his local roadmaster to use this employee "also as [a] general man about the yards, cleaning the switches, frogs, etc., [in] what spare time he has."[15]

Steam locomotives filled the air with noxious fumes. When British novelist Robert Louis Stevenson changed trains in Chicago in 1892 he entered "a great and gloomy city" where smoke blocked out the sun. Locomotives covered much of urban America with soot and grit, so

much so that air pollution became a subject of government regulation in the 1890s. In that decade American municipalities adopted smoke-abatement ordinances aimed at factories and railroads. St. Louis had a particularly active smoke-control campaign. The Engineers' Club experimented with smoke-reduction technology, and voluntary societies like the Civic League and the Wednesday Club advocated legislative restrictions.[16]

The city of Chicago passed a smoke-abatement ordinance in 1881 to eliminate "dense smoke" but without defining that key phrase. After an initial flurry of activity, enforcement virtually stopped. A subsequent city ordinance established the Department of Smoke

Inspection in 1907, but it was less effective than the efforts of the railroads themselves to reduce smoke. Chicago-area railroads employed thirty-eight smoke inspectors to teach engineers and firemen how to run their engines more efficiently, lowering coal consumption and decreasing the amount of smoke locomotives emitted. Illinois railroads also employed traveling engineers to instruct engine crews in the science of reducing coal consumption to save money and eliminate excess smoking. Noxious smoke was an indication that the engines were creating "clinkers," a hard residue left after burning coal, which reduced efficiency and required time-consuming cleaning of the locomotive's smoke-box. The Chicago Great Western even ranked engineers and firemen by fuel efficiency, but only the introduction of diesels and electrics eliminated smoke pollution.[17]

Antismoke activists advocated electrifying suburban lines to clear the air. Chicago's smoke-inspection officials photographed offending locomotives and encouraged the city to levy fines on the companies. But railroad corporations and the brotherhoods fiercely opposed legislation on these issues because of the cost of electrification, the dangers of live wires above workers or third rails at ground level, and the power city council wielded by forcing railroads to pay for the pollution they caused. Lobbying by the companies led to the dismissal of Paul Bird, a particularly zealous chief smoke inspector for the city of Chicago, and pressure from the Pennsylvania Railroad helped tone down the conclusions of a 1915 Chicago Association of Commerce study of railroad electrification.[18]

Despite the railroads' opposition, the Chicago City Council enacted the 1919 Lake Front Ordinance, requiring the Illinois Central to end its use of steam-powered locomotives within city limits by 1927. This legislation, passed after lobbying by the Chicago Anti-Smoke League, pertained only to the Illinois Central because its busy lines ran south from Central Station along the lake front, through Grant Park, and into politically influential neighborhoods. Electrification of the Illinois Central suburban line was completed by the city's deadline. Efforts to force other lines to electrify failed, in part because of the adoption of diesel locomotives and in part due to the financial constraints imposed by the Great Depression.[19]

State and municipal regulation achieved limited gains before 1900. Regular appeals for federal oversight developed in the 1870s, and some railroad officials welcomed the discussion of national rules because local and state requirements could seem capricious.[20] Congress regularly debated bills calling for railroad regulation after 1871, and demands for federal intervention increased in volume as mergers during the 1880s further concentrated ownership. In 1883 President Chester Arthur urged Congress to consider legislation to protect the public from abuses by railroads, and in 1886 a Senate select committee, chaired by former Illinois governor Shelby M. Cullom, recommended a federal regulatory commission to oversee the railroad industry. The ICC, created as a result of the Cullom Committee's report and in the wake of the *Wabash* case, assumed this role. Formation of the commission, though it was weak and ineffectual until the beginning of the twentieth century, meant the railroading landscape would never be the same, and events in Illinois had played a key role in altering it.

PANIC AND INNOVATION

egulators could do little to help the railroad industry in the face of global economic downturns, though their strictures did not help the bottom line. The capital needed to build railroads came from the Netherlands and Great Britain, from New York and Rock Falls. Financiers and farmers proffered their savings in hopes of earning a profit, but sometimes disaster struck. Connecting with a transatlantic economy could prove painful, as events in 1873 would demonstrate. In that year another of the recurring crises of capitalism forced numerous railroads into bankruptcy, demonstrating the dangers of relying on the invisible and far-flung forces of capital accumulation.

THE PANIC OF 1873

The vulnerability of railroads to financial forces they unleashed but could not control was stunningly demonstrated in 1873. Railroad construction virtually stopped and operations were threatened when the New York office of the country's largest private banker, Jay Cooke, suddenly closed its doors. This unexpected catastrophe was the culmination of a series of smaller failures and precipitated a downturn lasting on and off to the end of the century. The Panic of 1873—which initiated a frenzied effort to convert stocks, bonds, and savings into cash—revealed the dangers of overcapitalization and overbuilding. The cultural scale tipped against speculators again, and a new round of corporate consolidations kicked off.[1]

The panic was primarily a railroad affair. The Northern Pacific Railroad, which had no direct contact with or presence in Illinois, dominated Cooke and Company's portfolio. The crisis began when Northern Pacific bond sales failed to meet investors' unrealistic expectations. The bubble of overblown predictions burst when the "weakest of all the confidence operations of the speculators" collapsed in a softening economy. The Franco-Prussian War of 1870 (which scared off German capitalists), rumors that the Rock Island was in trouble, a small but newsworthy fire in Chicago, and a sudden sell-off of western railroad shares all contributed to the panic. The last straw came when country bankers who annually invested farmers' earnings with New York financial houses at high rates of interest withdrew their House of Cooke deposits. Short of cash due to those smaller-than-expected Northern Pacific bond sales, Cooke's Wall Street branch closed on September 18, 1873. Other banks followed suit. Railroads unable to pay the interest on securities began declaring bankruptcy: twenty-five across the country in the last quarter of 1873, seventy-one in 1874, and a further twenty-five in 1875. By 1876 railroad companies operating roughly a quarter of the national railroad network had entered receivership.[2]

Illinois railroads experienced a range of effects from the panic. The sudden contraction of the economy "paralyzed all business," and capital fled Chicago for the relatively safer havens of New York and Boston. Limited access to credit temporarily slowed a C&NW program of expansion, the value of its common stock fell by a third, and earnings declined in successive years, but by 1878 the picture brightened as share prices and revenues began to rise. The Illinois Central, an equally well-managed line, saw annual revenues drop between 1874 and 1877, when, responding to low income and a projected drop in dividends, it reduced officers' salaries by a quarter. Illinois Central lines south of Cairo—recently consolidated into the New Orleans, St. Louis & Chicago—were not so fortunate. Earnings barely covered payments on the ICRR's $21 million debt, but the road survived without either the harrowing experience of receivership or losing the faith of its investors.[3]

For some lines, however, the Panic of 1873 exacerbated preexisting problems. The Toledo, Peoria & Warsaw, for example, saw traffic levels fall and revenues plummet in late 1873 and into 1874. Beginning and ending in remote rural outposts, the TP&W's only real asset was the stretch of line between Gilman and El Paso, which the Illinois Central used as a connection between its charter lines. The ICRR temporarily operated the TP&W in 1874 to protect its access to this link. Elsewhere, railroad construction projects fell victim to the panic, including the Wabash Railroad's proposed line from central Illinois coal fields near Litchfield to Quincy. The situation improved very slowly. A credit squeeze in 1874 resulted in the virtual halving of crop plantings in Illinois, significantly reducing railroad traffic at harvesttime. The Alton experienced a 24 percent drop in corn haulage and—because of a miners' strike and competition from other lines—watched helplessly as coal-traffic volumes fell for the first time in the company's history.[4]

Other railroads profited from the Panic of 1873. One in particular was the New York Central (NYC), created in 1867 when Cornelius Vanderbilt merged several smaller roads into a single system. Vanderbilt wanted a direct route into Chicago from New York City, but his line ended at Buffalo. He sought to merge with other lines and two options existed. The Michigan Central operated from Buffalo to Chicago through Canada, while a number of small roads linked Buffalo with Toledo along the south shore of Lake Erie, connecting with the Michigan Southern into Chicago. After stock manipulation by speculators Jay Gould and Jim Fisk briefly delayed him, Vanderbilt purchased a controlling share in the Michigan Southern. The chairman of the Michigan Central, James F. Joy, approached the Commodore in an effort to connect his ailing road with the NYC, but Vanderbilt thought the price Joy demanded was too high. The Michigan Central then fell into Vanderbilt's lap in 1877, when he bought it inexpensively out of receivership.[5] This heralded a new era of competition between the NYC and the Pennsylvania Railroad on the Chicago to New York route.

INNOVATION

Crisis encouraged innovation, and new forms of financing gained currency in the wake of the Panic of 1873. Income bonds, which paid interest only when company revenues exceeded expenses, became popular with railroads seeking to lower their indebtedness. Though holders had a claim on the assets of the company in the event of bankruptcy, income bonds were not particularly popular with investors. The Erie Railroad guaranteed payment of bond interest on the bankrupt Chicago & Atlantic Railroad, its line into the Windy City. But after itself falling into receivership in 1884, the Erie ceased paying interest. Dutch bondholders then facilitated reorganization by purchasing the majority of second mortgages. This lasted until 1890, when the Chicago & Atlantic was renamed the Chicago & Erie with a lower debt and fewer bondholders.[6]

Investors turned to other financial instruments as the nineteenth century wound to a close. Debenture bonds, an idea imported from Great Britain, paid interest only when the company made money. Holders obtained what was essentially a lien on the property of the railroad, which meant they controlled it until the debt was repaid. Debenture holders could vote on the election of directors, and their claim on the company was perpetual, for debentures had no termination date. These were popular with railroad directors, but investors did not like them because they did not pay dividends when a corporation failed to earn a profit. Overall, they remained rare in the United States.

Not every railroad could ride out panics or overcome losses by floating new stock offerings or reorganizing. In an emergency a company could issue short-term, high-interest notes to raise capital, but failure to repay them could mean bankruptcy. Railroads used another increasingly common measure, the equipment trust, to lease rolling stock from investors when capital was either unavailable or too expensive. When the narrow-gauge Toledo, Cincinnati & St. Louis—which operated a line through central Illinois from Indiana to East St. Louis—entered receivership in 1885 most of its rolling stock had to be returned to the owners, primarily financial institutions, which then leased it to other railroads. The Toledo line's fleet of locomotives shrank from 101 to 16, and the number of freight cars fell from 3,410 to 450, hardly a recipe for recovery.[7]

Large sums of money attracted swindlers as well as entrepreneurs, though sometimes the categories overlapped. Swindles were all too common in the railroad age, and overseas investors were particularly vulnerable to stock speculation and manipulation. A commonplace trick in the early days of railroading was selling stock in companies that existed only on paper and in the imaginations of their promoters, a particular problem during the late 1860s and early 1870s. Another type of fraud preyed on the supposed ignorance of European financiers who might unwittingly purchase worthless shares in companies either on the verge of bankruptcy or actually in receivership. Just before the Panic of 1873, the Rockford, Rock Island & St. Louis Railroad had sold securities worth $9 million in Europe. Speculators in Germany and Holland purchased them, unaware that the prospectus erroneously claimed that the company would receive federal land grants and that coal mines alongside its tracks would generate traffic. No land grants were forthcoming, and the mines did not exist. Local financing in Beardstown and Byron was available, but the company failed during the 1873 panic after news that its treasurer had absconded with $245,000. In 1876 German bondholders purchased the foreclosed line and sold it to the CB&Q for barely fourteen cents on the dollar. Stories like this, splashed across the pages of industry newspapers such as London's *Railway Times,*

made investors cautious, and American railroad shares became hard sells in European capital markets.[8]

THE HINCKLEY ROADS

Illinois produced its share of railroad magnates, albeit on a smaller scale than that of Gould and Vanderbilt. A prime example was transplanted New Yorker Francis E. Hinckley.[9] Born in 1834, Hinckley moved to Galesburg and attended Knox College for six years without graduating before becoming a partner in a bridge-building firm. In 1867 he joined a group of railroad speculators who wanted to construct a line from the village of Oregon to the town of Aurora. Hinckley raised money for the Chicago & Iowa, which took traffic away from the Chicago & North Western by providing cheaper transit between the Illinois Central at Forreston, near the Mississippi River, and the Burlington, near Aurora, from where trains ran into Chicago. When the line opened in 1872 it so pleased locals that they renamed the village of Squaw Grove "Hinckley" in his honor.

Expanding his empire, in 1872 Hinckley invested in a line from Pekin to Streator, which he redirected south toward Effingham. Though he had the backing of the president of the National City Bank of New York, in 1877 things started to go badly wrong, and his ambitious vision collapsed. He published a prospectus promising to extend the line north to Chicago and south to Paducah, Kentucky, but it barely reached Effingham, and then only after a last-ditch effort to raise capital in London. Those funds soon returned to haunt him: Hinckley was arrested on charges of fraud brought by English investors unhappy with the abrupt termination of the road two hundred miles short of its intended goal. To save his holdings Hinckley placed his lines in receivership, losing control of the Chicago & Iowa to the CB&Q, and renamed the Effingham line the Chicago & St. Louis Railway and then the Chicago & Paducah (C&P). For locals along the route, however, it was known simply as the "Hinckley line." In 1879 the Wabash bought the section from Effingham to Fairbury, including a branch to Streator. In 1886 the Chicago, Santa Fe & California (chartered to extend the Atchison, Topeka & Santa Fe from Kansas City to Chicago) purchased the

Figure 9.1. ATSF tracks cross C&A and the Rock Island near Joliet's iconic Union Station. Library of Congress Prints and Photographs Division.

dilapidated C&P track from Chicago to Ancona, extending it to Joliet and then Chicago while building elevators en route to help move local grain. Divided, Hinckley's empire fell into the hands of others, but the town kept his name, and he served a six-year term as trustee of the University of Chicago before returning to New York, where he died in 1900.[10]

GAUGE COMPLICATIONS

In the aftermath of the Panic of 1873, the railroad industry underwent a period of consolidation, including attempts to adopt a single gauge. The most common gauge—the distance or width from the head of one rail to the other on a single track—was 4 feet 8.5 inches. This was probably used for the simple reason that George Stephenson, the British railroad pioneer, was familiar with it from his work with coal mines. Stephenson employed that gauge on the Stockton & Darlington, the world's first modern railroad, and it spread from there by emulation and intent. In the United States it became the standard when President Abraham Lincoln authorized building the transcontinental to the 4-foot-8.5-inch gauge rather than the 5-foot gauge he personally preferred.

The Iron Road in the Prarie State

Figure 9.2. ATSF grain elevators at Ransom, near Streator. Library of Congress Prints and Photographs Division.

Not everyone followed Stephenson, however, and from the very beginning of the railroad age engineers adopted a variety of gauges. Different gauges could be found in the railroads of Illinois in the 1850s, including the six-foot Ohio & Mississippi, designed by engineers from the East Coast's famous six-foot-gauge New-York & Erie Rail Road. From Chicago, the broad-gauge Illinois & Wisconsin—likewise promoted by a former Erie engineer—headed north in 1851 but ran out of money and switched to standard gauge when building recommenced in 1855. After the Civil War most new non-standard-gauge track was narrow, but some broad-gauge lines existed. Narrow-gauge lines continued to be built in Illinois into the 1880s despite the national trend toward standardization, mainly because advocates claimed—often without reason and frequently on false assumptions about costs—that they were cheaper than standard-gauge lines.[11] But as standard gauge became universal, the costs of exchanging traffic from one gauge to another proved prohibitive, and tracks were slowly but surely converted to the standard.

This did not stop Rantoul lawyer Benjamin Gifford. Angry at what he considered exorbitant rates for freight shipments on the Illinois Central, Gifford financed and built a three-foot-gauge line to bypass the ICRR in the 1870s. His Havana, Rantoul & Eastern drove seventy-five miles from Le Roy to West Lebanon, Indiana, where it interchanged with the Wabash. Passenger service between Rantoul and West Lebanon began in 1877 and soon extended to Le Roy. Gifford, an outspoken advocate of what historian George Hilton labeled "the narrow gauge ideology," hoped his line would connect at Havana with the Fulton County Narrow Gauge, built in the 1870s, but that did not happen.[12]

Instead, tired of running a railroad, Gifford offered his poorly constructed and underfinanced line for sale. Jay Gould bit, adding it to his Wabash system in 1880. Gould may have envisioned the Havana, Rantoul & Eastern as part of a projected transcontinental, a patchwork quilt of lines stitched together from Atlantic to Pacific, but historian Roger Grant pronounced the purchase "foolish." Overreaching and struggling to fund its enormous debt, the Wabash entered receivership in 1885, and the Illinois Central stepped in to lease the Havana line the next year. Having spent $575,000 building and operating the narrow-gauge line, Gifford and his fellow investors received $100,000 from the receivership proceedings. In 1887, after issuing $1 million in gold bonds to upgrade the line, the Illinois Central rebuilt it to standard gauge.[13] For customers, this meant direct access to the rapidly expanding Illinois railroad network, but for small investors like Gifford it suggested that the railroad game was now out of their reach.

Another narrow gauge, the Clover Leaf, began life as the Toledo, Delphos & Burlington (TD&B) before striking oil and adopting the four-leafed symbol of good luck in celebration. The TD&B entered Illinois in August 1882, reaching Charleston and then dramatically redirecting itself from Burlington, Iowa, toward East St. Louis. Service between St. Louis and Toledo, Ohio, began in May 1884, with the *St. Louis Express* traversing the six-hundred-mile route in twenty-four hours, suggesting that the moniker "Express" could have been misleading. The promoters of what was now called the Toledo, Cincinnati & St. Louis wanted it to connect with a line running from St. Louis to the Mexican border at Laredo, Texas, nicknamed the "Grand Narrow

Gauge Trunk." Despite other Illinois projects claiming a place in the "trunk line of narrow gauge road from the East to the West," the larger project did not materialize, and the TC&StL entered receivership in 1883. Branches were cut and service was reduced to a single daily mixed train (i.e., part passenger and part freight) in each direction. Renamed the Toledo, St. Louis & Kansas City after being purchased by bondholders, it was saved from further ignominy only after natural gas and oil were discovered along its right-of-way. The Clover Leaf's days as the longest narrow-gauge railroad east of the Mississippi River were numbered, however. Between 1887 and 1889 the line was converted to standard gauge, and passengers had to endure lengthy delays while they waited at gauge-change points to switch trains.[14]

Gauge conversion could not cure all problems. A case in point was the Ohio & Mississippi Railroad, which converted to standard gauge in 1871 to take advantage of promised traffic off the Baltimore & Ohio. The process of lifting and moving one rail took just seven hours on July 16 and cost $1,066 per mile plus the added expense of changing rolling-stock gauges. Derailments, flooding, and other difficulties continued to plague the line. Expansion did not prove to be a solution either. The company plunged into receivership just two years after its 1875 purchase of a branch from Shawneetown to Beardstown. The sparse population of southern Illinois and the poor state of the roads, which turned into impassable quagmires in wet weather, caused the Baltimore & Ohio Railroad to delay adding the O&M to its holdings. Not until 1900 was the O&M formally merged into the B&O as part of the new Baltimore & Ohio Southwestern Railroad, a 922-mile line from St. Louis to Marietta, Ohio.[15]

Other lines in and around Little Egypt had better luck. The Mobile & Ohio Railroad—itself recently converted from the five-foot gauge—leased the narrow-gauge St. Louis & Cairo in 1886 and immediately standardized it. The Illinois Central had extensive experience with the intricacies of conversion to standard gauge, having narrowed the five-foot-wide rails of the Chicago, St. Louis & New Orleans, its 547-mile line south of Cairo, between dawn and midafternoon on July

29, 1881. Much of the South followed suit five years later, smoothing the interchange of traffic between different railroads and the two sections of the country.[16]

The Illinois Central had a habit of buying and standardizing narrow-gauge railroads. The Springfield, Effingham & Southeastern found almost immediately that its poorly constructed trackbed and bridges limited operations. Opened in 1880 as the somewhat ambitiously named Cincinnati, Effingham & Quincy, it merged in 1883 with an Indiana short line famous locally for converting decrepit coal wagons into uncomfortable passenger cars and for owning two locomotives that habitually broke down or derailed. On a good day the fifty-six-mile trip from Effingham to the Wabash River took six hours or more. Approaches to its bridge over the Wabash River collapsed in the winter of 1881, and heavy rains swept away long stretches of track on an irritatingly regular basis. Further bridge failures, derailments, and washouts created three disconnected segments and led to receivership, after which the line was converted to standard gauge in 1887. But this was not the end of its problems, and things improved only after the Illinois Central purchased it at foreclosure in 1900, renamed it the Indiana & Illinois Southern Railway, and extended it to Indianapolis.[17]

Other narrow-gauge lines in Illinois experienced varying fates. The eleven-mile Chicago, Millington & Western—the only narrow gauge to enter the Windy City—was sold under foreclosure to the Burlington after just three years of operation in the 1870s and abandoned. Around the same time the Danville, Olney & Ohio River—one of several coal-shipping lines either built or proposed in the 1870s—was converted to standard gauge in 1881 but, after being owned by several different railroads over the next thirty years, was sold in segments at the close of the First World War. A third line, the Fulton County Narrow Gauge, was built with technical assistance from the Burlington because it terminated in Galesburg. The Burlington operated it as an independent feeder road until converting it to standard gauge in 1905 and absorbing it three years later. A much smaller coal road to the north, the three-foot-six-inch-gauge Moline & Southeastern, operated eight miles of track from Moline to Coal Valley between 1879 and 1885, but it proved unprofitable, and the company closed down, its track lifted and sold.[18]

Recovery from the Panic of 1873 was in full swing by the 1880s. In that decade 2,018 route miles of new track were built in Illinois, followed by another 1,067 miles in the final decade of the century. Revenue for the Illinois Central and other strong Prairie State lines had recovered to prerecession levels by the early 1880s. Railroads began the long process of consolidation, spanning rivers as new building techniques improved bridges and new lines—the so-called Little Grangers—entered Illinois.

10

BRIDGE BUILDING AND "OVERBUILDING"

*I*llinois railroad expansion began to fall behind national growth rates in the 1870s and 1880s. For the decade of the 1870s, railroads built 3,095 route miles in Illinois, adding 64 percent compared with 76 percent nationally, but in the 1880s, Illinois's 26 percent fell dramatically behind the nation's 79 percent of added mileage. The reasons were simple: railroads continued to push farther west, while the development of new lines slowed in the Prairie State as it did elsewhere east of the Mississippi River. Nationally, more track was laid during the 1880s than in any other decade in US history. The 73,741 route miles built between 1881 and 1890 represented a two-thirds increase over all rail laid in the United States before 1880.

By 1880 some observers began to complain of "overbuilding" east of the Mississippi, by which they meant that newly constructed lines duplicated existing routes and, consequently, neither could be profitable. In Illinois approximately two thousand route miles were built in the 1880s, still an impressive amount. In northern Illinois the "Little Grangers" made tentative forays into the state, while the Atchison, Topeka & Santa Fe finalized its long-awaited entrance into Chicago. Though the construction of new lines slowed, the railroads themselves grew in importance. Trains became longer and faster, passenger travel became more comfortable, and direct services across new bridges helped to center Illinois in the railroad network.

RIVERS, BRIDGES, AND BEYOND

Illinois is bounded and bisected by water. The Illinois River cuts the state in two from southwest to northeast, where the magic of engineering connects it—via the Illinois and Michigan Canal and the Chicago River—to Lake Michigan. The Mississippi River forms the western border, the Ohio River the southern, and, for much of the eastern boundary with Indiana, the Wabash River and Lake Michigan complete the outline of the state. Bridging the Mississippi, Ohio, and Wabash Rivers represented giant strides in extending the reach of Illinois-based railroads. These were no ordinary waterways. Highways for boats and barges, they presented formidable obstacles to railroad expansion. Ferry boats carried passenger and freight cars across them until steel construction and new engineering techniques were widely adopted after the Civil War. Bridges provided vital links in the chain of railroads reaching out from Illinois because they allowed trains to run nonstop, ending the delays caused by the need to transfer onto the river for the trip to the other side.

The first bridge across the Mississippi River, the Rock Island swing bridge to Davenport, opened in 1856. The original charter of January 17, 1853, required that it be built "in such a manner as shall not materially obstruct . . . navigation" on the river. The structure consisted of five fixed 250-foot-long spans and, close to the

Figure 10.1. Bridges needed constant attention. Here a bridge near Princeton on the CB&Q is repaired in 1899. Special Collections and Archives, Knox College Library, Galesburg, Illinois.

Illinois riverbank, a 286-foot pivoting span for river traffic to pass. This was left open until a train approached. The bridge was built on the model patented in 1840 by William Howe from Massachusetts. The Howe Truss design used triangular vertical and diagonal beams to strengthen the bridge by distributing the weight to be carried across it. The original Rock Island bridge used pine and oak beams held together by iron bolts. White lead paint protected it from the elements, though not, it transpired, from fire.[1]

Its construction caused resentment and fear among steamboat operators. Between August 1856 and September 1857, at least seven boats had been harmed when they hit bridge piers, and another thirteen hit the bridge but did not sustain damage. The news of its destruction by the *Effie Afton* on May 6, 1856, was received with rejoicing by ship owners, who expected that traffic from St. Louis lost to the railroads would return to the river. Rebuilding the Rock Island bridge renewed the fears of merchants in St. Louis and other river towns that freight would remain with the railroad. Steamboat owners had cause for alarm: within eighteen months of the bridge opening, two-thirds of the freight that had traveled on the river between Davenport and St. Louis was carried by rail. In April 1858 the House of Representatives Commerce Committee declared the bridge "a material and dangerous obstruction to the navigation of the Mississippi" but did not recommend further action. The next month a St. Louis steamboat operator, James Ward, sued to have the bridge removed as an obstacle to navigation, and although he won a favorable judgment in Iowa, the US Supreme Court reversed the decision, a ruling upheld in 1867.[2] But the structure could not support the heavier locomotives of the postwar period, and a steel replacement was built in 1872.

Despite the obvious success of the Rock Island bridge it was a decade before the Mississippi would once again be spanned from Illinois. Low traffic densities, the dominance of short hauls, and limited access to capital blocked bridge building until after the Civil War. In the eight years immediately following cessation of hostilities, seven new railroad bridges crossed the Mississippi River from Illinois. Railroad bridges were usually built to the Howe Truss pattern using iron and wood, though by the time of the Civil War steel beams were replacing their wooden counterparts. The first new bridge, forty miles north of Rock Island, crossed the Mississippi River from Fulton to Clinton, Iowa. A Chicago & North Western project, it was built by the Albany Bridge Company and opened in 1865. The Chicago, Burlington & Quincy followed suit with bridges at Quincy and Burlington in 1868, the same year the Illinois Central inaugurated a span from Dunleith to Dubuque, Iowa. In 1871 the dual-use Hamilton to Keokuk, Iowa, bridge for rail and road traffic opened under the joint control of three companies, including the Toledo, Peoria & Warsaw, and in the same year the Wabash inaugurated its new bridge at Hannibal, Missouri. The Chicago & Alton was forced to build across the Mississippi at Louisiana, Missouri,

by the persistent freezes halting the ferry boat on its line from Roodhouse to Kansas City. In 1873 the new bridge opened, ending those weather-related delays.[3]

Bridging the Mississippi at St. Louis proved no easy task. The Illinois and Missouri Rivers drained into the Mississippi just north of St. Louis, significantly widening an already forbidding impediment and presenting considerable challenges to bridge builders. Long unhappy about losing ground to Chicago, regional business boosters created the Illinois and St. Louis Bridge Company shortly after the Civil War, but design problems and money woes compounded by opposition from ferry operators and the Army Corps of Engineers slowed progress.

The project's principal engineer, James B. Eads, began building in 1867, but sickness and financial troubles slowed him considerably. Eads, whose family's arrival in St. Louis had almost ended in disaster when their boat caught fire and sank, made a fortune by recovering sunken vessels from the Mississippi riverbed. He designed the bridge to his own exacting specifications, his perfectionism exasperating Andrew Carnegie, among others. He also devised a cure for the "bends" afflicting his workers in deep water. The bridge, later called the Eads Bridge in his honor, opened in May 1874 at a cost of $13 million, but it was not an immediate success. The railroads entering St. Louis squabbled over the charges they had to pay to use the bridge, and traffic across it developed slowly in part because terminal facilities west of the river compared poorly with the extensive yards of East St. Louis.[4]

Traffic came too slowly, it transpired. Riverboat operators equaled or bettered the bridge company's attempts to attract customers. When it halved the tolls, ferrymen matched it; when it offered free ice water to teamsters, the boat operators retaliated with complimentary whiskey. The biggest problem facing the bridge company was its inability to provide adequate depot and terminal facilities in St. Louis, where switching tracks covering 20 acres of land were supposed to provide the same services as 660 acres in East St. Louis. Unable to meet the needs of the railroads and buffeted by competition from riverboat operators, the Illinois

The Iron Road in the Prarie State

Figure 10.2. The Eads Bridge in 1903. Library of Congress Prints and Photographs Division.

and St. Louis Bridge Company and the St. Louis Tunnel Company—which owned the tracks leading to the Eads Bridge—defaulted on their mortgages and entered receivership in April 1875. Less than a year after it had officially opened, the first bridge across the Mississippi at St. Louis was bankrupt.[5]

In 1886 the rival St. Louis Merchants Bridge Company inaugurated its own span and began operations north of the Eads Bridge. Championed by local businesses seeking a cheap alternative to the Eads Bridge, the company suffered from approaches built at awkward angles and poor switching facilities. Concerned about access for his own railroads, Jay Gould bought both bridges to rationalize the challenges of interchanging

traffic in St. Louis. Then in 1894 St. Louis Union Station opened. It was notable for the largest train shed in the world at the time: it was 630 feet long and 606 feet wide, and it contained 42 tracks on 10 acres. The Chicago & Alton began to operate over the Merchants Bridge into the new depot, allowing it to cooperate with other railroads on direct Pullman services to Los Angeles and San Francisco. Soon thereafter it began operating passenger trains to Arkansas, Texas, and Mexico and from Chicago to Denver over the Union Pacific.[6]

In 1894 the Chicago, Burlington & Quincy opened a bridge across the Mississippi at Alton and began regular commuter service into St. Louis. Two trains, one from the west and a second from the east, marked the

Figure 10.3. View of the CB&Q bridge at Alton clearly showing the swing section (1900). Library of Congress Prints and Photographs Division.

occasion by stopping in the middle of the new structure for speeches and the smashing of a bottle of champagne "on the heavy steel work." At the same time, facing competition from the Atchison, Topeka & Santa Fe, which had entered Chicago in 1888 from Kansas City, the Burlington began a five-year project to replace the Quincy bridge over the Mississippi in order to increase traffic on the newly acquired Quincy, Omaha & Kansas City Railroad. Opened in 1902, the new bridge was part of a plan to compete against the arriviste Santa Fe by offering customers a shorter route to Kansas City.[7]

Along the southern border of the state, the Ohio River proved equally difficult to span. The first bridge over the Ohio from Illinois, built by the Paducah and Illinois Bridge Company, opened on October 29, 1889. The company was formed in the immediate aftermath of the Civil War, and its promoters yearned to heal the wounds of conflict by including two Union generals and two Confederate generals among its directors. Despite this nod at reunification, actually raising the required capital proved slow going, and only in 1887 did work on the massive structure begin, complicated by the need

The Iron Road in the Prarie State

to build lengthy approaches across treacherous swampland. When it finally opened, it allowed Illinois Central trains to run directly into Kentucky and from there to the Gulf Coast.[8]

Another span vital to the growth of Illinois railroads crossed the Ohio River in Indiana. The Louisville & Nashville purchased the St. Louis & Southeastern Railroad, which opened in 1871 through southern Illinois to Evansville, Indiana, from its receivers in 1879. The somewhat circuitous route followed those of the Southern Railway and the Illinois Central from St. Louis east to Belleville, where the L&N split off toward the villages of Nashville and Mt. Vernon. At the latter it turned southeast toward McLeansboro and Carmi before reaching the Wabash River across from Evansville, Indiana. The line received a boost when it opened a bridge across the Ohio River from Evansville to Henderson, Kentucky, in 1885. Before then its St. Louis-to-Nashville passenger trains had to be ferried in sections across the Ohio River. Uninterrupted travel, further facilitated by the adoption of standard gauge over the entire system, allowed passengers from southern Illinois to enjoy sleeper service over the L&N to Atlanta, Georgia, and Jacksonville and St. Petersburg, Florida.[9]

Bridging rivers enabled Illinois to consolidate its status as the crossroads of the nation's railroad network. The links across the Mississippi, the Ohio, and the Wabash facilitated the direct movement of passengers and freight to the west, south, and east. Despite opposition from riverboat and ferry operators, the railroads defended their right to cross rivers while making appropriate compromises for continued river traffic, usually in the form of swing sections, which opened to enable boats to pass. Bridges also encouraged Illinois railroads to continue expanding to the west. In 1887 the Illinois Central reached Sioux Falls, South Dakota, which became its westernmost outpost. In 1894 the Chicago, Burlington & Quincy, seeking a route to the West Coast, connected with the Northern Pacific at Huntley, Montana, and gained running rights over thirteen miles of NP track from there into Billings, a booming railroad town. The Milwaukee Road unwisely built a "Pacific Extension" from South Dakota to Seattle between 1905

and 1909. The resulting competition led Chicago & North Western officials to contemplate expanding to the Pacific coast, but the cost seemed prohibitive, and the North Western remained a regional carrier—sensibly, as it turned out. The combination of the high price of the extension, an economic downturn in 1907, careless mergers, and the opening of the Panama Canal in 1914 pushed the Milwaukee into receivership in 1925.[10]

EXPANSION AND CONSOLIDATION WITHIN ILLINOIS

Complementing the expansionist mood symbolized by new steel bridges was the growth of tracks within the state. Existing Illinois railroads expanded piecemeal during the 1870s and 1880s by adding strategic lines. After pursuing cautious policies to ride out the worst of the economic storm of the 1870s, the North Western—which neither defaulted nor entered receivership during that cataclysmic period—added mileage in the 1880s. Most of this growth occurred in Iowa, Minnesota, Michigan, Wisconsin, and South Dakota, but the North Western did purchase two short lines in Illinois. The narrow-gauge Galena & Southern Wisconsin connected Galena with Platteville, Wisconsin, while the Chicago & Tomah ran from Freeport to a scattering of small communities in southwest Wisconsin. These lines, totaling some ninety miles, were physically linked to and absorbed by North Western subsidiary Milwaukee & Madison Railway, and most of them were widened to standard gauge in the mid-1880s.[11]

Of greater significance was the seventy-six-mile Northern Illinois Railway, built by the C&NW in 1885 to gain access to coal in Bureau County. Beginning in Belvidere, the new line crossed the main Chicago to Omaha route at DeKalb and continued south to Spring Valley. Trains operated between Sycamore and DeKalb over the Sycamore & Cortland branch, a formerly independent company built in 1859, and on a second line linking Sycamore with DeKalb, which meant three short branches converged on that bucolic burg, which the main CGW trunk passed through. In the late 1880s the North Western added mileage in Chicagoland, including a six-mile line from Batavia to Aurora and

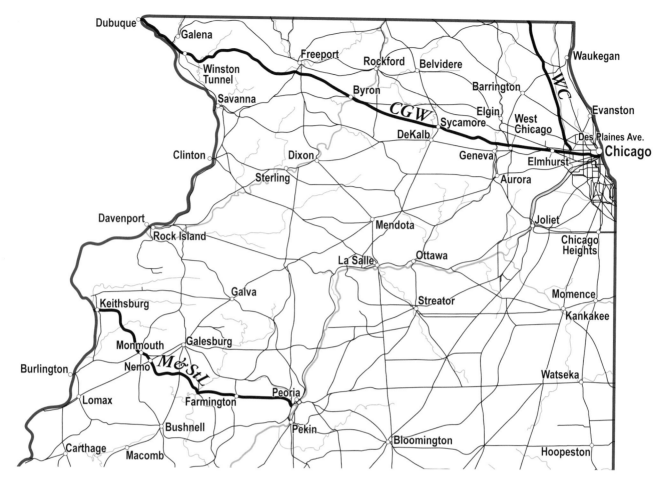

Map 10.1. The "Little Grangers" in Illinois. Courtesy of Christopher Sutton.

an extension to its Junction Railway within the city limits.[12]

A group of local promoters attempted to make Bloomington—already an important north-south junction—into a crossroads. The Lake Erie & Western, resulting from an 1879 merger of three lines linking Bloomington with Fremont and Sandusky, Ohio, reached Peoria in April 1888 and inaugurated passenger service between Peoria and Sandusky. Farther south, the Peoria, Decatur & Evansville Railway (PD&E), chartered from 1857, originated as the eighteen-mile-long Decatur & Lincoln Railway, linking Pekin and Delavan in 1870. The PD&L acquired the Decatur, Sullivan & Mattoon Railroad in 1879 to create the PD&E. The new corporation then purchased the Grayville & Mattoon Railroad in 1880 and pushed the line to Evansville, Indiana, by 1881, adding a short branch to New Harmony, Indiana, in the same

year. In 1893 the PD&E acquired the Chicago & Ohio River Railroad, a line from Olney to Sidell. This put the PD&E into receivership in 1894, and the C&OR was sold off in 1899. The PD&E itself was acquired at auction by the Illinois Central in 1900 and absorbed into that system, ending its independent existence.[13]

THE LITTLE GRANGERS

The 1880s was a decade of expansion with unanticipated long-term consequences. Four new companies—the Minneapolis, St. Paul & Sault Ste. Marie Railroad (often called the Soo Line after the pronunciation of "Sault"); the Iowa Central Railway (IC); the Minneapolis & St. Louis Railroad (M&StL); and the Chicago Great Western Railway (CGW)—became known collectively as the Little Grangers because they passed through much of the same country as the original Granger

The Iron Road in the Prarie State

Roads. The Little Grangers built into Illinois, but only the Chicago Great Western entered Chicago directly. Two of these new lines—the Soo and the M&StL—were promoted by Minnesota industrialists unhappy with the rates charged by Chicago railroads, and the former ran trains into the Windy City over the Wisconsin Southern.[14] The other two developed in response to the perceived greed of the railroads and the desire for local control of transportation arteries.

Chartered in 1883 as the Minneapolis, Sault Ste. Marie & Atlantic, the corporation that would eventually become the Soo Line was planned to connect the Twin Cities with the Lake Superior port of Sault Ste. Marie, Michigan, and thereby bypass Chicago completely. The company built into the lumber and ore lands of northern Minnesota and west to grain-rich North Dakota, but low traffic densities meant it needed a Chicago gateway, which it found in a strategic alliance with the Wisconsin Central. This line, built between 1871 and 1886 and partially financed by federal land grants, reached St. Paul in 1884 and Chicago in 1886. After a brief flirtation with the Northern Pacific (a dalliance unceremoniously ended by the Panic of 1893), the WC operated independently until the Soo leased it in 1909. The two lines operated a seamless service from Minneapolis to Chicago. To the uninitiated all the trains seemed to belong to the Soo, but Wisconsin Central locomotives had the letters "WC" discretely stenciled onto their cabs. This arrangement lasted until the Wisconsin Central declared bankruptcy in 1932.[15]

Iowa railroad investors championed their own local projects, one of which, the St. Louis, Iowa & St. Paul Railway, was designed to transport coal from southern Iowa and lumber from Minnesota. Delayed by the Panic of 1857 and then abandoned during the Civil War, the project was regenerated in 1865 as the Iowa Central Railroad to provide a locally owned alternative to Chicago lines. Though it attracted investment from financial giants like Jay Cooke and J. Edgar Thomson, it entered bankruptcy during the Panic of 1873. Called "Hook and Eye" because of the shape of its logo, the Iowa Central did not control its own destiny. It grew north and south but not far enough in either direction. Stopping at

Mason City, Iowa, near the Minnesota border and Albia, Iowa, to the south, it relied on the St. Paul for access to Minneapolis and on the Wabash to gain St. Louis.[16] Dependence upon competitors could only weaken it.

In 1883 the Iowa Central reached the Mississippi River across from Keithsburg, Illinois, and its president, Isaac M. Cate, announced his intention to extend the line to Chicago. But the proposed route—roundabout and liable to upset the Chicago-based companies on which the Central relied for much of its traffic—was eventually dropped in favor of terminating at Peoria. The Iowa Central adopted two unfinished Illinois projects, the Peoria & Farmington Railroad and the Monmouth & Illinois River Railroad, which it completed in 1882 and 1883, halting at Keithsburg until it bridged the Mississippi in 1886. Opening the bridge did not solve all problems because weight restrictions required trains to stop, break into two parts, and move separately across it. To overcome the delays and backups this caused, the Iowa Central built a new bridge, with a 233-foot lift span, in 1910.[17]

The third Little Granger, the Minneapolis & St. Louis Railroad, known for its meandering, isolated routes, never reached St. Louis. The railroad was chartered by Minneapolis flour merchants in 1870 to build south to the border with Iowa, and Jay Cooke temporarily leased it to connect with his Lake Superior & Minnesota Railroad. The expected traffic never materialized, and Cooke's company relinquished the lease during the Panic of 1873, when the company was shedding just about anything it could move. The next year the M&StL entered receivership and did not reach Albert Lea, Minnesota, a growing town near the Iowa border, until 1877, and only then by exchanging traffic with the Burlington, Cedar Rapids & Northern (BCR&N). Jointly operated by the Chicago, Burlington & Quincy and the Rock Island Railroads, the BCR&N connection pointed to the future for the M&StL. After building a line southwest to Fort Dodge and Des Moines and another, albeit much shorter, branch west to Lake Minnetonka, the M&StL entered into an agreement in 1880 with the BCR&N and the Rock Island to operate trains from Minneapolis to Chicago.[18]

The M&StL was a bit player in a large market. In 1886 James J. Hill, who had a keen eye for such matters, confidently asserted that the principal shareholders might be profiting but the company as a whole was "not a financial success." By then three other railroads challenged the M&StL for Twin Cities traffic to Chicago, but the M&StL had the longest route (532 miles compared with 407 for the shortest, jointly operated by the Chicago & North Western and the Chicago, St. Paul, Minneapolis & Omaha). Competition for lumber, coal, flour, and other commodities intensified, as did the battle for passengers. The M&StL fared poorly in both contests. Two years after Hill's not-so-idle speculation, it was unable to pay the interest on its bonds and entered receivership.[19]

This time it took six years for the M&StL to emerge from bankruptcy, and when it did it had a board of directors made up entirely of New Yorkers. This shift from local to distant control caused a fair amount of consternation among Minnesotans, but not much changed at first. In 1895 the M&StL cooperated with the Rock Island on an overnight train from Chicago to Des Moines and Omaha.[20] But earnings lagged, and the M&StL seemed unable to grow.

The appointment of Edwin Hawley as president in 1897 signaled a new direction. A New Yorker with experience as a clerk on the Rock Island, Hawley learned about railroad financing from Collis P. Huntington, one of the founders of the first transcontinental. Seeking to build a midwestern railroading empire, Hawley convinced M&StL directors to finance an extension into southeastern Iowa, creating new communities to encourage settlement and traffic. Colonization, Hawley believed, was crucial to the road's future. In 1901 he initiated passenger service in cooperation with the Illinois Central from Albert Lea, Minnesota, to Chicago, ending the now unstable relationship with the Rock Island and sizing up opportunities elsewhere. In 1905 he detached the Des Moines & Fort Dodge Railroad from the Rock Island by convincing DM&FD shareholders to allow its lease with the Rock to expire. This piece of negligence placed the Rock Island in the ridiculous position of paying the M&StL to reach its own branch to Gowrie, Iowa, over track it had previously controlled.[21]

In 1907 Hawley purchased the Iowa Central, becoming chairman of the new company and appointing his business partner, Theodore P. Shonts, as president. Shonts, a Monmouth College graduate who had served on President Theodore Roosevelt's Isthmian Canal Commission, was a technocrat who believed in centralizing control in Chicago, but he proved unable to put his plan into effect. His abrupt manner alienated the line's managers, who were reeling under the challenges facing the jointly owned Iowa Central and M&StL. Competition with other lines and their status as "short haul" railroads (which meant they moved freight as single segments of longer shipments involving other railroads) kept earnings below optimal levels. Unable to improve revenue, Shonts was shunted aside in 1912. A new investor, Newman Erb, joined Hawley's group and had himself appointed president of the Iowa Central and the M&StL. For financial reasons, including the desperate need to refinance a capital-absorbing South Dakota extension, Erb urged a merger of the two roads. Hawley agreed, and in 1912 the Iowa Central and the M&StL began operating as a single railroad. Only the M&StL name survived, attached to a 1,586-mile railroad operating in Illinois, Iowa, Minnesota, and South Dakota.[22]

M&StL directors decided against building to Chicago because of a fourth Little Granger, the Chicago Great Western Railway. Created by A. B. Stickney, a Yankee from Maine who had served as president of the Central of Iowa and director of the M&StL, it was often criticized as "one road too many." The CGW opened to traffic in 1885, a boom time for railroad building. An "astute iconoclast," Stickney had settled in St. Paul, Minnesota, and worked for the "Empire Builder," James J. Hill, from whom he learned a thing or two about turning a tidy profit. He gathered a group of investors from Minnesota and Great Britain to revitalize the moribund Minnesota & Northwestern Railroad by purchasing its charter and ten thousand shares, allowing him to benefit from some very favorable stipulations. Most beneficial was the clause exempting the line from taxation because it had been chartered before Minnesota gained statehood. Beginning with this advantage, Stickney created a

Figure 10.4. Freight handling at Nemo, where the M&StL interchanged with the ATSF main line to Chicago. John W. Barriger III National Railroad Library, St. Louis Mercantile Library, UMSL.

finance company to pay himself and his closest partners the difference between what he charged the railroad for construction and what he actually paid to contractors.[23]

Building south and east from St. Paul through Minnesota and Iowa, Stickney turned his eyes toward Illinois. He reached Dubuque, Iowa, a river city of thirty thousand people located 175 miles from Chicago, by merging the Dubuque & Northwestern—planned but not built—into his own company. In November 1886 the first passenger services ran between St. Paul and Dubuque, and investors exchanged five Dubuque shares for two preferred and three common shares in Stickney's Minnesota & Northwestern. By then Stickney had chartered the Minnesota & Northwestern Railroad Company of Illinois to reach his destination on Lake Michigan.

In 1886 construction commenced on a twenty-seven-mile segment from Forest Home west to St. Charles using the right-of-way of an abandoned but partly graded line, the Chicago, St. Charles & Mississippi. From St. Charles the line continued to South Freeport. Regular service began in July 1887, with trains running into Chicago over the confusingly named Chicago & Great Western, which would later become the Baltimore & Ohio Chicago Terminal. Stickney's Chicago Great Western then built west through the hilly terrain of northwestern Illinois to the Mississippi River across from Dubuque, a segment that included the half-mile-long Winston Tunnel, the longest in Illinois. The completed line between Chicago and Dubuque—and from there to St. Paul—opened in February 1888.[24]

Figure 10.5. A CGW 4-6-2 locomotive rests between runs in Chicago. Author's collection.

Indebtedness outpaced earnings and rate wars among midwestern railroads reduced profits. Preferring to compete rather than cooperate, Stickney refused to join traffic pools. Falling earnings and imminent loan repayment deadlines demanded action. Stickney and his partners created the Chicago Great Western Railway Company, eliminating debt by issuing $70 million in securities, of which $15 million took the form of debenture stock paying 4 percent in gold, another $15 million in Preferred A stock paying 5 percent, $10 million of Preferred B at 4 percent, and $30 million in common stock. The result was a mortgage-free company with only a lien on its income, an arrangement urged by its British shareholders as

fiscally prudent. With no outstanding debt, the CGW was in a position to survive the perilous economic times ahead.[25]

In its early days the line had been built cheaply, and it showed. One station agent wrote that accidents were so frequent that he "always kept a stretcher and a supply of first aid remedies on hand and they proved very beneficial." Travel was slowed by the terrain through which the line ran, the surveyors having taken it over the few hills to be found in eastern Iowa and northwestern Illinois. The Chicago Great Western nonetheless earned a well-deserved reputation for "innovation and self-promotion." It was the first railroad to issue, in 1891, a brochure advertising travel to the Columbian Exposition

Figure 10.6. The CGW *Minnesotan* crosses the Fox River after leaving Chicago. Center for Railroad Photography and Art, Madison, WI.

of 1893. The CGW aggressively lowered its rates to attract and retain customers. For example, barbed wire manufactured in DeKalb was transported six miles by horse-drawn cart to the CGW depot in Sycamore for shipment to St. Paul in preference to the closer but higher-priced Chicago & North Western.[26]

No friend of railroad regulation, Stickney did advocate government action to ensure uniform rates for carrying goods from one terminal to another. This, he hoped, would encourage competition on the basis of service, a test he felt his road could pass easily. Local newspapers advised businessmen to contact the road for information about new opportunities; "homeseeker excursions" and "colonist tickets" took settlers to

Canada, the South, the Midwest, and the West; and a joint service with the Santa Fe ran over CGW tracks from Chicago on its way to Los Angeles.[27]

Chicago Great Western officials used statistics to improve performance and efficiency, still relatively rare in the 1880s. They developed tonnage ratings for locomotives and maintained graphs of revenues and expenditures to help make operational decisions. Creative accounting also played a role in the company's contests for traffic. CGW officials, inveterate rate cutters, ingeniously placed categories such as canned goods under unusual headings ("peas and other canned goods") to circumvent the published rates so agents could beat competitors' prices. The CGW was also one of the first

Bridge Building and "Overbuilding"

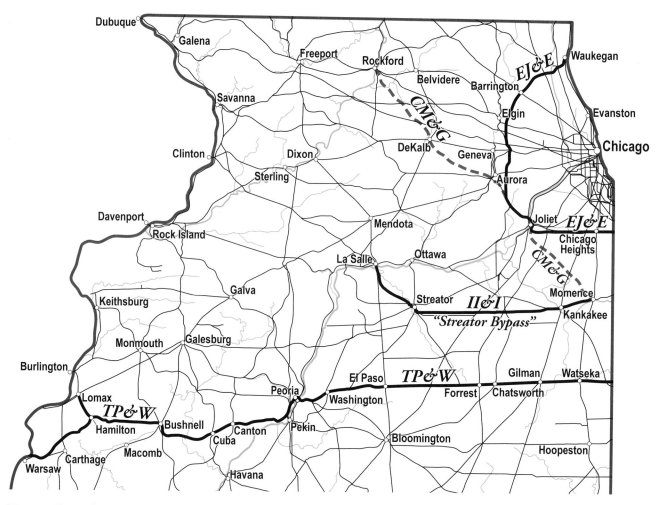

Map 10.2. Chicago bypass railroads. Courtesy of Christopher Sutton.

railroads to offer long-term contracts to shippers as a hedge against rate increases.[28]

The CGW generated positive publicity in a variety of ways. When gossip had it building a belt line around Chicago to Joliet, farmers were "well disposed toward the new road and willing to do the fair thing, as they saw that it was sure to go through." The citizens of Sycamore were thrilled, envisioning their town as the point from which the belt road would swing southeast toward Indiana. The Chicago bypass did not materialize, but locals remained enthusiastic, repeating Stickney's boast that the line would soon be "leading all competitors in the matter of equipment and train service." Investors in DeKalb financed the branch to their town from Sycamore, the county seat through which the CGW main line ran, after a normal school had been chartered there in

1895. Their hope was that the people of DeKalb would "feel jubilant" at living in "a city with competitive railroads." Rumors of a merger between the CGW and the Northern Pacific and Great Northern—rumors an inspection tour by James J. Hill and J. P. Morgan did nothing to dispel—led Sycamore boosters to enthuse, "It places this city on the main line of the greatest railway system in the United States."[29]

CHICAGO BYPASS RAILROADS

Rumors of a new line around Chicago were not without foundation. As the twentieth century opened, Chicago possessed a maze of railroads crossing and recrossing one another. Trains entering the city encountered delays, frustrations, and added costs. In November 1902, for example, railroad officials estimated they needed three months to unclog Chicago's rails after a bumper harvest. This situation convinced St. Louis investors—still smarting about losing traffic to the Windy City—to build a bypass, which they rather grandly and somewhat misleadingly named the Illinois, Iowa & Minnesota Railway (II&M) to allow trains to glide around the congested city. There was only one problem, and it was a big one: Chicago already had a belt line. The fifteen-year-old Elgin, Joliet & Eastern (EJ&E) operated 129 route miles from Joliet to Waukegan on a radius roughly 30 miles from the Loop. Owned by U.S. Steel, the consistently profitable operator was unlikely to welcome a competitor with open rails.[30]

Chartered in 1903, the II&M built a twenty-eight-mile line from Aurora northwest to DeKalb. Planned to avoid gradients, it followed a flat but winding course through sparsely populated countryside. The first train traveled from Aurora to DeKalb in October 1904, and the next year its rails reached Rockford from DeKalb. Now nicknamed the "Rockford Route," the II&M completed its line from Momence to Joliet in the same year, thereby attaining its northern and southern termini. But a forty-mile segment between Aurora and Joliet remained unbuilt, so the II&M signed an agreement to run trains over its competitor, the EJ&E, at the exorbitant rate of seventy-five cents per car mile. It did build the five-mile Rockford Belt Railway in 1905 to generate new customers from factories constructed as the city became an important industrial center. The metropolitan area expanded as furniture, watch, plough, and paper manufacturers took full advantage of the new line.[31]

Derisively but appropriately labeled "two tails without a middle," the II&M suffered as competition for Chicago suburban traffic intensified. The Joliet, Plainfield & Aurora Railroad opened in 1904, followed two years later by the Chicago, Aurora & DeKalb, which initially operated with steam traction but soon electrified. These and other lines siphoned off much of the passenger traffic. The II&M seemed to encourage its competitors by operating trains that simultaneously (and slowly) pulled freight and passenger cars. Customer service was a low priority, and the schedule was more a work of fiction than a depiction of reality. One Rockford Route executive acknowledged his trains regularly ran "from one to three or four hours late," and, as it owned almost no passenger cars, the few travelers it did entice often rode in its bumpy cabooses.[32] Perpetually in the red, it paid neither interest on its bonds nor dividends to its shareholders, but it never tasted bankruptcy and would eventually be sold to the Chicago, Milwaukee & St. Paul, which, ironically, it helped drag into receivership.

Avoiding Chicago proved an elusive goal. One early attempt, the 1869 Kankakee & Illinois River Railroad (K&IR), sought to connect Streator with railroads in Indiana. The K&IR captured the attention of neighboring Putnam County taxpayers, who promised $200,000 in share subscriptions to bring the line through their neighborhood. In 1871 the K&IR was folded into the Plymouth, Kankakee & Pacific Railroad (PK&P), projected to run from Plymouth, Indiana, to Bureau Junction through Momence and Streator. Unhappy about the switch, a local man, George Nugent, sued the Putnam County supervisors on the grounds that the county had an irrevocable contract to buy shares in the K&IR. In December 1873 *Nugent v. Putnam County Commissioners* reached the US Supreme Court, where Nugent lost on the grounds that the PK&P had a right to all of the assets of the K&IR.

The PK&P was leased to, and probably originated by, the Pennsylvania Railroad. Its trustees were J. Edgar Thomson, president of the Pennsylvania, and General George Cass, president of the Pittsburgh, Fort Wayne & Chicago. The Pennsylvania connection fell through, and investors proposed another railroad, the Kankakee Belt, to run from South Bend to Zearing, where it would connect with the CB&Q. This fell victim to the Panic of 1873. It emerged from receivership in 1881 as the so-called Three-I Railroad, the Indiana, Illinois & Iowa (III), and building commenced. In 1883 the section from Momence to North Judson, Indiana, was completed, and a decade later it reached South Bend. The west end through Putnam County and across the Illinois River was completed by 1902. In 1906 the III was purchased by the Chicago, Indiana & Southern Railroad, itself owned by NYC constituent Lake Shore & Michigan Southern. Poorly built and easily ignored, it failed as a

Chicago bypass but survived as a coal and grain road of local importance, like so much of the Illinois railroad network.[33]

By the 1880s, so many new lines had been proposed and so much capital had vanished that one contemporary wrote that "the country was full of singed cats." Capital did return to the railroads and construction recommenced, primarily to block competing companies from entering a specific area, and improvements continued to be made. In the 1880s and 1890s CB&Q branch line additions were guided by the rule of thumb that a farmer hauling grain with a horse and wagon could travel only about ten miles; therefore, branches through agricultural lands tended to be built in a grid pattern some fourteen miles apart. In the 1870s most tracks in Illinois were unballasted, which meant they sat on level ground without the small rocks facilitating drainage and smoothing the ride. In the next decade,

as speeds and the weight of traffic increased, ballasting programs were undertaken for the safety and comfort of passengers and freight. By the end of the 1880s nearly all Chicago & Alton tracks had been ballasted. The Iowa Central had a reputation for a rough ride, its main line ballasted with gravel, but soil, cinders, and slack (small pieces of coal) formed the trackbed on nearly half its lines in 1910.[34]

New bridges and more lines brought Illinois railroads to every part of the state and beyond. Expansion was not perpetual, however, as bankruptcy hit the Chicago, Rock Island & Pacific, while a movement to improve roads across the nation presented a new challenge to the railroads. Victims of their own success, railroads had cultivated a yearning for movement, and the aptly named automobile lay just beyond the horizon to meet that desire.

11

EXCURSIONS AND INTERURBANS

Railroads created new markets by advertising special excursion trains for vacationers. Long-distance holiday services gained in popularity as Niagara Falls, the Florida coasts, and other locales became fashionable destinations for escape-minded Illinoisans. Growth in this area did not hinder the development of locally oriented interurban railroads around the turn of the twentieth century. Usually powered by overhead electrical wires and using lightweight equipment, interurbans attracted capital and customers in the first twenty or so years of the new century by offering speedy trips between towns. Illinois was home to two of the nation's largest interurban networks, including one audacious but unsuccessful attempt to link Chicago with St. Louis. Interurbans signaled the desire for fast, frequent, comfortable services and, ultimately, for the types of freedom and mobility automobiles would offer.

EXCURSIONS

Taking a vacation of any distance in the nineteenth century involved riding a train. Railroads catered to a growing taste for travel by operating popular and inexpensive excursions, giving rise to the somewhat exaggerated saying "it was cheaper to travel than to stay at home." Excursions—literally, to run out—provided cheap vacations for people whose horizons might otherwise remain restricted to their immediate surroundings. Group outings were commonplace and often garnered positive press coverage, serving as early tourist advertisements.

An account of a trip to Madison, Wisconsin, for example, described the destination as "the most attractive point for an excursion . . . the prettiest city in the northwest," where the visitors were treated "with great cordiality." Methodists created camp-meeting grounds across Illinois and hired trains to get there, highlighted by the Des Plaines gathering of 1860, which attracted twenty thousand people. The CRI&P offered Illinois Oddfellows special fares to Denver between September and October 1887, for example. The Chicago & Alton sold "excursion tickets" to any station within two hundred miles of its line, offered in cooperation with nine other railroads serving Kansas City. Organizations booked round-trip journeys to special events, as with the Chicago-area teachers' "Grand Excursion" on the Michigan Central for the 1896 National Education Association convention in Buffalo, New York. This included a stop at Niagara Halt "overlooking the grandest panorama in the country."[1]

Niagara Falls was a popular destination for vacationers. Unfortunately, one trip to "the grandest panorama in the country" ended in disaster of historic proportions. On the sultry night of August 10, 1887, at the height of an uncommonly dry summer, two Toledo, Peoria & Western locomotives pulled fifteen cars carrying nine hundred vacationers east toward Niagara. Behind the locomotives were a baggage car, the TP&W superintendent's car, five ordinary passenger coaches, two chair cars, and six Pullman sleeping cars. Widely publicized long before the date of departure and greatly

Figure 11.1. Excursion trains, like this North Shore special for the 1926 International Eucharistic Congress in Mundelein, were sometimes highly decorated. Lake Forest College Library Special Collections.

anticipated by people in the region, the train originated at LaHarpe and made numerous stops to pick up passengers. At Bushnell a coach brought down from Galesburg on the Chicago, Burlington & Quincy was added to the train. Though the train was running ninety minutes late when it left Chatsworth (about seventy miles east of Peoria), the mood was festive as the excursion sped toward the Indiana state line.

Reports about the speed of the train after it left Chatsworth varied—some said it reached thirty-five miles per hour, others sixty—but whatever the case, the engineers were trying to make up for lost time.

As the train entered a downward-sloping prairie, the driver on the lead locomotive panicked when he saw hazy smoke rising from a culvert just three hundred feet ahead of him. A freight engineer with limited passenger-train experience, his first impulse was to shut off steam in order to stop the train. Realizing he did not have enough time to do this, he tried to speed the train over the culvert. The first engine accelerated safely across the burning wooden trestle, but the bridge collapsed under the weight of the coal tender and the second locomotive fell into the culvert, killing its engineer and fireman, followed by the first ten cars. Survivors

Figure 11.2. Telescoped coaches after the Chatsworth wreck (1887). Library of Congress Prints and Photographs Division.

recalled a sudden stillness, then a shock wave and a crashing sound as four of the wooden passenger cars telescoped into each other and "the occupants were simply crushed and mangled almost out of all semblance to human beings." The six Pullman sleeping cars at the end of the train remained undamaged and their passengers escaped with scrapes and bruises. Wood-burning stoves and smoldering grasses threatened to set the wreckage alight, but quick thinking by survivors made sure they did not. For four hours passengers threw soil onto the flames to quench them, keeping fire at bay until a thunderstorm blew through

the area. A total of eighty-five people died as a result of the crash, and many more were maimed.[2]

When the engineer on the first locomotive recovered his senses he continued to Piper City, without the tender, to raise the alarm. People from the area rushed to the scene to pull survivors out of the wreckage and lend what assistance they could. The Illinois Central dispatched a relief train at Gilman, and the Wabash Railroad did the same from Forrest. In Chatsworth the town hall, an engine house, and the TP&W depot served as temporary morgues, while the wounded were sent to private homes around town. On learning of the wreck,

Figure 11.3. Chatsworth wreck remains (1887). Special Collections and Archives, Knox College Library, Galesburg, Illinois.

Chicago newspapers chartered special trains to take their reporters and stenographers to the site, providing fast if not entirely accurate coverage for the next day's papers.[3]

The cause of the accident was a subject of much speculation. Some passengers claimed later to have seen thieves moving through the smashed cars stealing watches, wallets, and jewelry from the dead and dying. This led to a theory that the bridge had been sabotaged by accomplices of the "fiends in human form" who robbed victims. A pile of empty wallets and purses found in the field next to the culvert lent credence to the story that an "organized gang" of "human hyenas" staged the crash. Others claimed that sparks from an earlier train had set the bridge on fire or that the poor state of the track caused the train to derail. Picking up an old theme, the *Chicago Tribune* laid the blame squarely

at the feet of Jay Gould, "who wrecked the road" by stripping it of all rolling stock of value and employees of merit when he had owned it between 1879 and 1884.[4]

In the immediate aftermath, responsibility was pinned on Timothy Coughlin, foreman of the section gang that maintained that stretch of line. The coroner's jury found Coughlin culpable for not examining the line after excess foliage had been burned off earlier in the day to prevent sparks from passing trains setting fires. By failing to do this, he neglected to follow a direct command from the superintendent of the line. The jury heard that sectionmen under his authority had been burning grass just sixteen feet from the bridge and found Coughlin "guilty of gross and criminal carelessness in leaving fires burning along the track in such a dry season and with such a wind blowing." The jury exonerated the TP&W but criticized the company for requiring the burning during dry weather. Coughlin was sent to prison pending a grand jury hearing.[5]

The wreck provided ample opportunity for sensationalistic press coverage. One widely reprinted report opened, "All the railway horrors in the history of this country were surpassed three miles east of Chatsworth last night." It painted the picture as dramatically as possible: the dead had been "mangled in the most frightful manner, many of them having their faces torn away, leaving their brain exposed, while their jaws, fingers, and legs had been torn off," and the injured "passed through a maelstrom more fearful than all the whirling waters they were travelling to see." Compounding the terror were "thieves snatching breastplates and jewelry from the dead and insensible victims," many of whom had been "crushed into a pulp." Journalists reported that the railroad company was quietly disposing of bodies to lower the death count, that it refused to pay claims for damages, and that a criminal gang had destroyed the train for personal gain.[6]

The official report into the derailment, issued in December 1887 by the Illinois Railroad and Warehouse Commission, dismissed these and other fabrications. It found that "all the rumors of tramp malice and diabolism proved to be without basis." It concluded that the "accidental burning" of the bridge over the thirteen-foot-wide gully caused the crash, an event for which the railroad management was to blame for not making a complete and proper survey of the line immediately before the train operated over it. The report recommended checking wooden bridges regularly and replacing them with iron or stone structures. The commission found that the TP&W had issued an order for a full inspection of the line and that the section in which the crash occurred was checked before the train ran into it. The fire, it concluded, began after sparks from an earlier freight train had caught hold in "partly decayed timbers piled against the bridge in place of earth embankments." The report recorded that Coughlin and his men had inspected this part of the road and found the bridge "in sound and good condition." Coughlin, who had posted bail, was released by the grand jury for lack of evidence.[7]

Victim compensation was paid within nine months of the accident despite predictions that the hearings would last a decade or more and that the crash "will make a great big lawsuit . . . that will furnish new precedents and rulings." Rumors about a "scale of payment" offering from $2,000 to the family of a husband killed ($600 more than the death of a wife) down to $500 for the loss of an eye proved unfounded. The Toledo, Peoria & Western never admitted responsibility for the wreck, but it did pay about $500,000 in damages, settling the last claim in May 1888. Two benefit concerts held in Peoria for victims raised $1,444, but an attempt to stage a play in Chicago failed, though the $145 gained from advance ticket sales was donated, along with $25 from the principal performer, to the relief fund.[8]

The name Chatsworth quickly became synonymous with disaster. Passengers on board a Peoria, Decatur & Evansville Railroad train avoided "another Chatsworth horror" when their carriages remained upright after derailing near Mount Pulaski. Excursionists returning from a fishing expedition on the same line reported that a bridge over the Mackinaw River was in such bad condition that "there will soon be a repetition of the Chatsworth horror." At a deadly crash on the Chicago & Atlantic near Kouts, Indiana, "the worst horrors of Chatsworth were repeated." A Wabash passenger train escaped "another disaster similar to that at Chatsworth" when it safely passed over a burning cattle guard near Tolono, and when a Christmas excursion on the Minnesota & Northwestern derailed and fell down an embankment near Freeport "the wonder is that the Chatsworth horror was not repeated." A popular song, "The Chatsworth Wreck," cemented the association with disaster in stanzas such as "A mighty crash of timbers, a sound of hissing steam; / The groans and cries of anguish, a woman's stifled scream" and "The dead and dying mingled with the broken beams and bars; / An awful human carnage, a dreadful wreck of cars." For survivors, solace came from meeting with others who had lived through the disaster, and until 1937 they held annual reunions in Chatsworth.[9]

Figure 11.4. The C&EI Dixieland takes travelers to Florida. Lake Forest College Library Special Collections.

THE FLORIDA "DIXIES"

Despite well-publicized wrecks like Chatsworth, excursions grew in popularity. In the 1890s the state of Florida made a concerted effort to attract tourists. The Chicago & Eastern Illinois took full advantage of this development. Originating in 1849, three small companies merged in 1877 to form the C&EI and operate trains between Chicago and Evansville, Indiana. In 1902 the C&EI was acquired by the St. Louis & San Francisco Railroad (the "Frisco," itself soon purchased by the Rock Island) and C&EI passenger services switched

from Dearborn Street to LaSalle Street station, though the Rock returned to Dearborn Street station in 1913.[10]

A short line by the standards of the day, the C&EI survived by cementing a lucrative alliance with the Louisville & Nashville Railroad (L&N), enabling it to carry more people from Chicago to Florida than any other line and, unusually, to register more passenger-train miles than freight-train miles.[11] Known as the "Dixie Line," the two railroads offered the shortest route between Chicago and Atlanta at 735 miles. C&EI Florida services began running as temporary trains bringing people from the southeastern United States to

The Iron Road in the Prarie State

the World's Columbian Exposition of 1893 in Chicago. These short-term services proved so successful that railroad managers decided to make them permanent in 1896. In 1901 the *Chicago and Florida Limited* began operating, soon to be replaced by the famous *Dixie Flyer* with Pullman cars to Jacksonville.[12]

The C&EI benefited from a vigorous marketing campaign positioning Florida as a desirable tourist destination. Countless booklets, pamphlets, and advertisements promised first-class hotels, gourmet dining, instant relief from respiratory problems, and cures for virtually every disease. One 1904 guidebook went so far as to assert that visitors would encounter no problems with insects or reptiles. The Illinois Central, which also operated passenger services to Florida, produced its own pamphlet called *Florida: The Land of Sunshine*. It held out visions of "luxurious automobiles loitering while Chicago's most famous debutante rains smiles on the young banker from Cedar Falls, Iowa, and silver-templed men stop to comment on the latest tourney of golf, tennis, or polo. The flower of America promenading, resting, or playing—in the sunlight."[13] The publicity paid off, as railroad traffic to Florida continued to grow into the 1920s, yet (as the ICRR pamphlet suggested) the automobile had penetrated the public consciousness. Tourists took the train to familiarize themselves with the Sunshine State but came back by car. State and private tourism facilities catered to their needs, and another railroad monopoly would be fractured.

A NEW COMPETITOR: THE INTERURBANS

As the twentieth century opened, competitive pressure grew from a relatively new form of mass transit, the interurban. Beginning with a series of inventions making the long-distance transmission of electricity technologically feasible and safe, interurban railroads used electric power instead of steam to provide fast, smooth, reliable passenger service. Interurban trains consisted of passenger cars with cabs at both ends for the engineers, known as motormen. These trains specialized in passenger traffic at a time when railroads focused on freight; in fact, passengers constituted between three-quarters

and four-fifths of total interurban revenue in 1910, the opposite of traditional railroads. Interurbans became so extensive nationally that in 1909 one lawyer used them to travel from New York City to Chicago. The journey took five days, and he stayed in hotels each night en route, estimating his travel time at just over thirty-one hours, compared with about twenty hours on the Pennsylvania Railroad.[14]

Illinois became a significant player in the growth of interurbans, and its 1,422 route miles of interurban rails placed it fourth in the nation.[15] Two men dominated interurbans in the state: William B. McKinley and Samuel Insull. Both made the transition from owning electric companies to electric trains, and both built extensive networks, McKinley downstate and Insull in the Chicago area and north into Wisconsin. But their career paths diverged as McKinley rode his popularity and integrity into the US Senate while Insull, cheerfully optimistic in the face of the depression of the 1930s, expanded his empire into heavy debt, bankruptcy, personal disgrace, and self-imposed exile in France.

An investment broker from Champaign, McKinley began building what would become a state-wide network of interurbans in 1900 when he put together a partnership to purchase the unfinished street railway in Danville. By 1906 he had built interurbans to connect his Danville line with other towns, including Springfield, Bloomington, Peoria, and Decatur. His Illinois Traction System (IT) reached Granite City and built the McKinley Bridge across the Mississippi into St. Louis in 1910, the only bridge owned by the line running across it in the area at the time. McKinley flirted with the idea of building to Chicago and running interurbans from the Windy City to St. Louis but settled instead on his four-hundred-mile network, the second largest system in the nation. Unusually among interurbans, the IT attracted extensive freight, which it interchanged onto the Chicago & Eastern Illinois at Glover for the trip into Chicago. But McKinley's dream of a seamless interurban passenger route traversing the state did not reach fruition because he was unable to build a line into the Windy City. Illinois Traction was the first interurban to offer overnight service using sleeping cars, and its

Peoria–to–St. Louis limiteds became known for their luxurious appointments.[16]

In 1927 McKinley's Illinois Traction System became the Illinois Terminal Company, taking the name of an Alton-based line chartered in 1895. The original Illinois Terminal had expanded to provide passenger service on the Illinois side of the Mississippi River and was folded into McKinley's Illinois Traction as the St. Louis & Alton Division. The line became the first interurban to carry a US president on an official visit when it took President William Howard Taft from Decatur, where he had addressed students and faculty at Millikin University, to Springfield, where he served as keynote speaker for the Lincoln Centennial Association, on February 11, 1919.[17]

The other Prairie State interurban king, Samuel Insull, learned about electricity from one of its pioneers. Insull emigrated from England at the age of twenty-one to become Thomas Edison's private secretary, rising in eleven years to the presidency of two Chicago electric companies. He merged them in 1907 to monopolize the market and later added People's Gas to his holdings. A financial innovator, Insull used open-ended mortgages with no maturity date and long-term (up to forty years) bonds to acquire the near-bankrupt Chicago elevated railway in 1914. Two years later he bought the Chicago & Milwaukee Electric Railroad, which he renamed the Chicago, North Shore & Milwaukee Railroad. In 1924 Insull created the Chicago Rapid Transit Company by consolidating four elevated lines in the city of Chicago and its suburbs, and he continued to acquire interurbans, building a business empire worth $3 billion in 1926.[18]

Interurbans often redefined residential and business patterns, serving to stimulate the growth of commercial districts around depots and suburbs. From its debut in 1902, the Aurora, Elgin & Chicago Railway (AE&C) did just that in obscure rural villages like Warrenville, which became one of the many "streetcar suburbs" in the Chicago area. Nicknamed "the Great Third Rail" because it used a ground-level electric rail to power the trains, AE&C trains entered Chicago on the Garfield Park elevated line to avoid street-level running. In 1922 it became part of the Chicago, Aurora & Elgin, which

Samuel Insull bought four years later. Criticized for his extensive monopolistic holdings and facing competition from cars and buses during the Great Depression, Insull declared bankruptcy in 1932 and moved to France, where he died from a heart attack while waiting for a train on the Paris Metro.[19]

Not every interurban line was part of a major system, and not every interurban service used electricity. One minor line, the Macomb & Western Illinois, began operations in 1904 with a small Fornay steam locomotive. A planned conversion to overhead electricity was scrapped because of low traffic density and lower profits, a gas-electric locomotive being purchased instead. A connection to the CB&Q at Macomb fell victim to municipal politics, and a proposed extension south was abandoned when the money ran out. Financial difficulties created by the lack of investors led Macomb & Western Illinois promoter C. V. Chandler to file for bankruptcy. In receivership, it was going to be sold for scrap, but local businessmen rescued it. The steam engines puffed away until the line finally closed in 1930 after it had hauled materials to pave a road parallel to much of its route.[20]

Like many interurbans, the Southern Illinois Light & Power Company combined electricity generation with transportation. Created by merging six localized power companies with two small interurbans (the Sangamon Railway and the Hillsboro Railway) in 1913, it briefly operated the Sangamon Valley Railway. Farther south the similarly named Southern Illinois Railway & Power Company opened a seventeen-mile line from Eldorado, where it connected to the Illinois Central, to Carrier Mills. It combined passenger with coal traffic but failed in 1931 because of the Great Depression. In some areas interurbans saved existing street railroads. After the struggling Rockford Street Railway switched from horses to electricity, extended its lines out to Belvidere, Beloit, Janesville, and Freeport, and changed its name to the Rockford Interurban, it averaged around six hundred thousand passengers annually in the first decade of the twentieth century.[21]

Relations between interurbans and railroads ranged from antagonistic to affable. The Chicago & North

Figure 11.5. Suburbia personified: Lake Forest Station on the C&NW (1900). Library of Congress Prints and Photographs Division.

Western viewed two major interurbans, the CA&E and the Chicago, North Shore & Milwaukee, as enemies. Railroads in the midsection of the state, particularly the Chicago & Alton, were hurt by IT and tried to ignore it. Striking a competitive pose, the Illinois Central announced plans in 1905 to provide its own interurban service from Decatur to Bloomington in an effort to forestall a proposed IT line between those two cities. The ICRR also used lightweight equipment on its Champaign-to-Decatur branch and withdrew the mixed-freight trains it had been running. Nearer Chicago the Illinois Central took a cooperative attitude, hooking Chicago & Indiana Air Line (so named because it was straight) carriages to its own trains for the last leg of their journey into downtown Chicago. It later rented space on its tracks into the city after the route became the Chicago, South Shore & South Bend and operated its own trains. The Chicago Great Western maintained friendly relations with the electric interurbans springing up around it. The CGW interchanged traffic and passengers with the CA&E, Chicago, Aurora & DeKalb, and DeKalb & Sycamore, incorporating their train times into its own timetables to facilitate connections.[22]

The age of the interurban, like the era of excursions, was brief. By 1920 interurbans were retrenching, and by 1950 most of them would be out of business. One notable survivor, still operating today, is the South Shore line, part of the Chicago-area Metra commuter system. Originating as the Chicago & Indiana Air Line, it was purchased and expanded by Samuel Insull, who renamed it the Chicago, South Shore & South Bend Railroad. For other interurbans, road construction and the shift to the automobile for commuting and for recreational travel spelled their doom.

12

COAL AND COMPETITION

Coal lies beneath two-thirds of Illinois and has been mined at one time or another in three-quarters of the state's counties. More than 7,400 mines have operated within the Prairie State's borders. Illinois is in a bituminous (soft coal) field also covering much of Indiana, Ohio, and western Pennsylvania, providing a source of power for individuals and industries along the East Coast and into the Midwest. The price of Illinois coal fluctuated with national demand trends and regulatory shifts, creating periods of boom and bust over which mining companies had almost no control.[1] Railroads were likewise at the mercy of the marketplace until they built lines into coal fields, contracting directly with the mines for the resource.

Coal was vital to the financial health of the railroads, but the operational and commercial problems of finding and transporting it were not the only challenges the railroads faced at the beginning of the twentieth century. In 1915 between three-quarters and four-fifths of total rail revenue came from freight, but the rates being charged in 1915 were virtually the same as they had been in 1900 despite prices rising by 30 percent. The Interstate Commerce Commission (ICC) refused to grant anything other than minimal rate increases.[2] This situation, coupled with a disastrous takeover, led to the Rock Island's first bankruptcy.

Railroads created, met, and built demand for personal mobility, establishing the cultural and psychological preconditions for the automobile. The railroads facilitated their competitors by supporting the Good Roads movement. They hoped to make a profit, to better serve their customers, and to burnish their reputations as public-spirited companies. Ultimately, this backfired. The state embarked on an ambitious program of paving dirt paths and building new roads, which caused passengers to choose cars and shippers to try trucks. Railroads unwittingly participated in their own demise.

REACHING SOUTH FOR COAL

Railroads and coal enjoyed a symbiotic relationship. Steam locomotives need a combustible substance to burn. This boils water, and the steam created, released under pressure, turns rods to power the wheels. Iron and later steel production consumed vast quantities of coal in the quest for high furnace temperatures. On the prairies, wood remained in short supply and coal quickly became a key resource for domestic and industrial use. In 1835 a visiting New York physician recognized the importance of coal to the state's future. Warming himself in front of a fire at a tavern in Ottawa, Chandler Gilman wrote that coal "will be of incalculable advantage to the country" because the limited supply of trees "will very speedily lead to a scarcity of wood." By 1860 nearby LaSalle had become the coal-mining heart of northern Illinois.[3]

Amply endowed by nature and time with a wealth of natural resources, Illinois possesses rich seams of coal, most of it close to the surface. Native Americans used lumps of coal for decoration and jewelry, but it did not become a natural resource to be exploited for its energy

Figure 12.1. A CB&Q coal train strains as it pulls its load near the mining town of Ziegler in southern Illinois.
Lake Forest College Library Special Collections.

until Europeans arrived. Explorers such as Louis Jolliet and Père Marquette recorded outcroppings of coal, and as early as 1679 coal was mined along the Illinois River near Ottawa. This coal appears to have been consumed locally, but in 1810 miners dug a tunnel directly into a seam on the eastern bank of the Big Muddy River in Jackson County. Scottish miners created a temporary village at the site and loaded the coal onto barges destined for New Orleans. Twenty years later, the first railroads in Illinois were built at coal mines. Around 1830 a Belleville mining company constructed a railroad to connect its mine with the Mississippi River, and at

The Iron Road in the Prarie State

Figure 12.2. Locomotives in the ICRR roundhouse in Carbondale wait for their call to duty. Lake Forest College Library Special Collections.

about the same time miners near Murphysboro built an iron road to bypass shallow waters and reach barges.[4]

Coal provided a reliable source of power for locomotives and a profitable commodity for the corporate bottom line. Illinois Central Railroad coal experts reported finding "exhaustless quantities" of coal near its lines that could be mined "under the most favorable circumstances," and the railroad soon replaced wood-burning locomotives with coal-fired engines. Though no Illinois railroads became as dependent upon coal as the large coal-hauling companies in the East—the Virginian Railway springs to mind—it did help keep the trains on track and the books in the black. The Peoria-based Chicago & Illinois Midland (C&IM) was the closest equivalent, a line jointly owned by a utility and a mining company whose traffic relied heavily on coal extracted near its tracks. By 1906 the Chicago & Alton could justifiably be labeled a coal line because 53 percent of its freight

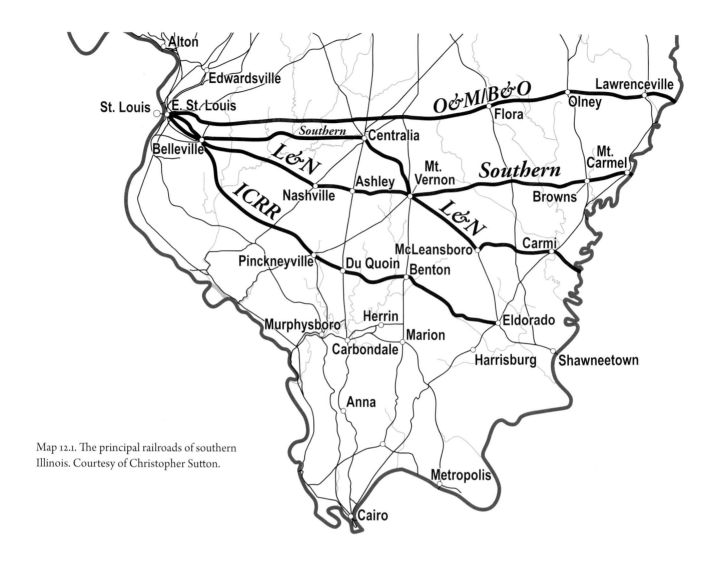

Map 12.1. The principal railroads of southern Illinois. Courtesy of Christopher Sutton.

was coal.[5] Long, heavy trains carrying coal for homes and factories became a common sight all across Illinois.

Southern Illinois was known for its rich deposits of carbon, leading one journalist to write, "The most remarkable and at the same time most valuable feature of Southern Illinois is the immense coal formation that underlies a great part of its surface." In 1855 a Scottish visitor examining coal pits owned by the Illinois Central near Du Quoin encountered a shaft dug through limestone into a coal seam seventy feet below the surface. The entire coal reserve covered several square miles, reaching west to the Big Muddy, down which mining companies floated coal to St. Louis. Carbondale—despite its name, a center of cotton cultivation in the decades after the Civil War—was the gateway to some of the most productive coal mines in the state. But not

all seams were equal, and mining was not eternal. When the Civil War made it impossible to bring coal across the Ohio River from Kentucky, the naval yards at Cairo and Mound City temporarily purchased it from new mines at Bowlesville, near Shawneetown. The end of hostilities reopened access to Kentucky coal—cheaper to mine and purchase—and by 1890 Bowlesville was out of the coal business.[6]

Railroad demand for coal increased as the number and duration of runs expanded, locomotives grew larger, and steel rails replaced iron. Coal mining gave railroads a reason to build into southern Illinois. Four main lines crossed Little Egypt from East St. Louis to the Indiana line, each one constantly on the lookout for new traffic. The northernmost, the Ohio & Mississippi Railroad, became part of the Baltimore & Ohio

Railroad (with which it had long been associated) with formation of the B&O Southwestern in 1893. This line was frequently identified as the border of Little Egypt, below which three lines radiated out from Belleville: the Jacksonville, Louisville & St. Louis Railway (the Southern Railway of Illinois after 1900), which operated the line to Mt. Carmel via Centralia and Mt. Vernon; the St. Louis & Southeastern (merged into the Louisville & Nashville in 1879 shortly after it opened) through Mt. Vernon and Carmi; and the St. Louis, Belleville & Southern through Du Quoin and Eldorado to Shawneetown, built as the Cairo Short Line but operated by the Illinois Central. The ICRR completed a direct route from Chicago to St. Louis in 1899, when it began operating the ninety-seven-mile "Wing Road" through Litchfield.[7]

Harrisburg, platted in 1851 seventy-five miles northeast of Cairo, grew to prominence as a mining center in the 1870s after the Cairo & Vincennes Railroad (C&V) came through. By 1890 the C&V had become part of the "Big Four" (Cleveland, Cincinnati, Chicago & St. Louis Railroad), and the town had grown into the center of an extensive and expanding mining district. In an effort to reach this field, the Chicago & North Western constructed an eighty-five-mile branch from Peoria to Nelson, on its Chicago to Clinton, Iowa, main line. Laid in 1902 and 1903, it was the first stage of a route to St. Louis and into the southern Illinois coal-mining region. At Peoria, the North Western ran its trains over the Peoria & Pekin Union and became a tenant in the Peoria passenger depot. In 1913 the St. Louis, Peoria & North Western extended the Nelson line another ninety miles south to Girard, near the tip of the southern Illinois mining region, where it interchanged with the Macoupin County Railway, also controlled by the North Western. In the same year, the North Western reached East St. Louis, a crucial freight hub, via the Litchfield & Madison Railway, the self-proclaimed "St. Louis Gateway Route." The result was a catastrophe for the already beleaguered C&A, which recorded a record deficit in 1914 largely because of coal traffic shifting to the more convenient North Western.[8]

The Chicago, Burlington & Quincy put corporate consolidation ahead of physical expansion. The CB&Q was a group of independent but operationally linked lines—a system—in which each member was a separate corporate entity with its own general manager, an expensive luxury. Ready to refinance its debt and unable to collect data because of a confusing jumble of financial arrangements and jealous territorial magnates, it began consolidating its holdings in 1899. The first move was to purchase outright the Chicago, Burlington & Northern (CB&N), the CB&Q's line to the Twin Cities, by exchanging stock and purchasing lines the parent corporation leased east of the Mississippi River. The Burlington issued a fifty-year Illinois Division mortgage worth $85 million, which served as a first lien on the CB&N. In 1900 the company did the same for lines it leased in Missouri and Iowa, and by 1910 the CB&Q had replaced the hodgepodge of nominally independent entities with a unified corporate structure. This program left only a few branch and narrow-gauge lines to be purchased, which the company did in the second decade of the twentieth century.[9] The process of streamlining the Burlington's finances allowed it to exploit increased traffic opportunities across the Midwest.

Merger fever gripped the railroad industry in the 1890s. Rumors of a new transcontinental line combining the Great Northern and the Northern Pacific with the Chicago, Milwaukee & St. Paul and an unnamed eastern line circulated, though those rumors proved unfounded. James J. Hill of the Great Northern and the Northern Pacific took control of the Burlington in 1901 and immediately demanded faster, more efficient services. New ties, longer passing sidings, grade reductions, curve widening, and improved terminal facilities accelerated the flow of traffic. Ever vigilant, the penny-pinching Hill noticed that four daily freights from Savanna to St. Paul loaded only four hundred tons on average, while the locomotives were rated for two thousand tons. He ordered fuller loads and longer but fewer trains to reduce costs and spent $1.5 million rebuilding the West Burlington, Iowa, shops to service heavier

Figure 12.3. A CB&Q switching move near Herrin, in the heart of Little Egypt coal country. Lake Forest College Library Special Collections.

locomotives. Other Hill-driven innovations included buying a headquarters building near Chicago's Union Station to centralize administration and installing a new type of printing telegraph to improve communications on the line between Chicago and Galesburg.[10]

Coal remained a prime commodity for railroads, and Hill soon turned his eagle eyes to that resource. Before 1900 the CB&Q's main source of the mineral was around Herrin, but that type of coal did not suit the ever-more-powerful locomotives being introduced. Hill sent a coal specialist to evaluate deposits elsewhere in southern Illinois and subsequently bought an existing line from Concord to Centralia, which he extended fifty-five miles to Herrin. Opened in 1906,

this line allowed the company to carry better-quality coal from Franklin, Williamson, and Saline Counties into the Burlington heartland and to St. Paul for the other Hill lines. The Burlington then pushed farther south to Neilson, where it interchanged with the Chicago & Eastern Illinois Railroad in 1909. The next year the Burlington built a line from West Vienna, on the C&EI, to Metropolis, on the Ohio River. In 1917 it bridged the Ohio River to Paducah for direct access to the Nashville, Chattanooga & St. Louis Railway to interchange passenger and freight trains, including Kentucky coal.[11] The consequence was an expanded traffic base, solidifying the Burlington's place as a major regional railroad.

The Iron Road in the Prarie State

Around 1890 the adoption of the "holding company" changed railroading. Holding companies were corporations engaged exclusively in financial transactions, operating no trains and carrying no freight or passengers. They could be used in any industry and seemed to legitimate what earlier generations had considered manipulation and theft. The introduction of a holding-company structure led to disaster for one stalwart of the railroad landscape, the mighty Chicago, Rock Island & Pacific Railway (CRI&P), when a financial group known as the Reid-Moore syndicate bankrupted it for the first time in its existence.

Corporate lawyers William H. and James H. Moore, sons of a New York banker, made their fortunes in mechanized biscuit and match manufacturing before forming a tin plate partnership with Daniel G. Reid and William B. Leeds. The syndicate sold its holdings to the new United States Steel Corporation around the turn of the century and looked to the railroad industry for other opportunities. Reid-Moore's sights settled on the Rock Island, until then a conservatively run and well-respected company. Rock shareholders had a reputation for holding on to stock in realistic expectation of increased value and regular dividends, and its management was known for caution and reliability. But by 1900 the company needed additional financing to build new lines and purchase better rolling stock to compete in a world of expanding track mileage, faster services, and sophisticated yard operations.[12]

The Reid-Moore syndicate quietly purchased Rock Island shares and took control in August 1902. Astutely retaining the patrician Ransom Cable, the company's long-serving septuagenarian president, as figurehead, the syndicate accelerated a program of expansion into the Southwest. It increased the capitalization of associated companies—like the BCR&N—to inflate the total value of its holdings and attract additional investment. The Rock Island reached into the growing markets of Texas and pushed its Oklahoma and New Mexico subsidiary toward a connection with the Southern Pacific at Tucumcari, New Mexico, for access to California.

In January 1903 Reid-Moore incorporated the Chicago, Rock Island & Choctaw Railway to build from Tucumcari east to connect with its Amarillo line.[13]

As its plans and proposals garnered positive publicity, the syndicate began "watering" the stock by issuing shares with a face value higher than the money borrowed to purchase them. Reid-Moore began by inflating the value of the original Chicago, Rock Island & Pacific *Railway* from $60 million to $75 million. But the syndicate did not yet control all of the Railway shares and the voting rights that came with them. To do this it created the Chicago, Rock Island & Pacific *Railroad,* incorporated in Iowa but existing only on paper. This holding company, capitalized at $125 million in stock and $75 million in 4 percent bonds, was designed exclusively to own the Railway shares and nothing else. The syndicate then incorporated a second holding company, the Rock Island Company of New Jersey, to issue $96 million in common stock and $54 million in preferred shares, the last of which endowed the directors—Moore, Moore, Reid, and their allies—with voting rights.[14]

The two holding companies increased the total book value of the syndicate's Rock Island investment from $60 million to $521 million. But there had been no commensurate improvements to the physical plant or to the operational efficiency of the railroad upon which the value of these shares was supposedly based. It was a paper growth only, a classic example of artificially inflating the value of a corporation by watering the stock. Reid-Moore offered $270 worth of shares in the holding company in exchange for $100 worth of outstanding Railway stock, taking advantage of the greed and gullibility of investors. This share-swap gave the syndicate control of the voting shares and with it the power to do whatever it wanted with Rock Island finances. One contemporary summarized the actions of the syndicate as transforming Rock Island shares "from investment securities to media for speculation." Of the three corporations bearing the name "Rock Island" only one, the original CRI&P *Railway,* actually operated trains. Reid-Moore then established a fourth corporation, the Rock Island Improvement Company, to protect rolling stock and other assets from liens under the Railway's mortgages.[15]

Figure 12.4. A Rock Island switch engine waits for work in Peoria. Author's collection.

With its financial position apparently secure and its power unrivaled, the syndicate set about increasing the size of the railroad by purchasing other lines. The Rock Island made a play for the Erie Railroad, leading observers to believe it wanted to create a true Atlantic to Pacific transcontinental. Conjecture then reached a climax when the Rock Island offered shareholders of the Frisco $120 worth of ten-year bonds in the Iowa and the New Jersey holding companies in exchange for $100 of Frisco shares. Soon investors and journalists speculated that the Rock Island was on the verge of entering into a strategic alliance with the Atchison, Topeka & Santa Fe to reach the Pacific Ocean. The Reid-Moore syndicate did make some purchases, and by the end of 1903 the New Jersey holding company controlled the Frisco, the

C&EI, the Chicago & Alton, and the Pennsylvania-based Lehigh Valley Railroad. The syndicate controlled 15,874 miles of railroad, an astonishing number by the standards of the day. In comparison, the CB&Q owned or leased 9,125 route miles; the Illinois Central 4,762; and the Union Pacific a relatively paltry 3,584 miles. Had the Rock persisted under Reid-Moore ownership it would have become the behemoth of the industry.[16]

But it did not last. The Reid-Moore scheme was underhanded, greedy, sharp, and completely legal; it was also a massive pretense, and it went badly wrong. Purchases had been hastily concluded, and the imperative to expand at all costs doomed it. By 1905 the Rock Island's reputation was in tatters as rumors of an unprecedented bankruptcy shocked Wall Street.[17] Though

The Iron Road in the Prarie State

Figure 12.5. How the railroads believed "good roads" would work: an M&StL delivery van. John W. Barriger III National Railroad Library, St. Louis Mercantile Library, UMSL.

receivership was avoided this time, the corporation's future looked bleak. The fatal weakness proved to be the Rock's obligation to repay outstanding Frisco bonds within ten years of purchasing that railroad. The Frisco, with its wandering lines and decrepit rolling stock, did not pay a dividend between 1903 and 1909, at which point it looked as if the syndicate would meet neither principal nor interest payments.

A member of the Rock Island board, Benjamin Yoakum, made the Reid-Moore syndicate an offer it could not afford to refuse. Playing the syndicate at its own game, Yoakum bought the Frisco and the C&EI from the

Rock Island for $37.50 per $100 of common stock, leaving the maturing bonds to be repaid by the New Jersey holding corporation. Yoakum could not make his new companies profitable, however, and in 1913 they filed for bankruptcy. In 1914 the Rock Island followed suit, and the Reid-Moore house of cards collapsed. Having burned through millions of dollars of investment capital and destroyed the reputation of a staid and famous railroad, the syndicate lost control of the corporation after a bitter boardroom battle in April 1915. By then Ransom Cable, its former president and the Reid-Moore figurehead, had been dead for five years, saved from

Figure 12.6. Members of the League of American Wheelmen, which lobbied for good roads, visit President William McKinley in Canton, Ohio. Library of Congress Prints and Photographs Division.

the humiliation of seeing the line he had so carefully managed brought low. Despite calls for the property to be dismembered and sold in separate sections, the Rock Island survived, for the time being.[18]

GOOD ROADS

As the railroads battled each other for traffic and fended off raiders, they missed an important development. In 1926 Illinois Central Railroad general manager George Patterson confidently asserted, "There is absolutely no danger of motor vehicles ever supplanting railroads." History would prove him wrong, but he was not alone

in failing to see how trucks and cars could replace trains. Application of the internal combustion engine to highway use seemed a natural complement to the iron horse. Railroad corporations therefore strongly supported the Good Roads movement, a loose confederation of government officials, automobile manufacturers, and road builders. Railroad executives went along for the ride because they thought weatherproof roads would allow customers to deliver freight at any time of the year, but the long-term impact could hardly have been more catastrophic. Astute lobbying and smart publicity, some of it exploiting public irritation with the railroad industry,

The Iron Road in the Prarie State

created a crescendo of support for using bricks, concrete, or macadam to pave the state's mud roads. Auto enthusiasts and well-advertised car races helped hype the new machines.[19]

It all began innocuously enough. Originating in the 1890s and promoted by the federal Office of Public Road Inquiry (OPRI, established in 1893 by the US Department of Agriculture), the gospel of good roads announced itself by laying a strip of hard road near the entrance to the New Jersey Agricultural College. Momentum accelerated with the formation of the National Good Roads Association in 1901, with state branches across the country.[20] In the Prairie State, the Illinois Good Roads Commission (IGRC), soon to be superseded by the Illinois Good Roads Association, promised that hard roads would end seasonal unemployment, eliminate trade recessions, and assist railroads ("the greatest sufferers of all") by guaranteeing year-round deliveries to depots, freight houses, and elevators. The OPRI estimated that paved roads would reduce transportation costs by as much as 60 percent.[21] Road builders and their allies rushed to stoke the fires of public opinion.

Successive groups kept the good roads agenda close to the surface of American public life. First came the League of American Wheelmen, which lobbied in the 1880s for better roads on behalf of socially elite bicyclists who wanted to escape from the masses and skip taking the train. The OPRI circulated an immense volume of literature and generated national awareness of the potential for widespread automobile ownership. Farmers, organized principally by the Grange, and advocates of rural free mail delivery (initiated by the Post Office in 1913) also made supportive noises about hard roads. The Illinois Highway Department got in on the act, sending out a fleet of speakers, most of whom addressed Grange meetings. The Illinois Highway Improvement Association (IHIA) played a crucial role in training legislators' eyes on road building, while paving interests such as the Danville Brick Company convinced Illinois county engineers to test bricks for road construction.[22]

Complaints about mud roads were as old as the state and advocates argued that paving them would reduce the cost of living. Good roads literature hinted at a redistribution of income from corporations to individuals, claiming "no man pays more than he is benefited and usually considerably less" because property taxes levied on manufacturers and other businesses would more than compensate for household payments. By 1920, six years before George Patterson's statement, "the era of good roads 'talk' gave way to the era of good roads 'construction'" and proponents promised that trucks would soon be "relieving the burden on the railroads" by carrying "milk, eggs, poultry, fruit, and vegetables" directly from farm to city. As a consequence, "the branch line railroad will yield its freight, at a time not far distant, to the motor truck and the good road." Writing in *Highway Magazine,* published in Chicago by culvert manufacturer Armco "in the interest of good roads," Illinois superintendent of highways S. E. Brandt justified using motor taxes to build new roads because motorists came from all walks of life. Perennial paving publicist Arthur L. Dahl argued that trucks would allow farmers to reach markets offering the highest prices instead of remaining captive to local buyers. "Verily," he exclaimed in a flourish characteristic of the proroad rhetoric of the 1920s, "the motor truck is a versatile, enduring and faithful friend of man."[23]

Americans learned to love their cars despite unreliable engines, poor infrastructure, and drivers more enthusiastic than skilled. The car offered personal mobility and freedom from the timetable. Get in and go: no ghastly waiting in the rain for a train that may or may not arrive; no hoping desperately for a clean seat in a warm spot; no discomforting delays or time-consuming transfers. Americans came to desire cars, though they were more aspiration than reality for most people until after World War II. Autotourists driving through and camping in the countryside could, with a little ingenuity and courage, travel almost anywhere, escaping railroads and hotels. Over three-quarters (77 percent) of all intercity freight and virtually every intercity passenger (98 percent) traveled by rail in 1916. But in that year private car registrations nationally reached 3.3 million, and just six years later 8.1 million registered cars motored across 390,000 miles of hard-surfaced roads. Illinois had 131,000 cars in 1910 (one car for every fifty

Figure 12.7. A "good roads" delegation meets with President Calvin Coolidge (far left) at the White House. Library of Congress Prints and Photographs Division.

inhabitants of the state), tripling to 375,000 by 1918 and exploding to 1.2 million in 1925 and 1.6 million in 1929, or one car for every five Illinoisans. In 1920 Americans averaged 50 miles of intercity travel by car and 450 miles by train. In 1930 those figures had shifted dramatically: train journeys fell to just 219 miles annually, while intercity car travel averaged 1,691 miles.[24] Cars were becoming ubiquitous, paved roads led the way, and the rails were hurting.

Road paving got off to a slow start in Illinois but soon gained traction. In 1913 counties began selling road-construction bonds, but that proved inadequate. In 1916 President Woodrow Wilson signed the Good Roads Act, authorizing the federal government to match state

funds for building interstate roads, a signpost to the future. The first federal appropriation was a modest $75 million; two years later, lobbying by the IHIA and the IGRA helped convince Illinois voters to pass a referendum authorizing the state to sell $60 million in road bonds. The bond, backed by automobile license fees, resulted in the construction of 4,800 miles of hard-surfaced roads by 1925, when a second bond was issued. No state politician embraced road-paving projects as enthusiastically as Len Small, who served as governor from 1921 to 1929. Small perceived road funding as a way to reward his friends and punish those who opposed him. After LaSalle County had rejected his handpicked proroad candidate for the state senate, he limited new

The Iron Road in the Prarie State

Figure 12.8. New automobiles arrive in Colchester (1913). Western Illinois University Libraries, Archives, and Special Collections.

road construction there to less than a mile during his two terms in office.[25]

Road openings became elaborate community rituals. Cook County road commissioners invited the public to participate in a Motor Pilgrimage to celebrate eighteen miles of new concrete roads in the suburbs of Chicago. A dedication ceremony in Des Plaines and a parade along the new hard road was followed by dinner at the Chicago Motor Club. Alice Roosevelt Longworth, celebrity daughter of recently deceased president Theodore Roosevelt, ceremonially opened Chicago's new Roosevelt Road in 1920. When the Chicago to Danville segment of the Dixie Highway opened in 1921, the *Chicago Tribune* hailed its 146 miles as "the longest stretch of modern road in Illinois." A new rural highway linking Sheffield, Neponset, and Kewanee in 1922 was celebrated with "parades, oratory, and concerts," culminating in a dance

along the new road. By the end of the 1920s such ceremonies had become so commonplace that organizers were reduced to begging residents and businesses to participate, though the opening of a major highway remained newsworthy. Route 2, stretching the length of the state from South Beloit to Cairo, was inaugurated in 1929 to a chorus of press praise.[26]

Ignoring warning signs about losing revenue to road traffic, railroads jumped aboard the good roads parade. Choosing to believe paved roads would serve their purposes by improving harvesttime deliveries, railroad corporations began advising farmers and businesses on how to create local chapters of the National League for Good Roads. The first Good Roads Train left Chicago for a three-month journey over Illinois Central Railroad tracks to New Orleans in 1901. This twelve-car train, subsidized by the OPRI, stopped in sixteen cities across five states. Road-grading machinery, classrooms, display areas, and two "hotel cars" rolled along the rails, spreading the message that roads were the future. Machines paved a mile or more of dirt road to demonstrate good road techniques using local materials. Public lectures about roads around the world by University of Illinois professors and government officials at venues like the Austin Opera House in Effingham and the Union Depot at Delavan informed local taxpayers. The propaganda worked. On January 7, 1929, the New York Central's Chicago to New York City *Twentieth Century Limited* set a one-day record for the most passengers carried by a single train. Many of them traveled to Gotham for an automobile show.[27]

Railroad expansion in Illinois had, by the 1890s, slowed to a few branch lines. Exploiting the rich Illinois coal fields was a crucial stage in the creation of new markets and the development of larger, more powerful locomotives. The economies of scale these engines offered allowed longer trains, fewer runs, and better service.

Building into southern Illinois made commercial and operational sense for lines like the Chicago & North Western and the Chicago, Burlington & Quincy. But all was not well.

The late nineteenth and the early twentieth centuries witnessed several troubling developments for the railroad industry. The bankruptcy of the Chicago, Rock Island & Pacific came as a shock despite concerns about the use of holding companies to inflate corporate values. By 1920 the future was no longer being shaped by railroads. In the nineteenth century the train had been a harbinger of modern life, its arrival a sign of industrial and social maturity, but the twentieth century would become the age of the automobile. Larger cultural shifts, especially the continuing move toward individualistic values, accompanied this change. Railroads would need to redefine their economic role, a process evermore-stringent government regulation and the forces of inertia slowed.

13

PROGRESSIVE REGULATION

The perceived excesses symbolized by the Reid-Moore syndicate's bleeding of the Chicago, Rock Island & Pacific Railway contributed to a political and social climate conducive to further regulation. Behind this renewed regulatory fervor was a fear of dependence on enormous economic entities. Corporations appeared to be getting too big, too powerful, and too likely to control an entire industry. Democratic republics were not supposed to give rise to monopolies dominating entire sectors of the economy, but that is precisely what seemed to be happening. When Minnesota-based railroader James J. Hill and Wall Street banker J. P. Morgan merged the Chicago, Burlington & Quincy into a holding company already containing the Northern Pacific and the Great Northern Railroads, the government called foul. President Theodore Roosevelt, spurning Morgan's gentlemanly offer to "send your man to see my man and tell him to fix it up," instead mobilized the might of the federal government and established a precedent for future trust busting.

But the creation of the Northern Securities Corporation was the culmination of a long-running process that had started innocuously enough when railroads established informal pools to share traffic and rationalize the railroad network. Though the system did not fit Illinois perfectly—there were simply too many different railroads reaching in too many directions—these so-called communities of interest did not technically become monopolies. This nuance escaped the regulators who then debilitated the industry by restricting railroads' ability to respond to changing market conditions. Trucks, cars, buses, and eventually airplanes benefited and subsequently competed successfully for passengers and freight.

TRAFFIC POOLING AGREEMENTS

Informal traffic pools developed to end rate wars when railroads serving the same areas agreed to charge uniform tariffs. Railroads had entered into rate agreements as early as 1856, but creation of the Chicago and Omaha Association in 1870, commonly known as the Iowa Pool, signaled a new departure. The Chicago & North Western, the Burlington, and the Rock Island agreed to divide freight carried between Chicago and Omaha. The Iowa Pool collapsed but was superseded by the larger, more official-sounding Western Freight Association in 1884.[1]

At least four types of pools had developed by the end of the nineteenth century: large associations covering great swaths of territory; small organizations operating in a single state or region; single-city bureaus or committees; and arrangements governing excursions and other types of special passenger services. Illinois lines to the east were covered by the Central Freight Association and a parallel Central Passenger Association, while railroads operating from Lake Michigan to the Rocky Mountains formed western equivalents. Because of its size and the complexities of its traffic patterns, Chicago had its own passenger association. But, like many informal arrangements, pools were not watertight: when the

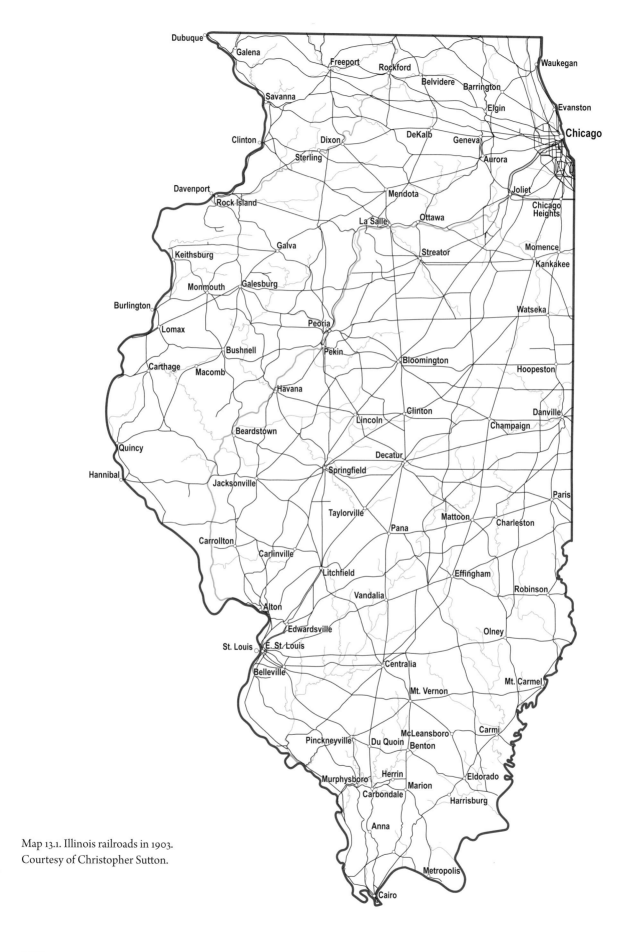

Map 13.1. Illinois railroads in 1903.
Courtesy of Christopher Sutton.

Central Passenger Association refused to admit the Chicago, Cincinnati & Louisville in the early twentieth century, it responded by offering a five-dollar fare, one dollar less than its competitors. Other companies followed suit, and the pool collapsed. This was at one level inevitable: pools failed because they had no legal standing even before being outlawed by the Interstate Commerce Commission in 1887. Railroads reorganized pools in that year to comply with federal antipooling regulations and again in 1898 after the US Supreme Court ruled against the revised version.[2] Carefully skirting the law, traffic pools increased in number, strength, and efficiency in the early twentieth century under communities of interest agreements.

COMMUNITIES OF INTEREST

So many railroads operated so much track in Illinois in the first decade of the twentieth century that one railroad manager likened the map of railroads to "a plate of wet spaghetti."[3] For many officials the jumble constituted an overbuilt network with too many railroads running too close together and generating too little traffic to be profitable. If consolidated ownership or informal pooling agreements were going to prove impossible to maintain, perhaps some sort of coordination might be feasible.

Upon closer inspection, the "wet spaghetti" revealed distinct patterns of interconnectedness. From the 1890s to the First World War regional clusters of loosely affiliated railroad corporations known as communities of interest, a form of self-regulation by the industry, replaced the pooling agreements of the second half of the nineteenth century.[4] The New York Central and the Pennsylvania controlled railroads in the Northeast and the mid-Atlantic, including the Baltimore & Ohio, the Erie, and the Norfolk & Western. Also in the Northeast, though primarily north of Boston and stretching into Maine, was the New Haven system, controlled by J. P. Morgan. A second Morgan-assembled syndicate owned the bulk of the main lines in the Southeast, while James J. Hill's firm grip on the Northwest—his empire stretched from Minnesota to the Pacific coast—gave him a virtual monopoly on the northern tier of the

United States. Edward H. Harriman controlled the two biggest systems in the West, the Union Pacific and the Southern Pacific, but could never quite integrate his Illinois Central into those other holdings.

Regional monopolies broke down in the Midwest and the Southwest. In the latter, the Gould Lines, including the Wabash, the Missouri Pacific (MoPac), and the Texas & Pacific, controlled a corridor from St. Louis into New Mexico, but other lines proliferated. The Midwest remained even more open. James J. Hill did gain control of the Burlington and operated it in concert with his Great Northern and Northern Pacific Railroads, but other lines—such as the Rock Island, the Chicago & North Western, the Milwaukee Road, and the Little Grangers—remained independent of each other.[5] Both the New York Central (via the Lake Shore & Michigan Southern Railroad) and the Pennsylvania (through its Pittsburgh, Fort Wayne & Chicago affiliate) boasted lines into the Windy City.

THE EMPIRE BUILDER ENTERS CHICAGO

Tucked away in a corner of the renovated St. Paul (Minnesota) Union Depot is a photograph of James J. Hill. Virtually invisible at the bottom of a display in the secluded "historic staircase," the placement minimizes Hill's impact on the railroads of the United States. And that impact was immense, his power reaching into Chicago and to the West Coast from his Twin Cities base. When the Burlington reorganized in 1899–1900 it attracted interest from the Union Pacific and the Great Northern Railway. Hill encouraged Burlington trains to run into St. Paul and Minneapolis over his Great Northern, hoping to foster good relations and smooth the way to a merger.[6]

An immigrant from Canada with a penchant for helping shovel snow when his lines were blocked, Hill gained his empire through a combination of vision, timing, and luck.[7] He pushed the Great Northern past Minnesota and across the Great Plains from St. Paul to the Pacific without land grants. When the neighboring Northern Pacific declared bankruptcy during the Panic of 1893 he joined forces with J. P. Morgan to engineer a takeover. The two oligarchs then set their sights on

Figure 13.1. James J. Hill, the "Empire Builder," who wanted the CB&Q to gain direct access to Chicago. Library of Congress Prints and Photographs Division.

acquiring the Burlington, but a powerful rival emerged in the shape of Edward H. Harriman, chairman of the Union Pacific. Harriman met with Burlington directors but they could not agree on a share price and the negotiations ended. Hill's interest was prompted by his desire to own a route from the Twin Cities into Chicago. He had three options but the one his board wanted, the Milwaukee Road, rejected an overture. That left the Chicago & North Western and the Burlington.

Hill and Morgan aimed for and got the Burlington, but not without a fight. As soon as it became clear his rivals had gained control of the CB&Q, Harriman stepped up his efforts to purchase stock in Hill's Northern Pacific. Harriman hungered for a direct path into the Windy City for his Union Pacific. The protracted bidding war for the CB&Q caused a minor national recession and wiped out the savings of thousands of investors. Undeterred, Hill and Morgan called a truce with Harriman and his primary backer, John D. Rockefeller, to create a holding company called Northern Securities to control the Northern Pacific and the Great Northern. Chartered in New Jersey (which had laws conducive to this type of arrangement), Northern Securities held a controlling interest in the two northernmost transcontinentals and, after 1900, the CB&Q. But the assassination of President William McKinley in 1901 and the

The Iron Road in the Prarie State

Figure 13.2. J. P. Morgan bankrolled Hill's Northern Securities holding company and tried to rebuff President Theodore Roosevelt's trust busting. Library of Congress Prints and Photographs Division.

Figure 13.3. E. H. Harriman almost upset Hill and Morgan's plans but was eventually brought onboard.
Library of Congress Prints and Photographs Division.

subsequent accession to the White House of his vice president, the progressive Republican Theodore Roosevelt, all but guaranteed such an arrangement would gain the attention of the federal government.[8]

HILL REBUFFED

Northern Securities smacked of monopoly to the new president. Though the Supreme Court rejected a petition from the state of Minnesota challenging the legality of Northern Securities, federal action against the holding company succeeded. After soliciting legal opinions on the matter, Roosevelt instructed the Justice Department to break up Northern Securities on the grounds that it was an illegal combination in restraint of trade. Using the Sherman Act, the federal government ordered Hill, Harriman, and Morgan to dismantle the holding

company. They appealed the decision, and, after two years of legal battles, the Supreme Court ruled 5–4 in favor of the federal government in 1904, establishing Roosevelt's reputation as a "trust buster" and cementing the powers of the ICC. One historian speculated that the Northern Securities case blocked the development of three or four supersystems to monopolize the American railroad industry, but the ruling did little to alter the balance of power in the railroad industry.[9]

Despite the Supreme Court decision, Hill remained adamant that the federal government had no right to interfere in business affairs. A thin-skinned Social Darwinist who had once removed a depot after the town's mayor sued the Great Northern, he defended trusts, telling a 1906 Senate committee, "The law of the survival of the fittest is a natural law that we can safely adopt."

He justified purchasing the CB&Q on the grounds that "nobody has lost anything by this transaction" and called the merger "merely an incident on the road to efficient service." The Supreme Court ruling had little practical effect, because Hill's other railroads owned 48 percent of Burlington, and the widely used phrase "Hill Lines" reflected the continuing reality of their financial and operational interconnectedness. They even cooperated to build the Spokane, Portland & Seattle Railway in 1905 to further that linkage in the Northwest. But the Northern Securities case represented the most important example of legal action under Sherman antitrust laws and demonstrated the power of the federal government.[10]

RATE REGULATION

Railroad rate setting favored large customers who could demand secret rebates and those in well-served areas for whom competition could mean lower rates. Railroads often gave rebates because shippers could threaten to use a competing line unless they received refunds on the official rates published by the ICC. In response to complaints about unfair discrimination, Congress passed the Elkins Act in 1903 to eliminate rebates. Pennsylvania Railroad president Alexander J. Cassatt consulted with President Roosevelt and the bill's namesake, West Virginia senator Stephen B. Elkins, while it was being drafted. The railroad's general counsel, James A. Logan, "largely wrote the actual bill." The 1903 law gave federal courts the power to enforce ICC rates. The Elkins Act also allowed the courts to punish rebating railroads and the recipients of refunds. Despite widespread evasion, the act stopped the loss of perhaps 10 percent of gross railroad revenues.[11]

Lawsuits under the Elkins Act revealed the magnitude of rebates. Eighteen railroads were charged in federal court in July 1905 with rebating livestock shipments. The defendants included the Alton, the Burlington, the Chicago Great Western, the Chicago & North Western, the Illinois Central, the Minneapolis & St. Louis, and the Rock Island. In September 1905 officials of the meatpacking firm of Schwarzchild and Sulzberger—including traffic managers in Kansas City and Chicago—were

fined $25,000 for conspiring to accept rebates from railroads. Honor among thieves is notoriously unstable and sometimes multiline rebate agreements broke down. In December 1905, for example, officials of the Alton, the Burlington, and the St. Paul, along with several major meatpackers, were indicted in Kansas City for providing rebates on shipments of meat from East St. Louis to New York. The refunds came to light when the empty-handed and indignant Lehigh Valley Railroad complained to the ICC because its cut of the income had been expended on rebates by other lines.[12]

But identifying rebates was not always simple, as the example of the Chicago & Eastern Illinois Railroad and Standard Oil demonstrated. In his 1908 address to Congress, President Roosevelt excoriated the "malefactors of great wealth" whose underhanded dealings were, he and other progressives felt, creating unfair advantages for large corporations. He specifically pointed to a rebate Standard Oil received for petroleum shipments over the C&EI from Dolton, near Chicago, to East St. Louis. The published rate was eighteen cents per one hundred pounds; the secret rate was six and a quarter cents, comparable to the six cents the Chicago & Alton charged Standard Oil to ship petroleum from Whiting, Indiana, to East St. Louis. Judge Kenesaw Mountain Landis, later to gain fame as baseball's first commissioner, fined Standard Oil $29.2 million on August 3, 1907, for violating the Elkins Act. Standard Oil successfully appealed the ruling—hardly a unique event for the controversial Landis—on the grounds that Dolton lay within the Chicago Switching District, in which low rates facilitated manufacturing in nearby towns.[13]

Provisions in the Elkins Act of 1903 only partly clarified the situation. After hearing numerous complaints about price discrimination (long-distance shippers paid lower per-mile rates than short-haul shippers), the ICC determined that differential rates (charging different per-mile rates to ship the same product) had to be eliminated. That way, simply producing more of a product or shipping it longer distances would not reduce shipping costs. Working together as regional rate bureaus, railroads collectively set rates—also called tariffs—under ICC regulation using a system called value-of-service pricing, by which customers of high-value products subsidized the rates of shippers who could not afford high transportation costs. Thus, steel manufacturers paid a premium in order to lower the cost of shipments for farmers and small-town merchants.[14]

The law did, however, create uncertainty about exactly what constituted a rebate. In March 1903 the Burlington sent station agents a list of what managers believed the Elkins Act banned. This included offering free or reduced tickets to hotel keepers and hotel employees, postal employees traveling on personal business, and "policemen and other municipal employes and those filling quasi-public positions." The company also believed the law made it illegal to offer reduced or free rates to theater agents, owners, managers, or actors. Reduced fares for "the families of army and navy officers, for clergymen and missionaries, and free or reduced rates for officers or leaders of [voluntary] societies" were also no longer legal, according to the letter. CB&Q managers feared the new law would punish station agents for discriminating against some shippers while favoring others. The circular may also have been a preemptive strike against free passes for customers, politicians, and lawmakers, which American railroad officials viewed as an expensive burden.[15]

The legislative focus returned to rate setting in 1906 after a series of highly publicized rate increases. Suffering under the twin stresses of inflation and their own success in attracting business, railroads across the country appealed for higher rates to generate much-needed investment in their physical plant. The railroads needed to improve capacity, efficiency, and safety. In 1906 Congress passed the Hepburn Act to strengthen the powers of the Interstate Commerce Commission and close loopholes in the Elkins Act. The Hepburn Act gave ICC rulings the force of law. Instead of relying on the courts to enforce regulations, the ICC could set mandatory maximum—though not minimum—"fair, just, and reasonable" rates. None of those three key words were defined, opening the door to multiple interpretations.

The new legislation also clarified the restrictions on free passes and mandated standard bookkeeping methods. Railroads were required to submit annual reports to the ICC, which employed professional staff to examine railroad accounts. The rule banning free passes helped the railroads by ending a practice bordering on extortion. Public criticisms of free passes as favors for which a return would be expected raised the specter of a corrupt quid pro quo. To offer two examples of officials "pestering" railroad officials for free travel, in July 1898 the Chicago Police Department requested passes from the CB&Q for a police lieutenant's daughters (Lizzie and Bessie) who "wish to spend the school vacation near Streator, Ills," and in December of the same year, the city's chief grain inspector requested passes for two of his inspectors to visit the towns of Oregon and Galesburg, though whether on business or pleasure is unclear. Both requests were granted, and revenue was lost. Yet, like the Elkins Act, the Hepburn Act created uncertainty among railroads. The C&EI, for example, began billing all shippers for switching their cars, a service they (and other roads) had been providing free of charge, to avoid running afoul of the law's prohibition on benefiting only selected customers.[16] The complexity of railroading created regulatory ambiguity and confusion.

HARRIMAN UNDER THE PROGRESSIVE MAGNIFYING GLASS

As one of a new breed of financiers imaginatively and legally leveraging small sums of money into giant returns, Harriman attracted controversy. His successful and highly profitable (to himself and his associates) financial maneuvers led to the rise of what one of his allies dismissively labeled the "Harriman Extermination League."[17] Roosevelt's elevation to the US presidency in September 1901 symbolically inaugurated the period of reform known as the Progressive Era, giving Harriman's enemies ammunition, as the new chief executive would become honorary leader of this imaginary "league." The kind of financial wheeling and dealing in which Harriman specialized came under intense scrutiny by Progressives who viewed the world through a moral lens. Harriman's actions were legal, but reformers argued that huge profits and the potential for developing monopolies acting against the public interest meant they should be outlawed.

Harriman became embroiled in a retrospective investigation of his takeover of the Chicago & Alton. This inquiry was part principled attack on unscrupulous deals and part political revenge. The Alton affair began innocuously enough in 1898 when Arthur Stillwell, a Kansas City railroader, and George Gould, who had inherited his father Jay's lines in the Southwest, were rumored to be interested in buying the C&A. Worried about a hostile takeover, Windy City banker John Mitchell, a major shareholder in the C&A, approached Harriman. The Alton was suffering in 1898 because of its insularity and its refusal to engage in rate wars or to join traffic pools. The railroads with which it connected began to interchange with the Santa Fe after that company's Kansas City to Chicago line opened in 1888 and with the Rock Island, which built a branch to connect Kansas City directly to its own main line. More interchange traffic was lost when the Illinois Central agreed to operate Cleveland, Cincinnati, Chicago & St. Louis Railway (Big Four) services into St. Louis. Harriman commissioned an investigation of the economic standing and prospects for the C&A from Samuel Felton, a financial specialist. Felton recommended Harriman buy the road, appoint a new management team, and invest $52 million to improve the C&A. Over President Timothy Blackstone's objections Harriman did just that, and the Alton was "reorganized financially, and extensively rebuilt and reequipped." Harriman transformed the Alton by spending some $15 million to straighten out curves; replace its old bridge over the Mississippi River at Louisiana, Missouri; and construct a second main line.[18]

But in 1906 the Alton became a political football when President Roosevelt asked the Interstate Commerce Commission to investigate Harriman's financial stewardship of the railroad. Harriman, who would soon lose control of the property, claimed the president was taking revenge for Harriman's refusal to donate funds to the Republican Party in 1906. In 1904, according to Harriman, Roosevelt asked for a $200,000 gift to the Republican Party for the election campaign of that year as part of what one critic labeled "a general shakedown" of corporations.[19] Harriman paid up but later asserted that he had provided funds for the New York governor's race in return for Roosevelt agreeing to appoint Chauncey Depew ambassador to France, a promise Harriman said Roosevelt failed to keep.

Relations between the two men, once quite friendly, cooled. In 1906 the Republican Party again approached Harriman for campaign cash, but this time he refused and supposedly told party leader James Sherman that Harriman "could buy whichever politician suited him on his own." Sherman related the story of this meeting to Roosevelt shortly afterward. Roosevelt claimed in 1906 that he did not ask Harriman to raise money for the 1904 campaign and publicly called him "an undesirable citizen." He later wrote that Harriman had asked him several times to appoint Depew to the ambassadorship, but Roosevelt had refused to make any such bargain. Roosevelt asserted that his communications with Harriman regarding the 1904 election pertained to the race for the governorship of New York and a message to Congress, not funding for a presidential campaign.[20]

Franklin Lane, chairman of the ICC, launched an official investigation of the Alton transaction at Roosevelt's request. The commission charged that a $6 million stock dividend—representing a 30 percent bonus to the members of the syndicate—paid from bonds was evidence of corruption. Harriman defended the payment by pointing out that the dividend derived from recapitalizing $12 million in permanent improvements written off by the previous management. Though "perfectly legal and justified," the payment raised ethical questions in the eyes of Roosevelt and other Progressives. The ICC published a formal report condemning Harriman for paying the dividend out of the proceeds of the bond sale. Selling bonds below par was also condemned, as was issuing $40 million in stock that had no face value. Illegal in some states, this practice was gaining ground at the beginning of the twentieth century but smacked of speculation to Progressives.[21]

Other commentators leaped to Harriman's defense, at the time and more recently. Journalist and explorer George Kennan, Harriman's first biographer, published a vindication of Harriman's role, incurring the wrath of Harvard professor William Z. Ripley by finding errors in the latter's analysis of the Alton case. Kennan charged Ripley with deliberately misrepresenting the facts. Ignoring the ethical mindset of the Progressives, historians sympathetic to Harriman have interpreted the Alton investigation as Roosevelt seeking "to embarrass Harriman and to pay him back for his refusal to generate campaign funds" and as evidence for the "archaic economic thinking of the Progressive era." Harriman, according to one historian, remained "undeterred by those less able to understand the way business in the new century was to be conducted."[22]

THE EIGHT-HOUR DAY

By 1910 railroaders outnumbered the combined workforce of the construction, cotton textiles, iron, and steel industries; railroad corporations employed 4 percent of all US workers and generated a total revenue of $3 billion, or 8 percent of GNP. Sections of this powerful labor force gained an important legislative victory in 1916 with passage of the Adamson Act. Named for William C. Adamson, chairman of the House Interstate Commerce Committee, the act established an eight-hour maximum workday for train crews—already the best-paid wage-earning railroaders—on interstate railroads. The Adamson Act passed because railroad presidents rejected the brotherhoods' demand for the shortened working day and rebuffed President Woodrow Wilson's attempts to broker a compromise. The brotherhoods called for a strike to begin on September 4, 1916 (Labor Day), and Wilson, fearing it would cripple preparations for the United States' entry into World War I, called on Congress to take action. The hastily drafted bill took effect on January 1, 1917. When the new

year arrived the railroads refused to implement it and the brotherhoods voted to strike. Pushed by the Wilson administration to test the constitutionality of the Adamson Act, the Supreme Court upheld it by a 5–4 vote on the grounds that the act operated in the public interest. The companies retreated, averting a strike.[23]

By setting an eight-hour precedent, the Adamson Act was a victory for all working people. Passage signaled a shift in the national political scene, with Democrats positioning themselves as the party of labor, while Republicans, slowly shedding their Progressive wing, appealed more overtly and more consistently to business than they had under Theodore Roosevelt. This change set the tone for the next seventy years as the American Federation of Labor (AFL), the brotherhoods, and other labor unions allied themselves with the Democratic Party, an alliance cemented by Franklin Delano Roosevelt's New Deal.

Prior to the First World War the railroads endured a period of public scrutiny and economic uncertainty. Some thirty-seven thousand route miles, almost 15 percent of the total, were owned by companies in receivership, including the Wabash, the Rock Island, the Frisco, and, on the East Coast, the New Haven.[24] From 1914 through 1918 war halted the fall, but rate regulations reduced income and blunted corporations' ability to attract investment capital to make vital improvements. But railroads were central to the nation's economy and remained the country's largest privately owned, nonagricultural industry, with over a thousand corporations operating 250,000 route miles and employing 1.7 million people on the eve of war.

The Iron Road in the Prairie State

14

WORLD WAR I AND THE 1920s

The First World War—or the "war to end all wars," as President Woodrow Wilson called it—nearly brought private ownership of the railroads to an end. Refusing to cooperate and unwilling to coordinate train movements, the lines became so congested in the East and so empty in the West that the federal government took them over. Plans were prepared, and seriously considered, to leave the trains in government hands at war's end. But the probusiness Republican Party regained power in 1920 and the owners regained their property. The 1920s witnessed a massive program of railroad improvements when as much total capital was expended on railroad physical plant and rolling stock as had been the case during the entire history of the industry up to 1920. Yet even as the railroads improved, public policy turned slowly toward highways. During the 1920s the state of Illinois ranked first in the nation for miles of concrete roadways, and a vibrant auto-building industry developed.[1] The Good Roads movement continued to gain adherents, and traffic switched slowly but surely from rail to truck, car, and bus with devastating long-term effects for Illinois railroads.

WAR AND FEDERALIZATION

The advent of war in Europe in 1914 overburdened the railroads. Foodstuffs and military supplies bound for Europe choked the ports, provisions rotting and matériel stagnating. The railroads could not keep up with the volume of freight being moved because rates

had remained unchanged since 1910 and vital infrastructure improvements were deferred as capitalists, wary of an industry that could not guarantee profits, refused to invest.[2] The one-way flow of traffic caused gridlock along the East Coast. As a means of preparing for war, the railroads fell at the first hurdle, and the situation had not improved when the United States entered World War I in 1917.

Suspicious of the government and of each other, railroad officials refused to cooperate in the national interest.[3] To make matters worse, a strike in the mining industry created coal shortages in the winter of 1917, raising fears of people freezing in their unheated homes and disaster if an economic downturn followed. President Wilson authorized a federal agency, the United States Railroad Administration (USRA), to run the railroads. As compensation for lost earnings, Congress passed the Railroad Control Act, which gave each company an annual subsidy equal to the average operating income for the previous three years. In a breathtakingly unrealistic gesture, the government promised it would return the railroads to private control in the same physical shape it had found them. All of this elicited undisguised anger from railroad officials, but Wilson believed there was no other way to get the trains running again. He appointed his son-in-law, investor and lawyer William Gibbs McAdoo, as director general for railroads.

The power of the USRA was one example of the expansion of the federal government during wartime. In 1916 the Council for National Defense created an

Figure 14.1. C&A shopmen at a "patriotic sing" in 1919. Three years later they would be on strike. McLean County Museum of History, Bloomington, Illinois.

advisory commission formed of representatives from industry, including Daniel Willard of the Baltimore & Ohio, to coordinate economic activity. But vast shortages remained, including, according to some estimates, the need for an additional 158,000 freight cars. Wartime priorities meant building locomotives for the European Allies and canceling orders at home. As a result American railroads had fewer locomotives in 1917 than in 1914, even though demand had increased.

Wartime conditions pushed prices and wages, and hence the cost of living, upward for all Americans. One of the challenges confronting railroads was a tripling in the price of coal mined in Illinois over the first three months of World War I. Only when the State Council

of Defense enacted price controls did the cost of coal drop. By then railroad employees were finding work in better-paid manufacturing industries all across the state, and many joined the army.[4] In response to increasing costs and competition for workers, McAdoo enacted 18 percent passenger and 28 percent freight rate increases in 1918, but these were soon canceled out by pay raises ranging from 16 to 48 percent. The Railroad Wage Commission mandated that employees who had been earning less than forty-six dollars a month should receive an additional twenty dollars, the largest proportional increase.[5]

Women represented one pool of potential workers to offset wartime labor losses. With a few exceptions and despite heady hopes that sex-segregated workplaces could be banished, women tended to be assigned to clerical and other occupations traditionally reserved for them. Seventy percent of the 101,785 women in railroad work in the United States in October 1918 entered clerical positions. Some women were assigned to the roundhouses and shops, where they were mostly to be found cleaning locomotives and operating turntables, but they were only 5 percent of all workers in those locations. Other women worked as welders and electricians, as crane operators and telegraphers. Railroads followed McAdoo's advice to keep them in work traditionally considered appropriate for women, though the CB&Q did train thirty-eight women in Chicago to work as claims agents investigating insurance cases. The Chicago Great Western's "Corn Belt Belles" were excluded from track or train work, being hired instead as clerks, agents, and cleaners.[6] The C&NW hired women as "coach cleaners, filing clerks, and depot custodians" and gave them other "low-level assignments," positions returning soldiers were only too happy to let the women keep once the global hostilities ended.

Before he told women where they could not work, McAdoo rationalized the national railroad network. He began by dividing the country into three regions, with all lines west of Chicago falling into a single unit headed by C&NW president Richard Aishton. Duplicate passenger services were eliminated, and the USRA demanded that all freight movements take the shortest possible route to minimize delays, creating winners and losers. The Chicago & Alton was one of the latter. It suffered because traffic into Chicago was diverted onto other railroads with shorter routes at Springfield, Bloomington, or Joliet. The circuitous main lines of the Chicago Great Western and the Minneapolis & St. Louis meant those Little Grangers also lost traffic to companies with more direct routes. The Toledo, Peoria & Western did not contribute in any notable way to the war effort, having entered receivership just prior to the USRA takeover and not leaving it until 1925.[7]

Healthy roads profited during the war. The Illinois Central benefited from prewar expenditures totaling almost $50 million, including new rolling stock and plans to increase freight car usage. In April 1917, as US armed forces entered the conflagration, the ICRR registered a new high of forty car miles per car day, compared with the national prewar average of twenty-six. By filling cars to maximum capacity, the CB&Q set new records for revenue ton miles in 1918, including a 20 percent increase in livestock and 10 percent increase in agricultural products. After the Panama Canal opened in 1914, oceangoing vessels saved approximately seven thousand miles of travel between the East and West Coasts of the United States. While this development contributed to the Milwaukee Road bankruptcy, other companies benefited. The Illinois Central enlarged its port facilities in New Orleans in order to stimulate traffic. To attract new business it hired agents in southeastern industrial and commercial centers and in ports serving canal traffic. Purchasing a controlling interest in the Central of Georgia, the Illinois Central inaugurated through passenger services from Chicago to Savannah, Georgia, and Jacksonville, Florida, and opened a direct line to Birmingham, Alabama. The Burlington accelerated work on its Chicago freight terminals with the outbreak of war, organizing the Burlington, South Chicago Terminal Railroad Company and buying land near the Calumet River adjacent to Chicago's Belt Railway for future expansion.[8] Improvement was the exception, however, and wartime demands pushed railroads as close to capacity as they could without substantially improving the physical plant. By the end of the conflict the system badly needed rebuilding.

Armistice signaled a controversy-riddled return to private control. The brotherhoods, many observers, and even some officials supported implementation of the Plumb Plan advocating federal control of the railroads, but the government followed the original timetable for reinstituting private ownership. Some railroads experienced significant deterioration despite government guarantees to the contrary. The Wabash was one of many lines demanding compensation from a $500 million federal fund for postwar repairs, though its request for $13 million was reduced to $1.5 million after investigation. The Pullman Company claimed $24 million to fix the rolling stock it leased to railroads but received only $7 million. Samuel Felton, president of the Chicago Great Western and director general of military railways, complained his line had suffered by losing hard-earned traffic to its competitors, while deferred maintenance left the track in shabby condition and its freight cars worn out. The $1.6 million it received from the federal government provided little solace. Grievances were commonplace, but compensation remained invariably lower than the demands railroad officials made.[9]

MILWAUKEE SINKS

The Chicago, Milwaukee, St. Paul & Pacific (known after 1900 as the Milwaukee Road) was the only western railroad to purchase track east of the Windy City. This line, the Chicago, Terre Haute & Southeastern (CTH&SE), ran from Chicago Heights to Westport, Indiana. In 1910 its creator, banker John R. Walsh, was imprisoned and a consortium of Chicago banks took it over. After trying unsuccessfully for a decade to sell the line, the consortium was on the verge of abandoning it when the Milwaukee Road showed up. Unfortunately for the latter, its president, H. E. Byram, a career railroader with no experience in large financial transactions, handled the negotiations disastrously. The leader of the banking consortium, Frank D. Wetmore, tricked Byram into paying full price for bonds worth only twenty-five cents on the dollar and ten dollars for CTH&SE shares selling at around one dollar each.[10] Wetmore had conned Byram into overpaying, weakening an already wounded Milwaukee Road.

Time was also running out for the independent Illinois, Iowa & Minnesota Railway after the war. The "Rockford Route" was reorganized in 1908 as the Chicago, Milwaukee & Gary Railroad (CM&G) and gained a new nickname, the "Gary Road." Though it never made money, the Gary did not lose too much of it either and even enjoyed moments of prosperity during World War I. It earned $77,658 in 1917 and $41,484 in 1918, but by 1920 passenger revenue had collapsed to a scant $98, and its owners were looking for a buyer. They found a willing partner in 1922, when the Milwaukee Road leased and then bought it.[11]

The purchase of the Gary Road by the Milwaukee Road was tinged with corruption. Takeover talk began in earnest at a 1915 dinner in St. Louis when a member of the syndicate owning the CM&G discussed it with Milwaukee investor Percy Avery Rockefeller, son of William Rockefeller. The younger Rockefeller liked the idea, but Milwaukee Road management rejected the Gary as financially unsound because of the cost of trackage rights over the Elgin, Joliet & Eastern between Aurora and Joliet. Rockefeller did not let the idea go, and his business partner, Samuel Pryor, convinced powerful investors to pressure the Milwaukee into purchasing the Gary Road. A private investment firm working with Rockefeller brokered the takeover, for which he and Pryor earned a substantial commission.[12]

The Milwaukee wanted the CTH&SE for access to southern Indiana coal fields and used the Gary Road to connect with the Terre Haute line. Both acquisitions were strategically smart but proved financially foolish: already in debt, the Milwaukee Road shouldered $23 million in additional liabilities from the two companies along with a combined operating deficit averaging nearly $5 million annually. Depressed business conditions in the Pacific Northwest, wartime wage increases, and the opening of the Panama Canal cut into traffic volume while raising costs. Poor business decisions and self-interested profiteering by directors didn't help. The added burdens of the Gary and CTH&SE were the proverbial straw breaking the camel's back, plunging the Milwaukee Road into the largest bankruptcy in American history to that point.[13]

THE 1922 SHOP WORKERS STRIKE

The poor condition of the railroads after World War I placed additional burdens on the workers who maintained rolling stock. In 1921 US railroads had 1,754 repair shops employing 418,455 workers in an almost exclusively male preserve. The second highest number of shop workers (36,070) was to be found in the 143 maintenance and repair facilities located in Illinois. In small towns like Taylorville and Carmi, railroad facilities provided important sources of employment, while at major junctions like Bloomington and Centralia they sustained

The Iron Road in the Prarie State

Figure 14.2. The busy C&A Bloomington shops, closed for the duration of the 1922 shopmen's strike. Library of Congress Prints and Photographs Division.

thriving economies. Shopmen worked in a variety of occupations, including machinists and carmen, painters and upholsterers, blacksmiths and metalworkers. To overcome shopfloor divisions, Illinois Central shopmen attempted early in the twentieth century to create a union, culminating in a strike from 1911 to 1915. The company used strikebreakers, outsourced repairs, and took out injunctions against picketing to end the strike and destroy the union.[14] Further organizing would need to be national in order to succeed.

Conditions had improved considerably during World War I. Shopmen enjoyed unparalleled job security and, under the auspices of the USRA, higher wages than ever before. Yet their pay lagged behind workers

in trades outside the railroad industry, and the groundwork for further action was laid in 1920, when shopmen recognized the AFL Railway Employees' Department (RED) as their bargaining agent. Simultaneously, the Transportation Act of 1920 authorized the Railroad Labor Board to adjudicate disputes between employers and employees while loosening the requirements for mergers, potentially weakening labor's position.[15]

Like other railroaders, shopmen had benefited from a modestly prolabor Wilson administration, but state sympathy ended in 1920 with the election of Republican Warren G. Harding. Harding's calls for a postwar return to "normalcy" encouraged capitalists to undo labor's wartime gains. Some railroads began by closing shops and laying off shopmen. Then the Railroad Labor Board, packed with Harding appointees, announced a 12.5 percent reduction in shopmen's wages to take effect on July 1, 1922. Shopmen retaliated by walking out that same day, taking their tools with them. Three-quarters of all shopmen joined the action, bringing the railroads perilously close to shutdown.

Trainmen initially stayed on the job, but there were exceptions. Crews at Roodhouse, a Chicago & Alton junction between Springfield and the Mississippi River, claimed the line was unsafe. They refused to report to work and used their automobiles to halt the few trains still running. Hundreds of passengers were stranded, one train from Roodhouse to Bloomington arriving twenty hours late, and for three days no freight trains ran between Roodhouse and Kansas City. The Chicago & Eastern Illinois detoured its trains onto other railroads to enter Chicago because a strike by signal repairmen rendered its line into the Windy City impassable.[16] At its height every shopman employed on the C&A, the CGW, and the Chicago Junction joined the strike. Ninety percent or more struck the C&NW, M&StL, the Milwaukee Road, and the C&EI, while 70 percent or so were out on the Rock Island and the Burlington. Of the principal Chicago-based roads only the Illinois Central saw a turnout below 50 percent, probably because of memories of the disastrous prewar strike.[17]

Shopmen on the Alton took a militant stand against the use of replacement workers. Brought to the Bloomington shops from around the state, these "scabs" met a hostile reception when they arrived and had to be unloaded in the relative safety of a stockyard. They could not live in the community because of the threat of violence against them, so the company built temporary accommodations in the C&A yard. The few permanent employees who remained at work suffered repercussions after the strike ended, including having bricks thrown at them by their fellow employees.[18]

Violence doomed the strike in the court of public opinion. Widespread community support and passivity among sympathetic local police forces could not defeat the antipathy of the national press and the alarmist rhetoric of business and government leaders. In Clinton a picketing shopman was injured and his fourteen-year-old son was killed by gunfire. Two strikers in Chicago were shot outside Illinois Central shops, and an attempt to arrest a striker in Aurora caused a riot. Fearing further troubles on the C&A, five National Guard companies traveled to Bloomington armed with barbed wire and a machine gun.[19]

Rising tensions caused both sides to dig in. Managers and clerks on the Minneapolis & St. Louis serviced locomotives. Shopmen at Roodhouse tarred and feathered a roundhouse foreman as a warning to others who refused to support them. The mayor of Moline was arrested for tearing down a copy of an injunction posted in a city park. The National Guard stood at readiness when protests threatened to become violent in Decatur. Governor Len Small appointed 251 deputy marshals to protect railroad property in Illinois.[20]

Shrinking coal supplies and Red Scare tactics labeling strikers Communists helped turn the American public against the shopmen. Coal miners had been on strike since April, and stockpiles were dwindling by July. To make matters worse, freight and passenger services were canceled in ever greater numbers, as locomotives had to be sidelined for lack of maintenance. For the striking workers themselves, alternative employment was difficult to obtain because they had to report daily to union offices in order to receive strike pay and participate on picket lines. In late July the RED tried to end the strike after the Harding administration promised to protect seniority and guarantee all strikers would be rehired, but railroad presidents refused to accept the terms.[21]

The railroads' intransigence and President Harding's failure to broker an agreement angered the four major brotherhoods, which had been sympathetic to the shopmen but had taken no action. The situation worsened on August 5, 1922, when a striker was killed in Joliet and National Guard troops, called in to keep the peace, shot at picketers. Newspapers responded hysterically to the discovery of a plan to dynamite a New York Central express train and derail an Illinois Central maintenance-of-way train, calling the plots a "reign of terror." The *Alton Hummer,* a C&A express from

Figure 14.3. Representatives of the AFL RED met with President Harding in an unsuccessful attempt to end the 1922 shopmen's strike. Library of Congress Prints and Photographs Division.

Chicago to Kansas City, was deliberately derailed by an open switch. The leader of the Brotherhood of Locomotive Engineers complained about Pinkertons endangering workers' lives, and locomotive crews went on strike until the guards left. The walkout spread to other lines, the shopmen's anger intensified, and acts of sabotage and shootings increased in frequency. Relations between railroaders and officials on the CB&Q became so heated that Aurora was virtually under martial law.[22] The 1922 national shopmen's strike proved to be the most violent railroad strike since 1877.

The federal government finally acted on September 1, 1922, with an injunction restraining strikers from interfering with the repair of rolling stock. An attempt to end the strike road by road was only partly successful, and farmers became worried about the prospects for shipping their harvests to market in the fall. After the RED brokered an agreement with the Baltimore & Ohio, ICRR shopmen returned to work in November, and others followed suit, but those on the Rock Island and the Burlington stayed out for two more years. The failure of the shopmen's strike demonstrated the power of management and the powerlessness of workers confronting aggressive owners, hostile newspapers, and an antagonistic federal government.[23]

The year 1922 would also be remembered as the year history caught up with the Chicago & Alton. Built to haul coal and agricultural products, its route had few manufacturing plants, it interchanged almost no industrial goods, and virtually all of its freight traffic took the form of unprofitable short hauls averaging 185 miles. Passengers on the line traveled a paltry sixty-five miles per trip, and the C&A operated three expensive freight terminals (Chicago, St. Louis, and Kansas City), owned only a thousand miles of track, and paid $500,000 annually for space at Chicago's new Union Station. In August 1922, owing $14 million and with little hope of repaying it, the C&A filed for bankruptcy.[24]

The receivers quickly realized the company was unlikely to meet its debt, and their task would be to reorganize it while running the trains and finding a buyer. Its most recent owner, the Toledo, St. Louis & Western, emerged from bankruptcy in 1923 as a subsidiary of the New York, Chicago & St. Louis Railroad (the Nickel Plate), but the Nickel Plate did not want the Alton. It took seven more years until finally, in December 1930, the Maryland Trust Company paid $23 million to buy the Alton on behalf of the B&O, which wanted to extend its operations in Illinois. The sale occurred after a ninety-minute open-air auction on the platform of the C&A station at Wilmington. The receivers agreed to a new financial package allowing Maryland Trust to purchase the C&A and pay dividends to bondholders, but shareholders lost their entire investment.[25]

THE BEGINNING OF THE END
FOR PASSENGER TRAINS

Passenger traffic increased dramatically during World War I but slowly fell thereafter. Short periods of recovery, most significantly the years of World War II, could not halt long-term decline. The Chicago & North Western carried 16.7 million passengers in 1917 but half that number, 8.1 million, in 1923. The Burlington experienced a drop of about a third during the 1920s. The situation was better on the Illinois Central because electrification of its Chicago commuter line attracted new riders. In the first quarter of the twentieth century, passenger revenues increased almost fourfold, though this did not keep pace with the sixfold growth of freight revenue. Between 1924 and 1928, however, ICRR passenger traffic dropped from 971 million passenger miles to 917 million

passenger miles, most of them lost to automobiles. For the decade, passenger traffic fell by one-fifth.[26]

The decline could be even more dramatic on smaller lines. Chicago Great Western officials watched helplessly as the total number of passengers plummeted from 2.5 million in 1920 to 730,730 in 1929. Trying to halt the losses, it created a luxurious overnight train from Chicago to the Twin Cities, the *Great Western Limited*, to compete against the North Western, the Milwaukee Road, and the Burlington. The Little Granger attempted to attract business travelers by arriving in St. Paul at 7:30 AM and in Chicago Grand Central Station at 8:30 AM, but the losses continued because the other lines were shorter and faster. The Toledo, Peoria & Western exceeded the million mark in passengers for the first time in 1911, but in 1924, when a new highway running parallel to much of its line from Peoria into Indiana opened, the number of passengers dropped to 421,629. By 1929 its few remaining passengers were riding in the caboose of a freight train listed on the timetable as a daily mixed service in each direction. Defeated by the automobile, all TP&W passenger services vanished in 1930.[27]

The Alton became the first railroad company in the country to launch a bus service, but that failed miserably. Trying desperately to reduce the number of loss-making rural passenger services, the C&A petitioned the ICC in 1925 to begin operating buses. Delays in obtaining authorization, complaints from private bus companies, and equipment problems meant the proposed road services never left the depot, and in 1933 the C&A sold its buses. The Chicago & North Western experimented by substituting buses for passenger trains on rural branches and using them as feeders for main line services in the 1920s. In conjunction with the Union Pacific, C&NW began a joint bus operation in 1929, offering direct carriage from Rockford to Omaha, Nebraska, and connecting to Union Pacific transcontinentals. In the 1930s the Burlington Transportation Company, an arm of the CB&Q, operated bus services on numerous routes, replacing a few unprofitable rural passenger trains and saving $175,000. In 1934 it even inaugurated long-distance runs from Chicago to Los Angeles and

San Francisco. Motor coaches did not supply a magic bullet to boost profits, however, and in that year the Burlington Transportation Company posted a deficit of $58,000.[28]

A FALSE MECHANICAL DAWN

Railroads constantly tinkered and experimented with locomotive designs. One radical concept, introduced in the late nineteenth century, tried to eliminate the locomotive completely by attaching gasoline engines to the undersides of passenger cars with control cabs for drivers. Lighter than steam locomotives, requiring less maintenance, and potentially being operated by a single engineer, they were in retrospect an early stage in the development of diesel power. Self-propelled in the sense that they did not have a power car separate from the passenger compartment, they were nicknamed "doodlebugs" because they seemed to scurry along the tracks.

In 1898 the CB&Q built a gas-electric railcar at its Aurora shops but abandoned it because the heavy prime mover became so hot that it melted the moving parts. The company tried again in 1922, when it built a coach on a Mack bus chassis. It also constructed six small self-propelled cars, though the two engines (one on each wheel-bearing truck) had the unfortunate habit of pulling in opposite directions simultaneously, the car moving in neither. [29]

Another innovator, the Chicago Great Western, experimented with a gasoline-powered Patton railcar in March 1898. Despite low fuel costs of one cent for every two miles, compared with fourteen cents for a coal-fired steam locomotive, the machine proved unreliable and quietly disappeared.[30] A decade later the CGW did buy McKeen gasoline-powered motor cars, primarily for its Iowa branches. Developed by the Union Pacific's superintendent of motive power, these distinctive cars had a knife-shaped front nose, a low-level central doorway, and porthole-like windows.[31] The CGW used them sparingly, and steam retained its stranglehold on most services.

A significant advance was registered in 1924, when the Electro-Motive Company (EMC) delivered the first of its gas-electric passenger cars, the M-300, to CGW. EMC made several key advances in gasoline-powered technology, including using distillate, a waste product left over from gasoline and benzene production, as a fuel. EMC also introduced an articulated truck bearing the weight of two carriages, a key to the development of diesel streamliners in the 1930s. The Burlington bought more of these EMC doodlebugs than any other railroad. The fifty-seven gas-electrics paid for themselves in savings on lightly traveled branches, delivering small freight, express packages, and the US mail.[32]

The Chicago & Alton, emulating the Burlington example of do-it-yourself, rebuilt two of its coaches into rail cars in 1924. Loud and unreliable, the jerry-rigged machines proved unpopular with passengers and maintenance crews alike, and the company scrapped the vehicles in 1928. At the same time, the Minneapolis & St. Louis acquired three gas-electrics from General Electric, putting one on the Peoria to Oskaloosa, Iowa, run in 1929. The C&NW purchased several gas-electric doodlebugs for rural branches in the 1920s, having also converted wooden coaches into gas-powered units.[33] Adopted to save money, these railcars met with varying degrees of success, but they could not arrest the declining number of people traveling by train.

The turmoil of wartime federalization and increased competition from road transportation were nothing compared to what awaited the railroads, along with the rest of the country, in the 1930s. The type of financial distress endured by the Rock Island and the Milwaukee Road would be confronted by virtually every railroad in the nation, and passenger traffic continued to fall, while freight also declined. But positive signs could be seen, especially the trend toward replacing steam locomotives with diesel and the railroad industry's impressive response to the exigencies of World War II.

DEPRESSION, DIESELIZATION, AND ANOTHER WAR

The Great Depression prepared the rail-road industry for another world war. The twin pains of unemployment and lost revenues forced railroads to reexamine their operations. Investment in building projects enhanced capacity, which, combined with new equipment, gave many companies the ability to respond quickly and positively to American entry into the war in 1941. Unlike World War I, the railroads performed admirably in the nation's hour of need. The coordinated, responsible actions of railroad leaders and workers staved off a repeat of the dreaded government control exerted during the earlier conflict. Railroad workers again benefited from wartime wage increases and resented the resumption of post-war "normalcy."

THE GREAT DEPRESSION

The collapse of share prices on October 24, 1929, was an unprecedented economic calamity, but it did not appear to be so at the time. *Railway Age* called it "a mild recession in business," and the stock market leveled off after the initial plunge. Many financiers continued as before, assuming they could weather the storm. Samuel Insull, for example, saw in the misfortunes of others an opportunity to expand his Chicago-area interurban empire. But consumer buying declined, industrial output tumbled, and the demand for railroad transportation collapsed. Auto sales plummeted from 4.6 million

units in 1929 to 1.3 million only four years later, and rail equipment suppliers likewise suffered. The American Locomotive Company (ALCO), which sold an annual average of six hundred locomotives during the 1920s, sold one in 1932.[1] The financial sector contributed to the crash: investors had been encouraged to purchase shares on margin—borrowing against the presumed perpetual increase in the value of their holdings—but found themselves unable to repay their loans when the value of their stock tumbled.

By 1932 40 percent of Chicago's workers—and a much higher proportion of Mexican immigrants and African Americans—were unemployed, while those still at work took pay cuts of up to 50 percent. Unskilled black workers were often the first to be fired when factory orders declined, while Mexican workers, recruited into meatpacking and steelmaking during labor shortages at the end of the 1920s, were forcibly repatriated by the federal government as jobs disappeared. Banks foreclosed on mortgages when homeowners could no longer meet payments, and evictions led to increased homelessness. The slow pace of recovery did not help matters: by 1939, industrial output nationally reached 84 percent of its 1929 level but Chicago's factories and workshops lagged behind, recovering to only 77 percent. Farmers and miners also felt the devastating effects of the Depression. Crop prices, already low during the 1920s, fell further, and farm foreclosures shot up. With one-half of the state's mines closed by 1931, coal miners confronted similarly dire circumstances.[2]

Railroad revenue and income declined precipitously during the early years of the Great Depression. From 1929 to 1932 revenue fell nationally from $6.2 billion to $26.2 million, while income over the same three-year period dropped from $3.1 billion to $1.4 million. For Illinois railroads the collapse of the economy, and with it their earning power, was nothing short of disastrous. Net operating income on the Chicago & Alton fell from $3.3 million in 1931 to $486,783 in 1932. Illinois Central common stock plummeted from $153.50 in 1929 to $4.75 in 1932. Traffic on its Chicago suburban line dipped 40 percent between 1929 and 1932, while total passenger revenue dropped by 50 percent over the same period. In 1932 nine railroad presidents, including Lawrence Downs of the ICRR, negotiated a national 10 percent wage cut with railroad unions. This was a start, but the Illinois Central—in common with many other railroads—borrowed money from the Reconstruction Finance Corporation, a federal stimulus agency established by President Herbert Hoover, to stay afloat. Red ink poured from ICRR accounts, and it staved off bankruptcy only by selling land and reducing expenditures, including firing or furloughing 55 percent of the workforce by 1933.[3]

The Burlington experienced a comparable decline. A 12 percent drop in income was matched by a similar reduction in the workforce in 1930 and maintenance programs were trimmed. Company officials could be excused for believing tough times were temporary after farmers delivered a normal harvest in the fall of 1930, and shareholders received dividends in June and December of that year. In 1931, however, traffic levels fell again. The usual seasonal recovery failed to materialize, and more cuts followed, including a massive fuel conservation program. Services were reduced, and two daily trains from Oregon to Aurora were discontinued in 1931. Despite the downturn, several major projects continued. Grade separation plans and construction of the new Railway Express Terminal in Chicago were completed, while a three-year program to rebuild and expand the Galesburg freight yard went forward.

Though hurting, the Burlington did not face disaster, posting small profits every year from 1933 to 1940 and staying solvent.[4]

Other Granger roads were not so fortunate. Each of the Burlington's three main competitors filed for bankruptcy protection during the Great Depression. The Rock Island, still suffering from the depredations of the Reid-Moore syndicate, went first in 1933. Two years later both the Milwaukee Road (for the second time in a decade) and the Chicago & North Western followed suit. The C&NW reorganized under a new federal bankruptcy law. Unfortunately, what should have been a three- or four-year process dragged into 1944 because of a dispute over the value of its shares.[5]

The Little Grangers fared just as poorly. The Minneapolis & St. Louis, damaged by war and the shopmen's strike, entered receivership in 1923 and had an application for a Reconstruction Finance Corporation loan rejected in 1932. Cutting back freight service and reducing passenger trains were last resorts, though M&StL did benefit from CB&Q's decision to abandon its Monmouth to Peoria line, large segments of which the M&StL took over, closing uneconomical portions of its nearby tracks on the same route. Farther north, the Soo Line entered receivership after fighting a rearguard action to improve traffic and retire debt. The Chicago Great Western slowed capital expenditures to the point where safety was seemingly compromised. The Sycamore City Council complained that postponing activation of a crossing signal in town resulted in several fatalities. The owner of a lumberyard adjacent to CGW tracks protested that road traffic sat for so long and made so much noise while waiting for trains to go through town that "it sounds as though there were a charivari in progress."[6]

One major source of railroad income, agricultural products, declined during the Depression years in part because of federal policy. In order to assist farmers, the Agricultural Adjustment Act (1933) subsidized taking land out of cultivation. This meant smaller harvests, and, because 40 percent of the wheat and cotton farmers receiving subsidies were in its territory, the Burlington suffered disproportionately. When droughts in 1933 and 1934 destroyed crops and wrecked harvests, the

Figure 15.1. Switchers like this Alco HH660 on the ICRR at the Water Street terminal helped reduce pollution in Chicago. Library of Congress Prints and Photographs Division.

company responded by cutting its rates to carry what was left to market. Even this did not help. Low prices meant farmers sometimes left their crops in the field to rot. Passenger traffic decreased downstate, and to save costs the Chicago & Alton—newly purchased out of receivership by the Baltimore & Ohio—convinced the ICRR and the Wabash to cut one daily service from their Chicago to St. Louis timetables.[7]

The Iron Road in the Prairie State

The most significant technological development of the Depression era was dieselization, or the replacement of steam-powered locomotives by diesel. Steam was expensive to maintain. Even the most reliable steam engines needed their fireboxes cleaned, tubes checked, water pipes examined, and movements lubricated on a daily basis. A single run between Denver and Chicago could require as many as six different locomotives. These tasks took time, labor, and capital, adding to the bottom line. In the 1890s German engineer Rudolph Diesel invented the engine bearing his name and Augustus Busch, the brewer, purchased the patent in the United States. The *American Railroad Journal* saw the potential for diesel traction as early as 1895. In 1898 a technical analysis of diesel motors praised them for offering "great possible advantages of superiority over the steam engine." But the weight-to-power ratio of diesel engines limited their utility well into the twentieth century. Gasoline engines used in the McKeen Rail Motor Car rated twenty-five pounds per horsepower, while the ratio for diesel was 60:1, making them too heavy for railroad use. Neither Diesel nor Busch made any meaningful attempt to apply diesel power to railroads, and not until the 1920s, when General Electric used diesel engines to drive electric traction motors, which turned the wheels, did diesel power gain a foothold in railroading.[8]

The first successful American diesel-electric locomotive was a switcher built at General Electric's Erie, Pennsylvania, plant in 1925 using an ALCO body and an Ingersoll-Rand engine, but it was heavy and slow. In 1932 General Motors developed a lightweight diesel engine sufficiently powerful for main line railroad use. The first market for the diminutive three hundred horsepower engines was provided by polluted urban rail yards and stations. Smoke-abatement rules, which had originally fostered electrification of the ICRR Chicago suburban lines, led to dieselization in the Windy City. In 1942 the city council amended the Lake Front Development Ordinance to ban all steam traction from the downtown lines of the Illinois Central. The ICRR purchased fifteen diesel switchers, lowering if not eliminating emissions.[9]

The diesel era dawned dramatically in the early 1930s. After four years of hard times, Americans prayed the worst was past but feared for the future. Chicago provided an important symbolic victory over the Depression when it hosted the Century of Progress Exposition in 1933. The exposition was designed to showcase advances since the city's founding, and railroads pitched in with exhibits and reduced-fare travel. General Motors, which purchased engine-maker Electro-Motive in 1930, entered its new lightweight Winton diesels, to the intense interest of Burlington president Ralph Budd. The fair was successful by every measure except retiring the debt its organizers had incurred, so a repeat was planned for 1934.

That year the Burlington made a historic contribution. At 5:05 AM on May 26, 1934, a stainless-steel, shot-welded, three-car passenger train powered by Winton diesels left Denver Union Station, waved off by an Indianapolis Speedway starter's flag. With guards posted at every crossing on the CB&Q main line, the lightweight speedster dashed the 1,015.4 miles to Chicago in thirteen hours and five minutes. Budd, who had been reading *The Canterbury Tales* and remembered the Zephyr, chose the name to signify the swift west wind the train sought to emulate and, because it began with the final letter of the alphabet, to position the new machine as the last word in engineering. Run like the wind it did, averaging 77.61 miles per hour and attaining a top speed of 112.5 miles per hour before reaching Chicago despite nearly grinding to a halt with mechanical problems soon after leaving Denver. Once in Chicago, it traveled on Illinois Central tracks from Halstead Street station to the exposition site where, in between demonstration runs across the country, it was displayed alongside the Union Pacific streamliner M-10000.[10]

The Burlington *Zephyr* heralded a new age of glamorous, streamlined, diesel-powered, high-speed train travel. Ralph Budd told the audience at its naming ceremony, "This sleek, glistening, streamlined streak symbolized progress." Burlington general manager J. H. Aydelotte described the run as an "excellent

Figure 15.2. The CB&Q *Twin Cities Zephyr* arrives at East Dubuque. The sleek, modern look of the *Zephyrs* created a sensation and set a streamlined fashion others would follow. Library of Congress Prints and Photographs Division.

demonstration of what science and research in engineering can accomplish when given the opportunity and a definite goal." Budd wrote that the trip demonstrated how "the morale of the men and officers of the Burlington is proved by the way this run has been planned and carried out," praised the condition of the railroad, and claimed the train performed "fully up to expectations."[11]

Following the inaugural run of the *Pioneer Zephyr*, the CB&Q deployed a fleet of diesel-powered *Zephyrs* across the Burlington system. The new trains made

quite an impression, hitting 122 miles per hour on a test run from Chicago to Denver in 1936 and garnering positive publicity for their futuristic looks. The *Zephyr* became something of a trademark, and the company clad a few steam locomotives in silver streamlining and ordered new diesel locomotives in *Zephyr*-style silver. When the company planned a new streamliner service from Chicago to Denver to replace the venerable *Aristocrat* it considered using steam power. Diesel won out because of reliability (96.1 percent for the *Zephyr* against 69.2 percent for a comparable steam locomotive),

The Iron Road in the Prarie State

Figure 15.3. Clad in its *Zephyr* streamlining, CB&Q Baldwin stands in for a diesel on a run in 1937. Author's collection.

durability (diesel required far less routine maintenance), and stamina (steam locomotives could only be expected to run up to a maximum of five hundred miles before an engine change would be needed, and coal and water stops en route slowed things down). The company ordered two stainless-steel *Denver Zephyr* sets from the Budd corporation. One of these established the world record for long-distance speed running on November 23, 1936, when it made the journey from Chicago to Denver in twelve hours and twelve minutes at an average speed of 83.33 miles per hour. *Zephyr* services were soon inaugurated from Chicago to Denver and then to Minneapolis–St. Paul, and, their resilience and timings confirmed, the fleet expanded.[12]

DIESEL STREAMLINERS

Other railroads copied the *Zephyr* example. In May 1935, using rolling stock borrowed from parent Baltimore & Ohio, the Alton introduced the first diesel service from Chicago to St. Louis. Two months later it inaugurated a new steam train, the *Abraham Lincoln,* soon augmented by the *Ann Rutledge,* nicknamed the "Blue Train" because it had B&O blue sides and gray roofs. A year later, in advance of the introduction of the Chicago to St. Louis *Green Diamond* on the Illinois Central, both the *Lincoln* and the *Rutledge* were dieselized. The ICRR celebrated a new articulated *Green Diamond* service with two radio broadcasts, including a live onboard

Figure 15.4. On its inaugural run, the ATSF Super Chief passes Joliet in 1937. Lake Forest College Library Special Collections.

show from "somewhere near Kankakee." Also in 1936, the *City of Portland* used Union Pacific diesel M-10001, a sleek aluminum-alloy, six-car, diesel-powered unit, on a forty-hour schedule over the 2,272-mile run from Chicago to Portland, Oregon. Crossing Illinois on C&NW tracks, it knocked eighteen hours off the previous schedule and was the first diesel streamliner to carry sleeping cars. In 1939, despite bankruptcy, the C&NW purchased new diesel-powered streamliner equipment with matching coaches for its four-hundred-minute express service from Chicago to Minneapolis, the aptly named *400*.[13]

The race to streamline sped up. The Rock Island, struggling to emerge from another bankruptcy reorganization, announced plans to introduce diesel-powered streamliners in 1937. These *Rock Island Rockets* began by operating Chicago to Peoria passenger services with comfortable new equipment. Fired by the *Rockets,* passenger revenues increased by $750,000 in 1937, a year in which freight revenues grew $2.7 million. *Rockets* were added from Chicago to Des Moines and Denver, bringing a touch of prestige back to the maligned but still-proud company. In 1936 the Santa Fe introduced the *Super Chief,* a forty-hour Chicago to Los Angeles service that regularly topped one hundred miles per hour on its journeys. The Santa Fe became the first railroad to employ diesel locomotives for long-distance freight runs, hooking four Electro-Motive units together for a combined 5,400 horsepower. Other railroads followed suit. Diesels were more expensive to purchase than steam locomotives, but better fuel consumption, significantly less maintenance, and longer working days made for overall savings. By 1951 railroads operated more diesel than steam locomotives, and the decline of the snorting beasts accelerated.[14]

The CB&Q *Zephyr* proved to be "the forerunner of the future of rail transport." From the elite Santa Fe *Super Chief* to relatively humble local services, a smooth, sleek look evoked speed and progress for travelers choosing between rail and road. Streamliners were "the finest, most modern trains in existence, incorporating every new development for making the traveler comfortable." Their advent represented "the most encouraging single thing that has happened" since the onset of the Depression.[15] Competing against automobiles and buses, railroads created a modernistic look with services to match.

SLOW STREAMLINERS

Not every streamlined train was fast. A modest attempt to put a modern foot forward was the Chicago & Eastern Illinois's *Egyptian Zipper.* Running between Villa Grove and Cypress, near Cairo, it replaced heavyweight steam-hauled coaches with two streamlined, custom-built American Car & Foundry Company diesel units. Each "motor coach train" had a rail post office and an express-parcels section along with room for sixty-one passengers and a cab for the engineer and fireman. The name *Zipper* was chosen out of fifty thousand entries in a public competition and applied first to the C&EI Chicago to St. Louis service. Inaugurated in 1925, the Villa Grove to Cypress *Egyptian Zipper* was extended to Danville in 1937 and a Tuscola radio station broadcast the first run of this extended service live. Host Clair Hull interviewed passengers, including Marybeth McGurk, the "Queen of the Western Railroads," and local politicians.[16]

The use of sleek-looking diesel railcars made the *Egyptian Zipper* a money spinner for the cash-strapped C&EI. Though the train stopped at all stations en route and took eight hours to travel the 225 miles from Danville to Cypress, it produced a 41 percent increase in passenger numbers and an 81 percent increase in revenue compared to steam traction. C&EI vice president J. B. Ford praised the smooth starts and stops of the new railcars, especially important on a service where the average distance between stations was just 4.5 miles. After six months with the new rolling stock, *Zipper* accounts recorded a 25 percent drop in operating costs compared with steam traction.[17]

Two slow streamliner services ran on the Illinois Central. Both employed ACF railcars similar to the C&EI *Zipper,* but their use was short-lived. In 1940 the ICRR purchased ACF Motorailer units called *Miss Lou* and *Illini* for use on the Champaign to Chicago run. This was a seasonal service operated during the University of Illinois academic year, and the units came with a baggage room and a buffet. A year later the ICRR inaugurated the *Land O' Corn* from Chicago to Waterloo, Iowa, using a two-car Motorailer consisting of a powered driving car and trailer. This unit had a lunch counter and seating for 109 passengers, but after an engineer died from his injuries when it struck a truck near Plano on February 18, 1942, the *Land O' Corn* unit was returned to ACF and replaced by a diesel engine hauling coaches. In 1947 the Champaign service was also switched to conventional equipment, and the Motorailers were sold to the New York, Susquehanna & Western Railroad of New York State. These streamliners proved an excellent source of publicity but not of revenue.[18]

DIESELS AND THE BROTHERHOODS

Diesel locomotives theoretically promised to reduce wage bills. A diesel locomotive does not need a fireman because there is no firebox, and the locomotive can be driven by a single engineer. The first diesels were operated without a fireman, but in December 1935 the Brotherhood of Locomotive Firemen and Enginemen voted to strike because the CB&Q ran its *Zephyr* and switcher fleets with only an engineer. Negotiations between the brotherhood and President Ralph Budd averted a strike at the last minute when firemen were put in the cabs of diesels as a safety measure. This precedent led to the National Diesel-Electric Agreement of 1937, which required firemen in virtually all diesel locomotives.[19]

The new labor agreement contributed to some rather absurd situations, exemplified by events in Galesburg on October 11, 1939. When the Denver to Chicago *Aristocrat* made its regularly scheduled stop, two passengers entered the station building to write postcards. The train left without them, but station staff, alerted to their predicament, had the train halted about three miles from the depot. This meant it was past the yard limit, a fact of no small significance. The two passengers boarded an empty carriage, which was then pulled out to the waiting *Aristocrat* by a yard engine. Fifteen minutes later, the *Aristocrat* resumed its journey to Chicago. Under the new bargaining agreement, taking the two negligent passengers out to their train cost the

company an additional ten days' pay because the two-man yard-engine crew received one day's pay for being asked to travel beyond the yard limit, the two switchmen and the yard conductor on board the special train received an additional day's pay for acting as road crew, and five crewmen on the extra list each received a full day's pay because they could have been the road crew but were bumped.[20]

INNOVATIONS AND CHALLENGES

Despite fiscal problems and the encroachment of competitors, railroads survived the Great Depression. The era was one of adaptation to straitened circumstances and improvisation in the face of a global economic crisis. Recovery occurred "inch by inch," though some technological progress was recorded. One advance passengers particularly welcomed was the installation of air-conditioning. Beginning in June 1932, the Alton cooled its Chicago to St. Louis services with equipment created by parent Baltimore & Ohio. In an increasingly competitive market, this forced the Illinois Central, the Wabash, and the C&EI to follow suit. By 1934 the Burlington began to air-condition its passenger car fleet, and three years later the Chicago Great Western, behind the curve for once, announced plans to do likewise.[21]

Long-distance automobile travel was inconvenient and difficult before the 1930s. The paucity of motels, gas stations, restaurants, and campgrounds and, in some places, the absence of paved roads made long trips uncomfortable. Trains offered meals, sleeping cars, comfy chairs, plenty of space, and even libraries and barbers. But the ambitious road-building programs of the 1920s and the construction of tourist facilities drew people away from the trains. Competition like this spurred the C&EI to revise its Florida services. In 1936 the *Dixieland* debuted, making the trip from Chicago to Jacksonville, Florida, in just twenty-four hours. In 1940 the C&EI began operating its first streamlined train, the *Dixie Flagler* to Miami. The C&EI operated the *Dixie Flagler* as part of a cooperative service with the Illinois Central's new diesel-powered *City of Miami* and the Pennsylvania's *South Wind,* allowing customers to ride any of the three trains regardless of who issued their tickets. Florida traffic generated over half of all C&EI revenue, and when the Louisville & Nashville proposed switching its trains onto the New York Central into Chicago the C&EI sued to retain the *Dixie* services. But the automobile grabbed hold of the popular imagination, and though railroads responded by introducing car rental services at main line stations, the competitor proved unbeatable.[22]

Railroads also faced increased competition for freight traffic from trucking companies. In 1925 there were 2.4 million trucks registered in the United States, most of which fed local traffic to the railroads. In 1926 an interurban, the Chicago, North Shore & Milwaukee, carried trucks on railroad flatcars for the first time. These services were soon to be called piggyback freights and the Chicago Great Western was the first major railroad to adapt this method, experimenting with it in 1935 between Chicago and the Twin Cities. In 1936 it inaugurated a regular trailer on flatcar (TOFC) train, an early example of switching freight among trains, trucks, and ships in a practice that would later become known as intermodal transportation. The Burlington did the same in 1939, and cooperation between rail and truck seemed to attest to predictions that railroads would benefit from good roads.[23]

But this did not last. Large-scale competition for freight between railroads and trucking companies in Illinois began in earnest during the drought of 1934, when truckers took below-capacity, or less-than-carload (LCL), shipments of animal feed to farmers and departed with distressed animals, lumber, or even coal. The railroads responded by working with "freight forwarding" companies, which combined multiple LCLs into single loads called "forwarder traffic." In 1937 the Burlington opened the Galesburg Truck Terminal, the first of many such innovations by the Burlington Transportation Company. Despite creative responses and efforts to accommodate trucking, by 1940 the combination of route flexibility and differential loadings meant that five million registered trucks were carrying about 10 percent of all intercity freight.[24] That proportion would continue to grow into the 1980s.

A second world war loomed as the 1930s drew to a close, bringing peril abroad and prosperity at home. But war fever failed to ignite in the United States. As the unofficial center of American isolationism, Chicago was particularly hostile to the idea of entering another "foreign" fight. Memories of World War I, a deep desire to remain neutral, and the presence of powerful noninterventionist voices like the *Chicago Tribune,* University of Chicago president Robert M. Hutchins, and Chicagoan Robert E. Wood, (chairman of the isolationist group America First), shaped public opinion in the city and the state. Concerns about further expansion of the federal government, its powers bloated by the combined effects of World War I and the Great Depression, fueled the desire to remain at peace.[25] Few people relished tax increases, and conservatives opposed government growth.

The urge for neutrality did not stop President Franklin Delano Roosevelt and his administration from planning for war. Preparations for the coming conflict, particularly the Lend-Lease program, had already increased railroad traffic when Germany invaded Poland in September 1939, pulling in Britain and France. By the time of the December 7, 1941, attack on Pearl Harbor, the US economy was geared up for war, and despite its isolationist outlook, Illinois contributed to the military machine springing to life. Federal contracts sparked production across the state after Chicago mayor Edward J. Kelly and Governor Dwight H. Green traveled to Washington to lobby for funding. The chairman of the War Production Board, Donald M. Nelson of Chicago-based Sears, Roebuck, funneled orders to his home state. Manufacturing companies converted to war production, including Pullman, which made tanks and aircraft components for the duration. The Rock Island Arsenal was modernized, and rail-served ordnance factories operated in Savanna, Kankakee, and Elwood, where a June 1942 explosion killed twenty-one workers. In southern Illinois a shell-loading plant opened at Crab Orchard, near Marion.[26]

The onset of World War II generated massive traffic increases comparable to those of World War I, but this time the railroads were ready and responded effectively to the nation's needs. Railroad industry leaders avoided a government takeover, except for a brief period when labor unions threatened to strike at the end of 1943. In fact, the consensus then and now is that the performance of American railroads during World War II provided a "sharp and happy contrast" to the chaos and hostility of World War I.[27]

Transporting military matériel and personnel boosted freight and passenger traffic. Railroads moved 83 percent of all civilian traffic in the United States between 1941 and 1944, 90 percent of military freight, and 97 percent of military personnel, reversing what had been a trend toward ever more road haulage. In 1941 railroads set a new high for freight traffic, 6 percent more than the previous record established in 1929. The Great Lakes Naval Training Center in North Chicago became the world's largest facility of its type, bringing more than a million sailors to the area during the war, most of them arriving and departing by train. Military instruction schools were reopened in Belleville, Chanute, Galesburg, Rantoul, and Rockford; the state's colleges and universities educated officers; and armaments bound for war rolled off assembly lines across the state. Railroads benefited: the Illinois Central alone served 142 facilities directly involved in the war effort.[28] The recession of 1938 faded into memory as the outbreak of war brought a windfall for railroads.

Farms, like the state's factories, also dramatically raised output as Depression-era fiscal restraints gave way to large-scale applications of herbicides, pesticides, and hybrid seeds. Bumper harvests translated into profits for the railroads. Freight on the Illinois Central jumped 59 percent between June and October 1939; other roads experienced traffic increases as crops, goods, and people took to the rails. The Minneapolis & St. Louis saw passenger numbers leap from 78,537 in 1940 to an unprecedented, and not to be repeated, high of 289,372 in 1945. Freight revenue on the M&STL doubled over the same period. Livestock production increased by almost a quarter, and harvests grew by 14 percent between 1941 and 1945, bringing more traffic onto the railroads. In 1943 the ICRR carried 24.6 billion

ton miles of freight, eclipsing the previous record of 16.2 billion ton miles set in 1923.[29]

Soon after war broke out in Europe, President Roosevelt consulted with CB&Q president Ralph Budd about the state of the railroads. Budd recommended allowing the railroads to remain in private hands but authorizing private and federal agencies to coordinate operations. This, he felt, was the most efficient way to confront the crisis.[30] In May 1940 FDR appointed Budd his commissioner of transportation to coordinate the movement of men and matériel among different modes of haulage. Depression-era infrastructure improvements and unhappy memories of World War I facilitated Budd's efforts.

After Pearl Harbor the game changed significantly. Budd returned to the Burlington, and FDR established a new Office of Defense Transportation (ODT) to continue the federal government's coordinating role. Contributing to the extra burden railroads bore during World War II were closure of the Panama Canal and declining coastal shipping at a time when the need for freight movements increased. Almost all waterborne oil traffic was forced onto the rails by the threat of U-boat attacks. War restrictions hurt the railroads, however, when the War Production Board (WPB) began rationing scarce resources. Despite the railroads' massive contributions, the WPB did not designate them essential to the war effort, and they could not gain access to sufficient quantities of steel, gasoline, replacement parts, and other materials for improvement projects and rolling stock maintenance.[31]

Railroads supported the war effort by sponsoring war-bond drives, opening railroad land to employee Victory Gardens, and hiring women to replace the men who joined the military. Most famously, Rosie the Riveter and her sisters answered the call to war work. In Illinois the number of women in manufacturing jobs—in steel mills, refineries, shipyards, and other formerly male preserves—more than doubled during the war years, and women working in all industries rose from 854,276 to 1,281,000 between 1940 and 1944. The North Western employed women as section hands and station agents and in more traditionally "feminine" occupations such as stenographers and clerks. In 1944 women railroaders formed their own "brotherhood," the National Association of Railroad Women, which would become the American Council of Railroad Women after the war.[32]

Wartime needs took precedence over railroad prerogatives, and in July 1945, even as the war seemed to be drawing to a close, ODT ordered sleeping cars off trains scheduled for less than 450 miles. This caused timetabling nightmares for Illinois railroads. The C&EI, for example, transferred its Chicago to St. Louis passenger trains from overnight runs to daytime and evening schedules, which proved unpopular with travelers. In the same month the ODT ordered railroads to discontinue passenger services averaging less than 35 percent occupancy. The Monon lost all of its Chicago to Indianapolis trains except one, though dieselization and the introduction of streamlined rolling stock under the stewardship of new president John W. Barriger III temporarily gave the road a competitive edge in that busy market. The Baltimore & Ohio had been losing money on passenger travel for two decades, with a brief wartime respite, and earned only 5 percent of its total revenue from passenger traffic in 1945. The B&O faced a sea of red ink that threatened to drown the road. The ODT directive enabled the company to focus on freight and allow passenger service to deteriorate.[33]

Smaller roads exhibited a mixed record. Bigger steam locomotives, a modest fleet of diesels, and a dedicated, resourceful maintenance department helped the Minneapolis & St. Louis overcome the drop from 198 to 101 engines between 1933 and 1943, though new units dribbled in from ALCO and Electro-Motive Division of General Motors (EMD) over the last two years of the war. The Wabash enjoyed dramatic increases in traffic and, defying its recent receivership, began paying dividends to stockholders. On some lines, however, the strain was too much. A 1942 decision to finish dieselizing the Alton had to be delayed, and the few diesels it did own broke down because of the volume of traffic. As a result, some trains were pulled by expensive double-headed steam locomotives.[34]

Labor shortages dogged the railroads during World War II, as they had in World War I. The Illinois Central was badly hit when, over the course of the second war, about a quarter of its total workforce joined the military. The company responded by opening training schools in Chicago and Carbondale to prepare sixteen- and seventeen-year-olds for railroad work. The Rock Island, in contrast, went the other way by lifting its maximum age for new hires, while the M&StL encouraged men to delay retirement. The Burlington looked farther afield and brought 3,449 immigrants from Mexico to help replace its over 8,000 employees on military service. Inflation eroded earning power, and as prices continued to rise the brotherhoods voted to strike in December 1943. The War Department stepped in, and for a month the railroads were federalized, and railroaders received pay raises, some retroactive to February 1943. Unlike World War I, the government administered with a light hand, and the actual management of the railroads remained with company officials.[35]

Wartime traffic growth allowed railroads to dig their way out of indebtedness incurred during the Great Depression. Financially, the period from 1941 to 1945 would prove to be a last burst of prosperity for two generations. The Burlington and the Illinois Central significantly reduced their debts, and many lines managed to place themselves in a stronger position for the postwar era. Dividend payments resumed, but real problems remained, and war only delayed their resolution. The biggest dilemma railroads faced could be seen in the map of Illinois: branch lines built during the era of mud roads and horse-drawn carts were now little used because road-surfacing programs encouraged automobiles and trucks.[36] Abandoning that track became a vital prerogative after the war.

In the 1950s railroads entered a period of decline many believed terminal. The traveling public, it seemed, responded positively to the convenience of cars. Railroads, despite offering fast, reliable, and comfortable transportation, could neither match the literally door-to-door service automobiles provided nor compete financially with roads and airports subsidized by taxpayers. Freight switched to the mostly unregulated and often cheaper trucking industry. By the end of the decade, long-distance travelers had begun choosing commercial airliners over trains. Railroad profitability teetered on the brink, and only the continued use of passenger trains by the US Postal Service kept many of them running. But the losses mounted, and while a few elite runs continued to break even, the end was near for private, common-carrier passenger trains.

16

POSTWAR CHALLENGES

World War II was the last golden age of railroading in the United States. Between 1935 and 1945 in Illinois, freight revenues more than doubled, passenger income increased by over 300 percent, and the network operated as smoothly as could be expected given the emergency conditions prevailing. Things would deteriorate after 1945, but that could not be known at the time and railroad executives exuded optimism following V-J Day. A bright postwar future appeared to beckon as new technological and safety developments promised to retain customers and grow traffic. To capture the festive postwar mood and commemorate a century of Chicago railroading, the Windy City hosted a lakefront Railroad Fair in 1948.

As joyful as the event proved, celebrating could not solve looming problems. Increased competition from other modes, deteriorating labor relations, and falling revenue posed massive challenges. Unlike the 1893 World's Columbian Exposition, which generated new traffic for and excitement about railroads, the majority of Railroad Fair attendees arrived by car. Passenger numbers declined as people drove locally and, increasingly, flew long-distance. The automobile returned with a vengeance after World War II, when gas and rubber rationing ended and creeping prosperity released pent-up demand. Factories shifted from producing tanks to making cars, suburban living encouraged auto ownership, and optimism in the future was reflected in a desire to take to the open road.[1] In the meantime, Illinois railroad passenger revenue plummeted by 36.7 percent in the ten years between 1945 and 1955, pointing to a grim future.

THE CHICAGO RAILROAD FAIRS

"Creaky Locomotives of Yesteryear" rolled into Chicago's Burnham Park for a Railroad Fair early in 1948 to celebrate the centennial of the city's first train. The *Pioneer*, the *DeWitt Clinton*, the *Tom Thumb*, and other replicas of celebrity engines shared the spotlight with cowboys, Indians, and sheriffs, giving visitors a brush with "the colorful, the bizarre, and the historic." Spectators watched Jolliet and Marquette land on the shore of Lake Michigan and initiate "the contest across the continent." Railroads monopolized the fair's "Wheels A-Rolling" historical reenactment through the nineteenth century. But when 1900 arrived, it became clear that, in the ominous words of the official guide to the fair, "the automobile is here to stay." Omitting the two world wars, a brief appearance by the *Pioneer Zephyr* was quickly followed by "the latest in motorcycles, automobiles, trucks and fire engines." To remind viewers of the existence of railroads after all those road vehicles, "a giant steam locomotive and a magnificent new diesel . . . slowly, majestically form the final curtain."[2]

Elsewhere in Burnham Park, individual railroad corporations sponsored thematic displays to advertise their services. The Chicago & Eastern Illinois featured Florida, treating visitors to Miami Beach, a Spanish colonial mansion, and Florida Citrus Queen Shirley Rhodes waving a signal flag made of a plastic called "gantron" that was supposedly visible for a distance of two miles. The Rock Island offered "the exotic romance of the southwest" in its "Rocket Village," while the Santa Fe populated a western-themed settlement with "125 tribesmen and women." The Burlington cooperated—not for the first time—with the Great Northern and the Northern Pacific to present a taste of the Old West, exhibiting caged bears, a working model of Old Faithful, a rodeo, and "gigantic caricatures of cowboys, Indians, Eskimos, and western animal life." Rolling-stock manufacturers Pullman, Budd, and ACF demonstrated construction techniques and reminded visitors of the role of the humble boxcar in keeping the economy moving.[3] As if that were not enough, three miles of track had been laid along the lakefront for a static display of locomotives, passenger cars, and freight vehicles.

Conceived by Frank Koval, head of publicity for the Chicago & North Western, and sponsored by thirty-eight railroads, the fair was a success. It exceeded expectations by attracting 2.5 million visitors from July to October 1948. The one-millionth visitor, a shy, twelve-year-old Chicago boy, stepped through a ceremonial entryway on August 11 to earn the multivolume *Encyclopedia Britannica*. Cheap tickets were sold to people from specific cities on certain days; competitions offered free entry to anyone with one hundred or more freckles; and group rail fares helped attract visitors. Attendees from Genoa, near DeKalb, expressed themselves "especially impressed with the beautiful pageant." Two busloads of elementary-school children from Sycamore took a field trip to the lakefront for the "Wheels A-Rolling" spectacle in October. On Illinois Central Day a Joliet-based special agent, Carol Bosworth, was crowned Miss Illinois Central, and a fireworks display depicted the emblems of that line's famous *Panama Limited* and *Green Diamond*. Toward the end of the summer, C&NW employee Kathleen Duffy was named queen of the Railroad Fair, beating out fourteen other contestants to win a $100 savings bond. An average daily attendance of 46,500 people encouraged organizers to hold a second fair in 1949. Nearly three million people visited that year's festival, many of whom arrived by car.[4]

Cheerful commemorations could not disguise significant challenges ahead. People "motored" to the lakefront fairs, and the harsh realities of postwar railroading contrasted with the celebrations.[5] Though railroads adopted new rolling stock and touted beautiful streamlined passenger trains, inflation cut into railroad earnings, and labor unrest, never far below the surface, boiled over. Canals and trucks took freight traffic while buses and airlines gained confidence, customers, and clout.

Strikes dogged the railroads immediately after World War II. One of the most violent strikes actually began during the war, in December 1941, on the Toledo, Peoria & Western and resumed afterward. Aggressively antiunion TP&W president George P. McNear Jr., refused to recognize labor organizations or match the wage increases larger railroads paid to offset inflation. Brotherhood members voted to strike. The fact that the corporation had returned to profitability before the end of the Depression and begun construction of a new line contributed to employees' anger because the money was being spent on the physical plant but not on their salaries. The paternalistic McNear, irritated by what he saw as betrayal by his men, hired replacement workers. Strikers retaliated by tearing up track and attacking bridges.

The situation became so volatile that the Office of Defense Transportation intervened. On March 17, 1942, ODT officials told John W. Barriger III he would have to run the railroad as federal manager, sidelining the controversial McNear. Two days later Barriger wrote, "The TP&W situation seems to have calmed down considerably and I am in hopes it will not be necessary [for me] to go to Peoria." The very next day, however, McNear forced the government's hand by sending President Franklin Roosevelt "a long message collect and then giving publicity to that fact." Roosevelt ordered ODT to run the railroad, and Barriger traveled to Chicago, where the military commander told him that five hundred soldiers had been equipped with rations, munitions, trucks, and orders to pacify TP&W territory by force if necessary. Guarded by three officers, Barriger rode the *Rock Island Rocket* to Peoria accompanied by ODT executives and accountants. Barriger spent his first day in Peoria meeting with McNear, labor leaders, and the press, concluding that "the situation can be handled without military assistance." His assessment proved accurate. The federal government began operating the railroad at midnight on March 25, and the brotherhoods, mollified, called off the strike.[6]

The TP&W remained under federal control for the remainder of the war, boosting morale and coaxing the road to record volumes of traffic. When the war ended ODT turned the corporation back to McNear, and the strike resumed. Tempers frayed. In February 1946 armed guards protecting a replacement crew fired into a group of strikers, killing two. McNear shut down the line and testified angrily before a congressional hearing about labor violence. Though fearing for his life, he refused to be intimidated and dug in his heels. On March 10, 1947, as he returned home from watching a Bradley University basketball contest, McNear was shot and killed. The murderer was never found, despite rewards totaling $41,155. In the aftermath of the slaying, the thirteen brotherhoods involved in the strike sat down with managers and reached a settlement. Employees gained higher wages in return for new work rules, and the line was reopened following a lengthy track-rebuilding program.[7]

The nation shared the Illinois railroad malaise. At war's end, journalist Wallace Abbey wrote, the railroads were "physically exhausted and mechanically worn out." World War II revived passenger traffic temporarily, but the decline in railroad travel evident during the Great Depression resumed at war's end. To make matters worse, an inflationary spiral followed the withdrawal of federal price controls and the ICC delayed increasing rates. A series of strikes in the automotive, coal, steel, and electrical industries hurt revenues. One of the worst hit was the B&O. Its wartime profitability proved short-lived, and expenses exceeded income less than one year after the spontaneous and heartfelt celebrations accompanying the end of the war. Despite the continued flow of grain to Europe, profits vanished, and a two-day strike by engineers and trainmen in May 1946 sparked a brief government takeover of the industry.[8]

Strikes gave investors pause and convinced customers to seek alternative modes of transportation. On the Minneapolis & St. Louis, a 1946 strike caused the cancellation of 98 percent of all trains. An industry-wide settlement with the brotherhoods created hard feelings between smaller roads like the M&StL and the larger companies. Regional carriers chafed under their powerlessness in the face of gargantuan neighbors, and the presidents of the Chicago & Eastern Illinois, the Chicago Great Western, the Monon, and the TP&W agreed when M&StL chief executive Lucian C. Sprague argued that the future for small railroads was dim.[9] Events would prove him right.

One smaller road facing an uncertain future was the Chicago & Alton. Confronting considerable and continuing losses, owner B&O filed a petition in Chicago to reorganize the line, calling in a receiver to retire its $48.4 million debt, some of it unpaid interest on bonds. The receiver proposed canceling the debts, but shareholders and bondholders understandably opposed the move. A newly organized railroad, the Gulf, Mobile & Ohio (GM&O), purchased the C&A in 1946 after Ralph Budd promised that the Burlington would lease a stretch of Alton track in Missouri. The GM&O paid $1.2 million, offering bondholders $500 in GM&O bonds for every $1,000 of Alton holdings, more than they had realistically expected.[10]

The glamorous and government-subsidized airlines posed a growing threat to railroads. New transportation modes represent investment opportunities and therefore attract political support. Railroads benefited from taxpayer investment and political protection in Illinois in the 1850s and, to a lesser degree, after the Civil War, which hurt canals and river shipping. In 1925 the federal government transferred some long-distance mail shipments from railroads to air carriers, and for the rest of the decade, federal expenditures on beacons, weather information, and airfields increased. Passenger air miles grew from one million in 1926 to one billion in 1940, when railroads recorded 23 billion passenger miles

Figure 16.1. A diesel at Glenn Railroad Yard in Chicago prepares for the day shortly after the GM&O purchased the C&A. Lake Forest College Library Special Collections.

nationally. From 1931 to 1940 rail passenger miles grew just 8 percent, while bus miles increased 100 percent and air a stunning 711 percent over the same period.[11]

Fearful of being left behind, some railroads attempted to enter the airline industry. A short-lived transcontinental service saw the Santa Fe, the Pennsylvania Railroad, and Transcontinental Air Transport provide a forty-eight-hour journey from New York to Los Angeles using airplanes during the day and trains at night. In 1943 the Burlington Transportation Company, a CB&Q subsidiary, tried to offer helicopter service from Peoria to Galesburg to connect with its *Zephyr* services.[12] Such initiatives failed, and the railroads opted

to compete against rather than cooperate with the airline industry.

A POSTWAR PASSENGER REVIVAL?

The most dramatic change in postwar railroading was the virtual death of passenger trains. Cash was not in short supply after the war, but raw materials for new rolling stock were. The railroads had collectively amassed over $1 billion by 1945, but strikes in the copper, steel, coal, and electrical industries created shortages that delayed much-needed infusions of new equipment. Passenger cars and locomotives waited half-complete on assembly lines for key components to be installed.

The automobile and air-travel sectors rushed ahead, the former capturing the public's attention with new models and the latter converting surplus military DC-3s to civilian use. As transportation lawyer Donald Itzkoff wrote, "Beaten at the starting gate, the railroads would never catch up."[13]

But that did not mean they retreated. Railroads attempted to compete with long-distance air travel by offering new cross-country passenger hauls and improving the comfort of the ride. In July 1946 the B&O's *Capitol Limited* attached sleeping cars to Santa Fe expresses in Chicago, creating the first seamless transcontinental passenger train, but high switching costs and low patronage doomed it. Later that same year the New York Central and the Pennsylvania began cooperating with western roads to operate sleepers from New York to Los Angeles and San Francisco via Chicago. The NYC and the Santa Fe exchanged passenger cars from the *20th Century Limited* and the *Super Chief* in Chicago for a New York to Los Angeles journey. The 3,184-mile trip in high-speed "super hotels" supplied glamour and "the finest foods available: prime beef; sole from the English channel and trout from Colorado and Idaho streams; guinea hen and pheasant in season; lobster and other sea delicacies; a wide variety of French and domestic wines." Despite such luxury, most of these expensive transcontinental services could not keep up with the burgeoning airline industry and had been discontinued by 1958.[14]

A more durable long-distance train, the *California Zephyr,* began running between Chicago and San Francisco in 1949, jointly operated by the Burlington, the Rio Grande, and the Western Pacific. Burlington managers envisioned the train as "a cruise ship on rails" providing opulence and a schedule conducive to enjoying the spectacular terrain through which it traveled. Designed to supply luxury on rails rather than compete directly with long-distance air travel, the fleet consisted of six new ten-car stainless steel streamliner sets. The westbound train left Denver after an overnight journey through the flat land between Chicago and the Mile High City, entering the scenic Rocky Mountains for a spectacular daytime run along the Colorado River. Passengers particularly enjoyed the new Vista-Dome

cars offering panoramic views of the unfolding scenery, described by one writer as "the Burlington's contribution to further breath-taking adventures on railroad's magic carpet." The CB&Q attracted coach passengers by adding low-fare Slumbercoaches (sometimes called Siesta coaches) containing forty one-person sleeping berths. By the beginning of 1949 forty-three different runs from Chicago used streamlined equipment put into service following World War II, testament to a recognition that something needed to be done to draw people back from their automobiles.[15]

TRAINS ANNULLED: EAST TO WEST

The 1950s witnessed the beginning of a full-scale retreat from passenger service because Vista-Domes, Slumbercoaches, and other innovations could not stem the flow of red ink. Passenger trains became increasingly unsustainable as losses jumped nationally from $140 million in 1946 to $705 million in 1953. In that same period, passenger revenues dropped by a third while the railroad's share of intercity travel fell by almost half. The picture in Illinois mirrored the national scene. Between 1945 and 1955 passenger revenues fell 37 percent, and passenger miles in the state dropped 30 percent to levels below those experienced at the height of the Great Depression.[16] The situation was unsustainable, and railroads began planning to annul passenger services.

Abandoning a passenger service required approval from the Interstate Commerce Commission for trains crossing state borders or from the Illinois Commerce Commission for intrastate services. This could be a lengthy and often futile process. As state-chartered common carriers railroads had a legal duty to transport anyone who wished—and could afford—to travel by train. Members of the public often protested against the withdrawal of "their" passenger run and, unless the railroad proved how financial costs far outweighed the social or economic benefits accruing from continuation, the ICC could—and often did—rule on the side of the traveling public. Nonetheless, the hurdles could be overcome and declining passenger numbers, the loss of railroad post office contracts, and increased costs were grounds for the often-controversial abandonments.

Figure 16.2. A Monon *Thoroughbred* leaves Chicago's Dearborn Street station in 1965. The service would be annulled two years later and all but the headhouse demolished eleven years after that. Lake Forest College Library Special Collections.

No service was immune to the ax. The Pennsylvania's *Broadway Limited* and the New York Central's *20th Century Limited*, elite trains between Chicago and New York, had their amenities reduced, were downgraded, and were eventually eliminated. The Pennsylvania sped up the *Broadway Limited* schedule in 1954 and attracted more passengers than the *20th Century Limited* after the NYC consolidated that train with the *Commodore Vanderbilt*, alienating its status-conscious clientele by converting it into "a run-of-the-road string of day coaches, sleepers, and baggage cars." The Pennsylvania experienced the nation's largest passenger deficit, losing $71

million annually in the 1950s and reducing the number of trains on its Pittsburgh to Chicago line while consolidating some of its New York–bound runs. Red-carpet service could not last forever, and in 1967 the Pennsylvania combined the *Broadway Limited* with the *General.* In that year NYC brought the curtain down on the *20th Century Limited.* The same line had applied in 1957 to end all of its St. Louis–originating services because ridership had fallen by almost two-thirds between 1946 and 1956. It was absorbing annual losses estimated at $1.2 million on trains through Illinois. By 1961 only three westbound trains ran, down from a postwar high of twelve.

The Iron Road in the Prarie State

These were two coach-only services to Cleveland and the overnight *Southwestern* to New York City. In 1967 one daily westbound service averaged an anemic 7.6 passengers, while its eastbound counterpart posted an even less robust 6.7 passengers a day. Only its RPO kept the train running, and when the postal service canceled the contract the ICC approved discontinuance.[17]

The Baltimore & Ohio ran two loss-making but prestigious trains between Chicago and Baltimore, the *Columbian* and the *Capitol Limited*. A less glamorous service, the Chicago to Washington *Shenandoah,* turned a profit, but even that began to lose money in the 1960s. Replacing dining cars with buffets serving frozen food and eliminating sleepers could not save it. Another service, the *Metropolitan Special,* traveled from St. Louis across central Illinois on its way to New York City, but it gradually gained so many express and mail cars that by 1958 the number of time-consuming stops required to switch cars in and out meant the train almost never arrived anywhere according to schedule. By 1962 it had begun terminating in Washington, and in 1964 it lost its "Special" designation, becoming primarily a mail and express-package train. The last B&O passenger run across southern Illinois, the *Metropolitan,* ceased operating from Cincinnati to St. Louis in 1968.[18]

The Monon, a company principally serving the Chicago to Indianapolis market, also ended passenger trains when mail contracts expired. In 1965 the government canceled the Monon *Thoroughbred*'s RPO. It took only two more years before the ICC allowed the company to annul its premier Chicago to Louisville service. A similar fate met that company's Chicago to Indianapolis trains. The Chesapeake & Ohio took sleeping cars off its Chicago to Grand Rapids trains in 1967, and when the C&O lost its mail contract in 1969, things got worse. By 1971 the *Pere Marquette,* a daily Chicago to Detroit train, operated with one locomotive and one coach.[19]

Passenger services across southern Illinois suffered as the Illinois Central, the Louisville & Nashville, and the Southern Railway sought to cut costs on their parallel lines from St. Louis to the Indiana border. The last surviving Southern Railway train was a St. Louis to Danville, Kentucky, local. It was also the final steam-hauled

passenger service anywhere on the Southern system and took more than fourteen hours to make its 367-mile trek, averaging barely 25 miles per hour. With an unfriendly schedule and declining patronage, only its RPO kept the service afloat. Survival became less likely when in 1949 the company prepared bankruptcy papers and terminated the train at East St. Louis to avoid paying to cross the Eads Bridge into Missouri. In 1952 the RPO contract ended, and the ICC authorized Southern to discontinue the service.[20]

In 1967 L&N announced plans to end the *Georgian* between St. Louis and Nashville, Tennessee, but these were stymied by vocal and well-organized patrons in southern Illinois. The new rolling stock with which the service had begun in 1946 was obsolete and uncomfortable by the 1960s. Armed with data about poor timings, dirty interiors, and the absence of onboard food, passengers fought a rearguard action in ICC hearings to save what had become the last train across southern Illinois between St. Louis and Indiana. In December 1967 the ICC authorized the L&N to discontinue the Evansville to Nashville segment of the *Georgian* but ordered it to keep both the Chicago to Evansville and the St. Louis to Evansville sections. The latter lost the name but had its run extended to Atlanta when the ICC authorized the C&EI to end its portion of the *Georgian* from Chicago to Evansville. The L&N informed the ICC that it intended to discontinue the St. Louis to Atlanta train at the end of 1969, reporting that it had lost over half a million dollars in the first six months of that year. Witnesses testified that the L&N had eliminated food service, reduced the train's maximum speed from seventy to fifty miles per hour, stopped cleaning the coaches, and ignored malfunctioning air-conditioning and unhygienic bathrooms. The ICC ruled that the loss of patronage was almost entirely down to corporate negligence and required it to keep one daily round trip from St. Louis as far as Evansville. As journalist Peter Lyon wrote at the time, "Did the passengers jump off the train, or were they pushed?"[21]

The Chicago & North Western faced a similar problem. When the post office began canceling mail cars on the Chicago to Clinton, Iowa, route, towns along the way had no rail-carried mail. The final C&NW long-distance train, the *Fast Mail* between Chicago and Council Bluffs, ran in March 1960, and the last nonsuburban passenger train was the April 30, 1971, *Kate Shelley* between Chicago and Clinton, Iowa. Thereafter the focus swung irrevocably to freight.[22]

Riding trains facing the ax could be an ordeal. In 1950 a college professor returning to Huron, South Dakota, from a Christmas celebration in Chicago wrote how "the Hades of the ancients must have been a Paradise in comparison" to her journey over the North Western's bumpy track in cold and dirty cars. Under new chairman Ben Heineman the C&NW began canceling long-distance passenger runs, starting in 1958 with Chadron, Nebraska, services, followed by trains to Omaha and Duluth. The North Western became so unreliable that Union Pacific switched its West Coast passenger services to rival Milwaukee Road in order to meet the schedule between Omaha, Nebraska, and the Windy City. The not-so-prestigious trains of the Chicago Great Western also hemorrhaged red ink, and in 1951 the trip from Chicago to the Twin Cities, until then a direct route, involved a two-and-a-half-hour layover in Oelwein, Iowa, to change trains. Even this tortuous trip was impossible to take after 1954.[23]

TRAINS ANNULLED: NORTH AND SOUTH

While airline competition threatened the future of transcontinental trains, optimists hoped railroads would remain competitive on runs of five hundred miles or less. A prime example was the Chicago to St. Louis corridor, where "creeping journeys to and from airports" canceled out airlines' faster times and four different railroads vied for traffic. The Alton, the Chicago & Eastern Illinois, the Illinois Central, and the Wabash competed for a dwindling supply of passengers, and each responded in its own way to the decline. The Alton, owned by the GM&O after 1947, lost $1.4 million on its Chicago to St. Louis route in 1957 due to "spiraling costs and declining income and passenger volume." It canceled all of its local passenger trains the next year while maintaining a fast service, including sleepers, for another decade but could not afford to stay in the race.

Chicago & Eastern Illinois customers suffered at the hands of the Missouri Pacific after it purchased the C&EI main line from Chicago to St. Louis. MoPac seemed "to treat the public like dirt and make sure they never came back" by offering late, overcrowded, and filthy trips remembered only as an excuse to drive next time. The railroads did not help themselves: a newspaper reader pointed out that the fastest way to travel by train between Chicago and St. Louis in 1955 was to transfer at Effingham from an Illinois Central train to a Pennsylvania service, cutting ten minutes off the fastest direct run even with a twenty-minute layover between trains.[24]

In 1949 the Chicago & Eastern Illinois began discontinuing its *Dixie* services as Florida-bound tourists switched to automobiles and airplanes. The company took off mail vehicles to accelerate the trains and came close to breaking even, but the losses returned, and in 1957 the C&EI withdrew the last sleeping services. The C&EI's principal partner in the *Dixie* trains, the Louisville & Nashville, carried a record 12.4 million passengers in 1944, but this figure tumbled to 2.6 million in 1950 despite extensive advertising of a new fleet of passenger cars. *Dixie* services from Chicago and St. Louis decreased throughout the 1950s, and soon the last *Dixie* train, the *Dixie Flyer,* carried primarily US mail and express parcels. It remained modestly profitable until the C&EI discontinued it between Chicago and Danville, leading to its demise in 1966. Another service to the southern United States, the Chicago to Atlanta, Georgia, *Humming Bird,* struggled on until the ICC allowed C&EI to discontinue the Chicago to Evansville, Indiana, segment in 1968. A year later, as soon as the ICC authorized it to do so, the L&N canceled the remaining *Humming Bird* service midroute and unceremoniously transferred surprised passengers to Greyhound buses.[25]

Despite a reputation for excellent service, Illinois Central passenger revenue declined by a quarter between 1946 and 1966. Well before then, branch-line passenger service abandonments had been commonplace, beginning in 1939, when trains from Peoria to Mattoon and from Mattoon to Evansville, Indiana, were discontinued. Three named trains, the *Chickasaw,* the *City of Miami,* and the *City of New Orleans,* operated

The Iron Road in the Prairie State

between St. Louis and Carbondale, where they connected with mainline services to Chicago and New Orleans. In 1955 the names were dropped, and one slow train in each direction made all station stops. Journey times lengthened, and would-be passengers sought alternative means of travel. In 1957 the railroad lost $800,000 on its St. Louis runs and the next year sought to reduce the service to a single train in each direction, eliciting customer complaints about overcrowding. In 1968 the Illinois Central began terminating the famous Chicago to St. Louis *Green Diamond* at Springfield, renaming it the *Governor's Special*.[26]

The Wabash introduced the Chicago to St. Louis *Blue Bird* in 1950. A fast streamliner using new stainless steel rolling stock with a buffet and dome cars for viewing the unfolding prairies, the service was an instant hit with the public until Route 66 became a four-lane highway. Automobiles displaced trains as the preferred mode of travel, and in 1970 the final *Blue Bird* carried only one lonely passenger. In 1950, after a sixty-year hiatus, the Wabash applied its famous *Wabash Cannon Ball* name to an existing St. Louis to Detroit service, but despite the shortest route between the two cities, the train lost money. In 1964 the ICC agreed to a proposal from the Pennsylvania, then leasing the Wabash, to merge the Wabash into the Norfolk & Western (N&W). Wabash trains through central Illinois from St. Louis, pulling cars painted in N&W color schemes, received severe blows in 1967 and 1968 when they lost Railway Express Agency contracts, feeder traffic from Kansas City, and RPO cars. When the N&W applied to the ICC to discontinue the loss-making *Cannon Ball* in 1967, passengers complained that the company had deliberately allowed the equipment to deteriorate to discourage riders, and the ICC refused the company's request. The N&W tried again in 1969 but was rebuked on the grounds that the *Cannon Ball* was the last passenger service between St. Louis and Detroit. Though the N&W lost approximately ten dollars per passenger to run the train, the ICC instructed the company to retain it because it connected with services to the Southwest. The N&W lost a lawsuit to overturn the decision, and the *Cannon Ball* limped into the Amtrak era, when it was finally canceled.[27]

The last of the great interurban systems in the state, Illinois Terminal, also fell on hard times after World War II. Between 1952 and 1956 IT replaced its electric-powered motors with diesels, which could pull half as much again for slightly more than the cost of using electricity or steam. A diesel locomotive cost about $60,000 to operate annually compared with $139,903 for a steam engine, making the decision to buy new ALCO diesels easy. The line slowly became an all-freight, all-diesel railroad between 1947 and 1957 because its electrical systems had been installed for relatively lightweight interurban passenger services, and it could not afford the cost of new wires for the increasingly heavy freight traffic it was hauling. In June 1950 the line ended service into Peoria and, three years later, discontinued loss-making suburban services between Alton and St. Louis and all Bloomington-area passenger services. The IT could no longer compete against the GM&O, the ICRR, and the Wabash, and what traffic those lines did not take away, the automobile did. In 1953 freight income subsidized passenger services to the tune of $500,000. Losses of this magnitude for a relatively small system were unsustainable and, despite public opposition, on March 3, 1956, the Illinois Terminal ran its last passenger train just before the wires came down.[28]

Another central Illinois service of local concern annulled in the 1950s was the Santa Fe's daily Pekin to Chicago doodlebug. The tortoise-like train ambled for five hours on its 154-mile voyage, stopping to pick up mail and express along with a few passengers and livestock. Departing Pekin at seven in the morning, it finally arrived at Dearborn Street Station just after noon and almost immediately left for its return. The ICC authorized discontinuance, and it made its last trip on January 29, 1955. Elsewhere across central Illinois, the Nickel Plate Railroad had begun regular passenger services from St. Louis to Cleveland in 1928. Given names (the *Blue Arrow* and the *Blue Dart*, westbound and eastbound, respectively) in 1956, the trains did not reach wartime traffic levels, and in 1959 the company terminated the service in western Indiana, eliminating the Illinois run-through. The C&EI applied to the ICC in 1961 for permission to abandon its Chicago to West

Vienna service, operated by a lone Budd Rail Diesel Car, after absorbing $116,890 in losses the previous year. Farther north the Soo Line lost $8.5 million on passenger services in 1952 and eliminated some trains completely while discontinuing sleepers and dining cars on others.[29]

RUNNING OUT OF TIME

Events across the 1950s seemed to push the American passenger train inexorably toward death, and at the end of the decade *Trains* magazine devoted an entire issue to the question, "Who Shot the Passenger Train?" The answer, suggested editor David P. Morgan, lay not in economic changes but in "psychological obsolescence." Morgan argued that the passenger train had been shot in the back by labor, regulators, railroads, and customers. Labor organizations unwilling to rewrite "reckless and, worse yet, self-defeating" work rules, irresponsible regulators who did not have to meet the costs of their rulings, ruinous tax bills, and taxpayer subsidies for lock-and-dam complexes, highways, and airports also contributed. Passenger services cost the railroads $161.86 in expenses for every $100 of gross income in 1957, but Morgan saw hope in the future and advocated saving them by separating passenger from freight operations, upgrading rolling stock, and renegotiating labor contracts.[30]

Few who read the issue heeded its recommendations. Improved cars—including popular observation cars—and a plethora of streamlined trains could not preserve passenger services. Ridership and revenue continued to tumble into the 1960s, and in 1968 less than 2 percent of the traveling public used railroads. Railroad executives knew that 40 percent of the profits from freight went to subsidize passenger operations, draining the bottom line and taking money away from capital improvements. The railroads themselves wanted to kill off passenger trains, their desire gaining momentum as the postal service accelerated the shift from rail to road and air for long-distance mail. In 1967 the post office, calculating that trucks and airplanes could provide a more reliable service, canceled mail contracts on virtually all intercity trains. "Head-end" units—railway

post offices and express-package cars coupled immediately behind the locomotives—were in many cases the only source of profit on passenger runs attracting a handful of customers. Railroads often had no financial incentive to continue a train when postal and parcel contracts ended.[31]

Formation of the Illinois Railroad Association (IRA) at a December 1950 meeting of the Chicago Railroad Presidents' Conference signaled a change in direction for the railroads' relationship with government. Instead of simply providing information to its members, the organization took an activist role. It tracked legislation, drafted bills, contacted member railroads, and testified in Springfield and Washington, DC, at hearings of concern to the state's railroads.[32] Like the Association of American Railroads, the principal national group lobbying for the industry in Washington, the IRA could do little in the short term to halt the decline, but in the long run AAR, IRA, and other pressure groups helped redefine railroading.

Commuter routes did get some investment in the 1960s. Though veering toward bankruptcy, the Rock Island leased new bilevel cars and improved customer service, breaking even by the end of the decade. After World War II, C&NW passengers grumbled about but had to endure old heavyweight carriages nicknamed "umbrella cars" because they sprang leaks during wet weather. Passengers had a nice surprise when, in the early 1960s, the company introduced refurbished locomotives and new double-decker stainless-steel carriages. This move brought a return to profitability for C&NW commuter services, aided by the closure of two competing interurbans, the Chicago, Aurora & Elgin (CA&E) and the Chicago, Milwaukee & North Shore. Construction of the Congress (later Eisenhower) Expressway devastated the CA&E because the line could no longer operate east of Forest Park, and its passengers were forced to transfer onto CTA subway trains, breaking what had been a seamless journey from the western suburbs into the loop. Plagued by mounting losses, it ended passenger services at 12:10 PM on July 3, 1957, stranding thousands of commuters in downtown Chicago. After repeated requests for abandonment, the North Shore

finally pulled down its wires in 1963, clearing the way for the C&NW to dominate suburban traffic north of Chicago.[33]

Elsewhere, riders on New York Central services complained about plans to close that line's East Side Station, even though its "waiting room is drafty, the roof leaks, doors don't close properly, and windows are poorly boarded up." Commuters riding the Chicago & Western Indiana's four passenger coaches—dating from 1926—lost their vintage train from Dolton to Dearborn Street Station in August 1964. On the other hand, the roughly forty thousand Illinois Central Railroad commuters woke up to good news when the federal government made $25 million available for the South Suburban Mass Transit District to purchase new double-decker, air-conditioned cars for ICRR suburban services.[34]

Commuter services into downtown Chicago survived because eliminating them would have further congested the city's already stressed streets. Establishing regional taxing authorities to subsidize mass transit offered one model for saving services elsewhere in Illinois, where passenger trains proved surprisingly durable. When the federal government offered to operate passenger trains nearly every railroad corporation accepted the deal. The state of Illinois explored ways to save them, including providing taxpayer subsidies, though the Rock Island retained its *Rockets*. But that Granger Road was living on borrowed time and would become a victim of the shrinking demand for rail service, a trend only deregulation would halt.

Figure 16.3. The days are numbered for the CA&E as the way is cleared for the Congress Street Expressway, which will lead to the demolition of this elevated track and cut the interurban off from downtown Chicago. Center for Railroad Photography and Art.

17

NATIONAL SOLUTIONS?

The age of the private railroad passenger train finally ended in 1971. Declining revenues, customers siphoned off by other modes, and bad service precipitated the transfer of most common-carrier passenger trains from the railroads to the federal government. Railroad corporations, which had precious little time for celebrating glittering pasts, saving famous trains, or reducing large deficits, could then put all their energies toward surviving. Chicago remained the hub of the American railroad network, principally by default because no other city could be bothered to mount a serious challenge for a crown no one particularly wanted anymore. The state government of Illinois would step forward to contribute to saving and creating regional passenger services, and a few long-distance trains endured into the 1970s, but the romance and luxury of rail travel seemed the relic of a bygone era.

Government regulation came under renewed attack in the 1970s. The Interstate Commerce Commission botched merger after merger, finally losing the plot completely in the case of the attempt by Union Pacific and Southern Pacific to purchase and divide the Chicago, Rock Island & Pacific. That effort began in 1962, but opposition from other railroads slowed the process to a crawl. Moving at a snail's pace, the ICC failed to render a timely decision, which, along with the added costs of deferred maintenance, meant UP and SP became less interested with each passing year. The Rock Island died amid renewed calls for dismantling the rate-making regime.

FROM RAILPAX TO AMTRAK

In 1970 the average number of daily passenger trains nationally was five hundred, down from a pre–World War II high of twenty thousand. Politicians recognized that something had to be done if American passenger trains were to be saved, and that something turned out to be a federal program that came to be known as Amtrak. The formation of Amtrak occurred in three stages. First, in October 1970 Congress passed the Rail Passenger Service Act creating Railpax, named after the telegraphic designation for passengers. A private corporation chartered and jointly funded by the federal government and the railroads, Railpax was authorized to design and operate a national passenger network. Either railroad companies could pay Railpax to run their passenger trains at a cost based on total passenger losses in 1969, or they could continue to provide the service themselves. The enabling legislation allowed Railpax to take up to $40 million in grants and loan guarantees from the federal government to operate trains from May 1, 1971.[1]

In the second stage of Amtrak's formation, which lasted from November 1970 until January 1971, Railpax negotiated with interest groups, labor unions, and the railroads to establish the new corporation's route map. The federal administrator in charge of Railpax, former defense contractor John Volpe, overrode Department of Transportation officials who wanted the new services concentrated in the

The Iron Road in the Prarie State

Figure 17.1. Three new Amtrak SDP40F diesels at EMD in LaGrange (1973). Lake Forest College Library Special Collections.

Northeast. Ignoring their advice, Volpe insisted on creating a national network, and his first attempt had trains from Chicago serving New York, Cincinnati, Detroit, Houston, Los Angeles, Miami, New Orleans, St. Louis, San Francisco, Seattle, and Washington, DC. The only other passenger train to operate in Illinois was a service from St. Louis to the nation's capital through the center of the state.

By January 1971 the passenger train schedules of the United States had been completely revised to the satisfaction of almost no one. Small towns with proud railroad roots and multiple daily trains lost service completely. Gilman, for example, straddled the

Toledo, Peoria & Western and two Illinois Central lines but saw passenger service fall from thirty-two trains within living memory to none when Amtrak began operations. Experts thought the Chicago to Miami route poorly planned because it bypassed Indianapolis and Atlanta, while members of Congress in underserved or excluded states demanded their share of the action. Despite Volpe's stance, most of the proposed trains did run in the Northeast, while three of the five projected long-distance routes from Chicago to the West Coast operated three times a week instead of daily. Undeterred by the threat of lawsuits from communities and passengers, Railpax ended service on several Illinois routes. Decatur, on the Norfolk & Western, lost passenger trains to Chicago, as did communities along the Chicago & North Western from Clinton, Iowa. Illinois Central passenger trains from the Windy City to Springfield and Carbondale were annulled.[2]

The third phase in the creation of a federally subsidized railroad passenger network began when Railpax hired the New York design firm of Lippincott and Margulies to create a new image for rail travel. Lippincott invented the name Amtrak, created its first logo (quickly nicknamed the pointless arrow), and optimistically announced that reviving passenger travel would take only three years. The firm consulted with airlines on computerized ticketing, meal service, special fares, baggage handling, and ways to improve passenger experiences.[3] But no amount of flashy branding and updated computer systems could instantly restore the tarnished reputation of the passenger train. That process would take decades.

When Railpax began operations as Amtrak in May 1971, twenty railroads gave cash, equipment, or service obligations totaling $190 million to the new corporation. Civic dignitaries and rail fans waved farewell to many trains as they operated for the last time. In Illinois only the dying Chicago, Rock Island & Pacific retained its passenger services, company officials calculating it would be cheaper than paying Amtrak to run them, but other railroads joyfully abdicated their passenger trains to the new entity. Amtrak compiled a unified equipment pool and used existing rolling stock without regard for their origins. "Rainbow trains" of cars from multiple railroads began appearing all over the country. Following the Lippincott line, Volpe and other officials claimed Amtrak would turn a profit within three years, establishing what they hyped as a model for other countries to follow. Given the constraints under which they operated, especially speculation that the Nixon administration wanted to strangle rail travel and the fact that Amtrak paid rent to other railroads to run its trains, these officials should not have been surprised when their prediction failed to come true.[4]

Amtrak experienced many false starts, working as it did to pick up the pieces of passenger travel or, more accurately, to force the phoenix to rise from the ashes of its recent immolation. Though it owned the former Pennsylvania mainline between Washington, DC, and New York City, called the Northeast Corridor, Amtrak encountered resistance and resentment from the railroads over whose track its train operated elsewhere. Santa Fe officials, for example, complained that Amtrak's old rolling stock and poor performance tarnished its storied *Super Chief* name because the train looked like "a French whorehouse." The Santa Fe reduced the potential profitability of the train by restricting its length and refusing to allow Amtrak to remove the loss-making first-class diner. The same company rebuffed an attempt by Amtrak to use its main line between Chicago and Chillicothe as part of a route to Peoria, condemning that service to extinction. Just a month after Amtrak began operations, the *City of New Orleans* derailed near Tonti, south of Effingham, killing eleven passengers. Widely publicized photographs of passenger cars lying on their sides with bent rails piercing their roofs did little to boost the image of rail travel.[5]

Problems beset Amtrak's Chicago to New York services. Critics charged that Amtrak's version of the *Broadway Limited* was at best a pale imitation of its renowned Pennsylvania Railroad namesake and at worst an insult. New carpets faded, equipment frequently broke down, mice scurried around onboard, and a near-fatal case of food poisoning demolished any remaining luster the train may have had. By 1973 fewer than one in ten trips arrived at their destinations on time. Yet shortly after inaugurating the *Broadway Limited,* Amtrak added the *Lake Shore,* a Chicago to New York service via Cleveland over former New York Central tracks. As bad as the *Broadway* was, the *Lake Shore* was worse. State legislators refused to appropriate funds to subsidize it and low ridership plagued the train. After just eight months and losses totaling $3.6 million, Amtrak axed it.[6]

Chicago remained the hub of the passenger system, but the initial pickings were slim. The corporation centered services on Union Station, resulting in the closure of Central Station, Dearborn Street, and Grand Central by mid-1972. Amtrak attempted to revive the *California Zephyr,* which had lost its route over the Western Pacific into Oakland, forcing passengers to change trains at Ogden, Utah. Temporarily named the *City of San Francisco,* the Chicago to Oakland train amassed an atrocious on-time record. Not until the 1980s did Amtrak restore the *California Zephyr* name, and then only after delivery of new Superliner equipment more in keeping with the famous train's illustrious reputation than the rainbow consists of Amtrak's early years. The result was a revival of the "cruise ship on rails" concept Ralph Budd had envisioned when the train began running in 1949, inspiring one traveling journalist to call it "the most welcome comeback in recent railroad history, the New California Zephyr—still the most scenic single route through the American West."[7]

Other long-distance Amtrak trains from Illinois were not so fortunate. Chicago to Florida services had flourished in the early twentieth century and again immediately after World War II. Running over the tracks of thirteen different railroads, they had been popular with tourists until the automobile triumphed in the 1950s. Amtrak attempted to revive the Florida route with the *South Wind,* operating over Illinois Central, New York Central, Louisville & Nashville, and Seaboard Coast Line tracks between Chicago and Miami. To boost patronage, Amtrak changed the train's name to the *Floridian* and mounted a lavish marketing campaign. A slow schedule, bad track, breakdowns, and consistently late arrivals doomed it. In August 1973 the train reached a new low with an on-time record of only 6.2 percent. In 1974 it derailed four times on former New York Central tracks through Indiana. In 1975 the twelve-car train derailed near Pulaski, Tennessee, "hurtling eight cars into steep ravines on either side of the track and injuring most of the 82 passengers."[8]

Amtrak's already poor reputation suffered from the bad publicity. The chairman of the National Association of Railroad Passengers, an advocacy group, warned that "the law of averages tells me there will be an accident with multiple fatalities," and passengers testified to the ICC about cockroaches on dining-room tables, overbooked journeys on short trains of old cars, and motion sickness induced by swaying rolling stock. A detour necessary to avoid closed sections of track added two hours to the *Floridian* schedule, and an experiment with car-carrying "Auto-Train" equipment failed financially. After losing millions of dollars and being canceled and reinstated several times between 1977 and 1979, the *Floridian* made its final run in October 1979.[9]

Service downstate suffered, especially for east-west passengers. Just one train, the Kansas City to New York City and Washington, DC, *National Limited,* traversed southern Illinois longitudinally. It proved to be a train of lost opportunities: between St. Louis, Missouri, and Terre Haute, Indiana, it stopped only at Effingham, and no effort was made to connect with the north-south *City of New Orleans* there. Even after schedule adjustments made the connection possible, passengers faced waits of up to eight hours between trains. Dinner in the dining car could take two hours or more to consume because of "inefficient and unfriendly" servers. The *National Limited* operated over deteriorating Conrail track that Amtrak president Paul Reistrup characterized as "absolutely lousy." Though it briefly turned a profit and passengers praised it, the train racked up $15 million in losses, and Amtrak announced it was ending the service in September 1979. Passenger groups protested and the case reached the Supreme Court, where Chief Justice Warren Burger overturned a lower court ruling in favor of retaining the train.[10] The *National Limited* had run out of time.

ILLINOIS SPONSORS TRAINS

Unlike those in most other states, Illinois politicians were not prepared to let passenger trains die. They offered subsidies to Amtrak to operate trains in regions underserved by airlines or on routes where ridership growth seemed possible. One region in particular, west-central Illinois, desperately needed passenger service because it had no interstate highways and no long-distance buses but several colleges enrolling students from Chicagoland. When the Burlington Northern tried to discontinue its trains from Quincy

Figure 17.2. Amtrak Dash 8-32BWH, no. 507, at Joliet (April 7, 1992). Author's collection.

to Chicago, riders—especially from Quincy College and Western Illinois University—complained to the Illinois Commerce Commission. The state government invoked a clause in the Rail Passenger Service Act allowing it to subsidize a passenger service by covering two-thirds of its operating deficit. Legislators appropriated the funds, and, after negotiations with Amtrak and the Burlington Northern, the *Illinois Zephyr* was inaugurated in November 1971, becoming within three years "the most successful state-subsidized train anywhere in the country."[11]

Chicago to St. Louis trains, which enjoyed steady patronage from Springfield, received a boost in 1975 when Amtrak temporarily assigned a gas-turbine-powered Turboliner to the route. Leased from the French train builder ANF, the new equipment consisted of five-car units with driving cabs at both ends. They received favorable reviews from travelers and reporters, with one journalist writing that the new train was "a sheer delight." Unfortunately for passengers, the experimental equipment had to be removed from service after a truck drove into the side of the train near Elwood, injuring

The Iron Road in the Prarie State

thirty-nine passengers and causing over $1 million worth of damage to the lightweight four-car unit.[12]

Growing demand for Illinois Amtrak trains convinced the state government to establish an Intercity Rail Passenger Office in 1974 to oversee taxpayer-subsidized services. A few state-sponsored trains failed to thrive despite support from Springfield and the high hopes of advocates. The *Black Hawk* from Chicago to East Dubuque relied on patrons from midroute Rockford, but its almost two-hour schedule could never adequately compete with the ninety-minute journey time from there to the Windy City on Interstate 90. It began operating in 1974 but was discontinued in 1981 because of low passenger numbers and a poor on-time record caused by bad track and malfunctioning signals.[13]

Similar problems plagued the *Rockets* to Peoria and the Quad Cities, which Amtrak began operating after the Rock Island's bankruptcy. Hampered by the Santa Fe's refusal to allow them to run over its main line to Chillicothe, and despite stays of execution and promises of new routes over better track, the *Rockets* finally fizzled out at the end of 1978. By 1977 ridership had fallen to a daily average of twenty-six people on the *Quad Cities Rocket* and just thirteen on the *Peoria Rocket,* levels no state legislator could justify subsidizing. For a short while Amtrak replaced the *Rocket* with the *Prairie Marksman* between Chicago and East Peoria. Running over the Illinois Central Gulf to Chenoa and onto the Toledo, Peoria & Western for the remainder of the journey, it was never particularly popular, terminating as it did on the wrong side of the Illinois River for many would-be patrons. Within four months of its first run, as ridership hovered around seventy a day, state officials issued a "use it or lose it" warning to towns along its route. Despite a fare roughly one-fifth of the cost of flying, the service did not catch on. The probationary period of eighteen months came to an end in October 1981 with the target of 150 passengers daily unmet, and Amtrak ended the service. The Peoria area was without a passenger train for the first time in 140 years. Elsewhere, though, state-subsidized trains proved popular with passengers. Students at the University of Illinois riding from Chicago to Champaign found Amtrak's cleaner and more punctual service an improvement over Illinois Central passenger trains.[14]

BANKRUPTCY BLUE:
THE DEMISE OF THE ROCK ISLAND

The economy of Illinois suffered throughout the 1970s. It dropped from fourth to fifth place in the national population ranking between 1960 and 1970. In the decade of the 1970s almost a million more residents died or left than were born or entered. Industrial decline led commentators to label the Midwest the "Rust Belt" as jobs and people fled to the Sunbelt. Some parts of Illinois did benefit from a shift in manufacturing away from urban and to rural areas driven by the search for non-unionized, low-cost labor. This did not materially help the railroads, because small plants such as the International Shoe Company factory in Anna, near Carbondale, relied on trucks for shipping raw materials and finished goods.[15] Racial segregation in Chicago and towns such as East St. Louis, Joliet, Rockford, and Urbana bred unemployment and poverty. Illinois seemed out of step with the times, its reliance on heavy industry and its political cronyism retarding modernization.

Symptomatic of the problems confronting Illinois was the failed attempt by Union Pacific to purchase the Chicago, Rock Island & Pacific. The venerable but unprofitable Granger Road promised to meet the original transcontinental's need for a secure gateway to Chicago. But the Rock Island had never fully recovered from the bleeding administered by the Reid-Moore syndicate between 1902 and 1915. Controlled by businessman Henry Crown, who made a fortune in the building supply industry and owned Rock Island securities worth $29 million and a tenth of its common stock, it needed the new partner to survive in the shrinking midwestern market. Though amenable to a merger, Crown understandably wanted to turn a profit on the deal and derailed several proposals, losing his able president, Downing B. Jenks, to the Missouri Pacific in the process. Jenks would resurrect MoPac to the point where it became a desirable target for the Union Pacific, but only after UP ultimately refused to absorb Crown's ailing Rock.[16]

In late 1962 the Union Pacific reached out to its archenemy, the Southern Pacific, and suggested dividing the Rock Island. The UP still stopped where it had originally started, in Council Bluffs, Iowa, and transferred its freight and passenger trains onto the Grangers for the rest of the trip to Chicago. Blocked from purchasing the Burlington by that road's owners, the Great Northern and the Northern Pacific, UP wanted the Rock's northern routes, especially the Chicago to Omaha main line. The Southern Pacific would get the Rock's lower tier—which tied into its own system at Tucumcari, New Mexico, and in St. Louis—to strengthen the joint SP–Rock Island "Golden State" route from Chicago to southern California. In June 1963 the Union Pacific made a formal proposal to the Rock Island, whose managers were receptive, as was Crown. Alarmed, the Chicago & North Western applied to the ICC to gain control of the Rock for itself. This may or may not have been a sincere effort to create a large regional road, but it did have the effect of disrupting the proposed consolidation. It took a further four years of negotiation before the merger case even came before the ICC.

The proceedings proved protracted and complicated. Every railroad in the country seemingly took a direct interest in the proposal. The North Western and the Milwaukee Road relied on the Union Pacific for a steady flow of freight traffic off the transcontinental, and the two companies feared its loss would spell their doom. North Western chairman Ben Heineman marshaled the opposition. This included just about every other western road, one of which, the Missouri Pacific, demanded extensive running rights and compensation should UP and Rock Island merge. The Santa Fe objected to the Southern Pacific connecting with the Rock and demanded running rights of its own. The hearings dragged on as Heineman argued that his road, even if allowed to merge with the Milwaukee Road and the Chicago Great Western, would not survive the combination of the Union Pacific and the Rock Island.[17]

The wheels of regulation turned slowly. The ICC rendered its decision in several parts separated by almost three years. In July 1970 ICC examiner Nathan Klitenic ruled that the merger could proceed after meeting certain conditions without specifying what those were. In 1971 and 1972 Klitenic issued further reports clarifying the conditions but leaving the final details undecided. At last, in February 1973, after ten years of hearings and decisions and complaints and reports and counterreports, Klitenic threw a hand grenade into the proceedings. He unexpectedly published a scheme to restructure the entire railroading system west of the Mississippi River by creating four systems: the Burlington Northern, the Santa Fe, the Southern Pacific, and the Union Pacific. Simple, rational, and elegant, it was monumentally unrealistic. Everyone involved protested, and another delay had been added to an already overlong process. Finally, the ICC gave the Rock Island mergers a green light, but UP backed out, and SP offered a ridiculously low purchase price for the southern lines. It was, as historian Richard Saunders wrote, "the most disastrous merger case ever."[18]

No one could have anticipated a ten-year delay from formal proposal to final ruling, but the refusal of the Rock Island board to authorize expenditures on maintenance during the hearings was inexcusable even under these circumstances. Claiming it could not "provide adequate service to the public" without the merger, the Rock Island did invest $24.4 million in new locomotives, freight cars, and cabooses. Under President Jervis Langdon Jr., the Rock Island launched a track renewal program on the Tucumcari line to improve its connection with the Southern Pacific. Unit grain trains and direct freight service from Silvis to Elkhart, Indiana, earned it the Railway Progress Institute's Silver Freight Car Trophy for innovation, but losses mounted. Langdon needed a rapid conclusion to the hearings to resolve his line's growing financial difficulties, but he did not get it. It was all downhill for the Rock.[19]

As the merger hearings dragged on Langdon retired, the track—especially on branch lines and spurs—deteriorated, and rolling stock showed signs of wear and tear. Henry Crown fretted that his investment would be lost, while his despondent employees worried for their livelihoods. Slow orders caused by bad track were plentiful but customers, driven away by the malaise, were not. Ultimately, there was nothing worth buying—so the

UP didn't. In 1974 the Rock Island repainted its locomotives and cabooses in a symbolic but futile attempt to hide the recent past. A year later the line entered receivership, earning its new color the nickname "bankruptcy blue." In that year the *Chicago Tribune* opined that "government delayed is no government at all" and recommended eliminating the ICC on the grounds that it "has long outlived its usefulness."[20] Such a move was just around the corner.

In 1980 the Rock became the first major railroad in the United States to be closed and its assets sold off. Others had been merged or divided, but the Rock was dismembered. A precipitous strike by disgruntled clerks, the loss of a vital contract to transport General Motors vehicles, and Congress's refusal to finance its recovery were the final nails in its coffin. Rock Island service terminated at 11:59 PM on March 2, 1980, and the sell-off began. Henry Crown was overjoyed: he would get a return on his investment after all. Rock lines were sold to existing railroads, made into new ones, or closed down completely and lifted. In Illinois its main line was divided at Bureau, with the track east to Chicago becoming the property of B&O while a new company, Iowa Interstate—successor to the short-lived Iowa Railroad—operated from Bureau through Rock Island to Council Bluffs. The Iowa Interstate later resurrected the derelict Rock route south from Bureau along the Illinois River to Peoria. Elsewhere, Cotton Belt, the North Western (which purchased the "spine line" from the Twin Cities to Kansas City and agricultural branches in northwestern Iowa), and the Katy obtained the majority of the trackage.[21] A long and mostly glorious chapter of Illinois railroad history ended when the Rock Island—that "mighty fine line"—disappeared.

CHAOS ON THE EAST COAST, CHICANERY IN LASALLE

As the slow demise of the Rock Island unfolded, railroading on America's East Coast nearly expired. The two giants of the Northeast, the Pennsylvania Railroad and the New York Central, applied to the ICC in 1962 for permission to merge. The commission took its time but formally accepted the proposal to create Penn

Central in 1968. The two corporations, whose combined revenue represented a fifth of the industry total, had unaccountably done little advance planning and failed in their attempt to unify two very different operations. Clerks and crews were ill prepared when the new company closed yards to save money. Loaded freight cars vanished for up to a month at a time as the two systems collided, neither side willing to alter its operating procedures. Both companies owned lines across central Illinois from Indianapolis to St. Louis, the Pennsylvania via Effingham and the New York Central farther north along the former Big Four line through Mattoon. Penn Central downgraded the NYC line, which meant that cars for customers on that route had to travel east on the former Pennsylvania all the way to Indianapolis before switching onto the NYC to return west. The added transit time drove customers away.[22]

The Penn Central merger created opportunities for skillful entrepreneurs willing to skirt the law. In central Illinois a company leasing space from the fifteen-mile-long LaSalle & Bureau County Railroad (LS&BC) did just that. The LS&BC switched with the Illinois Central, the Burlington, the Milwaukee Road, and Penn Central, connecting with every point on the American railroad compass. In the 1970s it rented sidings and shops to Magna Earth, a subsidiary of New Jersey–based Diversified Properties. Like other companies, Diversified purchased damaged boxcars to rehabilitate and resell or lease. So far so good, but Penn Central record keeping left a lot to be desired, and boxcars kept vanishing.

When federal investigators discovered some of the missing Penn Central boxcars on LS&BC sidings in March 1971 they seized the records of the railroad. "There is more here than meets the eye," one railroad official told the Associated Press. But an LS&BC railroader claimed the case was not clear cut, because at least some of the cars were legitimately owned by Diversified and were repainted at Magna Earth. Diversified had bought 466 damaged boxcars, but 638 were delivered, many in good condition. Magna Earth employees painted over the Penn Central logos, added LS&BC reporting marks, and sent the boxcars out to earn their keep. Loaned on a per diem basis to railroads around the country, some found their way into revenue service for Penn Central, which meant that the railroad was unwittingly paying to rent boxcars from itself.[23]

The federal government charged Diversified Properties with stealing boxcars, and the case came before a grand jury in Philadelphia. Joseph C. Bonanno, president of Diversified and the unfortunate holder of the same name as a Mafia don then in the news (Joseph "Joe Bananas" Bonanno), proclaimed his innocence. An agent with the Federal Task Force on Organized Crime suggested otherwise, asserting that Penn Central computers had been "manipulated . . . to make it appear the freight cars had not vanished." The boxcars, he charged, "had definitely been stolen, not accidentally lost or misrouted."[24]

In June 1971 Penn Central announced that 199 of the missing boxcars had been found on the railroad's own lines, but at least 215 others were in use elsewhere, many bearing LS&BC markings. The LS&BC had legitimately purchased 466 boxcars owned by Equitable Assurance Society upon the expiration of their leases with the Penn Central, but an extra 153 boxcars had mysteriously fallen into LS&BC hands. Those cars were returned to the Penn Central. Because its own records were a shambles, Penn Central settled out of court, taking possession of the missing boxcars and $150,000 in cash. No guilt was assigned, but the LS&BC quickly became known as the Let's Steal Box Cars Railroad. Bonanno moved on to pursue his railroading career in Florida, where, a year later, he incurred the wrath of West Virginia congressman Harley O. Staggers for ruining the Marianna & Blountstown by clogging its rails with boxcars his employees were storing and refurbishing while neglecting its customers.[25]

In the grand scheme of things, a few misplaced boxcars were the least of Penn Central's worries. The combined road simply was not earning enough revenue to meet its costs, and financiers restricted its access to lines of credit. Like many other businesses, it suffered during an unusual period of simultaneous recession and inflation. Unable to repay outstanding loans, Penn Central declared bankruptcy in June 1970. Its demise proved "an astonishing denouement to the high hopes for improved service and financial strength stirred by the merger of two giant railroad systems" just two years before. Creditors demanded that the road be closed and its assets sold off, but Penn Central was too big to fail. Had it stopped operating, half the nation's factories would have shut their doors. So great was its importance to American business that economists estimated GNP would fall by 2 percent within weeks if Penn Central stopped running. Something had to be done. With no buyers on the horizon, the federal government converted Penn Central into the Consolidated Rail Corporation (Conrail) in 1976 to keep the trains moving. Conrail was a private, for-profit railroad with a federal charter; creditors of its bankrupt predecessors owned its stock, but it did not turn a profit until the 1980s. It did, however, set the stage for the recovery of the American railroad network.[26]

The American passenger train appeared destined for extinction. By 1975 only three main line termini remained in Chicago: Union Station, LaSalle Street Station, and the Northwestern Station. All three were redeveloped—torn down and relocated one block to the south, in the case of LaSalle Street—as Amtrak trains moved exclusively to Union Station. For suburban commuters, however, passenger services remained vital. In 1974 voters in the six-county Chicago metropolitan area authorized creation of the Regional Transit Authority to fund commuter service. By then, the North Western had already handed over its few remaining passenger services to Amtrak, which took the rolling stock and chose not to run any trains over C&NW tracks.[27]

The creation of Amtrak and the provision of secure taxpayer funding for commuter rail relieved the railroads of loss-generating passenger trains. The other great weight on their shoulders, government regulation, was about to be lifted. Recovering from the demise of the Rock Island and the near extinction of eastern railroading, railroads would end the twentieth century as profitable, freight-focused enterprises allowed to shed traditional ways and compete unhindered for lucrative traffic. Just as significant, railroads learned to cooperate with trucking companies, barge operators, and shipping lines to provide intermodal service.

18

SALVATION

The collapse of the Rock Island and the failure of Penn Central sent shockwaves throughout the railroad industry and beyond. The former suggested that recovery would be a slow process, while the latter indicated that mergers alone could not save the trains. A dramatic shift was needed or they would vanish completely. The ICC paid attention to the consequences of delaying merger proposals, and a period of consolidation followed. Then, in 1980, reacting to the continued decline of the industry, the federal government passed legislation to deregulate railroads. The new law, called the Staggers Act in honor of one of its House sponsors, generated an immediate and positive upswing in virtually all railroad indices. The number of railroad corporations and route mileage in use continued to shrink, but the survivors enjoyed a renaissance, competing effectively with long-distance trucking, creating new markets for their services, and finding favor with Wall Street. Profitability followed.

Deregulation worked because archaic ICC rules caused economic sclerosis. The Staggers Act encouraged long-haul business and generated a renewed emphasis on mergers. Within fifteen years of its passage there were only seven major railroads, labeled "Class I" under the industry classification system, in the United States.[1] Illinois was the only state served by all seven. The Staggers Act indirectly encouraged consolidation by allowing railroads to limit access to important junctions and termini (gateways), meaning other companies could not hope to compete in those locations.

Elsewhere, truckers and railroads discovered a mutually beneficial relationship. The Preston Trucking Company, for example, expanded west by signing a contract with the ATSF to carry its trailers from Chicago, as did J. B. Hunt, seeking "faster, more reliable service" between the Midwest and the West Coast for time-sensitive, high-margin, imported commodities such as computers and video equipment.[2] For Illinois, however, the new age meant taking a reduced role in the financing and operations of the industry as headquarters moved out of the Prairie State and trains sought more efficient ways to run through it.

PARALLEL MERGERS

After withdrawing its application to purchase the Rock Island, the Union Pacific looked elsewhere to expand. It obtained the Missouri Pacific and the Western Pacific in 1983. MOPAC came with a bonus: a direct route to Chicago along the former Chicago & Eastern Illinois main line from St. Louis via Woodland Junction. Underfunded, losing the last remnants of its Florida traffic, and desperately needing new rolling stock and bridge repairs, the C&EI began seeking a buyer in 1960. In 1965 the ICC allowed MOPAC to purchase the C&EI line from St. Louis to Chicago, while the Louisville & Nashville bought the route from Woodland Junction south to Evansville. After opposition from the competing Illinois Central and disputes over stock ownership, the C&EI ceased to exist as an independent entity on October 15, 1976.[3]

The ICC made unwanted headlines when it rejected a proposed merger of the CB&Q, the GNR, and the NPR on April 27, 1966, the day it approved Penn Central. Trying to protect the Milwaukee Road, the ICC garnered negative press but only delayed the combination. The ICC approved a revised proposal granting the Milwaukee Road access to gateways and traffic rights on May 10, 1967. Opposition culminated in a Supreme Court hearing that concluded on February 2, 1970, with a 7–0 vote in favor of the new Burlington Northern (BN). The joining of the three "Hill roads" created the first of what some analysts called a "super railroad," holding an almost exclusive grip on the northern tier of the United States.[4]

With the CB&Q gone and the Milwaukee tottering, the era of the Grangers appeared to be drawing to a close. The North Western, one of those venerable and vulnerable roads, had to change. Maverick C&NW chairman Ben Heineman, whose fierce defense of the interests of his own road alienated executives on other railroads and helped torpedo the UP–Rock Island merger, had long talked publicly about the need for a single large midwestern railroad. In Heineman's ideal world this would be a combination of the North Western, the Rock Island, and the Milwaukee Road, along with some of the smaller regional and local companies.[5] He began by purchasing the Litchfield & Madison in 1958, giving the North Western access to St. Louis, and, two years later, bought the Minneapolis & St. Louis Railway. That acquisition created bad blood because the two companies had similar routes with the same terminals, and the North Western allowed M&StL track and facilities to deteriorate. A slightly smoother merger occurred in 1968, when the North Western purchased Chicago Great Western. It did so primarily because CGW owned a traffic generator called Roseport Industrial Park just outside the Twin Cities.[6]

A bigger prize lay in merging with the Milwaukee Road. Consolidation talks were an on-again, off-again proposition in the early 1960s, when the brotherhoods became concerned about repeated mention of the savings to be effected by eliminating the "substantial mileage of overlapping and parallel lines, duplicating yards and other facilities in the Midwest region." Job guarantees and retirement packages for union members were then added to the merger agreement. In September 1964 negotiations appeared to have concluded successfully, and four years later the ICC approved the merger. But the deal unraveled after Milwaukee shareholders sued to improve their side of the bargain and Northwest Industries, the holding company that owned the North Western, withdrew the offer.[7] By 1970 the North Western–Milwaukee Road merger was dead, and midwestern railroading stayed in the doldrums.

In an effort to shake off the cobwebs and reinvigorate the railroad, new president Larry Provo sold it from Northwest Industries to its employees in October 1970. The North Western became the first railroad and one of the largest corporations ever to be employee owned. The *Chicago Tribune* gently applauded the move as a step toward "that primitive form of private enterprise" in which employee and stockholder realize they have a mutual interest in the profitable operation of the company. It was, the *Tribune* claimed, "putting the eggs of management, labor, and the owners all back in the same basket." For $19 million and the assumption of $340 million in debt, the railroad became the property of the people who operated it. Only about a thousand of the fourteen thousand employees took advantage of the stock offer, and in 1981 the phrase "employee owned," which had been added to company logos and letterhead, was dropped because it did not reflect reality. Ultimately, employee stock ownership worked for those who took advantage of the initial offering: opening at $50, shares split within a year and were soon worth $650 each.[8]

No amount of financial tinkering could obscure the North Western's reliance on Union Pacific traffic for survival. The two companies signed a 1974 freight interchange agreement using the recently opened Fremont, Nebraska, "cutoff" to avoid the delays caused by running trains through Omaha. Ninety percent of all UP freight destined for Chicago ran over the North Western within a year. The increased volume of traffic meant C&NW needed to upgrade its line from Chicago to Omaha, part of which had been single-tracked as an economy measure during the 1960s. The company obtained federal funds and loan guarantees under the so-called 4-R Act, passed as one of the responses to the demise of Penn Central in 1970. The act authorized the government to purchase railroad bonds with a low interest rate and a long maturity, allowing the C&NW to upgrade its track. The old rails then cascaded down to other parts of the North Western system, and improvements rippled all the way to its freight yards.[9]

DEREGULATION

New rails and operational consolidations would not save the industry. Federally mandated rate structures and harrowingly slow adjustment procedures had long restricted railroads' ability to compete against other modes of transportation, particularly the mostly unregulated trucking industry. Railroaders and regulators therefore watched with great interest as the Canadian government began deregulating transportation north of the US border in 1967. Ottawa's Transport Commission acknowledged the obvious fact that railroads no longer enjoyed a monopoly on long-distance shipping and stated that the government's role should be to "encourage competition among carriers and free them from some of the federal restraints on rate-making."[10] In Washington, DC, the ICC took note and deregulated fruit and vegetable shipments, long lost to trucks, from the West Coast. US railroads grabbed the opportunity to gain additional traffic and, more importantly, to show how they would respond in a deregulated world. The ICC authorized further rate revisions on a case-by-case basis. The Illinois Central signed innovative contracts with the food-processing colossus A. E. Staley, and the C&NW procured new business with corporate giants Proctor & Gamble and General Foods. These and other moves helped divert traffic from road to rail, strengthening the case for complete deregulation of the industry.

Not everyone was pleased. Many shippers dependent on railroads to supply raw materials and deliver finished products appreciated the relatively low and usually slow-changing rates. Especially attractive to business was the inflexibility of ratemaking, a result of the ICC appeals process. The glacial pace of pricing adjustments for freight railroad services meant that transportation costs remained stable even as other costs increased during the inflationary 1970s. Hearings, complaints, and consultations delayed the hikes railroads needed to keep up with inflation and to fund track and rolling-stock improvements. But when the federal government began deregulating the airline industry in 1978 it was clear change was coming, and a wave of cautious optimism rippled through railroading.

Shipper resistance undid the first attempt to formulate a bill deregulating railroad ratemaking. Introduced in 1979 by two Democrats, Representative Harley O. Staggers of West Virginia and Senator Howard Cannon of Nevada, the bill was withdrawn in July 1980. The bill's opponents were legion and their coffers large. Industrial and commercial customers claimed that deregulation would mean higher shipping rates, while truckers feared losing business to the railroads. President Jimmy Carter, facing a close race for reelection against Republican challenger Ronald Reagan, sought a compromise and found it by setting maximum rates on "captive commodities," such as coal and iron ore, where no intermodal competition existed. This allowed the bill to move through Congress, and President Carter signed the Staggers Act into law on October 14, 1980, three weeks before the election he would lose.[11]

The Staggers Act ended a century of regulations banning differential pricing. Rate setting in a competitive, multimodal environment required earning revenue sufficient to allow reinvestment. Railroads after 1980 negotiated with shippers within a legal and political framework tolerating "a degree of market dominance and price differentiation." These types of minimonopolies had been unpopular because shippers and consumers formerly accepted regulation on the grounds it protected small manufacturers. In short, Staggers turned that world upside down by privileging large-scale shippers and encouraging market-driven pricing.[12]

The immediate response to Staggers, subsequently labeled "among the most consequential pieces of railroad legislation in history," came from shippers.[13] While the railroads waited for the ICC to finish writing new rules, their customers took full advantage of a clause creating a 180-day window for challenging existing rates.

Requests for lower rates poured in from shippers, but the railroads generally played a waiting game. Thomas White of the Association of American Railroads, predicting a via media, believed the railroad industry was entering "uncharted waters" in which a "shake down period" would see some rates increase, while others would fall. John Kenefick, president of the Union Pacific, worried that competition among railroads for business could lead to "a serious downward price movement" and prove disastrous for the industry. In contrast, James R. Wolfe, chief executive of the North Western, embraced deregulation. Declaring himself pleased with Staggers, Wolfe told journalists, "We consider ourselves entrepreneurs and if you're an entrepreneur, you like the freedom to act and the freedom to manage." The act promised railroads a type of liberty they had not known for a century, for good or ill, and railroad managers gained the ability to negotiate with shippers freely without fearing the ICC would reject innovative pricing strategies.[14]

The transition to a relatively free market in rail transportation did not go smoothly. One sticking point was the definition of "captive commodities." Bulk goods difficult to ship long distances by road such as coal, grain, and chemicals were usually included in that category, but exceptions arose. The ICC, gutted and marginalized by the antigovernment administration of President Ronald Reagan, ruled that coal exports were not covered because they were marketed by brokers. With their newfound freedom to respond to market conditions, railroad corporations raised rates selectively, causing unhappiness despite the fact that in some cases rates fell below pre-Staggers levels and mining corporations were enjoying abundant profits. Shippers complained to congressional subcommittees in 1983 that railroads were charging exorbitant rates to carry coal and grain. Adversarial interest groups developed. On one side were those who demanded revising Staggers (CURE, or Consumers United for Rail Equity, funded by coal mines and utilities), and on the other were its defenders (CARS, which stood for the Committee Against Revising Staggers, whose sponsors included Sears, Roebuck). Legislative attempts to reregulate coal

rates failed, and Staggers survived, but the railroads learned to tread lightly.[15] The free market, they discovered, had a human face.

Staggers enabled railroads to benefit from existing projects and the continued development of intermodal traffic. In the 1960s coal from the Powder River Basin of Montana and Wyoming became economical to mine and ship. With exploitable coal reserves estimated at 25 billion tons, the Powder River coal field represented an impressive source of low-sulfur—and therefore clean-burning—coal, increasingly attractive to power plants after the Clean Air Act of 1970. Extracting it was relatively simple compared to extracting the high-sulfur reserves buried beneath southern Illinois, and as the West boomed, anger and fear moved across Illinois as mines closed and unemployment rose.[16]

But Powder River coal was a long way from its users, which is where the railroads came in. The North Western's Coal Line Project culminated in August 1984 with the first Powder River coal train running over the line it owned jointly with the Burlington Northern. After delays and apparent obstruction by the Hill roads, which began operating their own trains out of the basin from Big Sky, Montana, to St. Paul, Minnesota, on May 1, 1969, the North Western commenced running unit coal trains south to Shawnee Junction and then over a connecting line to UP tracks at Joyce, Nebraska, and into Illinois.[17]

The other side of salvation came in the form of containers that were technically known as COFCs, or "containers on flatcar." Rectangular steel boxes capable of carrying virtually anything from toys to computers and stoves to scrap iron, COFCs are a crucial component in intermodal transportation because they can be lifted from a railroad flatcar onto a truck trailer or a ship and thereby eliminate the need for repacking. Stacked two high (double stacks) on trains and nine or more high in the holds of oceangoing vessels using removable corner posts, COFCs provide an economical means of transporting commodities. The Illinois Central was one of the pioneers in the container revolution, which integrated railroads more completely into global commerce and gave long-distance merchandise freight a new lease

The Iron Road in the Prarie State

on life.[18] Virtually scrapping the boxcar, railroads across the state took full advantage of the economies of scale containerization created.

The C&NW began operating double-stack container trains in 1984, interchanging with the Union Pacific for service from the West Coast to Chicago. This proved popular with shippers, and by the mid-1980s container mileage had surpassed piggybacks. The North Western increased capacity when it purchased Robey Street Yard from the B&O Chicago Terminal and combined it with the adjacent Wood Street Yard into a massive new container yard called Global One in 1986. Global One allowed the number of container trains on the C&NW to grow from eight per week to fourteen; by 1988 the company took an average of thirty-eight per week and opened Global Two at its Proviso Yard near the Chicago passenger station to further expand volume.[19]

When the Union Pacific renewed its interest in acquiring the North Western at the end of the 1980s, the latter was a lean, focused railroad. It had abandoned nearly two thousand miles of branch lines representing 40 percent of total mileage but returning only 4 percent of revenue. As truck competition cut into grain haulage and manufacturing plants fled Illinois for the low-wage Sunbelt, company officials had turned to coal and containers. In 1989 the North Western, recovering from two strikes and the unexpected death of President James R. Wolfe, fended off an attempt by corporate raider Japonica Partners to buy it and sell off its assets. The price of survival in this case was a pact with the Union Pacific. The North Western assumed $750 million in debt to thwart Japonica and granted UP trackage rights to Chicago. Union Pacific obtained permission from the ICC to convert the North Western shares it had purchased in the Japonica fight into voting rights and continued purchasing C&NW stock. By 1995 the UP controlled 30 percent and announced it would buy the rest. After spending $1.2 billion it succeeded, and the Chicago & North Western existed no more as an independent entity.[20]

TOWARD A BIPOLAR WESTERN WORLD

Mergers after 1980 followed a new pattern and fundamentally redrew the railroad map. Combinations of parallel routes were common in the pre-Staggers era because overbuilding had resulted in the duplication of poor service, low track utilization, and high per-unit costs. Thus, the C&NW's purchases of the M&StL and the CGW allowed the dominant corporation—the North Western—to abandon much of the track it had bought to concentrate on a few key routes. The Rock Island merger with SP and UP would in contrast have been an end-to-end combination, an idea ahead of its time. In the 1960s the ICC approved some fourteen parallel mergers but only two end-to-end combinations, a situation dramatically altered by the Staggers Act.[21]

The ICC authorized Burlington Northern to purchase the St. Louis and San Francisco (Frisco) in 1980, an end-to-end merger creating the largest railroad in the nation. The only real opposition to the consolidation came from the Missouri, Kansas & Texas (Katy), which feared a loss of interchange traffic off the Burlington. But the ICC had learned from the Rock Island experience and took just three years to approve the action. Its rulings began to distinguish between strong and weak carriers, and, taking a Darwinian view of the railroad world, the ICC redefined "public interest" to allow weak corporations to expire. Any valuable lines worth saving would be purchased by other railroads, and duplicate or loss-making track could be abandoned. In the estimation of the ICC, the Katy (which was "visibly dying" at the time) needed to disappear. The commission authorized it to abandon over a thousand miles of unprofitable rural branch lines, almost half its total, which made the Katy a more attractive acquisition. In 1988 the Union Pacific bought most of what remained.[22]

The growth of the Burlington Northern and the Union Pacific weakened other western roads, including the Atchison, Topeka & Santa Fe. The ATSF and Southern Pacific explored merging, going as far as to create a holding company for the assets of the two corporations and adopting a shared locomotive paint scheme. But in July 1986 the ICC ruled against the merger on the grounds that it would create a railroad monopoly between southern California and Texas. The Santa Fe hired away SP's president, Robert Krebs, and then sold SP to the Denver & Rio Grande Western. The sale left the Santa Fe holding a rich portfolio of land and minerals formerly owned by the Southern Pacific but bereft of a clear path forward.[23]

But the Santa Fe had Krebs. To save money he moved its headquarters from the fabled Railway Exchange Building on Chicago's lakefront (which continued to bear the words Santa Fe in giant letters on its roof until 2012) to the Chicago suburb of Schaumberg, best known for what was then the world's largest shopping mall, Woodfield. In a masterstroke he made Mike Haverty president of the railroad. Haverty, a fourth-generation railroader born in Atchison, Kansas, recognized the benefits of aggressively expanding the intermodal side of the business, already an important source of income. A major coup occurred in 1989, when J. B. Hunt Trucking signed with the Santa Fe after a fast, smooth run from Chicago to Los Angeles. Haverty and Hunt traveled together in a business car attached to an intermodal express train. Impressed, Hunt had agreed to do business with the Santa Fe by the time the train reached Galesburg, just three hours out of the Windy City and still two days from its destination. The agreement was unusual in that it marketed factory-to-store shipping directly to customers using dedicated trucks and trains, reducing California to Chicago transit times from four or five days to three days.[24]

The Santa Fe had found its future. A focus on container traffic brought rich rewards: in 1990 intermodal constituted 35 percent of the company's business but only 10 percent of its income; four years later it was 44 percent of all traffic and 20 percent of income. This made Santa Fe an attractive merger partner for BN. The two lines served different parts of the West and concentrated on different commodities. The northern-tier-positioned BN was a coal-hauling road, while the Santa Fe was a southwestern-oriented company staking its future on long-haul intermodal traffic. In June 1994 the two companies announced that they had reached an agreement on an exchange of stock. The merger would get BN into California and give the Santa Fe access to the Northwest and the Southeast. To smooth the way, the two companies offered trackage rights to the Southern Pacific and the Kansas City Southern. Expected opposition from

the Union Pacific did not emerge during the first round of ICC hearings, and the path seemed open to regulatory approval.[25]

But the Union Pacific did not remain quiet for long. In October 1994 UP offered $17.71 per share of Santa Fe stock, a full third higher than the BN price. Investors were wary: they feared the ICC would reject the merger on antitrust grounds if delays caused by competitors did not scupper the deal before it reached that point. In the end Union Pacific bowed out, but not before the sale price had risen from the original $2.7 billion to $4 billion. The merger went ahead, and the Burlington Northern Santa Fe (BNSF) named Krebs its new president and CEO. Teething problems included implementing a $150 million project to make Santa Fe computer software compatible with the rest of the system and a clash of cultures Krebs resolved by taking railroad executives to a retreat in Fort Worth to write a vision statement. But these were minor compared with the chaos of the Penn Central combination of 1968 or what happened next on the Union Pacific.[26]

THE FINAL PIECE OF THE PUZZLE?

The final piece in the puzzle of western railroad consolidation was a big one, and it almost didn't fit: the combination of Southern Pacific and Union Pacific. After the Southern Pacific–Santa Fe merger collapsed in 1986, the Denver & Rio Grande Western purchased the SP. Hampered as it was by lengthy routes over high mountains, the Rio Grande had survived by emphasizing customer service and leadership, exemplified by the highly successful twenty-year presidency of University of Illinois graduate Gus Aydelott. But the Union Pacific acquisitions of MoPac and Western Pacific cut the DRGW off from its most important connections. Isolated, DRGW investors welcomed Denver oilman Philip Anschutz when he gained a controlling interest in 1985. Three years later the ICC authorized the DRGW (2,248 total track miles) to purchase SP (11,605 miles), and the merged company was branded the Southern Pacific Rail Corporation.[27] A revitalized Southern Pacific gained direct access to the Windy City when it purchased the old Alton main line from St. Louis to Chicago, ending that route's brief and unprofitable existence as the Chicago, Missouri & Western.

The Union Pacific wanted SP's efficient port facilities in Long Beach, California, and its high-speed intermodal line, the Sunset Route through Arizona, New Mexico, and Texas into Louisiana. It offered a stock swap worth $3.9 billion, but shippers worried that operational problems experienced in the wake of the Union Pacific–North Western merger would be duplicated. Some customers raised fears of monopoly, especially on the so-called Chemical Coast of Louisiana and Texas, where oil refineries relied almost exclusively on one of the two companies for long-haul bulk transport. To quell antitrust concerns, the Union Pacific signed an agreement giving BNSF three thousand miles of trackage rights, allowing the latter to run its trains over UP track, to maintain competition. But opposition emerged from Conrail, which wanted Union Pacific to sell one of its Gulf of Mexico routes; from Kansas City Southern, which all but accused the UP and the BNSF of collusion in planning the combination; and from the nation's largest freight-shipper lobbyists and the powerful Texas Railroad Commission, all fearful of higher rates. In the middle of the mess, the federal government abolished the ICC, ending its 108-year reign as regulator of the railroad industry. Its successor, a unit of the Department of Transportation called the Surface Transportation Board, stunned the railroad world by unanimously authorizing the merger, which became effective in September 1996.[28]

What happened next will go down in history as one of the greatest railroad operational disasters of all time. The newly combined companies failed spectacularly. Southern Pacific technicians and middle managers accepted parachute payments and left, taking their accumulated knowledge and experience with them. Demonstrating how little had been learned from the Penn Central debacle, the two cultures collided. Wall Street, which had funded Union Pacific's purchase of SP, wanted immediate returns, obtainable in the short term by closing or consolidating facilities and laying people off. UP failed to prepare either its computers or its personnel for the takeover and unnecessarily and prematurely forced a new operating plan onto the combined systems.[29] The UP had two yards in Houston, so it shut one of them, the former MOPAC Settegast Yard, and shifted traffic to the other, the SP's Englewood Yard. But Englewood had not been built to classify everything suddenly converging on it, and by the end of June 1997 it was clogged up. Trains idled in sidings all the way to California, which meant locomotives could not be moved to where they were needed, and freight delays lost the corporation money, goodwill, and ultimately customers. Crews on full pay sat in their locomotive cabs and then went home without moving an inch. The computer system designed to track cars could not keep up with the demands placed on it, and, in another echo of Penn Central's problems, shipments vanished only to resurface weeks later hundreds of miles from their destinations.

Shippers groused. Ed Rastatter, director of policy for the National Industrial Transportation League, complained of the merged corporations, "They promised shorter transit times and more efficient routings and cost savings that would result in rate savings, but it looks like they delivered gridlock."[30] Things got so bad that UP paid BNSF to operate some high-priority intermodal services to avoid losing the contracts. On one day, October 8, 1997, 550 trains were stationary across the Union Pacific system because no locomotives were available to move them. Crews working twelve-hour shifts for seven days a week occasionally fell asleep, and accidents happened, several of them fatal.

The Surface Transportation Board stepped in and declared a transportation emergency on October 31, 1997. Safety inspectors closed down the railroad for twenty-four hours on Thanksgiving Day, 1997, and slowly the congestion around Houston eased. But instead of dissipating, it headed to Bailey Yard in North Platte, Nebraska, the largest railroad yard in North America. A winter snowstorm snarled the system, and traffic across the northern transcontinental line was halted. To regain use of the yard after snow removal, 126 trains were sent east and 130 west, where containers began to pile up at Long Beach, and ships were diverted to other ports. Fearing the merger would be negated and, worse, government regulation reinstituted, BNSF and UP jointly dispatched the busy tracks between Houston and New Orleans. Slowly the Union Pacific recovered, but some harsh lessons about mergers had been revisited. Delayed shipments and service interruptions totaled about $1 billion, and the public-relations losses were incalculable.[31]

DOWN THE MIDDLE

Fifty-seven railroads carried the word "Chicago" in their names in 1913, another ten contained "Illinois," and two had both. By the year 1999 no major railroad contained either noun, and though Illinois is still an important railroad center, the symbolic value of this shift is worth noting. Consolidation and closures had trimmed the American railroad network of its dead wood. As the twentieth century gave way to the twenty-first, BNSF and UP ruled in the West, while CSX (the operating name given to the 1986 merger of the Chessie and Seaboard rail systems) and Norfolk Southern dominated the East. These four megasystems met in the center of the country, where three smaller but no less important railroads operated: the Kansas City Southern, the Canadian Pacific, and the Canadian National.

KCS emerged from the 1980s in good shape because of revenue from taking Powder River Basin coal trains off the BNSF at Kansas City and its intermodal-oriented east-west route, bolstered by purchase of the Illinois Central Railroad's Shreveport, Louisiana, to Jackson, Tennessee, and Meridian, Mississippi, line. In 1995 it hired Mike Haverty away from the Santa Fe to explore the possibilities created by the North American Free Trade Agreement (NAFTA), which ended tariffs on most commodities traded across Mexico, the United States, and Canada. KCS expanded rapidly, including gaining access to CSX and Conrail across Illinois through St. Louis and purchasing the former Chicago & Alton line from Kansas City to Roodhouse. A traffic agreement with I&M Rail Link, a former Soo line, gave KCS entry into Shoreham Yard in Chicago.[32]

While the Kansas City Southern grew, the Milwaukee Road slowly shrank. The Milwaukee Road Restructuring Act of 1979 allowed it to abandon track without obtaining ICC permission. First to go was the Pacific Extension, closed down from Seattle to Miles City, Montana, in 1980 and, two years later, between Miles City and Ortonville, Minnesota. Branches in the upper Midwest followed. Then, in February 1985, a bitter bidding war with the Chicago & North Western ended with the Milwaukee Road declaring bankruptcy and a federal judge granting the Soo line permission to purchase what remained. The Soo line, controlled by Canadian Pacific, then converted the neglected Milwaukee Road line from Chicago to Savanna, on the Mississippi River, into a vital artery. At the same time the Illinois Terminal finally neared the end of its days. The ward since 1956 of a consortium of railroads interested in keeping it out of the clutches of the Santa Fe–controlled Toledo, Peoria & Western, it was subsumed into the Norfolk & Western as the loss of revenue from Peoria and the failure of its Chicago gateway, the Rock Island, made deep cuts in the road's income. The new owner closed facilities and furloughed half the workforce, absorbing parts of the system and abandoning most of it.[33]

The other major road in the midsection, the Illinois Central, had followed the fashionable path of diversification in the 1960s. It formed a holding company called Illinois Central Industries in 1962 in an effort to lower its exposure to risk and boost profits. Real estate, financial services, and manufacturing diverted the corporate focus away from railroading, making the loss of passenger service to Amtrak in 1971 simply a sensible fiscal calculation. But following the creation of Illinois Central Gulf Railroad (ICG)—a short-lived merger of the Illinois Central with the Gulf, Mobile & Ohio in 1972—the holding company tried to quit the rail business. It could not find a buyer until 1989, by which time it was called Whitman Corporation after the candies it made.[34]

Before 1989 the ICG had sold off many of its own routes to other railroads, especially north of the Mason-Dixon line, concentrating on serving New Orleans, Mobile, and Chicago. The corporation had closed, abandoned, or sold much of its mileage. By the end of the 1980s almost two-thirds of its route miles had been relinquished. This led to the creation of three

Map 18.1. Chicago area railroads in 2000. Courtesy of Christopher Sutton.

new minisystems: the Chicago, Central & Pacific; the Chicago, Missouri & Western (the former Chicago & Alton, soon to be divided between the Santa Fe and the Southern Pacific); and the Paducah & Louisville.[35] In 1996, seeking to reinvigorate its east-west connections, the Illinois Central repurchased the Chicago, Central & Pacific line from Chicago through Rockford to Fort Dodge, Iowa, where it split northwest to Sioux City and southwest to Council Bluffs.

That acquisition, along with the other improvements, made the Illinois Central profitable and a likely takeover target. In 1997 the Canadian National (CN), which had left government ownership two years earlier, did just that. The CN purchase of Illinois Central caused heartache among Chicago-based industry watchers and rail fans. Though remaining the nation's railroad hub, the Windy City would no longer host a major railroad company headquarters. The BNSF had moved south to Fort Worth, Texas; the C&NW had gone west to Omaha with the UP; the Monon, the Chicago Great Western, and the Chicago & Eastern Illinois had all disappeared as independent entities; and the Milwaukee Road and the Rock Island had been carved up. The Surface Transportation Board approved the acquisition in 1998, and the Illinois Central became part of the Canadian National system, headquartered in Calgary. The ICRR executive suites were not even in the United States anymore, let alone in Illinois.[36] Trains continued to run into Chicago, but the profits they generated went elsewhere.

The Canadian National–Illinois Central merger connected ICRR to the Grand Trunk Western, which operated CN lines in the United States, at Harvey. But the Canadian National wanted to bypass Chicago completely and run trains from north to south. In 2008 it purchased the Elgin, Joliet & Eastern. Reinvigorating this aging belt line angered residents living adjacent to its tracks who had become comfortably acclimated to its slow-moving, infrequent trains and dreaded the noise and inconvenience the purchase would cause. The CN also acquired Wisconsin Central, revived under the stewardship of the entrepreneurial Ed Burkhardt, from Canadian Pacific subsidiary Soo Lines, offering another route into Chicago from the north.

The reduction in the number of route miles and, most stunningly, of the number of major railroads was the culmination of a process first evident in the 1950s. Road and air competition revealed the full extent of overbuilding. Privately operated passenger trains, whether stabbed in the back, as some observers asserted, or undercut by government-subsidized competitors, vanished with the formation of Amtrak. Railroads seemed to be hurtling toward oblivion when Penn Central and the Rock Island entered receivership. But the industry avoided extinction with a little help from the government. Recognizing that burdensome ICC regulations stymied competition, the Carter administration brokered the Staggers Act to deregulate railroad pricing. Though no magic elixir, Staggers opened the doors to consolidation and innovation, and railroads rushed through.

By 1997 seven "supersystems" offering lengthy runs and competitive pricing ruled the railroad scene, two in the West (the Burlington Northern Santa Fe and the Union Pacific), two in the East (CSX and Norfolk Southern), and three in the center of the country (Kansas City Southern plus subsidiaries of Canada's two great transcontinentals, the Canadian National and the Canadian Pacific). Short lines bridged gaps in the network or connected industrial and agricultural facilities to the megasystems, but there was little in between. All had access to Chicago, and all owned track in the Prairie State. There were plenty of losers—shareholders in and employees of defunct railroads chief among them—but the industry thrived as the twenty-first century opened. Illinois, now more a place to pass through than a destination, retained its central role in what has become a less important but still vital industry.

EPILOGUE

own into the success of the railroad industry were the seeds of its own decline. Well into the twentieth century the trains went everywhere and carried everything, exercising a power critics called monopolistic and dangerous. Farmers and small businesses resented their dependence on the railroads, believing the corporations were squeezing inordinately large and unjustified profits out of small producers. Responding to popular grievances, state officials in Illinois created the first meaningful regulatory regime in the 1870s, culminating in formation of the federal Interstate Commerce Commission in 1887. The ICC slowly constructed a complex and inflexible rate-setting system, introducing a dangerous degree of ossification into pricing. By 1900 railroads had become virtually incapable of responding to market fluctuations, their rates fixed for them and their customers unwilling to negotiate.

Regulation alone did not spell the end of the railroad monopoly. Railroad travel fueled a growing taste for motion, a taste automobiles sated. The Illinois railroad network contracted after 1920 as state and local politicians—unaware of the environmental and social costs involved—voted to pave roads, often with federal subsidies and support from the railroads themselves, and encourage car use. Competition from bus and truck companies and, after World War II, airlines also cut into railroad ridership. Peacetime factories produced cars for a new mass audience, and gas stations appeared on street corners to supply fuel and repairs. Several high-profile bankruptcies, including the Chicago, Rock Island & Pacific, led to a dramatic downsizing, and by 1975 the industry appeared to be in terminal decline.

But railroads did not vanish. Amtrak allowed them to focus on freight and deregulation enabled them to respond rapidly to new opportunities. Labor-force reductions, satellite technology, computerized car-tracking and cost-accounting systems, continuous welded rail, intermodal traffic, and an emphasis on long hauls using dedicated "unit trains" increased operational efficiency. The private corporations came to grips with the delicate balance between having too much track, which cost money to maintain, and too little, which created congestion. Consolidation into a few megasystems saved the industry but ended the place of Illinois as the unchallenged epicenter of railroading. Railroad headquarters left the state for places like Fort Worth, Omaha, and Calgary, taking well-paid railroad executives and prestige with them.

Despite these blows, Illinois railroads continued to prosper into the twenty-first century. With 6,986 route miles in 2012, the state retained second place in the nation, while the volume of freight originating and leaving it remained buoyant. There were 13,152 railroad employees living in Illinois, also the second highest number in the United States. Passenger service, negligible though it may have been in contrast to the early twentieth century, prospered compared to other states. In 2012 ten Amtrak routes originated in Chicago, three of which operated almost exclusively within the state. Trains from Chicago to Carbondale, Milwaukee, St. Louis, and Quincy received state subsidies, though no Amtrak services traversed Illinois from east to west outside the Windy City and the only trains downstate came from Chicago. Additional trains and faster timings translated into an 85 percent increase in ridership between 2006 and 2011, from 947,000 to 1,749,900 people.[1]

The ambitious dreams of 1837 had, by 2012, come and gone, with one observer claiming the railroad belonged to a lost age of blast furnaces, pizzerias, gangsters, and air pollution. The obituary proved premature for the smaller but more vibrant railroad industry, which remained financially healthy and commercially vital. Railroad route mileage in Illinois had peaked in 1920 at 12,128 and, though half of that had been abandoned by the beginning of the twenty-first century, private equity firm Berkshire Hathaway's $34 billion purchase of BNSF in November 2009 looked like a statement of faith in railroading. Warren Buffett, Berkshire Hathaway's chairman and CEO, justified the investment as "an all-in wager on the economic future of the United States" while noting, "Our country's future prosperity depends on its having an efficient and well-maintained rail system."[2]

That immediate future rests on the twin pillars of coal and containers. Relying on these two key sources of revenue made Illinois railroads dependent on power plants and consumer spending. In 2011 the 81.3 million tons of coal brought by train into Illinois made up 51.3 percent of all railroad shipments terminating in the state. About 18 million tons of coal originated there. Intermodal traffic ranked second among arriving freight, at 16.1 percent, and almost a quarter of all trains originating in Illinois were TOFC and COFC. Farm products, long the foundation of railroad wealth in Granger country, represented 6.3 percent of arrivals and 20.6 percent of traffic starting from the state.[3] In 2011 Illinois ranked second in the United States behind Wyoming for freight originations (112.3 million tons) and second behind Texas for terminating freight (158.7 million tons).[4] Other commodities began to filter into the railroad universe in ever greater quantities, notably oil and ethanol, but changing

air pollution standards, the increased use of wind and solar to generate electricity, and a weakening economy translated into reduced coal and merchandise traffic. Despite concerns over the volatility of Bakken crude oil and several highly publicized explosions, the environmental advantages of trains over trucking continue to give an edge to the railroad industry.

Forty railroad corporations operated in Illinois in 2012, including all seven Class Is. The other thirty-three railroads were either regionals or short lines (Classes II and III, as defined by the Surface Transportation Board) ranging from the Iowa Interstate, operating five hundred miles of former Rock Island lines from Council Bluffs, Iowa, to Bureau and Peoria, to the mile-long Chicago Port Railroad. Many of the short lines were owned by holding companies such as Iowa Pacific Holdings (headquartered in Chicago and led by former C&NW and Amtrak executive Ed Ellis), Peoria-based Pioneer Railcorp (whose lines included the Keokuk Junction, operating the west end of the former Toledo, Peoria & Western), and Genesse and Wyoming (owner of former TP&W tracks east of Peoria along with the Illinois & Midland Railroad south to Taylorville). Purchasing segments of track from Class I railroads, they operated as gateways to industry or bridge roads from one Class I to another. Several, such as the Joppa and Eastern (running coal trains into an Ameren power plant on the Ohio River) and the Bloomer Line (a fifty-mile short line owned by the Alliance Grain Company in Central Illinois), are the properties of the industries they serve.

Railroad financing originated in a mix of private capital and government assistance through stock subscriptions, land grants, and favorable treatment. Though primarily private corporations, railroads garnered public subsidies in the nineteenth century because of their status as common carriers and their origins as state-chartered businesses. That situation has not entirely changed. A case in point was CREATE, the Chicago Region Environmental and Transportation Efficiency program. Designed to unravel Chicago's knotted railroads, CREATE was a public-private partnership between the federal government, the Illinois Department of Transportation, the City of Chicago, Amtrak, Metra,

The Iron Road in the Prairie State

Figure E.1. The enduring fascination of railroading: a North Shore railfan special in 1940, running in a long tradition that continues to this day across the state of Illinois. Lake Forest College Library Special Collections.

and eight freight railroads. CREATE funded projects to elevate train tracks over roads by building bridges; to separate the railroads of different corporations to avoid bottlenecks; and to close grade crossings to increase rail capacity, speed, and safety. In 2012 the estimated cost of these improvements had reached $3 billion, of which $230 million (about 8 percent) was to be supplied by railroads, with the remaining $2.77 billion coming from federal, state, and local tax monies.[5]

The congestion CREATE was intended to ease is one indication of how railroads fell victim to their own success. Lobbying by competing industries, fear of monopolies, and, ultimately, a growing demand for instant personal mobility ended the railroad dominance but could not extinguish the industry itself. The Staggers Act of 1980 created the conditions for the economically healthy contemporary railroad scene, but what might the future hold? If history is any guide, bankruptcy and further mergers are in the cards for the railroad industry.

External factors have also been responsible for changes. The physical plant is in excellent shape and the services railroads provide are crucial to a strong consumer economy. Chicago remains the most important railroad city in the country, a status CREATE was designed to preserve. But publicly traded corporations have been raided before—witness Reid-Moore—and will be again. It is probably in the best interests of the major American railroads that they all survive and remain strong, but there is no guarantee of this or of a secure future. Moving away from dependence upon coal in an era of ever-stricter environmental controls and on shrinking consumer spending in a recession are crucial to the long-term health of the industry, but if there is one lesson to be learned from the history of American railroads, it is their ability to adapt and survive. The trains rush on, fewer in number and longer in length but just as crucial to American economic power.

NOTES

PREFACE

1. Davis, *Frontier Illinois*, 49.

2. Stover, *Life and Decline*, 154–155; and AAR, *Railroad Facts*, 46.

1. PRELIMINARIES

1. Biles, *Illinois*, 4.

2. Farnham, *Life in Prairie Land*, 14–15; and Regan, *Emigrant's Guide*, 35.

3. See Hadfield, *The Canal Age*, chaps. 1 and 2; and Hepburn, *Artificial Waterways*, 1–9.

4. Ward, *Railroads*, 31.

5. Quoted in Clarke, *History of McDonough County*, 101.

6. *American Railroad Journal*, January 21, 1832, 49.

7. Botkin and Harlow, *Treasury of Railroad Folklore*, 71; and Grant, *We Took the Train*, 15. The "Outburst" first appeared in the *Vincennes Western Sun*: see Ward, *Railroads*, 120.

8. Licht, *Working for the Railroad*, 7; and Fetters, *Charleston and Hamburg*.

9. Miner, *A Most Magnificent Machine*, 319; and Cronon, *Nature's Metropolis*.

10. *Chicago Daily Tribune*, December 28, 1850, 2.

11. *Prairie Farmer*, March 1, 1850, 29.

12. Young, *The Iron Horse*, 7–10; and Matile, "John Frink," 125.

2. DEVELOPMENT DELAYED

1. Owen, *A Brief Practical Treatise*, 20–21.

2. Faragher, *Sugar Creek*, 175; and *Sangamo Journal*, May 7, 1836, 1.

3. *Sangamo Journal*, August 2, 1834, 4, and January 30, 1836, 2; and *American Railroad Journal*, January 14, 1832, 37.

4. Gerstner, *Early American Railroads*, 506–507; and Allen, *Legends and Lore*, 136–137.

5. *Sangamo Journal*, May 23, 1835, 2.

6. Bonham, *Fifty Years' Recollections*, 460; Johannsen, *Stephen A. Douglas*, 49; and Glendinning, *Chicago and Alton Railroad*, 5.

7. Glendinning, *Chicago and Alton Railroad*, 49–50; and Starr, *Lincoln and the Railroads*, 20–21.

8. Young, *The Iron Horse*, 13; Sutton, "Illinois' Year of Decision," 37; and Grant, "The Iron Horse," 3.

9. Miner, *A Most Magnificent Machine*, 182; Russell, "The Planning and Failure," 196; and *American Railroad Journal*, September 10, 1836, 562.

10. Biles, *Illinois*, 307.

11. Johannsen, *Stephen A. Douglas*, 51; *Sangamo Journal*, September 23, 1837, 4; and Grant, "The Iron Horse," 3–4.

12. Gerstner, *Early American Railroads*, 491–505.

13. *American Railroad Journal*, February 11, 1837, 83, and December 16, 1837, 671.

14. See Bonham, *Fifty Years' Recollections*, 43; Thomas and Baldwin, *Complete Pronouncing Gazetteer*, 893; Gates, *Illinois Central*, 68; and Miner, *A Most Magnificent Machine*, 76, 80.

15. The following account of the Panic of 1837 draws heavily on Reynolds, *Waking Giant*.

16. McLear, "Speculation," 135–138, 142–143; and Howard, *Illinois*, 181.

17. *Sangamo Journal*, June 14, 1839, 2.

18. *American Railroad Journal*, April 1, 1837, 194; Thomas and Baldwin, *Complete Pronouncing Gazetteer*, 893; and *Illinois Free Trader*, April 30, 1841, 2.

19. *Illinois Free Trader*, December 4, 1840, 1; Bonham, *Fifty Years' Recollections*, 57, 459; Sutton, "Illinois' Year of Decision," 38–39; and Adler, *British Investment*, 10, table 1.

3. OPTIMISM REVIVED

1. Bradsby, *History of Bureau County*, 405; and Hevlin, *Historical Encyclopedia*, 705.

2. Klopfenstein, *Foundations Strong*, 38.

3. *Chicago Daily Tribune*, August 4, 1877, 5; Grant, *The North Western*, 8; Lundin, *Rockford*, 40; and McLear, "William Butler Ogden," 286, 290.

4. Miner, *A Most Magnificent Machine*, 181.

5. Originally called Turner Junction and sometimes simply Turner, the town officially changed its name to West Chicago in 1896. See Grant, *The North Western*, 11–12.

6. *New-York Daily Tribune*, May 6, 1852, 8; Elizabeth F. L. Ellet, "By Rail and Stage to Galena" (1852), reprinted in Angle, *Prairie State*, 272; and *The Rail-roads*, 4.

7. Grant, *The North Western*, 16; and Botkin and Harlow, *Treasury of Railroad Folklore*, 180–181.

8. *American Railroad Journal*, June 24, 1854, 399; and Miner, *A Most Magnificent Machine*, 183–188.

9. Botkin and Harlow, *Treasury of Railroad Folklore*, 113; and Hofsommer, *Steel Trails of Hawkeyeland*, 8–9.

10. Dirck, *Lincoln the Lawyer*, 95; Jackson, *Rails across the Mississippi*, 3; *Nashville Union and American*, May 11, 1856, 3; *New-York Daily Tribune*, July 9, 1856, 5; and *Daily Nashville Patriot*, August 10, 1857, 3. See chap. 10 for more on the legal status of bridging the river.

11. Dirck, *Lincoln the Lawyer*, 91.

12. *Ottawa Free-Trader*, November 11, 1851, 2.

13. Michael W. Blaszak, "Chicago Railway History," in Solomon et al., *Chicago*, 23.

14. Overton, *Burlington West*, 36; *Miscellaneous Documents of the Senate of the United States*, 38th Cong., 2nd sess. (Washington, DC: Government Printing Office, 1865), 9; and Stringham, *Toledo, Peoria & Western*, 4.

15. Botkin and Harlow, *Treasury of Railroad Folklore*, 79.

16. Russell, "The Planning and Failure," 200–204; and *Ottawa Free-Trader*, November 28, 1845, 2.

17. Johannsen, *Stephen A. Douglas*, 211, 306–308.

18. Gates, *Illinois Central*, 101.

19. *New-York Daily Tribune*, September 20, 1850, 8; *Ottawa Free-Trader*, September 28, 1850, 2; and *New Orleans Daily Crescent*, September 25, 1850, 2.

20. Hill, *Highways of Progress*, 146; Gates, *Illinois Central*, 325–327; Anna Centennial Committee, *Centennial History*, 17–18; and White, *Kankakee River Area Assessment*, 138.

21. Brownson, *History of the Illinois Central*, 45; and Gates, *Illinois Central*, 59.

22. Johannsen, *Stephen A. Douglas*, 37, 211, 316–317; and Stephen A. Douglas to James Washington Sheahan, April 6, 1855, in Douglas, *Letters*, 388.

23. *New-York Daily Tribune*, April 30, 1852, 5; Brownson, *History of the Illinois Central*, 60; and Corliss, *Main Line of Mid-America*, 56.

24. Gates, *Illinois Central*, 58; Johannsen, *Stephen A. Douglas*, 316–317; and Stover, *Iron Road to the West*, 190, 210.

25. Brownson, *History of the Illinois Central*, 51; and Corliss, *Main Line of Mid-America*, 48–50, 57.

26. Andreas, *History of Chicago*, 255; and Corliss, *Main Line of Mid-America*, 91.

27. Thomas and Baldwin, *Complete Pronouncing Gazetteer*, 893.

28. Faragher, *Sugar Creek*, 173, 179. For more on Dwight and his dubious financial dealings, see chap. 5; Glendinning, *Chicago and Alton Railroad*, passim, esp. chap. 3; and White, "Captain Benjamin Godfrey," passim.

29. Glendinning, *Chicago and Alton Railroad*, 67.

30. Sanders, *Limiteds, Locals, and Expresses*, 46; and Stover, *Iron Road to the West*, 212.

31. Part of the Indianapolis and St. Louis, the THA&StL merged with the "Big Four" (Cleveland, Cincinnati, Chicago, and St. Louis) in 1889 and would later be controlled by the New York Central.

32. Churella, *The Pennsylvania Railroad*, 275, 279–80.

33. Stringham, *Toledo, Peoria & Western*, 10–11; and Sanders, *Limiteds, Locals, and Expresses*, 49, 169, 138.

34. Schwieterman, *Terminal Town*, 126–127; Sanders, *Limiteds, Locals, and Expresses*, 73; and *Prairie Farmer*, November 15, 1860, 13.

35. Quoted in Miner, *A Most Magnificent Machine*, 191; and George, *Forty Years*, 137–138.

4. CULTIVATING THE PRAIRIE

1. Faragher, *Sugar Creek*, 39.

2. Biles, *Illinois*, 39–40; and Gates, *The Illinois Central*, 99–100.

3. *American Railroad Journal*, May 9, 1835, 277, and November 21, 1835, 723; *Sangamo Journal*, May 5, 1835, 2; Haeger, "The Abandoned Townsite," 165–183; and *Prairie Farmer*, August 1, 1848, 2.

4. Stover, *History of the Illinois Central*, 115; and *Prairie Farmer*, May 1, 1852, 34.

5. Overton, *Burlington West*, 3–5; and Gates, *The Illinois Central*, 100–103, 149.

6. Gates, *The Illinois Central*, 105–108.

7. Miner, *A Most Magnificent Machine*, 183; and Gates, *The Illinois Central*, 171, 188–190.

8. Gates, *The Illinois Central*, 173, 286; and Ward, *Railroads*, 97–98.

9. *Illinois Farmer*, June 1, 1858, 16.

10. The transition from outrage to subsidized complicity can be traced in the *Prairie Farmer*: May 1, 1852, 34; February 1, 1854, 2; June 1, 1854, 34; and February 1, 1855, 2.

11. Gates, *The Illinois Central*, 173–181.

12. Gates, *The Illinois Central*, 142, 151–152, 238–239; Lansden, *History of the City of Cairo*, 120; and George, *Forty Years*, 204.

13. Faragher, *Sugar Creek*, 62–63; and George Flower, "The English Prairie," in Havighurst, *Land of the Long Horizons*, 180–181.

14. Bardolph, "Illinois Agriculture," 416; Hudson, *Making the Corn Belt*, 7, 88, 98; and Peter Cartwright, "Riding the Sangamon Circuit," in Havighurst, *Land of the Long Horizons*, 202.

15. Cobden, *The American Diaries*, 151; Trollope, *North America*, 155; Bogue, *From Prairie to Corn-Belt*, 72–73; and Faragher, *Sugar Creek*, 64.

16. Faragher, *Sugar Creek*, 71.

17. Trollope, *North America*, 161–162.

18. *Chicago Daily Tribune*, December 3, 1852, 2; Belcher, *The Economic Rivalry*, 38–39, 191; and Bardolph, "Illinois Agriculture," 418–419.

19. *Sangamo Journal*, August 2, 1834, 4; Lundin, *Rockford*, 42; and quoted in Cronon, *Nature's Metropolis*, 84.

20. Trollope, *North America*, 157.

21. Biles, *Illinois*, 226.

22. Cronon, *Nature's Metropolis*, 114–117, 120–123.

23. Cronon, *Nature's Metropolis*, 180–184.

24. See Fogel, *Railroads*.

5. FINANCING RAILROADS

1. Gustav Unonius, "Chicago" (1857), reprinted in Angle, *Prairie State*, 292; Stover, *History of the Baltimore and Ohio*, 24–25; and Churella, *The Pennsylvania Railroad*, xiv.

2. *Ottawa Free Trader*, February 23, 1850, 2.

3. *Glasgow (MO) Weekly Times*, October 2, 1851, 2; Dodd, *Robert J. Walker*, 29; Veenendaal, *Slow Train to Paradise*, 58–59; and Flesher, Previts, and Samson, "Early American Corporate Reporting," 9.

4. *New-York Daily Tribune*, February 9, 1852, 8; Gates, *Illinois Central*, 73; and Adler, *British Investment*, 55, 63–64.

5. *Wheeling Daily Intelligencer*, July 11, 1854, 2; *Ottawa Free Trader*, July 29, 1854, 2; Stover, *History of the Illinois Central*, 35–36; Gates, *Illinois Central*, 76; and Veenendaal, *Slow Train to Paradise*, 59–60.

6. Adler, *British Investment*, 172–173; Gates, *Illinois Central*, 72, 74; and Veenendaal, *Slow Train to Paradise*, 76.

7. *Sycamore True Republican*, July 11, 1877, 2; Veenendaal, *Slow Train to Paradise*, 84, 113–115; Stover, *History of the Illinois Central*, 198–199.

8. For an interpretation of Gould's actions as being at odds with the picture of him as a classic robber baron, see Klein, *Life and Legend*; and see Mercer, *Railroads and Land Grant Policy*, 48.

9. Veenendaal, *Slow Train to Paradise*, 85–86; Stringham, *Toledo, Peoria & Western*, 27–31; and Grant, *"Follow the Flag,"* 68.

10. *American Railroad Journal*, March 10, 1855, 145; *Sangamo Journal*, November 29, 1834, 2; and see Glendinning, *Chicago and Alton Railroad*, 20–24, 27–32, 39–45.

11. Glendinning, *Chicago and Alton Railroad*, 20.

12. *American Railroad Journal*, July 22, 1854, 455, and June 12, 1855, 301–302; and Glendinning, *Chicago and Alton Railroad*, 32, 39–43, 52.

13. White, "Captain Benjamin Godfrey," 485.

14. Glendinning, *Chicago and Alton Railroad*, 59–60.

15. Corliss, *Main Line of Mid-America*, 347–348.

16. *Prairie Farmer*, July 22, 1858, 8; and *Illinois Farmer*, June 1, 1857, 24.

17. Gates, *Illinois Central*, 274–288; and Grant, *The North Western*, 94.

18. Grant, *The North Western*, 49; Overton, *Burlington West*, 271–274, 403–404; and Hayes, *Iron Road to Empire*, 112.

19. Glendinning, *Chicago and Alton Railroad*, 114–115.

20. *Chicago Tribune*, July 8, 1876, 7; *American Railroad Journal*, May 23, 1874, 668; Hilton, *American Narrow Gauge Railroads*, 383. Canda, along with his brother Charles, was a principal partner in the Chrome Steel Works in Brooklyn and the Ensign Car Company of Huntington, West Virginia: Veenendaal, *Slow Train*

to Paradise, 103; *New York Times*, July 31, 1874, 12; and *Eleventh Annual Report*, 9–10.

6. CONFLAGRATIONS AND EXPANSION

1. Data from Stover, *Life and Decline*, 154–155; Glendinning, *Chicago and Alton*, 114; and Young, *The Iron Horse*, 169.

2. Biles, *Illinois*, 131.

3. *Chicago Tribune*, May 11, 1861, 2, and October 11, 1862, 2; Allen, *Legends and Lore*, 290; Brownell, *The Other Illinois*, 152–153; and Biles, *Illinois*, 102–103, 106.

4. Thomas, *The Iron Way*, 77.

5. Weber, *Northern Railroads*, 39–40, 177–178; and Thomas, *The Iron Way*, 77, 89.

6. Ward, *Railroads*, 46; and Weber, *Northern Railroads*, 86–89, 98.

7. See Corliss, *Main Line of Mid-America*, 127–128; and Stover, *History of the Illinois Central*, 94–95.

8. Weber, *Northern Railroads*, 226; Stover, *History of the Illinois Central*, 95–96; Gates, *Illinois Central*, 204, 261, 283.

9. Lind, *Illinois Central Story*, 131; and Biles, *Illinois*, 102–103; the description is from William H. Russell, "From Cairo to Chicago by Train" (1861), reprinted in Angle, *Prairie State*, 336; Allen, *Legends and Lore*, 48, 306; and Corliss, *Illinois Central*, 129.

10. Weber, *Northern Railroads*, 63–64; Licht, *Working for the Railroad*, 69; and Glendinning, *Chicago and Alton Railroad*, 63–65.

11. Grant, *The North Western*, 28; and Weber, *Northern Railroads*, 89–91.

12. See Wade, *Chicago's Pride*, chap. 3.

13. Weber, *Northern Railroads*, 21, 222.

14. Weber, *Northern Railroads*, 14, 223, 11, 69, 229, 94, 127. See also Taylor and Neu, *American Railroad Network*, chap. 1.

15. *Urbana Daily Courier*, June 5, 1906, 1.

16. Burford, "Twilight," 161; and Ives, *Wayfaring Stranger*, 48.

17. Gates, *Illinois Central*, 281.

18. Sir James Caird, "A Bird's Eye View of Illinois," reprinted in Angle, *Prairie State*, 318; Butler et al., *Magnificent Whistle Stop*, 13.

19. Butler et al., *Magnificent Whistle Stop*, 15, 17–18; Burlington Northern Timetable, October 25, 1970, table 1.

20. Gates, *Illinois Central*, 124; Cavalier, *North American Railroad Stations*, 15; "St. Charles Branch," http://encyclopedia.chicagohistory.org/pages/1189.html; Grant, *The North Western*, 66.

21. Grant and Bohi, *The Country Railroad Station*, 3–4; *Sycamore True Republican*, April 30, 1892, 4; Burford, *The Chatsworth Wreck*, 16–17; Faragher, *Sugar Creek*, 178, 180.

22. This section is based on Schwieterman, *Terminal Town*, 12–53; Brian Solomon, "Chicago's Classic Passenger Terminals and Trains," in Solomon et al., *Chicago*, 82–97; and Gates, *Illinois Central*, 91.

23. See Hartley, "A Touch of Class."

24. Transcript of an interview with George M. Pullman (December 1, 1897), 01/01/01, folder 113, box 8, Pullman Company Archives, Newberry Library, Chicago; and Glendinning, *Chicago and Alton Railroad*, 69–73.

25. *Chicago Tribune*, April 25, 1880, 9; and Glendinning, *Chicago and Alton Railroad*, 55–56, 80. For the town of Pullman, see Buder, *Pullman*.

26. Sheahan and Upton, *The Great Conflagration*, 46.

27. *Reminiscences of Chicago*, 25, 95; and Biles, *Illinois*, 124–125.

28. Glendinning, *Chicago and Alton Railroad*, 92; Sheahan and Upton, *The Great Conflagration*, 80, 147; and Stover, *History of the Illinois Central*, 182.

29. Young, *The Iron Horse*, 101; Grant, *The North Western*, 38; *Reminiscences of Chicago*, 42; Sheahan and Upton, *The Great Conflagration*, 124, 140; and Colbert and Chamberlin, *Chicago and the Great Conflagration*, 338.

30. Glendinning, *The Chicago and Alton Railroad*, 94; Young, *The Iron Horse*, 101; Sawislak, *Smoldering City*, 93–94; and Stover, *History of the Illinois Central*, 182–183.

31. Stover, *Iron Road to the West*, 107; and *Official Proceedings*, 14, 16.

32. Mercer, *Railroads and Land Grant Policy*, 33.

33. *Chicago Tribune*, May 1869, 1.

34. Mercer, *Railroads and Land Grant Policy*, 147. For a particularly trenchant critique of the transcontinental railroads, see White, *Railroaded*.

7. ILLINOIS RAILROAD LABOR

1. This division follows categories found in the Interstate Commerce Commission, *Second Annual Report*, 16.

2. Licht, *Working for the Railroad*, 44; and Black, "Experiment," 444–459; *Chicago Daily Tribune*, January 1, 1856, 3; Corliss, *Main Line of Mid-America*, 348; and see *Chicago Daily Tribune*, August 7, 1856, 2.

3. *Eleventh Annual Report*, 321. For the number of employees, see *Tenth Census*, 1:705.

4. Gates, *Illinois Central*, 94; and Stover, *History of the Illinois Central*, 47–48.

5. Lightner, "Construction Labor," 285–288; Stover, *History of the Illinois Central*, 48, 289; and Corliss, *Main Line of Mid-America*, 52–53.

6. Stover, *History of the Illinois Central*, 49.

7. Corliss, *Main Line of Mid-America*, 54–55; and Lightner, "Construction Labor," 296–300.

8. Licht, *Working for the Railroad*, 81, 105; and Hofsommer, *The Hook and Eye*, 106–107.

9. Licht, *Working for the Railroad*, 56, 104, 111–114, 134, 167–168.

10. Licht, *Working for the Railroad*, 94, 96; *Chicago Daily Tribune*, January 9, 1856, 3, and September 5, 1856, 3; *Ottawa Free Trader*, December 1, 1855, 2; and *Tallula Express*, January 18, 1896, 1.

11. *Chicago Tribune*, August 24, 1879, 3; and *Urbana Daily Courier*, April 2, 1904, 8, and September 15, 1906, 3.

12. This paragraph is based on reports in the *Chicago Tribune*, December 25, 1912, 4; *New York Times*, December 25, 1912, 15; *Rock Island Argus*, December 26, 1912, 1; and *Urbana Daily Courier*, December 26, 1912, 1.

13. Licht, *Working for the Railroad*, 144–146, 203–206.

14. Licht, *Working for the Railroad*, 26–27; and Black, "Experiment," 445.

15. See Hayes to Catlin, April 3, 1866, ICRR 11 N 1.5 1856–85, Illinois Central Railroad Archives, Newberry Library, Chicago (hereafter ICRR Papers); Chicago Fraternal Societies, Small Collections of Chicago Topics, F, Miscellaneous Collection, Chicago History Museum; and Lightner, *Labor*, 193–195.

16. United States Bureau of Labor, *Bulletin 2* (1897): 41–45; W. A. Gardner, "Railroad Rewards and Pensions," *Independent*, March 28, 1901, 730; Grant, *"Follow the Flag,"* 124–126; Grant, *The Corn Belt Route*, 42–43; Licht, *Working for the Railroad*, 144; Richardson, *The Locomotive Engineer*, 104, 105; Stromquist, *A Generation of Boomers*, 194; and Holbrook, *The Story of American Railroads*, 244.

17. United States Bureau of Labor, *Bulletin 3* (1898): 555, 588.

18. Cordery, "Mutualism," 263–279; Cordery, *British Friendly Societies*; Ducker, *Men of the Steel Rails*, 133; Commons et al., *History of Labor*, 2:63; Salmons, *The Burlington Strike*, 32. See also Chandler, *The Railroads*, 135; and McMurry, *The Great Burlington Strike*, viii.

19. Arnesen, *Brotherhoods of Color*, 66, 80.

20. Licht, *Working for the Railroad*, 249.

21. ICRR Board of Directors Minutes, Papers, and Accounts, box 4, folder 76, Telegrams and Dispatches, July 26 and 27, 1877, IC 3.4, ICRR Archives; and Lause, "'The Cruel Striker War,'" 90–91.

22. *Chicago Daily Tribune*, July 27, 1877, 8; and *Sycamore True Republican*, July 28, 1877, 1.

23. Stover, *History of the Illinois Central*, 186–187; Taillon, *Good, Reliable, White Men*, 71; and Grant, *"Follow the Flag,"* 70–72.

24. Grant, *The North Western*, 94; and Hall, *The Great Strike*, 40–45.

25. White, *Railroaded*, 345–346; Stromquist, *A Generation of Boomers*, 58; and Salmons, *The Burlington Strike*, 5.

26. They wanted faster appeals, "a reasonable time" to prepare for work, different pay scales for different types of passenger and freight runs, definitions of what constituted delays, minimum pay rates and overtime for passenger runs, published rates of pay for work train, helper, snow plough, weed train, suburban, hostling, and light engine duties; see Hall, *The Great Strike*, 29–34.

27. Overton, *Burlington Route*, 211.

28. Hall, *The Great Strike*, 32–34.

29. Overton, *Burlington Route*, 211–212; Hall, *The Great Strike*, 48–50, 50–51, 52; White, *Railroaded*, 346; McMurry, "Labor Policies," 165–166; and Botkin and Harlow, *Treasury of Railroad Folklore*, 309.

30. Ely, *Railroads and American Law*, 254; and Overton, *Burlington Route*, 212.

31. Overton, *Burlington Route*, 213; and McMurry, "Labor Policies," 165–166.

32. P. Ryan to F. R. Doty, February 19, 1888; C. A. Beck to A. B. Minton, August 24, 1888; F. R. Doty to P. Ryan, July 3, 1890; and J. C. Jacobs to F. R. Doty, November 7, 1891, all in Doty In-letters, IC 1, D6.1, ICRR Archives.

33. J. M. Forbes to C. E. Perkins, April 11, 1888, 33 1880 9.76; and C. E. Perkins to R. Harris, December 7, 1877, 33 1870 3.6, both in Chicago, Burlington & Quincy Railroad Company Papers, Newberry Library, Chicago (hereafter cited as CB&Q Company Papers).

34. "Statement of Medical Expenses 1875," 33 1870 1.81; "Burlington Hospital Bills, 1882," 33 1880 8.12; Burlington Voluntary Relief Department, broadside announcing formation, May 15, 1889, +33.8, no. 14; Burlington Voluntary Relief Department, poster announcing election results, December 12, 1889, 3 D 2.1; and C. E. Perkins, "Memorandum of Understanding," June 27, 1891, 33 1880 8.6, all in CB&Q Company Papers.

35. Grant, *The Corn Belt Route*, 35.

36. See Buder, *Pullman*, 18–20; Corliss, *Main Line of Mid-America*, 352; Young, *The Iron Horse and the Windy City*, 125–126; Pacyga, *Chicago*, 143–146; Susan Hirsch, "The Search for Unity among Railroad Workers: The Pullman Strike in Perspective," in Schneirov, Stromquist, and Salvatore, *The Pullman Strike*, 45; Licht, *Industrializing America*, 171; and Salvatore, *Eugene Debs*.

37. Eggert, *Richard Olney*, 24–25, 50–53; Taillon, *Good, Reliable, White Men*, 110; Stromquist, *A Generation of Boomers*, 19; White, *Railroaded*, 417–418; and *Chicago Daily Tribune*, January 4, 1894, 7.

38. *Sycamore True Republican*, July 4, 1894, 1; and Melvyn Dubofsky, "The Federal Judiciary, Free Labor, and Equal Rights," in Schneirov, Stromquist, and Salvatore, *The Pullman Strike*, 164; and Eggert, *Richard Olney*, 139.

39. Eggert, *Richard Olney*, 140–141, 144–146; Biles, *Illinois*, 170; Grant, *"Follow the Flag,"* 83; *Chicago Daily Tribune*, July 4, 1894, 5, and July 6, 1894, 2, 5; McMurry, "Labor Policies," 178; *New York Times*, July 31, 1894, 2; and White, *Railroaded*, 450.

40. Taillon, *Good, Reliable, White Men*, 110–111.

8. A KALEIDOSCOPE OF REGULATIONS

1. Grant, *The North Western*, 35–36; and Stromquist, *A Generation of Boomers*, 12–13.

2. McCabe, *History of the Grange Movement*, 99–100.

3. Gallamore and Meyer, *American Railroads*, 17; Harrison, *Congress*, chap. 3; and Stover, *Life and Decline*, 90.

4. Miller, *Railroads*, 62; *Prairie Farmer*, August 2, 1860, 9; *Illinois Farmer*, August 1, 1862, 4; and *Ottawa Free Trader*, February 9, 1867, 2.

5. *Prairie Farmer*, April 2, 1870, 5, and January 20, 1872, 1; Biles, *Illinois*, 123; and Ely, *Railroads and American Law*, 86.

6. *First Annual Report*, 20; Burns, *Railroad Mergers*, 11; and Ely, *Railroads and American Law*, 87.

7. *First Annual Report*, 150, 126.

8. Ferris, "The Disgrace," 204–205, 209–212.

9. Ely, *Railroads and American Law*, 86, 89; and Glendinning, *Chicago and Alton*, 97–98.

10. Young, *The Iron Horse*, 141.

11. *Farmers Review*, December 27, 1883, 8.

12. *Sycamore True Republican*, December 15, 1886, 2; *Chicago Tribune*, January 24, 1887, 4, and November 12, 1886, 6; *New York Times*, December 20, 1886, 4, and October 26, 1886, 3; and Grant, *"Follow the Flag,"* 74–75.

13. *Chicago Tribune*, October 27, 1886, 4; and Stover, *Life and Decline*, 92.

14. Ade, *Stories of Chicago*, 51; Young, *The Iron Horse*, 149; Glendinning, *Chicago and Alton*, 143, 172; Burgess and Kennedy, *Centennial History*, 521; Overton, *Burlington Route*, 295; and *Daily Illini*, November 19, 1922, 10.

15. J. C. Jacobs to F. R. Doty, October 16, 1891, Doty In-letters, folder 134, box 35, ICRR Archives.

16. Grant, *We Took the Train*, 49; and *American Railroad Journal*, January 1894, 48; Mrs. Ernest R. Kroeger, "Smoke Abatement in St. Louis," in Stradling, *Conservation*, 78–79; and Jenkins, *The Illinois Terminal Railroad*, 141–142.

17. Chicago Association of Commerce, *Smoke Abatement*, 82–96; Stover, *History of the Illinois Central*, 299; and Aldrich, "Energy Conservation," 12.

18. Stradling and Tarr, "Environmental Activism," 694, 696.

19. See *Progress of Reconstruction*, 1; Young, *The Iron Horse*, 151; Stover, *History of the Illinois Central*, 298–299; and Stradling and Tarr, "Environmental Activism," 693.

20. Kolko, *Railroads and Regulation*, 3.

9. PANIC AND INNOVATION

1. Lubetkin, *Jay Cooke's Gamble*, 278, 283.

2. *Chicago Daily Tribune*, November 30, 1873, 9; White, *Railroaded*, 83–84; and Grant, *The North Western*, 44.

3. *Chicago Daily Tribune*, December 21, 1873, 8; Grant, *The North Western*, 29, 44; and Stover, *Illinois Central*, 137, 161, 184–185.

4. Stringham, *Toledo, Peoria & Western*, 23–25; Glendinning, *Chicago and Alton*, 100, 135.

5. See Stiles, *The First Tycoon*, 441–442, 479–488; Sanders, *Limiteds, Locals, and Expresses*, 94; and Stover, *The Routledge Historical Atlas*, 68–69.

6. Veenendaal, *Slow Train to Paradise*, 88–89.

7. Veenendaal, *Slow Train to Paradise*, 51–53, 57; Hilton, *American Narrow Gauge Railroads*, 478.

8. Veenendaal, *Slow Train to Paradise*, 110–112, 119; *Sycamore True Republican*, April 20, 1870, 1, and October 5, 1870, 4; and *New York Times*, December 6, 1872, 2.

9. The next two paragraphs are based primarily on Gernon, "Hinckley's Railroad Empire."

10. Grant, *"Follow the Flag,"* 54; Bryant, *History*, 136; and Marshall, *Santa Fe*, 202–203.

11. Puffert, *Tracks across Continents*, 117; and Hilton, *American Narrow Gauge Railroads*, chap. 3, esp. 59–63.

12. Hilton, *American Narrow Gauge Railroads*, 52, 56, 387.

13. Grant, *"Follow the Flag,"* 59; Hilton, *American Narrow Gauge Railroads*, 389; and Sanders, *Limiteds, Locals, and Expresses*, 222.

14. Hilton, *American Narrow Gauge Railroads*, 473–479; Burlington, Monmouth, and Illinois River RR, 3; and Sanders, *Limiteds, Locals, and Expresses*, 163–164.

15. Stover, *History of the Baltimore and Ohio*, 150–151, 191; and Puffert, *Tracks across Continents*, 138.

16. Veenendaal, *Slow Train to Paradise*, 103; *New York Times*, July 31, 1874; and *Eleventh Annual Report*, 9–10; Stover, *Life and Decline*, 67; and Corliss, *Main Line of Mid-America*, 206–207.

17. Sanders, *Limiteds, Locals, and Expresses*, 224; *Eleventh Annual Report*, 269; and Hilton, *American Narrow Gauge Railroads*, 390.

18. Hilton, *American Narrow Gauge Railroads*, 383–389.

10. BRIDGE BUILDING AND "OVERBUILDING"

1. Riney, *Hell Gate*, 4–6.

2. Riney, *Hell Gate*, 173–174; Jackson, *Rails across the Mississippi*, 3; and House of Representatives Committee on Commerce, *Report*, 5.

3. Glendinning, *Chicago and Alton Railroad*, 100.

4. See Jackson, *Rails across the Mississippi*, passim.

5. Jackson, *Rails across the Mississippi*, 210–214.

6. Glendinning, *Chicago and Alton Railroad*, 105–106, 123–124.

7. *Rock Island Argus*, May 3, 1894, 1; and Overton, *Burlington Route*, 232, 268–269.

8. Corliss, *Main Line of Mid-America*, 226–231.

9. Sanders, *Limiteds, Locals, and Expresses*, 208.

10. Corliss, *Main Line of Mid-America*, 225; Overton, *Burlington Route*, 229; and Grant, *The North Western*, 93. For the Milwaukee Road catastrophe, see chapter 8.

11. Grant, *The North Western*, 47.

12. Grant, *The North Western*, 65–66.

13. Sanders, *Limiteds, Locals, and Expresses*, 158.

14. Dorin, *The Soo Line*, 11; and Suprey, *Steam Trains*, 3.

15. Dobnick and Glischinski, *Wisconsin Central*, 11, 16–17.

16. Hofsommer, *The Hook and Eye*, 5–14.

17. Hofsommer, *The Hook and Eye*, 58–63, 71–72, 96–97. Hilton, *American Narrow Gauge Railroads*, 474, calls the line the Burlington, Monmouth & Illinois River Railroad, a successor to the similarly unconsummated Illinois & Mississippi Railroad.

18. Hofsommer, *The Tootin' Louie*, 8–17, 38–39.

19. Hofsommer, *The Tootin' Louie*, 41.

20. Hofsommer, *The Tootin' Louie*, 51–52.

21. Hofsommer, *The Tootin' Louie*, 66–68; and Hayes, *Iron Road to Empire*, 175. Hayes calls this a "major mistake" by the Reid-Moore syndicate.

22. Hofsommer, *The Tootin' Louie*, 116–121; and Hofsommer, *The Hook and Eye*, 107, 120.

23. Grant, *The Corn Belt Route*, 4–5, 20.

24. Grant, *The Corn Belt Route*, 7–13.

25. Grant, *The Corn Belt Route*, 32–34; and *Chicago Daily Tribune*, March 23, 1892, 9.

26. Grant, *The Corn Belt Route*, 19, 29.

27. *Sycamore True Republican*, May 10, 1899, n.p.

28. Grant, *The Corn Belt Route*, 41–42.

29. *Sycamore True Republican*, January 20, 1892, 4, January 21, 1893, 2, March 20, 1895, 3, and September 4, 1897, 1.

30. *Chicago Daily Tribune*, November 18, 1902, 15. For data regarding the profitability of the Elgin, Joliet & Eastern Railway between 1910 and 1921, see *Poor's Intermediate Manual*, 1073.

31. *Poor's Manual of Railroads*, 440; Grant, *Twilight Rails*, 151–156, 162; and Bateman and Selby, *Historical Encyclopedia*, n.p.

32. Grant, *Twilight Rails*, 163, 166.

33. Snyder, *American Railways*, 391.

34. Corliss, *Main Line of Mid-America*, 220; Overton, *Burlington Route*, 408; *First Annual Report*, 8; Glendinning, *Chicago and Alton*, 119; and Hofsommer, *The Hook and Eye*, 102.

11. EXCURSIONS AND INTERURBANS

1. *Sycamore True Republican*, June 12, 1886, 4, and September 3, 1887, 3; Keating, *Chicagoland*, 115–116; *Tallula Express*, December 28, 1895, 1; and *Prairie Farmer*, May 18, 1896, 15.

2. *Chicago Daily Tribune*, December 10, 1887, 6; and *Sycamore True Republican*, August 20, 1887, 1.

3. *Chicago Tribune*, August 12, 1887, 7; *St. Paul Western Appeal*, October 1, 1887, 2.

4. *St. Paul Daily Globe*, August 12, 1887, 1; and *Chicago Daily Tribune*, August 28, 1887, 4.

5. *St. Paul Western Appeal*, August 27, 1887, 2.

6. *Sycamore True Republican*, August 20, 1887, 2.

7. *Chicago Daily Tribune*, September 3, 1887, 1, and December 11, 1887, 4; and *Sycamore True Republican*, October 26, 1887, 4.

8. *Sycamore True Republican*, August 20, 1887, 2; *Daily Illini*, November 14, 1887, 7; *Ottawa Free Trader*, May 12, 1888, 3; and *Chicago Daily Tribune*, September 10, 1887, 2, and September 6, 1887, 5.

9. *Chicago Daily Tribune*, August 24, 1887, 1, October 10, 1887, 1, October 24, 1887, 1, December 10, 1887, 6, and December 24, 1887, 1; Peters, *Folk Songs*, 242; Burford, *The Chatsworth Wreck*; and Haine, *Railroad Wrecks*, 56–61.

10. Sanders, *Limiteds, Locals, and Expresses*, 195.

11. Sanders, *Limiteds, Locals, and Expresses*, 193.

12. Sanders, *Limiteds, Locals, and Expresses*, 196; Klein, *History*, 182; Cox, *Rails across Dixie*, 131, 149.

13. Revels, *Sunshine Paradise*, 27; and *Florida: The Land of Sunshine*, 1.

14. Stover, *History of the Illinois Central*, 252; Hilton and Due, *The Electric Interurban Railways*, 312; and Grant, *We Took the Train*, 98–101.

15. Hilton and Due, *The Electric Interurban Railways*, 335.

16. Middleton, *The Interurban Era*, 192–201; Stringham, *Illinois Terminal Railroad*, 12, 35; and Jenkins, *Illinois Terminal Railroad*, 300.

17. Jenkins, *Illinois Terminal Railroad*, 68, 90–91.

18. Borzo, *The Chicago "L,"* 71, 76; Hilton and Due, *The Electric Interurban Railways*, 335–336; and John F. Due, "Samuel Insull," in Bryant, *Railroads*, 226–228.

19. Schwieterman, *When the Railroad Leaves Town*, 64–65; and Johnson, *Aurora 'n' Elgin*, 1–2.

20. See Hicks, *The Little Road*.

21. *Street and Electric Railways*, 338; and Blakemore, *Moody's Analyses*, 540; Schwieterman, *When the Railroad Leaves Town*, 60; and Lundin, *Rockford*, 96–97.

22. Grant, *The North Western*, 204; Glendinning, *Chicago and Alton Railroad*, 146; *Urbana Daily Courier*, April 29, 1905, 5, and

June 3, 1905, 3; Stover, *Life and Decline*, 254–255; and Grant, *The Corn Belt Route*, 83.

12. COAL AND COMPETITION

1. See Robert Paul Jordan, "Illinois," reprinted in Angle, *Prairie State*, 579; and Chenoweth and Borino, *Directory of Coal Mines*, 1.

2. Stover, *Life and Decline*, 118.

3. Chandler R. Gilman, "By Stage and Packet," reprinted in Angle, *Prairie State*, 157; and Sir James Caird, "A Bird's Eye View of Illinois," reprinted in Angle, *Prairie State*, 157.

4. Allen, *Legends and Lore*, 135–137.

5. *Chicago Daily Tribune*, May 13, 1856, 1; and Glendinning, *Chicago and Alton Railroad*, 160.

6. *Prairie Farmer*, July 1, 1855, 4; William Ferguson, "Through Illinois in the Illinois Central," reprinted in Angle, *Prairie State*, 307; and Allen, *Legends and Lore*, 338–339.

7. Corliss, *Main Line of Mid-America*, 284.

8. Schwieterman, *When the Railroad Leaves Town*, 59–60; Grant, *The North Western*, 90–91; Grant, *Twilight Rails*, 150; and Glendinning, *Chicago and Alton Railroad*, 172.

9. Overton, *Burlington Route*, 244–246.

10. *Chicago Daily Tribune*, January 5, 1901, 1, and April 26, 1901, 11; and Overton, *Burlington Route*, 280–282, 295.

11. Overton, *Burlington Route*, 278, 295; and Grant, *Twilight Rails*, 150.

12. Albro Martin, "William H. Moore," in Bryant, *Railroads*, 309–310; Stuart Daggett, *Railroad Reorganization* (Boston: Houghton and Mifflin, 1908), 314–317; and Hayes, *Iron Road to Empire*, 147–148.

13. Daggett, *Railroad Reorganization*, 321; and Hayes, *Iron Road to Empire*, 171.

14. White, *Railroaded*, 35–36; and Hayes, *Iron Road to Empire*, 158.

15. Daggett, *Railroad Reorganization*, 322; and Hayes, *Iron Road to Empire*, 166–169.

16. *Farm, Field and Fireside*, July 25, 1903, 2; *Chicago Livestock World*, February 26, 1903, 7; Hayes, *Iron Road to Empire*, 166–167; Martin, "William H. Moore," 311–312; and Glendinning, *Chicago and Alton Railroad*, 157. The Frisco was the St. Louis & San Francisco Railroad, which ran from the Mississippi River city into Kansas, Indian Territory, and northern Texas but not California. Mileage data are from the Interstate Commerce Commission, *Twenty-Sixth Annual Report*.

17. *Chicago Livestock World*, December 15, 1905, 2.

18. *Chicago Daily Tribune*, November 13, 1909, 9; and Hayes, *Iron Road to Empire*, 187–189.

19. *Daily Illini*, February 25, 1926, 1; Ladd, *Autophobia*, 15–16; and Cord Scott, "The Car Race of the Century," in Reiss and Gems, *The Chicago Sports Reader*, 92–103.

20. *New York Times*, November 24, 1894, 9.

21. *Report of Illinois Good Roads Commission*, 18; and Hugill, "Good Roads," 329.

22. Wrone, "Illinois Pulls Out," 56; Hugill, "Good Roads," 329–330; *Sycamore True Republican*, March 20, 1918, 2; and *Farm Home*, July 1, 1916, 4.

23. *Better Farming*, April 1, 1920, 14, and April 1, 1922, 4; and *Highway Magazine*, April 1920, 9.

24. Belasco, *Americans on the Road*; Stover, *Life and Decline*, 121–122; Wrone, "Illinois Pulls Out," 68, 73; Biles, *Illinois*, 209; Stover, *American Railroads*, 193–194; and Grant, *North Western*, 145.

25. Wrone, "Illinois Pulls Out," 68–70, 73–74; Hugill, "Good Roads," 342; Glendinning, *Chicago and Alton Railroad*, 181; and Biles, *Illinois*, 149–150.

26. *Chicago Daily Tribune*, September 6, 1918, 9; Cordery, *Alice*, 291; *Chicago Daily Tribune*, August 12, 1921, G4 (the Dixie Highway included segments in Florida, Georgia, Indiana, Kentucky, Michigan, Ohio, and Tennessee); *Daily Illini*, November 3, 1922, 9, and September 19, 1922, 9; and *Sycamore True Republican*, July 10, 1929, 3.

27. Goddard, *Getting There*, 51–52; *Sycamore True Republican*, July 27, 1901, 1, and March 12, 1902, 2; *Daily Illini*, January 27, 1906, 4, and February 24, 1906, 1; and Sanders, *Amtrak*, 76.

13. PROGRESSIVE REGULATION

1. Kolko, *Railroads and Regulation*, 8; and Johnson and Huebne, *Railroad Traffic and Rates*, 166. For more on the Iowa Pool, see chapter 8.

2. Johnson and Huebne, *Railroad Traffic and Rates*, 167–168; and Kolko, *Railroads and Regulation*, 73.

3. Quoted in Grant, *The North Western*, 83.

4. See US Congress, *Industrial Commission Final Report*, 57th Cong., 1st sess., 1902, reprinted in Chalmers, *Neither Socialism nor Monopoly*, 47–48; Stover, *Life and Decline*, 93–97; Kolko, *Railroads and Regulation*, 67, 96; and Glendinning, *Chicago and Alton Railroad*, 129. Pools failed because they were technically illegal and therefore easy to evade: see Kolko, *Railroads and Regulation*, 8–11, 17–20, 82–83; and Burns, *Railroad Mergers*, 10.

5. Martin, *Enterprise Denied*, 18–19.

6. Overton, *Burlington Route*, 247–248. For the CB&Q corporate consolidation, see chapter 11.

7. Botkin and Harlow, *Treasury of Railroad Folklore*, 150.

8. Overton, *Burlington Route*, 248–251; and Saunders, *Merging Lines*, 20–22.

9. Martin, *Enterprise Denied*, 102.

10. Botkin and Harlow, *Treasury of Railroad Folklore*, 150; Chalmers, *Neither Socialism nor Monopoly*, 63; US Senate Committee on Interstate Commerce, *Hearings on the Regulation of Railway Rates*, 59th Cong., 1st sess., 1906, reprinted in Chalmers, *Neither Socialism nor Monopoly*, 63; Hill, *Highways of Progress*, 131–132, 133; Saunders, *Merging Lines*, 24; and Gallamore and Meyer, *American Railroads*, 12. In 1970 the CB&Q, GNR, NPR, and SPS finally consummated the merger by forming the Burlington Northern Railroad.

11. Churella, *The Pennsylvania Railroad*, 664–665.

12. *Urbana Daily Courier*, July 19, 1905, 5, September 23, 1905, 4, and December 16, 1905, 9.

13. "Special Message of the President to the Two Houses of Congress 31 January 1908," http://www.theodore-roosevelt.com/images/research/txtspeeches/968.pdf, app. 1, 30–35; and Glendinning, *Chicago and Alton Railroad*, 153.

14. Gallamore and Meyer, *American Railroads*, 6, 32.

15. *Urbana Daily Courier*, March 19, 1903, 2; Overton, *Burlington Route*, 286; and White, "The Railroad Pass," 70–71.

16. 3 D2.1, CB&Q Company Papers; and Kolko, *Railroads and Regulation*, 149.

17. Kahn, *Our Economic and Other Problems*, 52.

18. Glendinning, *Chicago and Alton Railroad*, 130–132, 152; Bryant, *History*, 138; Martin, *Enterprise Denied*, 86–88; and *Rock Island Argus*, April 28, 1894, 8.

19. Dalton, *Theodore Roosevelt*, 328.

20. Glendinning, *Chicago and Alton Railroad*, 154–155; Martin, *Enterprise Denied*, 85; Dalton, *Theodore Roosevelt*, 328; and Theodore Roosevelt to James Schoolcraft Sherman, October 8, 1906, reprinted in Morison, *The Letters*, 5:447.

21. Martin, *Enterprise Denied*, 89.

22. Klein, *Life and Legend*, 13–17; Kennan, *Misrepresentation*, 33–34; Glendinning, *Chicago and Alton Railroad*, 155; and Martin, *Enterprise Denied*, 84.

23. Davis, *Power at Odds*, 11; Stover, *Life and Decline*, 120–122; Stover, *American Railroads*, 169; Taillon, *Good, Reliable, White Men*, 201.

24. Glendinning, *Chicago and Alton Railroad*, 175.

14. WORLD WAR I AND THE 1920S

1. Overton, *Burlington Route*, 371; and Biles, *Illinois*, 208–209.

2. Stover, *Life and Decline*, 112–113.

3. Stover, *Life and Decline*, 164.

4. Biles, *Illinois*, 190.

5. EuDaly et al., *Complete Book*, 47.

6. Goldmark, "Women in the Railroad World," 214–215; Brown, *Rosie's Mom*, 166, 176; Greenwald, "Women Workers," 163; and Grant, *The Corn Belt Route*, 89.

7. Grant, *The North Western*, 130; Glendinning, *Chicago and Alton Railroad*, 177; Hofsommer, *The Tootin' Louie*, 138; Grant, *The Corn Belt Route*, 89; and Stringham, *Toledo, Peoria & Western*, 45, 49.

8. Corliss, *Main Line of Mid-America*, 331–333, 340–341; and Overton, *Burlington Route*, 299–300.

9. *Chicago Tribune*, February 8, 1919, 3; *New York Times*, August 2, 1922, 13; Stover, *Life and Decline*, 174–175; Grant, *The Corn Belt Route*, 93; and Grant, *The North Western*, 133–134.

10. Lowenthal, *The Investor Pays*, 37–41.

11. Grant, *Twilight Rails*, 166–169.

12. Grant, *Twilight Rails*, 170.

13. Derleth, *The Milwaukee Road*, 206–207; *New York Times*, December 1, 1925, 40; Lowenthal, *The Investor Pays*, 36, 41–42.

14. Davis, *Power at Odds*, 13, 27–30; and for the official view by a company vice president, see Park, *The Facts*.

15. Davis, *Power at Odds*, 45–46; and Overton, *Burlington Route*, 315–317.

16. Glendinning, *Chicago and Alton Railroad*, 184; *Urbana Daily Courier*, July 17, 1922, 1.

17. The actual percentages are as follows: C&NW, 96 percent; M&StL, 93 percent; the Milwaukee Road, 91 percent; C&EI, 90 percent; CRI&P, 71 percent; CB&Q, 70 percent; and ICRR, 48 percent (Davis, *Power at Odds*, 67–68).

18. Matejka and Koos, *Bloomington's C&A Shops*, 5, 74.

19. Davis, *Power at Odds*, 84, 93, 95.

20. *Summer Illini*, July 9, 1922, 1; and Davis, *Power at Odds*, 97, 90, 92.

21. *Urbana Daily Courier*, July 21, 1922, 4; and Davis, *Power at Odds*, 103–110.

22. *Urbana Daily Courier*, August 31, 1922, 1; and Davis, *Power at Odds*, 112, 115, 129.

23. *Wallace's Farmer*, September 29, 1922, 4; and Davis, *Power at Odds*, 154, 158.

24. Glendinning, *Chicago and Alton Railroad*, 183–185, 203.

25. Glendinning, *Chicago and Alton Railroad*, 186, 188, 202–203.

26. Overton, *Burlington Route*, 319; and Stover, *Illinois Central*, 257, 290.

27. Grant, *The Corn Belt Route*, 95–96, 99; and Stringham, *Toledo, Peoria & Western*, 44–47, 51.

28. Glendinning, *Chicago and Alton Railroad*, 193–194; Grant, *The North Western*, 146–148; Overton, *Burlington Route*, 406; and Stover, *Life and Decline*, 202.

29. Morgan, *Diesels West!*, 26.

30. See *Farm, Field, and Fireside*, April 2, 1898, 5; Churella, *From Steam to Diesel*, 24; and Solomon, *The American Diesel Locomotive*, 29.

31. Grant, *The Corn Belt Route*, 78; and Lamb, *Evolution*, 13–16.

32. EuDaly et al., *Complete Book*, 158–159; and Morgan, *Diesels West!*, 25, 27–29.

33. Glendinning, *Chicago and Alton Railroad*, 193; Hofsommer, *The Tootin' Louie*, 156; and Grant, *The North Western*, 146.

15. DEPRESSION, DIESELIZATION, AND ANOTHER WAR

1. Hofsommer, *The Tootin' Louis*, 168, 171.

2. Biles, *Illinois*, 211–214; and Spinney, *City of Big Shoulders*, 192–193.

3. Grant, *The North Western*, 153; Glendinning, *Chicago and Alton Railroad*, 206; and Stover, *Illinois Central*, 315–327.

4. Overton, *Burlington Route*, 364–365, 383, 409; and *Sycamore True Republican*, May 11, 1932, 4.

5. Grant, *North Western*, 154, 164.

6. Hofsommer, *The Tootin' Louie*, 176; Dorin, *The Soo Line*, 105; and *Sycamore True Republican*, October 14, 1931, 1.

7. Overton, *Burlington Route*, 385–386; and Glendinning, *Chicago and Alton Railroad*, 206, 208.

8. Shaw, *Nine Thousand Miles*, 200–207; *American Railroad Journal*, February 1895, 57–58, and August 1898, 265; Lamb, *Evolution*, 27; and Stover, *Life and Decline*, 248–249.

9. Overton, *Burlington Route*, 393–394; and Stover, *Illinois Central*, 357.

10. Overton, *Burlington Route*, 395–398; and Morgan, *Diesels West!*, 50–55.

11. *New York Times*, April 19, 1934, 3; and *Sycamore True Republican*, May 27, 1934, 1.

12. *New York Times*, January 19, 1936, N2; Overton, *Burlington Route*, 400; and Morgan, *Diesels West!*, 82–84.

13. Glendinning, *Chicago and Alton Railroad*, 210–211; and *Chicago Daily Tribune*, May 17, 1936, NW6.

14. Hayes, *Iron Road to Empire*, 239–240, 245; and *Chicago Tribune*, May 15, 1936, 37.

15. *New York Times*, April 23, 1934, 19; and *Sycamore True Republican*, August 13, 1940, 4, and November 28, 1934, 6.

16. Curl and McQuown, "Passenger Train Operations," 59; *Daily Illini*, June 10, 1930, 3; and *Chicago Tribune*, May 23, 1937, NW4.

17. ACF Records; Miller with Shacklette, *My Brother*, 62, 99; Stout, *Route of the Eagles*, 86. Data from *Chicago Tribune*, August 18, 1937, 23; and *Chicago Tribune*, January 9, 1938, B7.

18. White, *American Railroad Passenger Car*, 2:623; Downey, *Chicago*, 95–96; *Daily Illini*, June 27, 1939, 2; and Gallamore and Meyer, *American Railroads*, 128.

19. Horowitz, "The Diesel Firemen Issue," 551; and Overton, *Burlington Route*, 435–436.

20. Overton, *Burlington Route*, 440–441.

21. Overton, *Burlington Route*, 384, 403; Baldwin, "History and Methods," 6; Glendinning, *Chicago and Alton Railroad*, 207; and *Sycamore True Republican*, October 2, 1937, 1.

22. Revels, *Sunshine Paradise*, 67–69; Sanders, *Limiteds, Locals, and Expresses*, 197–198; Stover, *Illinois Central*, 349; and Overton, *Burlington Route*, 406.

23. Grant, *The Corn Belt Route*, 119–121; and Overton, *Burlington Route*, 414, 417.

24. Overton, *Burlington Route*, 387–391, 416–417.

25. Biles, *Illinois*, 229–230.

26. Biles, *Illinois*, 231.

27. Overton, *Burlington Route*, 476. For a sense of the frequently self-congratulatory contemporary opinion, see *Chicago Daily Tribune*, March 17, 1942, 21; and *New York Times*, April 11, 1943, E10, and September 25, 1943, 43.

28. Grant, *The North Western*, 171; EuDaly et al., *Complete Book*, 49; Stover, *Life and Decline*, 180; and Corliss, *Main Line of Mid-America*, 441.

29. Biles, *Illinois*, 234–235; Hofsommer, *The Tootin' Louie*, 212–213; and Corliss, *Main Line of Mid-America*, 440.

30. Overton, *Burlington Route*, 478.

31. Overton, *Burlington Route*, 481; Grant, *North Western*, 171; Corliss, *Main Line of Mid-America*, 443–444; and Hayes, *Iron Road to Empire*, 252.

32. Grant, *North Western*, 173; Biles, *Illinois*, 232; and Overton, *Burlington Route*, 497.

33. Curl and McQuown, "Streamline Era Begins," 14; Hofsommer, *The Tootin' Louie*, 214–215; and Sanders, *Limiteds, Locals, and Expresses*, 21; Hilton, *Monon Route*, 187, 191; and Stover, *History of the Baltimore and Ohio*, 317–320.

34. Hofsommer, *The Tootin' Louie*, 216–217; Grant, *"Follow the Flag,"* 189–190 (the Wabash officially exited receivership on January 1, 1942); and Glendinning, *Chicago and Alton Railroad*, 217.

35. Hayes, *Iron Road to Empire*, 255; Hofsommer, *The Tootin' Louie*, 215; Overton, *Burlington Route*, 497; Grant, *North Western*, 174–175; and Stover, *Life and Decline*, 187–188.

36. Stover, *Life and Decline*, 189; and Grant, *North Western*, 175.

16. POSTWAR CHALLENGES

1. Ladd, *Autophobia*, 43–44.

2. *Chicago Daily Tribune*, July 2, 1948, 7; *New York Times*, July 4, 1948, X11; and Chicago Railroad Fair, *Official Guide Book*, 7.

3. Chicago Railroad Fair, *Official Guide Book*, 8–9, 11; *Chicago Daily Tribune*, July 3, 1948, A6, and August 14, 1948, 3; and *New York Times*, August 22, 1948, X11.

4. Grant, *The North Western*, 177–178; *Chicago Daily Tribune*, August 12, 1948, 19, September 23, 1949, 11, and September 23, 1948, 1; *Sycamore True Republican*, August 19, 1948, 11, and October 8, 1948, 2; and *New York Times*, August 22, 1948, X11.

5. See, for example, *Sycamore True Republican*, July 30, 1948, 3, and August 6, 1948, 7.

6. See the diary of John W. Barriger, 1942, entries for March 1942, John W. Barriger III Papers.

7. J. W. Barriger, "Report on Toledo, Peoria, and Western Railroad 1942," and George Voelkner to J. W. Barriger, August 28, 1942, correspondence to J. W. Barriger 1942, Barriger Papers; *Chicago Daily Tribune*, March 12, 1947, 6, and April 23, 1947, 16; Stringham, *Toledo, Peoria & Western*, 58–60; and *New York Times*, March 13, 1947, 23, and March 16, 1947, 37.

8. Abbey, "Railroads," 86; and Stover, *History of the Baltimore and Ohio*, 315.

9. Hofsommer, *The Tootin' Louie*, 223.

10. *Chicago Daily Tribune*, April 25, 1945, 29; and Glendinning, *Chicago and Alton Railroad*, 215, 221–223.

11. Gallamore and Mayer, *American Railroads*, 9; and Overton, *Burlington Route*, 420–422.

12. Stover, *American Railroads*, 196; and Overton, *Burlington Route*, 501–502. The Civil Aeronautics Board denied the request.

13. Itzkoff, *Off the Track*, 27.

14. *Chicago Tribune*, August 25, 1957, F30–31, 40; and Sanders, *Limiteds, Locals, and Expresses*, 39, 78, 114.

15. Overton, *Burlington Route*, 526; Farrington, *Railroading*, 140; *Chicago Tribune*, January 24, 1949, B3, and November 7, 1959, A5.

16. Sanders, *Limiteds, Locals, and Expresses*, 10; Illinois data from Clayton, *Illinois Fact Book*, 340.

17. *Chicago Tribune*, April 27, 1958, 1; Stover, *Life and Decline*, 193; and Sanders, *Limiteds, Locals, and Expresses*, 82–89, 115.

18. Sanders, *Limiteds, Locals, and Expresses*, 41–42, 51.

19. Sanders, *Amtrak*, 68.

20. Sanders, *Limiteds, Locals, and Expresses*, 236–238.

21. Klein, *History*, 470; Sanders, *Limiteds, Locals, and Expresses*, 216–218; and Lyon, *To Hell in a Day Coach*, 223.

22. *Sycamore True Republican*, July 18, 1961, 1.

23. Grant, *North Western*, 180, 183; Saunders, *Merging Lines*, 325; and Grant, *The Corn Belt Route*, 140, 156.

24. *Chicago Tribune*, May 3, 1946, 16, January 30, 1958, 14, and April 10, 1955, 16; Lyon, *To Hell in a Day Coach*, 224; Glendinning, *Chicago and Alton Railroad*, 232; and Saunders, *Merging Lines*, 308.

25. Sanders, *Limiteds, Locals, and Expresses*, 199, 213–214.

26. Lind, *Illinois Central Story*, 118, 129; Illinois Central, *Timetable*, April 24, 1955, table 2, and Illinois Central, *Timetable*, April 26, 1964, table 2; *Chicago Tribune*, January 16, 1958, D7; and *Daily Illini*, March 25, 1959, 4.

27. Grant, *"Follow the Flag,"* 112, 198–202, 250; and Sanders, *Limiteds, Locals, and Expresses*, 174, 176–177.

28. Jenkins, *Illinois Terminal Railroad*, 141–145, 154, 219–235.

29. http://www.minonktalk.com/doodle.htm; Sanders, *Limiteds, Locals, and Expresses*, 167; *Chicago Tribune*, February 7, 1961, B13; and Dorin, *Soo Line*, 81.

30. *Trains*, April 1959, 16–25, 34–44.

31. Stover, *Life and Decline*, 220.

32. http://www.illinoisrailroadassociation.com/aboutus.html.

33. Schneider, *Rock Island Requiem*, 96; Grant, *North Western*, 203–204; Saunders, *Merging Lines*, 324; Schwieterman, *When the Railroad Leaves Town*, 64, 66; and Johnson, *Aurora 'n' Elgin*, 1.

34. *Chicago Tribune*, March 27, 1958, S2, August 9, 1964, SW9, and December 31, 1968, 1.

17. NATIONAL SOLUTIONS?

1. Sanders, *Amtrak*, 2–5; and Stover, *American Railroads*, 234.

2. Solomon, *Amtrak*, 31–32; *Chicago Tribune*, April 30, 1970, 1; Sanders, *Amtrak*, 9–10.

3. Sanders, *Amtrak*, 7.

4. *Chicago Tribune*, April 30, 1971, 2, and May 2, 1971, 3; Stover, *American Railroads*, 235; Sanders, *Amtrak*, 7–8.

5. Sanders, *Amtrak*, 124–125, 246; *Chicago Tribune*, June 11, 1971, 1, and August 15, 1974, 10.

6. Sanders, *Amtrak*, 19–20.

7. *Chicago Tribune*, April 22, 1971, 1, and November 25, 1984, J16; Schwieterman, *Terminal Town*, 12–29; Sanders, *Amtrak*, 137–140.

8. *Chicago Tribune*, October 2, 1975, 5.

9. *Chicago Tribune*, July 7, 1974, 28; *New York Times*, March 5, 1975, 77.

10. *Chicago Tribune*, June 30, 1974, C2, April 14, 1978, C12, and October 1, 1979, 1; and Sanders, *Amtrak*, 44, 57, 61–62.

11. Sanders, *Amtrak*, 242–243; and *Chicago Tribune*, August 21, 1975, A4.

12. *Chicago Tribune*, August 1, 1975, A4, and November 20, 1975, 28.

13. *Chicago Tribune*, August 20, 1975, A4; and Sanders, *Amtrak*, 249.

14. *Chicago Tribune*, December 7, 1980, B18, and August 10, 1980, B12; Sanders, *Amtrak*, 246, 249; and *Daily Illini*, April 26, 1972, 7.

15. See Wilson J. Warren, "Beyond the Rust Belt: The Neglected History of the Rural Midwest's Industrialization after World War II," in Anderson, *The Rural Midwest*, 73, 86–88.

16. Grant, *Visionary Railroader*, 123–124; and Young, *The Iron Horse*, 194.

17. Saunders, *Main Lines*, 19; Schneider, *Rock Island Requiem*, 43–44; *Chicago Tribune*, August 16, 1966, C5, and September 29, 1967, C7; and Grant, *The North Western*, 213–214.

18. Saunders, *Merging Lines*, 332.

19. *Chicago Tribune*, August 20, 1966, F6, and July 10, 1970, C9; and Grant, *Visionary Railroader*, 148–150.

20. *Chicago Tribune*, November 15, 1974, A2.

21. Saunders, *Merging Lines*, 182; and Grant, *North Western*, 231. The former Rock Island line from the Twin Cities to Kansas City replaced the North Western's own winding, heavily graded line made up of former Minneapolis & St. Louis and Chicago Great Western trackage.

22. Saunders, *Merging Lines*, 382.

23. *Daily Illini*, March 19, 1971, 5; *New York Times*, March 19, 1971, 43, and March 19, 1971, 43; *Chicago Tribune*, March 20, 1971, 5, and March 25, 1971, 16; Daughen and Binzen, *The Wreck*, 215.

24. *New York Times*, March 20, 1971, 60. For "Joe Bananas," see *Chicago Tribune*, March 3, 1973, 17.

25. *Chicago Tribune*, April 9, 1971, 4, and June 17, 1971, A10; and *New York Times*, January 28, 1972, 41.

26. *New York Times*, June 23, 1970, 42; and Stover, *American Railroads*, 238.

27. Grant, *North Western*, 229.

18. SALVATION

1. The Association of American Railroads, an advocacy and coordination group, categorized railroads according to their operating revenues. In 2012 it defined Class I railroads as "line haul freight railroads with 2010 operating revenue of $398.7 million or more": http://www.aar.org/~/media/aar/Industry%20Info/AAR-Stats-2012-05-10.ashx.

2. *Chicago Tribune*, December 13, 1982, B1; and *New York Times*, August 1, 1982, F1.

3. Saunders, *Merging Lines*, 310–312.

4. Saunders, *Merging Lines*, 338–340.

5. Grant, *The North Western*, 213.

6. Grant, *The North Western*, 207–209, 213; and Saunders, *Merging Lines*, 336.

7. *Sycamore True Republican*, September 30, 1964, 1, 6; and Grant, *The North Western*, 212.

8. *Chicago Tribune*, October 8, 1970, 16, and November 26, 1970, E9; and Grant, *The North Western*, 216–220.

9. Grant, *The North Western*, 222–223.

10. *New York Times*, February 19, 1967, 208.

11. Saunders, *Main Lines*, 177–188.

12. Gallamore and Meyer, *American Railroads*, 243.

13. Wilner, *Railroad Mergers*, 220.

14. *Chicago Tribune,* August 2, 1981, D9; *New York Times,* January 11, 1981, NE34; and Gallamore and Meyer, *American Railroads,* 260.

15. Saunders, *Main Lines,* 193–198.

16. Robert Paul Jordan, "Illinois," in Angle, *Prairie State,* 590.

17. Solomon and Yough, *Coal Trains,* 110; Grant, *The North Western,* 230; and *Trains Magazine,* March 2011.

18. *New York Times,* January 21, 1968, S21; and see DeBoer, *Piggybacks and Containers.*

19. Grant, *The North Western,* 239.

20. Grant, *The North Western,* 220, 238–239, 251.

21. Gallamore and Meyer, *American Railroads,* 306.

22. Conant, *Railroad Bankruptcies,* 104–105; Saunders, *Merging Lines,* 417; and Saunders, *Main Lines,* 260–261.

23. Saunders, *Main Lines,* 262–270.

24. *Chicago Tribune,* December 13, 1989, B1.

25. Saunders, *Main Lines,* 301–303.

26. Saunders, *Main Lines,* 305–306; and Conant, *Railroad Bankruptcies,* 105.

27. Saunders, *Main Lines,* 272–273.

28. Saunders, *Main Lines,* 313–315; and *Wall Street Journal,* September 12, 1996, A2.

29. Gallamore and Meyer, *American Railroads,* 293.

30. *Wall Street Journal,* August 29, 1997, 1.

31. *New York Times,* November 3, 1997, D2, and November 23, 1997, B3; and Saunders, *Main Lines,* 329–336.

32. Saunders, *Main Lines,* 316–318.

33. Jenkins, *Illinois Terminal Railroad,* 253–254, 300.

34. Cox, *Rails across Dixie,* 117; Saunders, *Merging Lines,* 317; and Saunders, *Main Lines,* 288.

35. Cox, *Rails across Dixie,* 118; and Saunders, *Main Lines,* 284–287.

36. Saunders, *Main Lines,* 338–340; and Cox, *Rails across Dixie,* 118.

EPILOGUE

1. AAR, *Railroad Facts,* 46, 58, http://www.dot.il.gov/amtrak/amtrak.asp.

2. Richard C. Longworth, "The Political City," in Madigan, *Global Chicago,* 70; and http://www.bnsf.com/media/news-releases/2009/november/2009-11-03a.html.

3. https://www.aar.org/keyissues/Pages/Railroads-And-States.aspx#.U7qHuSjHo20.

4. https://www.aar.org/keyissues/Documents/Railroads-States/RANKINGS-2010.pdf.

5. *Progressive Railroading Daily News,* June 30, 2014.

BIBLIOGRAPHY

ARCHIVAL COLLECTIONS

Chicago History Museum
    Miscellaneous Collection
Mercantile Library, University of Missouri St. Louis
    ACF Records
    John W. Barriger III Papers
Newberry Library, Chicago
    Chicago, Burlington & Quincy Railroad Company Records
    Illinois Central Railroad Archives
    Pullman Company Archives

UNPUBLISHED PAPERS

Baldwin, Karl F., Jr. "History and Methods of Air Conditioning on the Baltimore and Ohio Railroad." Tau Beta Pi, University of Maryland, College Park, 1934. www.archive.org.
Smith, William Howard, Jr. "The Early Public Career of Stephen A. Douglas." PhD diss., Indiana University, 1963.

CD-ROM

Jenkins, Dale. *Illinois Railroads: Then and Now.* Decatur, IL: Dale Jenkins, 2012.

NEWSPAPERS

American Railroad Journal (1832–1899)
Chicago Daily Tribune (1850–2012)
Daily Illini (1874–1975)
Farm, Field and Fireside (1884–1906)
Illinois Farmer (1856–1864)
New York Times (1850–1980)
Prairie Farmer (1841–1941)
Sangamo (Springfield, IL) Journal (1831–1842)
Sycamore True Republican (1869–1968)
Tallula Express (1895–1896)
Urbana Daily Courier (1903–1935)
Western Rural (1868–1883)

ARTICLES

Abbey, Wallace W. "Railroads and the War." Special issue, "The Diesel Revolution," *Railroad History,* 2000, 81–88.
Aldrich, Mark. "Combating the Collision Horror: The Interstate Commerce Commission and Automatic Train Control, 1900–1939." *Technology and Culture* 34, no. 1 (January 1993): 49–77.
———. "Energy Conservation on Steam Railroads." *Railroad History,* no. 177 (Autumn 1997): 7–42.
Bardolph, Richard. "Illinois Agriculture in Transition 1820–1870." *Journal of the Illinois State Historical Society* 41, no. 4 (December 1948): 415–437.
Black, Paul V. "Experiment in Bureaucratic Centralization: Employee Blacklisting on the Burlington Railroad, 1877–1892." *Business History Review* 51, no. 4 (Winter 1977): 444–459.
Burford, Cary Clive. "The Twilight of the Local Passenger Train in Illinois." *Journal of the Illinois State Historical Society* 51, no. 2 (Spring 1958): 161–180.
Cordery, Simon. "Mutualism, Friendly Societies, and the Genesis of Railway Trade Unions." *Labour History Review* 67, no. 3 (December 2002): 263–279.
Curl, Ray, and Robert McQuown. "Passenger Train Operations." *C&EI Flyer* 12, nos. 1 and 2 (Spring and Fall 1993): 1–84.
———. "Passenger Train Operations: The Streamline Era Begins." *C&EI Flyer* 13, nos. 1 and 2 (Spring and Fall 1994): 1–85.
Davis, J. F. "Shifts in US Coal Production: Trends and Implications." *Geography* 66, no. 4 (November 1981): 304–309.
Downard, William L. "William Butler Ogden and the Growth of Chicago." *Journal of the Illinois State Historical Society* 75, no. 1 (Spring 1982): 47–60.
Ferris, William G. "The Disgrace of Ira Munn." *Journal of the Illinois State Historical Society* 68, no. 3 (June 1975): 202–212.
Flesher, Dale L., Gary J. Previts, and William D. Samson. "Early American Corporate Reporting and European Capital Markets: The Case of the Illinois Central Railroad, 1851–1861." *Accounting Historians Journal* 33, no. 1 (June 2006): 3–24.
Gernon, Blaine Brooks. "Hinckley's Railroad Empire." *Journal of the Illinois State Historical Society* 47, no. 4 (Winter 1954): 361–372.

Goldmark, Pauline. "Women in the Railroad World." *Annals of the American Academy of Political and Social Science* 86 (November 1919): 214–221.

Grant, H. Roger. "Chicago: America's Railroad Mecca." *Illinois History Teacher* 15, no. 1 (2008): 27–31.

———. "The Iron Horse Comes to Illinois." *Illinois History Teacher* 15, no. 1 (2008): 2–6.

———. "Railroad and Community Life." *Illinois History Teacher* 15, no. 1 (2008): 18–21.

———. "Still Hauling: Today's Railroads in Illinois." *Illinois History Teacher* 15, no. 1 (2008): 42–46.

Greenwald, Maurine Weiner. "Women Workers and World War I: The American Railroad Industry, a Case Study." *Journal of Social History* 9, no. 2 (Winter 1975): 154–177.

Haeger, John D. "The Abandoned Townsite on the Midwestern Frontier: A Case Study of Rockwell, Illinois." *Journal of the Early Republic* 3, no. 2 (Summer 1983): 165–183.

Hartley, Robert E. "A Touch of Class: Fred Harvey's Operations at Chicago Union Station." *Journal of Illinois History* 14, no. 3 (Autumn 2011): 218–220.

Hayter, Earl W. "The Fencing of Western Railways." *Agricultural History* 19, no. 3 (July 1945): 163–167.

Horowitz, Morris A. "The Diesel Firemen Issue on the Railroads." *Industrial and Labor Relations Review* 13, no. 4 (July 1960): 550–558.

Hugill, Peter J. "Good Roads and the Automobile in the United States 1880–1929." *Geographical Review* 72, no. 3 (July 1982): 327–349.

Lause, Mark A. "'The Cruel Striker War': Rail Labor and the Broken Symmetry of Galesburg Civic Culture, 1877–1888." *Journal of the Illinois State Historical Society* 91, no. 3 (Autumn 1998): 81–112.

Lee, Guy A. "The Historical Significance of the Chicago Grain Elevator System." *Agricultural History* 11, no. 1 (January 1937): 16–32.

Lightner, David L. "Construction Labor on the Illinois Central Railroad." *Journal of the Illinois State Historical Society* 66, no. 3 (Autumn 1973): 285–301.

Matile, Roger. "John Frink and Martin Walker: Stagecoach Kings of the Old Northwest." *Journal of the Illinois State Historical Society* 95, no. 2 (Summer 2002): 119–131.

McLear, Patrick E. "Speculation, Promotion, and the Panic of 1837 in Chicago." *Journal of the Illinois State Historical Society* 62, no. 2 (Summer 1969): 135–146.

———. "William Butler Ogden: A Chicago Promoter in the Speculative Era and the Panic of 1837." *Journal of the Illinois State Historical Society* 70, no. 4 (November 1977): 283–291.

McMurry, Donald L. "Labor Policies of the General Managers' Association of Chicago, 1886–1894." *Journal of Economic History* 13, no. 2 (Spring 1953): 160–178.

Meints, Graydon M. "Race to Chicago." *Railroad History*, no. 183 (Autumn 2000): 4–29.

Russell, Robert D. "The Planning and Failure of Cairo, Illinois 1838–1840." *Journal of Illinois History* 13 (Autumn 2010): 189–210.

Searles, William. "Railroad Construction across the Shawnee Hills." *Springhouse Magazine* 24, no. 1 (February 2007): 42–48.

Stradling, David, and Joel A. Tarr. "Environmental Activism, Locomotive Smoke, and the Corporate Response: The Case of the Pennsylvania Railroad and Chicago Smoke Control." *Business History Review* 73, no. 4 (Winter 1999): 677–704.

Sutton, Robert M. "Illinois' Year of Decision, 1837." *Journal of the Illinois State Historical Society* 58, no. 1 (Spring 1965): 34–53.

White, Elizabeth Pearson. "Captain Benjamin Godfrey and the Alton and Sangamon Railroad." *Journal of the Illinois State Historical Society* 67, no. 5 (November 1974): 466–486.

White, John H., Jr. "The Railroad Pass: Perk or Plunder?" *Railroad History*, no. 182 (Spring 2000): 58–71.

White, Roy. "Memo to America." *Railroad Magazine* 46, no. 4 (September 1948): 11–17.

Wrone, David R. "Illinois Pulls Out of the Mud." *Journal of the Illinois State Historical Society* 58, no. 1 (Spring 1965): 54–76.

REFERENCE WORKS

AAR. *Railroad Facts*. Washington, DC: Association of American Railroads, 2013.

Bateman, Newton, and Paul Selby, eds. *Historical Encyclopedia of Illinois*. Chicago: Munsell, 1900.

Carpenter, Richard C. *A Railroad Atlas of the United States in 1946*. Vol. 4, *Illinois, Wisconsin, and Upper Michigan*. Baltimore, MD: Johns Hopkins University Press, 2011.

Clayton, John, comp. *The Illinois Fact Book and Historical Almanac, 1673–1968*. Carbondale: Southern Illinois University Press, 1970.

Handy Railroad Atlas of the United States. Chicago: Rand McNally, 1973.

Penfield, T., ed. *The Rand-McNally Official Railway Guide and Hand Book*. Chicago: Rand-McNally, 1886.

The Rail-Roads, History and Commerce of Chicago. Chicago: Democratic Press, 1854.

Street and Electric Railways. Washington, DC: United States Printing Office, 1910.

Thomas, J., and T. Baldwin, eds. *A Complete Pronouncing Gazetteer or Geographical Dictionary of the World*. Philadelphia: J. B. Lippincott, 1856.

Walker, Mike. *Railroad Atlas of the United States: Great Lakes West*. Faversham, UK: Steam Powered Publishing, 1996.

The World Almanac 1892. New York: New York World Press Publishing, 1892.

BOOKS: PRIMARY

First Annual Report of the Railroad and Warehouse Commission of the State of Illinois for the Year Ending November 30th 1871. Springfield: Illinois Journal Printing Office, 1872.

Second Annual Report of the Railroad and Warehouse Commission of the State of Illinois for the Year Ending November 30th 1872. Springfield: State Journal Steam Print, 1873.

Eleventh Annual Report of the Railroad and Warehouse Commission of the State of Illinois for the Year Ending June 30th 1881. Springfield: H. W. Rokker, 1882.

Thirty-Second Annual Report of the Railroad and Warehouse Commission of the State of Illinois for the Year Ending June 30th 1902. Springfield: Phillips Print, 1903.

Ade, George. *Stories of Chicago.* 1941. Reprint, Urbana: University of Illinois Press, 2003.

Angle, Paul M., ed. *Prairie State: Impressions of Illinois, 1673–1967, by Travelers and Other Observers.* Chicago: University of Chicago Press, 1968.

Blakemore, Maurice N., et al., eds. *Moody's Analyses of Investments and Security Rating Books: Public Utility Investments.* New York: Moody's Investment Services, 1922.

Bonham, Jeremiah. *Fifty Years' Recollections with Observation and Reflections on Historical Events.* Peoria: J. W. Franks, 1883.

Botkin, B. A., and Alvin F. Harlow, eds. *A Treasury of Railroad Folklore: The Stories, Tall Tales, Traditions, Ballads and Songs of the American Railroad Man.* New York: Crown, 1953.

Burlington, Monmouth, and Illinois River RR: Its Location, Business Prospects, &c. Monmouth, IL: Review Steam Book and Job Print, 1876.

Chicago Association of Commerce. *Smoke Abatement and Electrification of Railway Terminals in Chicago.* 1915. Reprint, Elmsford, NY: Maxwell Reprint Company, 1971.

Chicago Railroad Fair. *Official Guide Book and Program for the Pageant "Wheels A-Rolling."* Chicago, 1948.

Cobden, Richard. *The American Diaries of Richard Cobden.* Edited by Elizabeth Hoon Cawley. Princeton, NJ: Princeton University Press, 1952.

Colbert, Elias, and Everett Chamberlin. *Chicago and the Great Conflagration.* 1871. Reprint, New York: Viking Press, 1971.

Douglas, Stephen A. *The Letters of Stephen A. Douglas.* Edited by Robert W. Johannsen. Urbana: University of Illinois Press, 1961.

Farnham, Eliza W. *Life in Prairie Land.* New York: Harper and Brothers, 1846. Reprint, New York: Arno Press, 1972.

Florida: The Land of Sunshine. Illinois Central RR, n.d.

George, Charles B. *Forty Years on the Rail.* 2nd ed. Chicago: R. R. Donnelly & Sons, 1887.

Gerstner, Franz Anton Ritter von. *Early American Railroads.* Edited by Frederick C. Gamst. Translated by David J. Diephouse and John C. Decker. 1842–43. Reprint, Stanford, CA: Stanford University Press for the Railway and Locomotive Historical Society, 1997.

Hall, John A. *The Great Strike on the "Q."* Chicago: Elliott and Beezley, 1889.

Havighurst, Walter, ed. *Land of the Long Horizons.* New York: Coward-McCann, 1960.

Henry, Robert Selph. *This Fascinating Railroad Business.* Indianapolis: Bobbs-Merrill, 1942.

House of Representatives Committee on Commerce. *Report: Railroad Bridge across the Mississippi River at Rock Island, April 1858.* Washington, DC, 1858.

Interstate Commerce Commission. *Second Annual Report on the Statistics of Railways in the United States.* Washington, DC: Government Printing Office, 1890.

————. *Twenty-Sixth Annual Report on the Statistics of Railways in the United States.* Washington, DC: Government Printing Office, 1914.

Ives, Burl. *Wayfaring Stranger.* New York: Whittlesey House, 1948.

Johnson, Emory Richard, and Grover Gerhardt Huebne. *Railroad Traffic and Rates: Passenger, Express, and Mail Services.* New York: D. Appleton, 1911.

Kennan, George. *Misrepresentation in Railroad Affairs.* 1916. Reprint, New York: Arno Press, 1981.

Lyford, Will H. *History of the Chicago and Eastern Illinois Railway to June 30, 1913.* Chicago, 1913.

Matejka, Michael G., and Greg Koos, eds. *Bloomington's C&A Shops: Our Lives Remembered.* Bloomington, IL: McLean County Historical Society, 1987.

McCabe, James Dabney. *History of the Grange Movement, or The Farmer's War against the Monopolies.* Chicago: National Publishing Company, 1874.

Morison, Elting E., ed. *The Letters of Theodore Roosevelt.* Cambridge, MA: Harvard University Press, 1952.

Official Proceedings of the Mississippi Valley Railroad Convention. St. Louis: M. Niedner, 1852.

Owen, Robert Dale. *A Brief Practical Treatise on the Construction and Management of Plank Roads.* New Albany, IN: Kent & Norman, 1850.

Park, W. L. *The Facts about the Shopmen's Strike.* Chicago: Illinois Central Railroad, 1911.

Poor's Intermediate Manual of Railroads. New York: Poor's Manual Company, 1917.

Poor's Manual of Railroads. New York: Poor's Manual Company, 1922.

President Theodore Roosevelt's Railroad Policy: Report of a Discussion before the Economic Club of Boston March 9, 1905. Boston: Ginn, 1905.

Progress of Reconstruction and Electrification of the Chicago Terminal. Chicago: Illinois Central Railroad, 1926.

Regan, John. *The Emigrant's Guide to the Western States of America.* 2nd ed. Glasgow: Oliver and Boyd, 1852.

Reminiscences of Chicago during the Great Fire, with an Introduction by Mabel McIlvaine. Chicago: Lakeside Press, 1915.

Report of Illinois Good Roads Commission to the Forty-Fourth General Assembly. Springfield: Illinois State Journal, 1905.

Ripley, William Z. *Railroads Finance and Organization.* New York: Longmans, Green, 1920.

Salmons, C. H. *The Burlington Strike.* Aurora, IL, 1889.

Shaw, M. M. *Nine Thousand Miles on a Pullman Train: An Account of a Tour of Railroad Conductors from Philadelphia to the Pacific Coast and Return.* Philadelphia: Allen, Lane and Scott, 1898.

Sheahan, James W., and George P. Upton. *The Great Conflagration. Chicago: Its Past, Present and Future.* Chicago: Union Publishing, 1871.

Snyder, Carl. *American Railways as Investments.* New York: Moody, 1907.

Stradling, David, ed. *Conservation in the Progressive Era: Classic Texts*. Seattle: University of Washington Press, 2004.

Street and Electric Railways. Washington, DC: United States Printing Office, 1910.

Tenth Census of the United States, 1880. Washington, DC: Government Printing Office, 1883.

Thompson, Slason. *Cost Capitalization and Estimated Value of American Railways: An Analysis of Current Fallacies*. Chicago: Gunthorp-Warren, 1908.

Trollope, Anthony. *North America*. Edited by Donald Smalley and Bradford Allen Booth. 1862. Reprint, New York: Alfred A. Knopf, 1951.

BOOKS: SECONDARY

Adler, Dorothy R. *British Investment in American Railways 1834–1898*. Edited by Muriel E. Hidy. Charlottesville: University Press of Virginia, for the Eleutherian Mills–Hagley Foundation, 1970.

Alexander, Edwin P. *Down at the Depot: American Railroad Stations from 1831 to 1920*. New York: Clarkson N. Potter, 1970.

Allen, John W. *Legends and Lore of Southern Illinois*. Carbondale: Southern Illinois University Press, 1963.

Anderson, J. L., ed. *The Rural Midwest since World War II*. DeKalb: Northern Illinois University Press, 2014.

Andreas, Alfred Theodore. *History of Chicago from the Earliest Period to the Present Time*. Vol. 1 ending with 1857. Chicago: A. T. Andreas, 1884.

Anna Centennial Committee. *The Centennial History of Anna, Illinois*. Cape Girardieu, MO: Missourian Printing and Stationery Company, 1954.

Arnesen, Eric. *Brotherhoods of Color: Black Railroad Workers and the Struggle for Equality*. Cambridge, MA: Harvard University Press, 2001.

Belasco, Warren James. *Americans on the Road: From Autocamp to Motel, 1910–1945*. Cambridge, MA: MIT Press, 1979.

Belcher, Wyatt Winton. *The Economic Rivalry between St. Louis and Chicago 1850–1880*. 1947. Reprint, New York: AMS Press, 1968.

Biles, Roger. *Illinois: A History of the Land and Its People*. DeKalb: Northern Illinois University Press, 2005.

Bogue, Allan G. *From Prairie to Corn-Belt: Farming on the Illinois and Iowa Prairies in the Nineteenth Century*. Chicago: University of Chicago Press, 1963.

Borzo, Greg. *The Chicago "L."* Charleston, SC: Arcadia, 2007.

Bradsby, H. C., ed. *History of Bureau County*. Chicago: World Publishing, 1885.

Brown, Carrie. *Rosie's Mom: Forgotten Women Workers of the First World War*. Boston: Northeastern University Press, 2002.

Brownell, Baker. *The Other Illinois*. New York: Duell, Sloan and Pearce, 1958.

Brownson, Howard Gray. *The History of the Illinois Central Railroad to 1870*. Urbana: University of Illinois Press, 1915.

Bryant, Keith L., Jr. *History of the Atchison, Topeka and Santa Fe Railway*. New York: Macmillan, 1974.

———, ed. *Railroads in the Age of Regulation*. New York: Facts on File, 1988.

Buder, Stanley. *Pullman: An Experiment in Industrial Order and Community Planning, 1880–1930*. New York: Oxford University Press, 1970.

Burford, Cary Clive. *The Chatsworth Wreck: A Saga of Excursion Train Travel in the American Midwest in the 1880's*. Fairbury, IL: Blade Publishing Company, 1949.

Burgess, George H., and Miles C. Kennedy. *Centennial History of the Pennsylvania Railroad Company 1846–1946*. Philadelphia: Pennsylvania Railroad Company, 1949.

Burns, James B. *Railroad Mergers and the Language of Unification*. Westport, CT: Quorum Books, 1998.

Butler, Kenneth B., et al., eds. *Magnificent Whistle Stop: The 100-Year Story of Mendota, IL*. Mendota, IL: Mendota Centennial Committee, 1953.

Casson, Herbert N. *Cyrus Hall McCormick: His Life and Work*. 1909. Reprint, Freeport, NY: Books for Libraries, 1971.

Cavalier, Julian. *North American Railroad Stations*. Cranberry, NJ: A. S. Barnes, 1979.

Chalmers, David M., ed. *Neither Socialism nor Monopoly: Theodore Roosevelt and the Decision to Regulate the Railroads*. Philadelphia: J. B. Lippincott, 1976.

Chandler, Alfred D., ed. *The Railroads: The Nation's First Big Business*. New York: Harcourt, Brace and World, 1965.

Chenoweth, Cheri, and Melisa Borino. *Directory of Coal Mines in Illinois*. Rev. ed. Springfield: Illinois Department of Natural Resources, 2004.

Churella, Albert J. *From Steam to Diesel: Managerial Customs and Organizational Capabilities in the Twentieth Century American Locomotive Industry*. Princeton, NJ: Princeton University Press, 1998.

———. *The Pennsylvania Railroad. Volume I: Building an Empire, 1846–1917*. Philadelphia: University of Pennsylvania Press, 2013.

Clarke, S. J. *History of McDonough County, Illinois: Its Cities, Towns and Villages*. Springfield, IL: D. W. Lusk, 1878.

Commons, John R., et al. *History of Labor in the United States*. New York: Macmillan, 1918–35.

Conant, Michael. *Railroad Bankruptcies and Mergers from Chicago West 1975–2001: Financial Analysis and Regulatory Critique*. Research in Transportation Economics. Vol. 7. Amsterdam: Elsevier, 2004.

Cordery, Simon. *British Friendly Societies, 1750–1914*. Basingstoke, UK: Palgrave-Macmillan, 2003.

Cordery, Stacy A. *Alice: Alice Roosevelt Longworth, from White House Princess to Washington Power Broker*. New York: Viking, 2007.

Corliss, Carlton J. *Main Line of Mid-America: The Story of the Illinois Central*. New York: Creative Age Press, 1950.

Cox, Jim. *Rails across Dixie: A History of Passenger Trains in the American South*. Jefferson, NC: McFarland and Company, 2011.

Cronon, William. *Nature's Metropolis: Chicago and the Great West*. New York: W. W. Norton, 1991.

Daggett, Stuart. *Railroad Reorganization*. Boston: Houghton and Mifflin, 1908.

Dalton, Kathleen. *Theodore Roosevelt: A Strenuous Life*. New York: Alfred A. Knopf, 2002.

Daughen, Joseph R., and Peter Binzen. *The Wreck of the Penn Central*. Boston: Little, Brown, 1971.

Davis, Colin J. *Power at Odds: The 1922 National Railroad Shopmen's Strike*. Urbana: University of Illinois Press, 1997.

Davis, James E. *Frontier Illinois*. Bloomington: Indiana University Press, 1998.

DeBoer, David J. *Piggybacks and Containers: A History of Rail Intermodal on America's Steel Highways*. San Marino, CA: Golden West, 1992.

Derickson, Alan. *Workers' Health, Workers' Democracy: The Western Miners' Struggle, 1891–1925*. Ithaca, NY: Cornell University Press, 1988.

Derleth, August. *The Milwaukee Road: Its First Hundred Years*. 1948. Reprint, Iowa City: University of Iowa Press, 2002.

Dirck, Brian R. *Lincoln the Lawyer*. Urbana: University of Illinois Press, 2008.

Dobnick, Otto P., and Steve Glischinski. *Wisconsin Central: Railroad Success Story*. Waukesha, WI: Kalmbach Publishing, 1997.

Dodd, William Edward. *Robert J. Walker Imperialist*. Chicago: Chicago Literary Club, 1914.

Dorin, Patrick C. *The Soo Line*. Burbank, CA: Superior Publishing, 1979.

Downey, Clifford J. *Chicago and the Illinois Central Railroad*. Charleston, SC: Arcadia, 2007.

Ducker, James H. *Men of the Steel Rails: Workers on the Atchison, Topeka and Santa Fe Railroad, 1869–1900*. Lincoln: University of Nebraska Press, 1983.

Duis, Perry R. *Challenging Chicago: Coping with Everyday Life, 1837–1920*. Urbana: University of Illinois Press, 1998.

Eggert, Gerald G. *Richard Olney: Evolution of a Statesman*. University Park: Pennsylvania State University Press, 1974.

Ely, James W., Jr. *Railroads and American Law*. Lawrence: University Press of Kansas, 2001.

EuDaly, Kevin, et al. *The Complete Book of North American Railroading*. Minneapolis: Voyageur Press, 2009.

Faragher, John Mack. *Sugar Creek: Life on the Illinois Prairie*. New Haven, CT: Yale University Press, 1986.

Farrington, S. Kip, Jr. *Railroading from the Rear End*. New York: Coward McCann, 1946.

Fetters, Thomas. *The Charleston and Hamburg: A South Carolina Legacy and an American Railroad*. Charleston, SC: History Press, 2008.

Fogel, Robert W. *Railroads and American Economic Growth: Essays in Economic History*. Baltimore, MD: Johns Hopkins University Press, 1964.

Gallamore, Robert E., and John R. Meyer. *American Railroads: Decline and Renaissance in the Twentieth Century*. Cambridge, MA: Harvard University Press, 2014.

Gates, Paul Wallace. *The Illinois Central and Its Colonization Work*. Cambridge, MA: Harvard University Press, 1934.

Glendinning, Gene V. *The Chicago and Alton Railroad: The Only Way*. DeKalb: Northern Illinois University Press, 2002.

Goddard, Stephen B. *Getting There: The Epic Struggle between Road and Rail in the American Century*. Chicago: University of Chicago Press, 1994.

Grant, H. Roger. *The Corn Belt Route: A History of the Chicago Great Western Railroad Company*. DeKalb: Northern Illinois University Press, 1984.

———. *"Follow the Flag": A History of the Wabash Railroad Company*. DeKalb: Northern Illinois University Press, 2004.

———. *The North Western: A History of the Chicago & North Western Railway System*. DeKalb: Northern Illinois University Press, 1996.

———. *Twilight Rails: The Final Era of Railroad Building in the Midwest*. Minneapolis: University of Minnesota Press, 2010.

———. *Visionary Railroader: Jervis Langdon Jr. and the Transportation Revolution*. Bloomington: Indiana University Press, 2008.

———, ed. *We Took the Train*. DeKalb: Northern Illinois University Press, 1990.

Grant, H. Roger, and Charles W. Bohi. *The Country Railroad Station in America*. Boulder, CO: Pruett Publishing, 1978.

Grodinsky, Julius. *The Iowa Pool: A Study in Railroad Competition, 1870–84*. Chicago: University of Chicago Press, 1950.

Gutman, Herbert G. *Work, Culture and Society in Industrializing America: Essays in American Working-Class and Social History*. New York: Vintage, 1977.

Hadfield, Charles. *The Canal Age*. New York: Frederick A. Praeger, 1968.

Haine, Edgar A. *Railroad Wrecks*. New York: Cornwall Books, 1994.

Hamblen, Herbert. *The General Manager's Story*. 1898. Reprint, Upper Saddle River, NJ: Greg, 1970.

Hamer, Jennifer F. *Abandoned in the Heartland: Work, Family, and Living in East St. Louis*. Berkeley: University of California Press, 2011.

Harrison, Robert. *Congress, Progressive Reform, and the New American State*. Cambridge: Cambridge University Press, 2004.

Hart, John Fraser. *The Land That Feeds Us*. New York: W. W. Norton, 1991.

Hayes, William Edward. *Iron Road to Empire: The History of 100 Years of the Progress and Achievements of the Rock Island Lines*. New York: Simmons-Boardman, 1953.

Hepburn, A. Barton. *Artificial Waterways and Commercial Development*. New York: Macmillan, 1909.

Hevlin, Jesse, ed. *Historical Encyclopedia of Illinois and History of Fulton County*. Chicago: Munsell, 1908.

Hicks, Frank G. *The Little Road: The Story of the Macomb, Industry & Littleton Railway*. Macomb: Western Illinois University, 2006.

Hill, James J. *Highways of Progress*. Garden City, NY: Doubleday, 1912.

Hilton, George W. *American Narrow Gauge Railroads*. Stanford, CA: Stanford University Press, 1990.

———. *Monon Route*. Berkeley, CA: Howell-North Books, 1978.

Hilton, George W., and John F. Due. *The Electric Interurban Railways in America*. Stanford, CA: Stanford University Press, 1960.

History of Fulton County, Illinois. Peoria: Chas. A. Chapman, 1879.

Hofsommer, Don L. *The Hook and Eye: A History of the Iowa Central Railway*. Minneapolis: University of Minnesota Press, 2005.

———. *Steel Trails of Hawkeyeland: Iowa's Railroad Experience*. Bloomington: Indiana University Press, 2005.

———. *The Tootin' Louie: A History of the Minneapolis & St. Louis Railway*. Minneapolis: University of Minnesota Press, 2005.

Holbrook, Stewart H. *The Story of American Railroads*. New York: Bonanza Books, 1947.

Howard, Robert P. *Illinois: A History of the Prairie State*. Grand Rapids, MI: William B. Eerdmans Publishing Company, 1972.

Huddleston, Eugene L. *Uncle Sam's Locomotives: The USRA and the Nation's Railroads*. Bloomington: Indiana University Press, 2002.

Hudson, John C. *Making the Corn Belt: A Geographical History of Middle-Western Agriculture*. Bloomington: Indiana University Press, 1994.

Huibregtse, Jon R. *American Railroad Labor and the Genesis of the New Deal, 1919–1935*. Gainesville: University Press of Florida, 2010.

Interurban to Milwaukee. Bulletin 106. Chicago: Central Electric Railfans' Association, 1962.

Itzkoff, Donald M. *Off the Track: The Decline of the Intercity Passenger Train in the United States*. Westport, CT: Greenwood Press, 1985.

Jackson, Robert W. *Rails across the Mississippi: A History of the St. Louis Bridge*. Urbana: University of Illinois Press, 2001.

Jenkins, Dale. *The Illinois Terminal Railroad: The Road of Personalized Service*. Hart, MO: White River Productions, 2005.

Johannsen, Robert W. *Stephen A. Douglas*. New York: Oxford University Press, 1973.

Johnson, James D., comp. *Aurora 'n' Elgin: Being a Compendium of Word and Picture Recalling the Everyday Operations of the Chicago Aurora and Elgin Railroad*. Wheaton, IL: Traction Orange, 1965.

Kahn, Otto Hermann. *Our Economic and Other Problems: A Financier's Point of View*. New York: George H. Doran and Company, 1920.

Keating, Ann Durkin. *Chicagoland: City and Suburbs in the Railroad Age*. Chicago: University of Chicago Press, 2005.

Keiser, John H. *Illinois Vignettes*. Springfield, IL: Sangamon State University, 1977.

Klein, Maury. *History of the Louisville and Nashville Railroad*. New York: Macmillan, 1972.

———. *The Life and Legend of E. H. Harriman*. Chapel Hill: University of North Carolina Press, 2000.

———. *The Life and Legend of Jay Gould*. Baltimore, MD: Johns Hopkins University Press, 1986.

———. *Unfinished Business: The Railroad in American Life*. Hanover: University Press of New England, 1994.

———. *Union Pacific: The Reconfiguration. America's Greatest Railroad from 1969 to the Present*. New York: Oxford University Press, 2011.

Klopfenstein, Perry A. *Foundations Strong: A History of Gridley, Illinois, 1856–1990*. Fort Scott, KS: Sekan Publications, 1990.

Kolko, Gabriel. *Railroads and Regulation 1877–1916*. Princeton, NJ: Princeton University Press, 1965.

Ladd, Brian. *Autophobia: Love and Hate in the Automotive Age*. Chicago: University of Chicago Press, 2008.

Lamb, J. Parker. *Evolution of the American Diesel Locomotive*. Bloomington: Indiana University Press, 2007.

———. *Perfecting the American Steam Locomotive*. Bloomington: Indiana University Press, 2003.

Lansden, John M. *A History of the City of Cairo, Illinois*. 1910. Reprint, Carbondale: Southern Illinois University Press, 1976.

Licht, Walter. *Industrializing America: The Nineteenth Century*. Baltimore, MD: Johns Hopkins University Press, 1995.

———. *Working for the Railroad: The Organization of Work in the Nineteenth Century*. Princeton, NJ: Princeton University Press, 1983.

Lightner, David L. *Labor on the Illinois Central Railroad 1852–1900: The Evolution of an Industrial Environment*. New York: Arno, 1977.

Lind, Alan R. *The Illinois Central Story: An Illustrated History of the "Main Line of Mid-America."* Park Forest, IL: Transport History Press, 1993.

Linroth, R. W. *A History of the CB&Q Illinois Pea Vine: The Galesburg to Savanna Branch*. Dahinda, IL: R. W. Linroth, 2009.

Lowenthal, Max. *The Investor Pays*. New York: Alfred A. Knopf, 1933.

Lubetkin, M. John. *Jay Cooke's Gamble: The Northern Pacific Railroad, the Sioux, and the Panic of 1873*. Norman: University of Oklahoma Press, 2006.

Lundin, Jon W. *Rockford: An Illustrated History*. Tarzana, CA: American Historical Press, 1996.

Lyon, Peter. *To Hell in a Day Coach: An Exasperated Look at American Railroads*. Philadelphia: J. B. Lippincott, 1968.

Marshall, James. *Santa Fe: The Railroad That Built an Empire*. New York: Random House, 1945.

Martin, Albro. *Enterprise Denied: Origins of the Decline of American Railroads, 1897–1917*. New York: Columbia University Press, 1971.

———. *Railroads Triumphant: The Growth, Rejection, and Rebirth of a Vital American Force*. New York: Columbia University Press, 1992.

McMurry, Donald L. *The Great Burlington Strike of 1888: A Case Study in Labor Relations*. Cambridge, MA: Harvard University Press, 1956.

Meints, Graydon M. *Railroads for Michigan*. East Lansing: Michigan State University Press, 2013.

Mercer, Lloyd. *Railroads and Land Grant Policy: A Study in Government Intervention*. New York: Academic Press, 1982.

Middleton, William D. *The Interurban Era*. Milwaukee, WI: Kalmbach Publishing, 1961.

Miller, Edward L., with Norbert J. Shacklette. *My Brother, the IC Railroad, and Southern Illinois, 1936–1942*. St. Louis: Railway Mediation Services, 2005.

Miller, George H. *Railroads and the Granger Laws*. Madison: University of Wisconsin Press, 1971.

Miner, Craig. *A Most Magnificent Machine: America Adopts the Railroad, 1825–1862.* Lawrence: University Press of Kansas, 2010.

———. *The Rebirth of the Missouri Pacific, 1956–1983.* College Station: Texas A&M University Press, 1983.

Morgan, David P. *Diesels West! The Evolution of Power on the Burlington.* Milwaukee, WI: Kalmbach Publishing, 1963.

Overton, Richard C. *Burlington Route: A History of the Burlington Lines.* Lincoln: University of Nebraska Press, 1965.

———. *Burlington West: A Colonization History of the Burlington Railroad.* 1941. Reprint, New York: Russell and Russell, 1967.

Pacyga, Dominic A. *Chicago: A Biography.* Chicago: University of Chicago Press, 2009.

Peters, Harry B., ed. *Folk Songs out of Wisconsin.* Madison: State Historical Society of Wisconsin, 1977.

Puffert, Douglas J. *Tracks across Continents, Paths through History: The Economic Dynamics of Standardization in Railway Gauge.* Chicago: University of Chicago Press, 2009.

Reinhardt, Richard. *Workin' on the Railroad: Reminiscences from the Age of Steam.* 1970. Reprint, Norman: University of Oklahoma Press, 2003.

Reiss, Steven A., and Gerald Gems, eds. *The Chicago Sports Reader.* Urbana: University of Illinois Press, 2009.

Revels, Tracy J. *Sunshine Paradise: A History of Florida Tourism.* Gainesville: University Press of Florida, 2011.

Reynolds, David S. *Waking Giant: America in the Age of Jackson.* New York: Harper Collins, 2008.

Richards, Jeffrey, and John M. MacKenzie. *The Railway Station: A Social History.* Oxford: Oxford University Press, 1986.

Richardson, Reed C. *The Locomotive Engineer 1863–1963: A Century of Railway Labor Relations and Work Rules.* Ann Arbor, MI: Bureau of Industrial Relations, 1963.

Riney, Larry A. *Hell Gate of the Mississippi: The Effie Afton Trial and Abraham Lincoln's Role in It.* Geneseo, IL: Talesman Press, 2007.

Rose, Mark H. *Interstate: Express Highway Politics 1941–1956.* Lawrence: Regents Press of Kansas, 1979.

Salvatore, Nick. *Eugene Debs: Citizen and Socialist.* Urbana: University of Illinois Press, 1982.

Sanders, Craig. *Amtrak in the Heartland.* Bloomington: Indiana University Press, 2006.

———. *Limiteds, Locals, and Expresses in Indiana, 1838–1971.* Bloomington: Indiana University Press, 2003.

Saunders, Richard, Jr. *Main Lines: Rebirth of North American Railroads, 1970–2002.* DeKalb: Northern Illinois University Press, 2003.

———. *Merging Lines: American Railroads 1900–1970.* DeKalb: Northern Illinois University Press, 2001.

Sawislak, Karen. *Smoldering City: Chicagoans and the Great Fire, 1871–1874.* Chicago: University of Chicago Press, 1995.

Schneider, Gregory L. *Rock Island Requiem: The Collapse of a Mighty Fine Line.* Lawrence: University Press of Kansas, 2013.

Schneirov, Richard, Shelton Stromquist, and Nick Salvatore, eds. *The Pullman Strike and the Crisis of the 1890s.* Urbana: University of Illinois Press, 1999.

Schwieterman, Joseph P. *Terminal Town: An Illustrated Guide to Chicago's Airports, Bus Depots, Train Stations, and Steamship Landings, 1939–Present.* Lake Forest, IL: Lake Forest College Press, 2014.

———. *When the Railroad Leaves Town: American Communities in the Age of Rail Line Abandonment.* Kirksville, MO: Truman State University Press, 2001.

Solomon, Brian. *The American Diesel Locomotive.* Osceola, WI: MBI Publishing, 2000.

———. *Amtrak.* St. Paul, MN: MBI Publishing, 2004.

Solomon, Brian, Mike Blaszak, Chris Guss, and John Gruber. *Chicago: America's Railroad Capital: The Illustrated History.* Minneapolis, MN: Voyageur Press, 2014.

Solomon, Brian, and Patrick Yough. *Coal Trains: The History of Railroading and Coal in the United States.* Minneapolis, MN: Voyageur Press, 2009.

Spinney, Robert G. *City of Big Shoulders: A History of Chicago.* DeKalb: Northern Illinois University Press, 2000.

Starr, John W., Jr. *Lincoln and the Railroads: A Biographical Study.* New York: Dodd Mead, 1927.

Stiles, T. J. *The First Tycoon: The Epic Life of Cornelius Vanderbilt.* New York: Alfred A. Knopf, 2009.

Stout, Greg. *Route of the Eagles: Missouri Pacific in the Streamlined Era.* Kansas City, MO: White River Productions, 1995.

Stover, John F. *American Railroads.* 2nd ed. Chicago: University of Chicago Press, 1997.

———. *History of the Baltimore and Ohio Railroad.* West Lafayette, IN: Purdue University Press, 1987.

———. *History of the Illinois Central Railroad.* New York: Macmillan, 1975.

———. *Iron Road to the West: American Railroads in the 1850s.* New York: Columbia University Press, 1978.

———. *The Life and Decline of the American Railroad.* New York: Oxford University Press, 1970.

———. *The Routledge Historical Atlas of the American Railroads.* New York: Routledge, 1999.

Stowell, David O. *Street Railroads and the Great Strike of 1877.* Chicago: University of Chicago Press, 1999.

Stringham, Paul H. *Illinois Terminal: The Electric Years.* Glendale, CA: Interurban Press, 1989.

———. *Toledo, Peoria & Western: Tried, Proven, and Willing.* Peoria, IL: Deller Archive, 1993.

Stromquist, Shelton. *A Generation of Boomers: The Pattern of Railroad Labor Conflict in Nineteenth-Century America.* Urbana: University of Illinois Press, 1987.

Suprey, Leslie V. *Steam Trains of the Soo.* 3rd ed. Mora, MN: B&W Printers, 1962.

Taillon, Paul Michel. *Good, Reliable, White Men: Railroad Brotherhoods, 1877–1917.* Urbana: University of Illinois Press, 2009.

Taylor, George Rogers, and Irene Neu. *The American Railroad Network 1861–1890.* 1956. Reprint, Urbana: University of Illinois Press, 2003.

Thomas, William G. *The Iron Way: Railroads, the Civil War, and the Making of Modern America.* New Haven, CT: Yale University Press, 2011.

Veenendaal, Augustus J., Jr. *Slow Train to Paradise: How Dutch Investment Helped Build American Railroads.* Stanford, CA: Stanford University Press, 1996.

Wade, Louise Carroll. *Chicago's Pride: The Stockyards, Packingtown, and Environs in the Nineteenth Century.* Urbana: University of Illinois Press, 1986.

Ward, James A. *Railroads and the Character of America 1820–1887.* Knoxville: University of Tennessee Press, 1986.

Weber, Thomas. *The Northern Railroads in the Civil War 1861–1865.* 1952. Bloomington: Indiana University Press, 1999.

White, John. *Kankakee River Area Assessment, Vol. 5: Early Accounts of the Ecology of the Kankakee River Area.* Springfield: Illinois Department of Natural Resources, 1999.

White, John H., Jr. *The American Railroad Passenger Car.* Baltimore, MD: Johns Hopkins University Press, 1978.

White, Richard. *Railroaded: The Transcontinentals and the Making of Modern America.* New York: W. W. Norton, 2011.

Wilner, Frank N. *Railroad Mergers: History, Analysis, Insight.* Omaha, NE: Simmons-Boardman Books, 1997.

Young, David M. *The Iron Horse and the Windy City: How Railroads Shaped Chicago.* DeKalb: Northern Illinois University Press, 2005.

Zakim, Michael, and Gary J. Kornblith, eds. *Capitalism Takes Command: The Social Transformation of Nineteenth-Century America.* Chicago: University of Chicago Press, 2012.

INDEX

Italics indicate an illustration or map

All place names are in Illinois, except where noted

Simon Cordery researches, writes, and rides the rails on both sides of the Atlantic. He is a historian specializing in the nineteenth century, with a particular interest in and appreciation for the railroad industry. He serves as chair of the Inductions Committee of the National Railroad Hall of Fame and as chair of the Department of History at Western Illinois University. A member of the Lexington Group of Transportation Historians, he has published two previous books and numerous articles and has lectured on the history of railroading across the state of Illinois.